SELF-INJURIOUS BEHAVIOR IN INTELLECTUAL DISABILITIES

SELF-INJURIOUS BEHAVIOR IN INTELLECTUAL DISABILITIES

By

JOHANNES ROJAHN
George Mason University, USA

STEPHEN R. SCHROEDER
University of Kansas, USA

and

THEODORE A. HOCH
Northern Virginia Training Center and George Mason University, USA

ELSEVIER

Amsterdam • Boston • Heidelberg • London • New York • Oxford
Paris • San Diego • San Francisco • Singapore • Sydney • Tokyo

Elsevier
Linacre House, Jordan Hill, Oxford OX2 8DP, UK
Radarweg 29, PO Box 211, 1000 AE Amsterdam, The Netherlands

First edition 2008

Notice
No responsibility is assumed by the publisher for any injury and/or damage to persons
or property as a matter of products liability, negligence or otherwise, or from any use
or operation of any methods, products, instructions or ideas contained in the material
herein. Because of rapid advances in the medical sciences, in particular, independent
verification of diagnoses and drug dosages should be made

British Library Cataloguing in Publication Data
A catalogue record for this book is available from the British Library

Library of Congress Cataloging-in-Publication Data
A catalog record for this book is available from the Library of Congress

ISBN: 978-0-08-044889-3
ISSN: 1871-1294

For information on all Elsevier publications
visit our website at books.elsevier.com

Printed and bound in The Netherlands

08 09 10 11 12   10 9 8 7 6 5 4 3 2 1

Working together to grow
libraries in developing countries

www.elsevier.com | www.bookaid.org | www.sabre.org

ELSEVIER   BOOK AID
International   Sabre Foundation

Contents

Dedications

Dieses Buch ist meinen verehrten, lieben Eltern gewidmet - meiner Mutter Johanna Rojahn, die ihren Glauben an mich nie verloren hat und im Andenken an meinen Vater Rudolf Rojahn, der sich davon überzeugen ließ.

This volume is also dedicated to all families of individuals with self-injurious behavior who persevere in supporting their loved ones in spite of their difficulties.

J.R.

"They came to the other side of the sea, to the territory of the Gerasenes. When he [Jesus] got out of the boat, at once a man from the tombs who had an unclean spirit met him. The man had been dwelling among the tombs, and no one could restrain him any longer, even with a chain. In fact he had frequently been bound with shackles and chains but the chains had been pulled apart by him and the shackles smashed, and no one was strong enough to subdue him. Night and day among the tombs and on the hillsides he was always crying out and bruising himself with stones" (Mark 5:1–5).

Preface

The focus of this book is on the pathological, malignant, and socially unacceptable form of self-destructive behavior among individuals with intellectual disabilities. That means that the subject is anchored by two criteria, the first one being a particular group of behaviors, and the second being a subgroup of individuals within the population at large in which those behaviors are observed.

As for the first criterion, at first glance it seems self-evident that self-destructive behavior is pathological and socially unacceptable. The notion of "deliberately" inflicting physical damage to our own bodies seems disturbing at best, if not repugnant and outright frightening. It may sound surprising therefore, to realize that it is not trivial trying to define self-injurious behavior and to distinguish forms that are aberrant and those that are not. The designation of what behavior is deemed normative and acceptable on the one hand and what is undesirable and pathological is not rooted in a priori, objective, and mutually exclusive categorical criteria. Nor can we hope that science will help us determine such criteria (e.g., Maddux, Gosselin, & Winstead, 2004). The designation is based on our prevailing values and sensibilities that are formed by our socio-cultural context. Whether behavior is seen as acceptable or as pathological depends on morals and traditions that are fluid within and variable across cultures. This is also true for self-injurious behavior.

Taking a very broad definition of self-injurious behavior, we find that we all engage regularly in behavior that causes destruction to our own body tissue, without raising alarms that some deviant behavior is being performed. In fact, not to engage in some of those tissue-damaging behaviors would have negative societal repercussions in many cultures. For instance, in our Western postindustrial societies we are normally expected to keep our fingernails in proper length and shape and we regularly cut and shave our hair. Of course these types of behavior are not considered harmful, probably because they do not cause pain. But many of us also condone or engage in behaviors that actually break the skin and even draw blood. For example, many people pick at sores, exacerbating wounds; or we scratch our itching skin after a mosquito bite. More drastic, but still socially sanctioned forms of self-inflicted tissue damage (or damage we freely permit others to inflict on us) include rather invasive procedures such as tattooing, piercing, and cosmetic surgery for face lifts, breast enlargements, or hair implants. The consensus on acceptability begins to crumble with self-harming practices for religious or spiritual purposes, with traditions such as male and particularly female genital circumcision, or the more radical practices of body-modification practiced by cultural fringe groups such as the Modern Primitives (Musafar, 1996; Vale & Juno,

1989). Few people would argue, we trust, that the removal of ones own eyeball or self-castration as it has been observed by people with schizophrenia are examples of healthy behavior. The same, we believe, is true for the various forms of self-injurious behavior seen in some individuals with intellectual disabilities.

The second boundary we set on the topic of this book is the population. Individuals with intellectual disabilities are biologically and behaviorally vulnerable and many of them run the risk of developing self-injurious behavior at one point or another during the course of their lives. Pathological forms of self-injurious behavior are of course also observed in persons without intellectual or developmental disabilities, and are typically so alarming to warrant the attention of mental health professionals. Unfortunately, there are only very few scientists or clinicians who focus on self-injurious behavior in both the general, intellectually typical, and the intellectually disabled population. The psychiatric literature, for instance, has traditionally not reflected much interest in self-injurious behavior in individuals with intellectual disabilities. Self-injurious behavior in that group has mostly been studied by behaviorally and later by biologically oriented psychologists. This schism within the scientific community into those who studied self-injurious behavior in the intellectually typical or superior population (essentially psychiatry, psychiatric nursing, etc.) and those who specialized in intellectual disabilities (psychologists and special educators) drove a wedge between those two camps that discouraged attempts to inform each other of their respective issues, concerns, and achievements. Theoretical papers, conceptual models and empirical research approaches on self-injurious behavior rarely bridged the gap between the two groups. The upshot is that we have no clear, integrated sense at this point in which aspects and to what extent self-injurious behavior across the intellectual spectrum is conceptually similar or different. Therefore, we will briefly discuss some selected theoretical models of self-injurious behavior as it occurs in the general public and in clinical groups without intellectual disabilities, especially those that seemed relevant, either due to their historical significance or due to their potential significance in expanding our thinking about self-injurious behavior among people with intellectual disabilities. We will also present empirical data on the epidemiology and the behavioral function of self-mutilation in those populations.

Our book is intended to give a broad overview of the literature in the area of self-injurious behavior in people with intellectual disabilities, but most of the text is dedicated to the review of the behavioral and biological research in this field. In fact, it is our view that the most promising heuristic approach for the advancement of our understanding of this phenomenon and for its management and treatment is likely the bio-behavioral perspective in which behavior can be studied at the intersect of learning and the biological bases of behavior. We will propose an overarching heuristic model, which we will call the Gene–Brain-Behavior Model of Self-Injurious Behavior that presents a platform to integrate disparate, and previously isolated scientific approaches.

A word about the terminology of intellectual disabilities: Although not unanimously and universally agreed upon, the term *intellectual disabilities* has been gradually adopted world wide to replace the term *mental retardation*, which, through its derogatory meaning in the vernacular, is seen by many to have become pejorative and insulting. In keeping with the prevailing sentiments among people with intellectual disabilities and their advocates, and with some of the decisions made by major national and international organizations (e.g., the former *American Association on Mental Retardation* has been renamed in 2006 to *American Association on Intellectual and Developmental Disabilities*), we are using the term "intellectual disabilities" throughout the book.

According to all major diagnostic classification systems, such as the *Diagnostic and Statistical Manual* (DSM-IV-TR) (American Psychiatric Association, 2000), the *International Classification of Diseases, 10th revision* (ICD-10) (World Health Organization, 1993), and the *Definition, Classification, and Supports* of the American Association on Mental Retardation (AAMR, 2002) intellectual disability (now referred to as intellectual disabilities) is a chronic, typically lifelong, and etiologically heterogeneous condition that is defined by three criteria:

1. Significant limitations in intellectual functioning,
2. Significant limitations in adaptive behavior, and
3. Manifestation of these limitations before the age of 18 years.

Largely overlapping but not identical with intellectual disabilities are developmental disabilities. Developmental disabilities are also severe, chronic, usually lifelong conditions due to diverse mental and/or physical impairments. People with developmental disabilities typically have limitations with major life activities such as language, mobility, learning, self-help, and independent living that must appear before 22 years of age. Typical diagnostic categories that can lead to a developmental disability are intellectual disabilities, autism, cerebral palsy, epilepsy, etc.

Chapter 1

Definition, Classification, and Epidemiology

1.1. Terms and Definitions

Someone interested in the topic of self-injurious behavior (SIB) who approaches the existing literature will encounter a whole host of terms for this puzzling and sometimes terrifying phenomenon. This diversity in the terminology hints at the state of our knowledge but also reflects a fragmentation of different scholarly disciplines, all of which have brought their own terms and approaches to the arena.

Perhaps it is useful to distinguish between two main groups of terms and definitions: Definitions developed by scholars with a primary interest in self-injurious behavior in the general population and psychiatric patients, and those focused on people with intellectual disabilities. The first group has traditionally come from a psychodynamic orientation and tends to use interpretative terms that imply intent or seemingly explain the causes of the behavior. Examples of such charged terms are *auto-aggressive behavior* (Freud, 1949), *self-aggressive behavior* (Cain, 1961), *partial and focal suicide* (Menninger, 1938), *localized self-destruction* (Menninger, 1938), *parasuicide* (Kreitman, Philip, Greer, & Bagley, 1969; Shneidman, 1985), *antisuicide* (Simpson, 1980), *aggressive behavior turned inward* (Cain, 1961), *deliberate self-harm syndrome* (Pattison & Kahan, 1983; Kahan & Pattison, 1984), *self-assault* (Cohen, 1969), *indirect self-destructive behavior* (Simpson, 1980), and *self-mutilation* (e.g., Favazza, 1996; Simpson, 1976; Walsh & Rosen, 1988). A more comprehensive discussion of such terms can be found in Walsh and Rosen (1988). Winchel and Stanley (1991) defined self-injurious behavior as "... the commission of deliberate self harm to one's own body. The injury is done to oneself, without the aid of another person, and the injury is severe enough for tissue damage (such as scarring) to result. Acts that are committed with the conscious suicidal intent or are associated with sexual arousal are excluded. Common forms of self-injurious behavior include cutting and burning, banging the hands and limbs, picking at wounds, and chewing fingers" (p. 306).

Behaviorally oriented scientists tend to use definitions based on observable characteristics of behavior. Tate and Baroff (1966) proposed a non-theoretical, descriptive definition of self-injurious behavior as a general term with inter-individual applicability that intends to capture all forms and types of *pathological* forms of self-injurious behaviors that ought to be included without veiled references to presumed causation or motivational explanation: "Repetitive acts by individuals directed toward their own body, which result in physical harm or tissue damage." A critical advantage of this term is that it avoids subterfuge of preconceived and unproven attributions (e.g., auto-aggressive behavior implies that self-injurious behavior is in fact aggressive behavior turned against oneself), *explanatory fictions*, and circular reasoning.[1] Its main disadvantage as a working definition is over inclusion.

Schroeder, Mulick, and Rojahn (1980) pointed out that even this definition fails to rely only on observable behavioral characteristics because it explicitly refers to socially undesirable and pathological behavior implied in the terms "harm" and "tissue damage," offsetting it from other forms of self-directed behavior that causes tissue alterations. Causing *damage* to ones own body is pathological and justifies, and even calls for intervention.

Others have developed variations of Tate and Baroff's definition. Grossman (1973, p. 195) for instance, defined self-injurious behavior as behavior exhibited "to damage or disfigure a body part by one's own action (e.g., biting or hitting self)." Matson described self-injurious behavior as a class of often highly repetitive and rhythmic behaviors that result in physical harm to the individual displaying the behavior (Matson, 1989). Many definitions used in epidemiological or survey research can be found in the Appendix. For instance, Oliver, Murphy, and Corbett (1987) defined self-injurious behavior as "Repeated, self-inflicted, non-accidental injury, producing bruising, bleeding, or other temporary or permanent tissue damage. Also, any such behavior which would produce bruising, bleeding or tissue damage were it not for protective devices, restraints, specific medical or psychological interventions in use." The *Behavior Problems Inventory-01* (Rojahn, Matson, Lott, Esbensen, & Smalls, 2001) uses an umbrella definition that applies to self-injurious behavior in general ("Behavior that causes, or at least has the potential to cause, manifest damage to the person's own body") and then lists specific topographies.

In this book we are using the term "self-injurious behavior," except when reporting the work of other researchers who explicitly adopted different parlance. This term has become common in the literature on individuals with developmental disabilities and beyond (e.g., Yates, 2004).

For the purpose of this book we define self-injurious behavior in persons with intellectual disabilities as self-directed behaviors that

(a) Are pathological in the sense that they are – according to the prevailing sensibilities of our society – clinically significant and require intervention;
(b) Involve relatively stable, idiosyncratic response pattern (i.e., they occur repeatedly and by large uniformly);
(c) Cause or have the potential to cause direct or indirect (cumulative) physical damage to the person's own body (i.e., observable damage has either already occurred,

---

[1] Skinner (1974) pointed out a common fallacy when explaining human behavior of turning an adjective (e.g., self-injurious) into a noun (self-injury), which then used as a pseudo explanation. A circular statement answers the question "Why does Rob bang his head?" "*because* he has self-injury," which later may become "*because* he has Borderline Personality Syndrome."

or is likely to occur if the behavior remains untreated or not prevented by physical or pharmacological means); and

(d) Topographies that are typically included as self-injurious behavior if they meet criterion are self-biting, head hitting or banging own body parts or with other objects, body hitting (excluding areas of the head), self-scratching, self-induced vomiting, self-pinching, stuffing or inserting dangerous objects into body orifices, pulling out finger or toe nails, poking or digging in orifices such as eye sockets or rectum, hair pulling, drinking excessive amounts of liquid, teeth grinding, pica (the swallowing of non-edible objects) and aerophagia (air swallowing).

The illegal literature in intellectual disabilities typically does not address, drug use abuse of nicotine and alcohol, or paraphiliac behaviors under the umbrella of self-injurious behavior.

1.2. Classification

One important question is whether all those different types of behaviors that cause self-harm do in fact constitute a meaningful entity or construct where all constituting exemplars show some common characteristics, above and beyond the fact that they cause physical damage to one's own body. For instance, do they have common etiological bases or behavioral functions, collective treatment indications, or similar relationships to other clinical constructs?

In order to get a better handle on the variety of behaviors, it might be useful to review some of the categorization attempts that have been proposed. We can distinguish two basic types of taxonomies or classification systems, structural and functional taxonomies. Structural taxonomies group behaviors on the basis of their similarities in observable dimensions (similar topography, outcome, etc.). Functional taxonomies, on the other hand, are independent of topography. Instead, they seek to group behavior on the basis of their functional similarities.

Before discussing ways of classifying self-injurious behavior in persons with intellectual disabilities, we will turn to taxonomies that were developed primarily with the intellectually typical population in mind.

1.2.1. Classification in Intellectually Typical Populations

1.2.1.1. Structural Classifications

Self-mutilation as a psychopathological phenomenon was probably first addressed comprehensively by Menninger (1935). Based on Sigmund Freud's Eros–Thanatos theory of the human psyche, Menninger postulated the existence of a death instinct, which represents an "adverse tendency within the personality," and which, under certain circumstances, can foment the development of self-harm. To organize the variety of different self-destructive manifestations Menninger proposed a classification system that distinguished between six types of self-mutilation, including a separation between pathological and normal behavior:

1. Abnormal self-mutilation
   a. Neurotic self-mutilation – nail biting, skin picking, disfiguring hair removal, etc.;
   b. Religious self-mutilation – ascetic self-flagellation, genital self-mutilations;
   c. Puberty rites – circumcision, clitoral alteration, hymen removal;
   d. Psychotic self-mutilation – self-enucleation, genital self-mutilation, ear removal, extremity amputation; and
   e. Organic self-mutilation – intentional fracturing of fingers, self-enucleation in patients suffering from encephalitis and other organic conditions.
2. Normal self-mutilation – nail clipping, hair trimming, shaving.

A couple of years later, in his book *Man against Himself* Menninger (1938) developed and refined his categorical scheme in which he viewed self-mutilation in the broader context of suicide. According to Menninger, the tendency to self-destructive behavior is fueled by self-punitive, aggressive, and erotic urges. On that basis Menninger then distinguished between three broad suicide or self-destruction types:

1. Chronic suicide or self-destruction: This type includes manifestations such as asceticism or martyrdom, neurotic invalidism (hypochondriacs, including individuals with actual physical symptoms), alcohol addiction, and psychosis.
2. Focal suicide: Self-mutilation, malingering, poly-surgery, purposive accidents, impotence, and frigidity.
3. Organic suicide: Destruction of own organs by way of hormonal or neuronal processes in the sense of psychosomatic conditions.

Pattison and Kahan (1983) developed a two-dimensional descriptive taxonomy of self-destructive behavior, the first being a dimension of "lethality," the second a dimension of "immediacy of damage." On the *lethality* dimension they distinguished four levels, ranging from high to low levels of lethality. The *immediacy* dimension has only two-levels (direct vs. indirect damage). In this scheme, specific self-destructive behaviors can be mapped. For instance, a single episode of successful suicide would be high on lethality with direct damage. In most cases, multiple-episode head banging will rank low-to-medium in lethality, and they can either cause indirect (cumulative) or direct damage. Other low lethality behaviors on the indirect dimension are habitual alcohol abuse, over-eating, and heavy cigarette smoking.

By including behaviors such as over-eating and alcohol abuse, Pattison and Kahan included socially acceptable behaviors among self-injurious behaviors. Walsh and Rosen (1988) made that inclusion more explicit in their four-dimensional classification system:

1. Behavior types
   a. Ear piercing, tattoos, cosmetic plastic surgery
   b. Ritualistic scarring
   c. Self-cutting, burning, wound excoriation
   d. Self-castration, enucleation, amputation

2. Degrees of physical damage
   a. Superficial
   b. Severe
3. Psychological states
   a. Benign
   b. Benign to agitate
   c. Psychic crisis
   d. Psychotic decompensation
4. Social acceptability
   a. Acceptable in most social groups
   b. Entirely unacceptable with all peers in all social groups.

In perhaps the most comprehensive classification attempt to date, Favazza (1996) proposed a two-category classification scheme of self-injurious behavior. It is the first one that explicitly addressed self-injurious behavior in people with intellectual disabilities. Favazza, a professor of psychiatry and neurology at the University of Missouri, is the founder of cultural psychiatry, and as such is interested in the role of self-mutilation as it appears in cosmogony, the occult, and in symbolism and cultural practices of pre-modern, modern, and post-modern societies (Table 1.1).

Favazza (1996) draws a clear distinction between culturally sanctioned and pathological acts of self-mutilation. *Culturally sanctioned self-mutilation* is presumed to play important roles in healing practices, spirituality, and the maintenance of social order (such as initiation rites). Among culturally sanctioned acts of self-mutilation Favazza distinguishes between rituals and practices. Cultural *rituals* are activities that are practiced by a group of people repeatedly and consistently over generations and they reflect symbolism, traditions, and beliefs of a society. They have an important role for the individual as well as for the entire community by correcting or preventing destabilizing conditions that may threaten the integrity and survival of a community. "The alteration or destruction of body tissue helps to establish control of things and preserve the social order" (p. 231). Anthropologists have described many examples of such rituals in Africa, Melanesia, and Asia (see Favazza, 1996). An example of a *cultural ritual* in Western societies is the "Mensur." Certain university fraternities (*Burschenschaften*) in Germany, Austria, and Switzerland (so-called *Schlagende*

Table 1.1: Self-injurious behavior classification by Favazza (1996)

Culturally sanctioned self-mutilation
    Rituals
    Practices
Deviant-pathological self-mutilation
    Major self-mutilation
    Moderate/superficial self-mutilation
    – Compulsive self-mutilation
    – Episodic self-mutilation
    – Repetitive self-mutilation
    Stereotypic self-mutilation

Verbindungen) require their members to engage in ritualistic sabers duels, called "Mensuren." During the Mensur, the two opponents (*Paukanten*) confront each other at a specified distance and exchange saber blows. The fencers, barely protected, are not permitted to move from their spot. There are no match winners or losers in a Mensur; the point is to show courage and to deny fear of injury. Stepping back from the determined spot is considered dishonorable. Such exercises may have group-cohesive and group-identity enhancing functions, such as the emphasis on tradition, honor, and fortitude. Characteristic scars (*Schmisse*) caused by saber blows are carried with pride.

Karl Menninger's (1938) chronic suicide (asceticism, martyrdom) and religious mutilations can be considered culturally sanctioned forms of self-injurious behavior in Favazza's classification format as well. Religious self-mutilation is a ubiquitous phenomenon, even in mainstream religions. Here are just a few examples:

- Male circumcision is practiced by several religions including Judaism and Islam has become a wide spread practice in the United States devoid of religious overtones.
- Although banned for many centuries by the official Roman Catholic Church, hooded flagellants can still be encountered in some predominantly Catholic countries, especially during Lent. Even in the U.S. today ritual self-mutilating behavior is performed. The *Hermanos Penitentes*, for example, a sect found predominantly in New Mexico and Colorado, atone for their sins by practicing self-flagellation, carrying heavy crosses, binding their bodies to a cross, and tying the limbs to hinder circulation of the blood (The Columbia Encyclopedia, 2002).
- The Hindu festival of *Thaipusam* is held to celebrate the birthday of Lord Murugan, son of Siva, and features pilgrims who engage in highly elaborate rituals of self-mutilation. Devotees will carry a *kavadi* (meaning "sacrifice at every step"), a heavy, adorned framework of wood or metal, attached to the body by fish hooks that are pierced through the pectoral and back muscles.
- Ashura is a time of mourning for Shi'a Muslims to commemorate the martyrdom of Husayn ibn Ali, the grandson of the Prophet Muhammad who was killed at the Battle of Karbala in AD 680. Ashura often involves pilgrims who beat themselves with whips or blades.
- Homicidal self-sacrifices of the modern day radical Islamic "jihadists" can also be considered a form of the ultimate self-mutilation, which is approved and encouraged within some Islamic subcultures and political groups. The self-destructive attacks of Japanese Kamikaze pilots in World War II are another example of sanctioned act of self-destruction in the name of a greater good.
- Young men of the North America Plains Indians used to practice the Sun Dance, a spectacular and important religious ceremony. A medicine man pushed a narrow spike of bone through a fold of the loose skin of the breast, which was tied to a rope that was attached to the top of the sun-pole. The devotee had to break loose from these fetters by tearing the spikes through the skin. This ritual symbolized rebirth, whereby the torture represented death from which the sun dancer is reborn, mentally and spiritually as well as physically (Schwatka, 1889/1890).

Self-mutilating *practices* on the other hand refer to faddish acts that lack deeper meaning and have no community-preserving properties according to Favazza.

Examples are piercing ear lobes and other body parts, tattooing, non-religious male circumcision, and plastic surgery to enhance appearance and physical attractiveness. Whether body modifications or "body play," as it is sometimes euphemistically called by members of post-modern movements such as the *Modern Primitives* (Musafar, 1996) are rituals, practices, or pathological behavior may well depend on whether or not one is an insider of such a movement. However, the group identity-building role of those body modifications in such groups is hard to deny.

Among the deviant and socially clearly unaccepted forms of self-mutilation Favazza distinguishes between three main types: (a) major self-mutilation, (b) moderate–superficial self-mutilation, and (c) stereotypic self-mutilation.

The category of *major self-mutilation* refers to highly dramatic and rare behaviors, which often have lasting effects. They are most commonly encountered in individuals who suffer from severe psychiatric conditions such as acute psychotic episodes, schizophrenia, mania, depression, and acute intoxication. Examples of major self-mutilations are acts of self-enucleation, self-amputation, and complete or partial self-castration.

In contrast to the major forms of self-mutilation Favazza describes *moderate/superficial self-mutilation* as less dramatic acts than the major forms of self-mutilation, although they can also be potentially very harmful. He groups *moderate/superficial self-mutilation* into three subgroups.

- *Compulsive self-mutilation* behaviors occur frequently and repetitively with more or less deleterious consequences. Typical forms of compulsive self-mutilation are hair pulling, and picking, or attempts to remove imaginary skin blemishes causing excoriations.
- *Episodic self-mutilation* involves deliberate acts that often have a clear functional component, such as a release of distressing thoughts and feelings or the recovery of self-control. Favazza discusses several cases of individuals who reported such effects as release of tensions, return to reality, and the relief from alienation as a function of having engaged in self-injurious behavior. In behavioral terms, such episodic self-mutilation refers to behaviors that are maintained by negative automatic reinforcement. In other persons self-injurious behaviors seem motivated by idiosyncratic positive automatic reinforcement, such as sexual orgasm, other forms of euphoria, or positive social reinforcement by the influence they exert on others. Episodic self-mutilation is often associated with psychiatric disorders such as anxiety disorders, depression, dissociative disorders, and personality disorders (borderline, antisocial, and mixed).
- *Repetitive* self-mutilation according to Favazza has characteristics of episodic self-injurious behavior, but it has become an overwhelming preoccupation to the point where the person assumes the identity of a "self-injurer," becoming a "cutter" or a "burner." The essential feature of repetitive self-injurious behavior is the recurrent failure to resist impulses to self-harm and a *lack of suicidal intent*. From a diagnostic perspective according to Favazza, repetitive self-injurious behavior should be listed on the DSM-IV, Axis I among the "impulse control disorders not elsewhere classified."

Stereotypic Self-Mutilation in Favazza's classification scheme approximates most closely the type of phenomenon that is the main focus of this book. Favazza describes stereotypic forms of self-mutilation as monotonous, repetitive, and sometimes rhythmical behaviors, which are common in chronic conditions such as intellectual disabilities (e.g., Lesch–Nyhan syndrome, de Lange syndrome, Rett syndrome, autism, schizophrenia and acute psychosis, neuroacanthosis, and Tourette's syndrome). Favazza emphasizes that it is usually not possible to "ascertain any symbolic meaning, thought content, or associated affect with the behaviors," and he states that "self mutilators seem to be driven by a primarily biological imperative to harm themselves *shamelessly* and *without guile*" (p. 237, italics added by the authors). Although Favazza's characterization of individuals with stereotyped self-mutilation comes across as derogatory and indifferent, his classification scheme is the first to explicitly acknowledge self-injurious behavior in people with intellectual disabilities as part of the broad phenomenon of self-mutilation, albeit distinguished from other forms of self-mutilation.

Favazza's classification system is a welcomed heuristic tool because it provides a comprehensive structure that incorporates all forms of the wide variety of self-injurious behaviors. Whether it will stand up to empirical validation remains to be seen.

Sachsse (1999) proposed a distinction between openly (overt) and secretly (covert) performed self-mutilation with the difference being that individuals who secretly self-harm are assumed to deny or dissociate their actions and, therefore, are less aware of their behavior than those who openly engage in self-mutilating behavior.

To explore this distinction empirically, Fliege, Kocalevent, Rose, Becker, Walter, and Klapp (2004) conducted a study with general hospital patients who either received psychosomatic–psychotherapeutic services or were referred to the outpatient department. First, using an expert rating assessment instrument, they identified a total of 63 patients who exhibited self-harm (overt or covert). For comparison, they included in the study 63 clinical patients without self-destructive behavior and 63 healthy controls matched for age and sex. Next, all participants completed a validated self-rating questionnaire measuring optimism and self-efficacy. No differences were found between patients with or without self-destructive behavior. However, patients with overt self-harm had significantly lower levels of optimism and self-efficacy than those who concealed their behavior. This was seen as a validation of the distinction between persons who performed their self-mutilation in full awareness or not.

This last study was an exception among topographical classifications mentioned so far in that it employed empirical methods of verification. All previously mentioned nosologies were speculative and lack empirical support. The degree to which they are pertinent to furthering our understanding of self-injurious behavior in general and in people with less severe degrees of intellectual disabilities in particular is an empirical question that remains to be answered.

1.2.1.2. Functional Classifications
Over the years clinicians who interacted with psychiatric patients with self-injurious behavior asked their patients to articulate the reasons (or functions) why they engaged in that behavior. Most of the early functional classifications were based on

psychodynamic reasoning, which led to many speculative, empirically non-verified classification schemes with little consistency across authors.

For instance, Simpson (1975) identified four reasons why individuals engaged in self-injurious behavior. It was assumed to

1. release tension,
2. promote reintegration/repersonalization,
3. vent anger, and
4. modulate affect.

A few years later, Leibenluft, Gardner, and Cowdry (1987) suggested that self-injurious behavior was driven either by

1. exhilaration,
2. distraction from psychic pain,
3. by seeking revenge,
4. rage dissipation,
5. escape from dysphoric states, or
6. the urge to express pain to others.

Favazza (1989) listed several reasons that were offered to him as explanations by non-psychotic patients. Among them were

1. tension release,
2. return to reality,
3. establishing control,
4. establishing security or uniqueness,
5. influencing others by gaining their attention, and
6. venting of anger.

Favazza also emphasizes that habitual self-mutilation and suicide are functionally very different phenomena in that suicide is a final act of escape that is intended to end life and to stop all feelings. Self-mutilation behavior, on the other hand, is considered to be an unhealthy form of coping and self-help.[2] The intent is to escape troublesome thoughts and feelings and to continue with life. In fact, Favazza suggested that self-mutilation is defined by a lack of conscious suicidal intent. This position was supported in part by recent empirical work on the intentionality of self-injurious behavior with borderline personality disorders (Brown, Comtois, & Linehan, 2002).

---

[2] It is important, however, not to dismiss entirely the possibility that self-injurious behavior may be a risk factor for suicide in some individuals. Muehlenkamp and Gutierrez (2007) showed that adolescents who engaged in non-lethal forms of self-injurious behavior and who also attempted suicide could be differentiated from adolescents who only engaged in (non-lethal) self-injurious behavior in terms of the degree of suicidal ideation and depression. Also, recent data have shown that repeated or multi-episode self-injurious behavior is associated with short-term and long-term increases in the risk of eventual suicide (e.g., Owens, Horrocks, & House, 2002; Zahl & Hawton, 2004).

Herpetz (1995) reported a similar list of functions of self-mutilation as

1. tension release,
2. expression of anger or revenge,
3. attention,
4. self-hatred and
5. self-punishment.

Suyemoto and MacDonald (1995) suggested eight differentiable theoretical models why female adolescents may want to resort to *self-cutting*. These were

1. behavioral,
2. systemic, to avoid
3. suicide,
4. sexual,
5. expression of affect,
6. control of affect, stopping
7. depersonalization, and
8. delineation of self-boundaries.

In 1998, based on a comprehensive literature review of the many hypotheses that have been suggested to motivate self-mutilation Suyemoto (1998) refined her hypothetical classification scheme to account for the various intra-psychic and interpersonal functions of pathological self-mutilation in general:

- *Environmental models* – self-injurious behavior produces responses from the environment.
- *Drive models* – which consist of antisuicide (suicide replacement) and sexually motivated behavior (conflicts over sexuality).
- *Affect regulation models* – which consist of behavior that lead to affect regulation (e.g., expression or control of anger, anxiety, or pain) and behavior that is designed to end or escape dissociation.
- *Interpersonal models* – self-injurious behavior to create a distinction between self and others.

Osuch, Noll, and Putnam (1999) empirically developed a functional self-report scale to systematize the intent to self-injure in psychiatric populations. The resulting instrument, the *Self-Injury Motivation Scale – Version 1* (SIMS) is a 35-item self-report scale with ten-point scales, ranging from "never" to "always." Each item begins with "I have injured myself to ...." The SIMS was administered to 99 inpatients in a tertiary psychiatric hospital who were recruited into the study consecutively as they were admitted to the hospital. Factor analysis supported a six-factor solution, which accounted for 88% of the variance and the instrument was found to have excellent reliability (Cronbach α ranged from .81 to .93). The factors and the resulting subscales were labeled and described as follows:

- *Affect Modulation* – refers to escape from emotional pain and discomfort such as feelings of fear, anger, shame, guilt, and suicidal thoughts.

- *Desolation* – also refers to escape from feelings such as loneliness, emptiness, and from bad memories.
- *Punitive Duality* – consists of items of self-punitive intent (for having positive feelings, for telling secrets, or just for deserving so), and of pleasing others (inside or outside voices, important figures (God, the devil, etc.)).
- *Influencing Others* – consists of items that refer to seeking support and caring from others, to show others how angry, hurt or hopeless one is, or to irritate, shock or take revenge on others.
- *Magical Control* – implies a wish to influence others such as the previous subscale, but in a more indirect and complicated way (protecting or controlling the behavior of others, to hurt others) and to eliminate threatening impulses (prevent oneself to hurt someone else, to kill part of oneself, and to control part of oneself that would otherwise be controlling).
- *Self-Stimulation* – refers to the induction of excitement, exhilaration, a drug-like "high," and sexual or quasi-sexual tension release.

Brown et al. (2002) examined self-reported reasons for suicide attempts and non-suicidal self-injurious behavior in chronically suicidal women with borderline personality disorders ($n = 75$) using the *Parasuicide History Interview*. They discovered that most of the women in their study reported that both types of behavior were intended to relieve undesirable emotions. However, it was more likely that non-suicidal self-injurious behavior was reported to be motivated by the desire for distraction, self-punishment, the restoration of normal feelings and expression of anger, while suicide attempts were more often reported as intended to benefit others. The authors suggested that it is likely that suicidal and non-suicidal forms of self-injurious behavior have multiple and partly differing functions.

Only recently have researchers who work primarily with intellectually typical populations incorporated the molar principles of behavior analysis to explain the functional properties of self-injurious behavior. Nock and Prinstein (2005) developed a functional-behavioral model of self-injurious behavior on the basis of four basic contingencies of reinforcement:

1. Automatic positive reinforcement
2. Automatic negative reinforcement
3. Social positive reinforcement
4. Social negative reinforcement.

Using the *Functional Assessment of Self-Mutilation* self-report measure (FASM) by Lloyd, Kelly, and Hope (1997), Nock and Prinstein (2005) conducted a study with 108 adolescent psychiatric inpatients who had been referred for self-injurious thoughts or behaviors. Their results supported the structural validity and reliability of the contingency-based functional model of self-injurious behavior. Most adolescents engaged in self-injurious behavior for automatic reinforcement, although a sizable portion endorsed social reinforcement functions as well.

Perhaps the most important aspects of the paper by Nock and Prinstein (2005) is their recognition of the significant role of behavioral principles of learning in the development and maintenance of self-injurious behavior in the intellectually typical population which could have direct implications for its treatment. Rationally linked treatment options such as certain forms of cognitive behavior therapy and dialectical behavior therapy, offer powerful remedies (e.g., Bohus, Haaf, & Stiglmayr, 2000; Linehan, 1993). In addition, Nock and Prinstein's study provides an opportunity to close ranks and to start a dialogue between scientists who work with people from different sections of the entire cognitive spectrum. An excellent review of the functions of self-injurious behavior in the general population was recently published by Klonsky (2007).

1.2.1.3. Combined Functional and Topographical Classification
Although functional and topographical approaches to classification are fundamentally different, they are not incompatible. It is not unreasonable to assume that specific topographies are more strongly associated with certain functions than with others. Indeed, some empirical evidence has been published to that effect. Rodham, Hawton, and Evans (2004), for instance, conducted an anonymous survey in 41 schools in England and were able to collect data on self-injurious behavior from 5,737 (of 7,433 invited) students. The two groups who represented the most prevalent forms of self-mutilation were compared, namely 220 adolescents who engaged in self-cutting with 68 adolescents who used poison to self-harm. The respondents were asked to express in their own words why they harmed themselves and the investigators coded their responses. In addition, the participants were asked to choose from a list of eight motives[3] that best described their reasons to carry out self-harming behavior. Differences between the motives to self-harm were found between the two groups as well as between gender. A significantly higher proportion of adolescents who had engaged in self-poisoning indicated that they wanted to die and to find out whether somebody loved them. In contrast, the most common motivation for both topographies was to escape from "a terrible state of mind." The topographical information about a behavior can guide the process of determining its current functional properties.

1.2.1.4. Psychiatric Diagnostic Systems
The *Diagnostic and Statistical Manual of Mental Disorders* (DSM-IV-TR) (American Psychiatric Association, 2000) classifies self-injurious behavior as a subcategory of a *Stereotypic Movement Disorder* (307.3). Stereotypic Movement Disorders are defined as repetitive, seemingly driven, nonfunctional motor behaviors that have persisted for four weeks or longer and markedly interfere with normal activities, or result in bodily injury that require medical treatment (or would result in injury if not prevented). Examples of such behaviors are hand shaking or waving, body rocking, head banging, mouthing of objects, self-biting, and hitting own body. If an intellectual disability is present, stereotypic movement disorder or self-injurious behavior must be of sufficient

---

[3] "I wanted to ... (1) show how desperate I was feeling," (2) die," (3) punish myself," (4) frighten someone," (5) get my own back on someone," (6) get relief from a terrible state of mind," (7) find out if someone really loved me," and (8) get some attention."

severity to become the focus of treatment. Excluded from 307.3 are behaviors that are better accounted for by other disorders such as in Obsessive Compulsive Disorder, or a tic disorder, or if it is part of a Pervasive Developmental Disorder. Also excluded are behaviors that are due to the direct physiological effect of a substance abuse disorder or general medical condition. According to DSM-IV-TR, a specification is required if the behavior results in bodily damage that requires specific treatment (or that would result in bodily damage if protective measures were no used). Hair pulling or tricho-tillomania (312.39) and pica (307.03) have their separate diagnostic category and are not coded under 303.02.

Similarly, in the *International Statistical Classification of Diseases and Related Health Problems*, 10th revision (ICD-10), (2006) self-injurious behavior appears un-der *Stereotyped Movement Disorders* (F98.4), which is classified as one of the behavioral and emotional disorders usually with childhood and adolescence onset in the chapter on Mental and Behavioral Disorders (F00-F99). The definition of F98.4 refers to "voluntary, repetitive, stereotyped, nonfunctional (and often rhythmic) movements that do not form part of any recognized psychiatric or neurological condition. When such movements occur as symptoms of some other disorder, only the overall disorder should be recorded. *The movements that are of a non self-injurious variety include: body rocking, head-rocking, hair-plucking, hair-twisting, finger-flicking mannerisms, and hand-flapping. Stereotyped self-injurious behavior includes repetitive head banging, face slapping, eye poking, and biting of hands, lips or other body parts*" (italics added by the authors). All the stereotyped movement disorders occur most frequently in association with intellectual disabilities (when this is the case, both should be recorded). If eye poking occurs in a child with visual impairment, both should be coded: eye poking under this category and the visual condition under the appropriate somatic disorder code. This diagnostic category excludes abnormal involuntary movements, movement disorders of organic origin, nail biting, nose picking, stereotyped behaviors that are part of a broader psychiatric condition, thumb-sucking, tic disorders, and trichotillomania. Also excluded from this diag-nostic category is pica.

Contrary to the more inclusive definition adopted for this book, ICD-10 and DSM-IV reserve separate diagnostic categories for hair pulling and pica and are thus not considered to be stereotyped movement disorders that results as self-injurious behavior. Also, if a person has a Pervasive Developmental Disorder (PDD), the diagnostic label of a Stereotypic Movement Disorder is not warranted because such behaviors are considered manifestations of PDD.

1.2.2. Classification in Persons with Intellectual Disabilities

Attempts to classify self-injurious behavior among individuals with intellectual disabilities were predominantly empirical or inductive rather than theory driven or deductive. Again, two general classification approaches will be distinguished: The structural/topographical classification and the behavioral/functional classification.

1.2.2.1. Structural Classifications

Self-injurious behavior topographies have many different overt features, all of which could potentially be used to classify the behaviors. Some of the more salient measurable features are:

1. Type or topography of behavior
2. Clusters of topographies
3. Number of different self-injurious behavior topographies per person
4. Behavioral parameters:
   a. frequency or rate
   b. duration per event
   c. intensity (velocity, impact force)
   d. chronicity
   e. sequential behavior patterns (single discrete behaviors type vs. bouts of single behaviors vs. massed bouts including behavioral sequences or behavior chains)
5. Harm inflicted (type of harm, site of harm, severity/lethality of the damage, immediate vs. protracted harm)
6. Comorbidity (concurrent neurological and psychiatric disorders, other coexisting behavior problems)
7. Person characteristics (age, sex, level of intellectual disabilities, etiology of intellectual disability, speech/language, motor skills, social skills, emotion regulation, impulse control, coping strategies, etc.).

1.2.2.1.1. Topographical Subtyping

The purpose of a topographical classification is to determine whether the term self-injurious behavior is merely descriptive applying to an assortment of heterogeneous types of behaviors or whether it refers to a class of behaviors that are bound by some meaningful common attributes such as a similar etiology, similar treatment, and similar prognosis. Typically, classical test theory and multivariate statistics have been used to determine structure, validity, and reliability of topographical classes or constructs and their assessment.

Boundaries   The assumption that self-injurious behavior may be closely related to aggressive behavior ("aggression turned inward") or stereotypic behaviors (e.g., DSM-IV) has been proposed repeatedly over the years. What we are asking from a topographic point of view is whether self-injurious behavior is sufficiently different and independent from these types of behavior to represent an independent entity. One of the earliest attempts to establish an empirical typology of a broad range of behavioral disturbances among people with intellectual disabilities was made by Leudar, Fraser, and Jeeves (1984) in the U.K. First, nurses and instructors from four adult training centers were interviewed to develop a list of problem behaviors among community residents who represented all levels of intellectual disabilities. Interview results were summarized, condensed, and formulated in a 20-item rating scale

(*Behaviour Disturbance Scale-1*, BDS-1) that was then completed for 45 residents. The BDS-1, which employed three-point frequency of occurrence rating scales contained only one generic self-injurious behavior item ("Physically aggressive to self"). A six-factor solution emerged via factor analysis, with one factor that was labeled "aggressive conduct." This six-item factor contained verbal and physical aggressive behavior toward others as well as the single self-injurious behavior item. The authors then revised and expanded the instrument which resulted in a 51-item version (*Behaviour Disturbance Scale-2*), which employed five-point rating scales ("never" to "very frequently"). Nurses and instructors completed the BDS-2, which contained two generic self-injurious behavior items ("Injures self deliberately" and "Injures self without apparent reason"). Again, six factors were derived with a factor analysis, which the investigators labeled *aggressive conduct, mood disturbance, communicativeness, antisocial conduct, idiosyncratic mannerisms*, and *self-injurious behavior*. The self-injurious behavior factor was made up of four items, namely two self-injurious behavior items and two suicide-related items ("attempts suicide," "has threatened suicide but never actually attempted it"). In other words, self-injurious behavior stood out as relatively independent of aggressive behaviors and of stereotyped behaviors, both of which formed their own factors. This finding was consistent with results from later studies (e.g., Rojahn, 1986).

Maisto, Baumeister, and Maisto (1978) surveyed 1,300 individuals in a state residential facility and identified 182 residents with self-injurious behavior. Thirty-one variables were factor analyzed with varimax rotation. These variables included demographic and medical information as well as behavioral data on self-injurious behaviors, stereotyped behaviors, and an aggressive behavior. A two-factor solution revealed that all self-injurious behaviors, stereotyped behaviors, and the aggressive behavior items loaded more highly on the first factor, which suggests that the self-injurious behaviors did not separate themselves from the aggressive and of stereotyped behaviors. Closer inspection of the factor loadings shows, however, that most of the self-injurious behavior items loaded much more strongly on that factor than the stereotyped and the aggressive behaviors.

Rojahn et al. (2001) conducted a confirmatory factor analysis of the *Behavior Problems Inventory* (BPI) (see Chapter 3 for a description of the scale) to examine the validity of the three a priori subscales, Self-injurious Behavior, Stereotyped Behavior, and Aggression/Destruction. The three-factor structure had a reasonably good fit with the a priori subscales, which means that self-injurious behavior was relatively independent of aggressive behaviors and of stereotyped behaviors.

This step was followed by an exploratory factor analysis. It was found that Aggression/Destruction items had the strongest factor loadings of the three subscales. Two self-injurious behavior items (stuffing objects, aerophagia) and one stereotyped behavior item (spinning objects) were not statistically related to their a priori factor. In summary, the Aggression/Destruction subscale represented a relatively more robust construct than stereotyped behavior and self-injurious behavior (see Table 1.2). From a psychometric view this means that those heterogeneous self-injurious behavior topographies formed a separate and independent construct, albeit a relatively loose and fuzzy one.

Table 1.2: Factor loadings (FL) and item-to-subscale-total correlations (I-S) of BPI-01 items by exploratory factor analysis (Rojahn et al., 2001)

Self-injurious behaviors	FL	I-S	Stereotyped behaviors	FL	I-S	Aggressive/Destructive behaviors	FL	I-S
Self-biting	0.3	0.5	Rocking	0.5	0.6	Hitting	0.7	0.8
Head-hitting	0.5	0.6	Sniffing objects	0.2	0.3	Kicking	0.6	0.6
Body-hitting	0.4	0.5	Spinning	0.6	0.5	Pushing	0.7	0.7
Self-scratching	0.6	0.6	Waving arms	0.5	0.5	Biting	0.7	0.7
Vomiting	0.2	0.3	Head rolling	0.1	0.2	Grabbing, pulling	0.5	0.5
Self-pinching	0.3	0.4	Whirling	0.6	0.4	Scratching	0.7	0.7
Pica	0.4	0.5	Body movements	0.6	0.7	Pinching	0.7	0.7
Stuffing objects	0.04*	0.1	Pacing	0.3	0.4	Spitting	0.5	0.6
Nail pulling	0.1	0.2	Twirling	0.2	0.3	Verbally abusive	0.3	0.4
Poking	0.3	0.4	Hand movements	0.6	0.6	Destroys	0.3	0.4
Aerophagia	0.08*	0.2	Yelling	0.2	0.3	Cruel	0.3	0.4
Hair pulling	0.4	0.4	Sniffing self	0.3	0.4			
Drinking	0.3	0.3	Bouncing	0.2	0.2			
Teeth grinding	0.2	0.4	Spinning	0.7*	0.1			
			Running	0.4	0.4			
			Finger movements	0.5	0.5			
			Manipulating	0.4	0.5			
			Sustained finger	0.5	0.6			
			Rubbing self	0.4	0.5			
			Gazing	0.4	0.5			
			Postures	0.2	0.3			
			Clapping	0.2	0.3			
			Grimacing	0.4	0.4			
			Hand waving	0.5	0.5			

* Non-significant factor loadings (confirmatory factor analysis).

Yet another strategy to explore the BPI factor validity was to examine item total correlations within (see Table 1.2) and across subscales (Rojahn et al., 2001). The mean item-subscale correlation for self-injurious behavior was .39 (SD = .15) with a range .14–.62. For the stereotyped behavior item the mean within category correlations was .41 (SD = .15) with a range .12–.68. The mean within category correlations for the Aggression/Destruction subscale was .59 (SD = .14) with a range .38–.78. All self-injurious behavior items correlated most highly with the self-injurious behavior subscale.

Before the issue can be settled whether different forms of self-injurious behaviors actually form a class of behaviors and to what extent this class can be viewed as separate from aggressive behavior on the one hand and from stereotyped behavior on the other, more research is necessary. This is especially so since other studies showed different outcomes (e.g., Aman & Singh, 1986; Maisto et al., 1978). Perhaps a multi-modal methodology involving repeated assessments with informant rating scales and direct observations could bring clarity. But despite the heterogeneity of the topographies, their widely varying prevalence rates and distribution patterns, quantitative data lend some support to the notion that it is relatively independent at least of other common behavior problems, such aggressive behavior and stereotyped behaviors.

Construct Robustness The robustness of the self-injurious behavior construct reflects to what extent the various types of self-injurious behaviors represent a homogenous and coherent entity. Rojahn (1986) examined 15 self-injurious behavior topographies among 431 individuals who had at least one form of self-injurious behavior with intellectual disabilities. Item selection was based in part on the Maisto et al. (1978) survey instrument. Given skewed distributions of the scores, the data for the self-injurious behavior items were reduced to dichotomous scores and entered into a single linkage cluster analysis of items. The correlation between two variables was used as the measure of similarity. Cluster analysis produced three self-injurious behavior clusters (Table 1.3). One could argue that Cluster 1 consisted of very noticeable, dramatic behaviors with a direct harmful impact, which may be more prone to draw immediate social attention, while Clusters 2 and 3 represented less noticeable behaviors, which have a protracted, cumulative destructive outcome, and which may be less likely to attract attention. However, those are speculations that lack empirical support.

Saloviita (2000) conducted a survey with 421 residents and identified 171 individuals with self-injurious behavior as measured by the original version of the *Adaptive Behavior Scale* (ABS) (Nihira, Foster, Shellhaas, & Leland, 1974). To determine the structure of self-injurious behavior he computed a principal axis factor analysis with varimax rotation that included 10 self-injurious behavior items, four demographic variables, and the ABS stereotyped behavior domain score. Using the scree-plot criterion, he discovered a two-factor solution (see Table 1.4).

Methodological Problems of Topographical Classification It is quite difficult to compare different studies on structural classification of self-injurious behavior because – among many other differences between studies – they were obtained with different assessment instruments and therefore include different behavior topographies (e.g., see Tables 1.3

Table 1.3: Results of a single linkage cluster analysis of self-injurious behavior items (Rojahn, 1986)

Cluster 1	Cluster 2	Cluster 3
Head targeted hitting with body parts	Rumination	Stuffing objects in body orifices
Body (non-head) targeted hitting with body parts	Teeth grinding	Pica
Head hitting with or against objects		Inserting fingers in body orifices
Body hitting with or against objects		Excessive drinking
Pinching		Air swallowing
Biting		
Scratching		
Hair pulling		

Table 1.4: Results of a principal axis factor analysis with varimax rotation that included self-injurious behavior items, demographic variables and the ABS stereotyped behavior domain score (Saloviita, 2000)

Factor 1	Factor 2
IQ	Age
Stereotyped behavior	Length of institutionalization
Bites or cuts self	Scratches or picks self causing injury
Slaps and strikes self	Picks at any sore he might have
Bangs head or other parts of the body	
Pulls own hair, ears, etc.	
Soils and smears self	

and 1.4). For instance, some studies use a broad item that includes any kind of body hitting or banging behavior (e.g., Johnson et al., 1988), while others break them down into subtypes (1) head hitting with own body parts (hands, knees, etc.), (2) hitting head with or against objects, (3) hitting body (not the head) with own body parts, and (4) hitting body parts (not the head) with or against objects (e.g., Maurice & Trudel, 1982; Rojahn, 1986) (see Table 1.7).

In addition, the use of multivariate statistical procedures can be troublesome from a methodological point of view. Here are some of the problems:

- Specific self-injurious behavior consists of many specific topographies with varying prevalence rates. Low prevalence items tend to have low item-factor loadings, item inter-rater agreement and test–retest item reliability.
- In a self-injurious behavior assessment instrument, given the multitude of equally significant topographies, each one is typically represented by a single item only.

This – by definition – makes that item unreliable. Generating more than one item to describe a specific topography would probably improve reliability, but it would also increase the number of items to an extent that would render the resulting instrument unfeasible. On the other hand, dropping the very low-frequency items runs the risk of reducing the clinical significance of the instruments.

- Self-injurious behavior topographies tend to have skewed frequency distributions, with more cases having low-frequency behaviors and fewer high-frequency behaviors.
- Finally, we lack a coherent theory about the structure of self-injurious behaviors.

In summary, to date, we have no clear and stable topographical structure of the different forms of self-injurious behavior. If we have learned anything, it is that the conglomerate of the various forms of self-injurious behavior constitutes a rather loose construct.

1.2.2.1.2. Dynamic Characteristics

In addition to the topographical forms, self-injurious behavior has also been studied with regard to its dynamic characteristics, such as temporal and sequential features and the force of impact. There is much less research to be found on the classification of self-injurious behavior according to dynamic as compared to the topographical characteristics. We will briefly discuss research on two salient dynamic characteristics, namely sequential characteristics (or cyclicity) and impact force.

Sequential Characteristics   Considering that self-injurious behavior is influenced by environmental as well as internal biological variables, it would seem reasonable to assume that the occurrences of discrete self-injurious behavior events are not randomly distributed over time. Indeed, it has been frequently observed in the literature that most self-injurious behavior tends to occur in somewhat predictable temporal patterns, although that may not become apparent by simple observation alone. For instance, self-injurious behavior in some individuals has the tendency to occur in a massed fashion, or in bursts, rather than as isolated, singular events. Behavioral sequence pattern can be explored in different time units, from seconds to months and even across the entire lifespan.

Using time-series analyses, Lewis, MacLean, Johnson, and Baumeister (1981) found temporal cycles in self-injurious behavior and stereotyped behavior with variable peak frequencies across five individual subjects. The participants had profound intellectual disabilities and were living in a residential institution at the time. Ultradian or less than 24-hour rhythms were discovered for each individual on each day and the authors concluded that the temporal characteristics of self-injurious behavior seemed to reflect the influence of periodic changes in the institutional environment and, to a lesser degree, an endogenous rest-activity rhythm. In a longitudinal study Lewis, Silva, and Gray-Silva (1995) found evidence for monthly cyclicity in self-injurious as well as in aggressive behavior.

Marion, Touchette, and Sandman (2003) set out to quantify the temporal characteristics of self-injurious behavior, stereotypic behavior, and agitated behavior. Their goal was to determine whether a unique sequential pattern of expression of self-injurious behavior would emerge. Forty sequential hours of observational data were collected in the natural environment of 45 individuals (aged 17–80 years) with developmental disabilities and a broad range of severe maladaptive behaviors. Conditional probability analysis found that successive episodes of self-injurious behavior were indeed sequentially dependent and that the sequential association was unrelated to the self-injurious behavior occurrence rate. Compared with other environmental and behavioral events such as stereotyped behaviors, agitation, staff and peer interactions, the best predictor of the occurrence of self-injurious behavior was intra-individual, namely an earlier self-injurious behavior episode.[4]

Kroeker, Touchette, and Engleman (2004) used survival analysis to determine how long the probability of occurrence of a self-injurious behavior remains elevated after a previous self-injurious behavior occurrence. Discrete self-injurious behavior events were grouped into bouts and the estimated bout length criterion time point was determined individually for 19 subjects with developmental disorders and severe self-injurious behavior. Bout length criterion estimates ranged from 0.6 to 15.5 seconds. When participants' self-injurious behaviors were grouped into bouts, the rate of bouts and the average number of self-injurious behaviors in each bout were found to be more stable than the rate of individual self-injurious behaviors. The authors argued that analyses of self-injurious behavior sequences might facilitate functional analysis of self-injurious behavior.

Impact Force   Impact force is another potentially interesting parameter for some forms of self-injurious behavior, from a scientific but even more so from a clinical point of view. Numerous cases have been reported, for instance, where individuals with a chronic history of head banging have suffered a partial or complete retinal detachment in one or both eyes and therefore blindness as a presumed result of incessant blows to the head. Newell, Sprague, Pain, Deutsch, and Meinhold (1999) measured the impact force of head banging of an eight-year-old girl with profound intellectual disabilities and an autistic disorder. The behavior was not only found to be highly consistent, but the impact force was similar to boxing blows and karate hits. This rather dramatic finding should not be surprising to any experienced clinician and practitioner who has worked with individuals with head banging.

Impact force measures may be relevant parameters and indices of change for some self-injurious behavior topographies, such as head banging, biting, teeth grinding, or scratching, but it may not be for others (e.g., pica, self-induced vomiting, or removing of finger or toe nails).

1.2.2.2. Functional Classification
The fundamental underlying assumption of the functional-behavioral approach to classifying self-injurious behavior is that behavior is learned, which means acquired as a lawful outcome of the individual's learning history. But every individual also

---

[4] This is consistent with the notion of a "contagious" distribution, which refers to a probability distribution, which is dependent on a parameter that itself has a probability distribution.

possesses a unique physiology due to her or his genetic endowment, which accounts for inter-individual differences in learning and a predisposition toward the development of certain behaviors. Functional analysis distinguishes types of behaviors on the basis of their common functional properties or consequences. It addresses primarily the behavioral mechanisms that currently maintain the behavior rather than its learning origin. Selecting treatments based on the specific controlling variables of the target behavior of a specific individual has been a mainstay of behavior therapy from its early days (e.g., Kanfer & Phillips, 1970; Kanfer & Saslow, 1969; Ullman & Krasner, 1965).

With regard to self-injurious behavior among people with intellectual disabilities, it was perhaps Lovaas, Freitag, Gold, and Kassorla (1965) who published the first systematic functional analysis of self-injurious behavior that appeared in the literature. Working with a nine-year-old hospitalized girl, they discovered in experimental fashion that the occurrence and magnitude of self-injurious behavior was directly related to environmental events, namely social reinforcement and extinction. Bachman (1972) published probably the first conceptual paper on the behavioral analysis of the acquisition and maintenance of self-injurious behavior, a paper that never received the attention that it deserved. Based on Skinner's work, and supported by clinical and animal research studies, Bachman distinguished between two main hypotheses, the avoidance hypothesis and the discriminative stimulus-conditioned reinforcement hypothesis:

- The avoidance hypothesis proposes that individuals might be "willing" to expose themselves to aversive stimulation (meaning the pain involved in self-injurious behavior), if they can thereby avoid even more aversive events (e.g., having to take a shower).
- The conditioned stimulus/conditioned reinforcement hypothesis states that (a) an originally aversive stimulus can become a conditioned reinforcer if it is repeatedly paired with a reinforcer that has maintained the behavior; and that (b) that originally aversive stimulus can also function as a discriminative stimulus for that behavior.

A more widely cited paper was Carr's (1977) *Psychological Bulletin* article titled "The motivation of self-injurious behavior: A review of some hypotheses." It introduced a broader readership to the lawful functional properties of self-injurious behavior in persons with intellectual disabilities. The paper by Iwata, Dorsey, Slifer, Bauman, and Richman (1982) presented for the first time a standardized method to conduct experimental functional analyses. Functional classification of self-injurious behavior will be discussed in more detail in a later section of this book.

1.2.2.3. Combined Functional and Topographical Classification
The question can be raised, whether differential topography-specific functional profiles exist. Or, more concretely, is head banging more likely to be maintained by social reinforcement than eye poking or skin picking?

Functional and structural-topographic classifications of self-injurious behavior emerged from opposing scientific traditions of assessment, namely the psychometric mentalistic tradition and the behavior analytic tradition, which emanated from radically different heuristic models, assumptions, and assessment approaches. However, functional and structural-topographic classifications are not mutually exclusive (Emerson & Bromley, 1995). In fact, combining them may reveal interesting information. Just as was seen earlier with regard to self-injurious behavior in persons of average or superior intellect, it is not unreasonable to assume that some forms of self-injurious behavior are more likely maintained by certain functional dynamics than others.

There is emerging evidence to support that view. For instance, Cannella, O'Reilly, and Lancioni (2006) discovered in a literature review that hand mouthing is typically maintained by automatic reinforcement. Also, self-injurious and aggressive behaviors, on average, seem to have different functional profiles (e.g., Bienstein, Smith, Rojahn, & Matson, 2006). In the context of psychopharmacological research, Garcia and Smith (1999) demonstrated a function- and topography-specific effect of naltrexone on self-injurious behavior. Conducting extended functional analyses during a double-blind placebo-controlled trial of naltrexone they found a differential effect depending on the topography of self-injurious behavior in one of two clients. While the medication reduced head slapping but not head banging during the escape condition, it did not reduce self-injurious behavior in the other conditions. Schroeder and some of his colleagues also found effects for different self-injurious behavior topographies, functions, and subjects in three functional analysis studies in their double-blind crossover program study of risperidone (Valdovinos et al., 2002; Crosland et al., 2003; Zarcone et al., 2004). In a clinical study by Rojahn, Hoch, Whittaker, and González (in press) six graduate students interviewed direct-care staff in an institution for people with intellectual disabilities using a functional assessment rating scale (*Questions About Behavioral Function*, QABF; Vollmer & Matson, 1995) for severe problem behaviors. The mean QABF results of the three most frequently observed self-injurious behavior topographies, head hitting, biting, and self-scratching are shown in Figure 1.1 Despite large inter-individual QABF score variations different behavioral topographies tended to have different functional characteristics.

Most of the evidence about an association between the self-injurious behavior topographies and their differential functions comes either from retrospective data analyses from convenience samples, or as secondary study outcomes. Exploring this issue with explicit hypotheses and a prospective research design may be worth pursuing. Valuable empirical information might be discovered to assists in treatment selection.

1.3. Epidemiology

1.3.1. Epidemiology in Intellectually Typical Populations

1.3.1.1. Self-Injurious Behavior Prevalence
The actual prevalence and incidence rates of self-injurious behavior in the general population are difficult to ascertain at this point due to many methodological challenges. For instance, many individuals who engage in self-mutilation do so secretly (e.g., Sachsse, 1999). Drawing firm conclusions from widely varying epidemiological

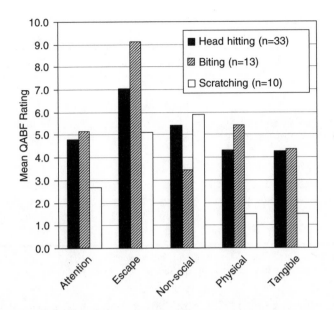

Figure 1.1: Differential profile of three SIB types on the QABF Rating Scale: Topography–function relationships (maximum score = 15).

data sets is also hampered by problems such as non-standard case definitions (e.g., inclusion or exclusion of suicidal behavior, self-poisoning) and questionable reliability of the survey instruments. To give an example, Klonsky, Oltmanns, and Turkheimer (2003) reported that approximately 4% of almost 2,000 military recruits self-reported deliberate self-harm. The sample consisted of 1,236 males and 750 females. Self-harm was defined by responses to two items of the *Schedule for Nonadaptive and Adaptive Personality* (Clark, 1996): "I have hurt myself on purpose several times" (4.2% males, 3.6% females), and "When I get tense, hurting myself physically somehow calms me down" (2.5% males, 1.7% females); 0.8% males and 0.5% females responded affirmatively to both items. Recruits who self harmed showed more symptoms of borderline and dependent personality disorders than those without. While these results are interesting, one has to be skeptical about the reliability of single-item assessments with vaguely defined behavior and the accuracy of self-report.

Nevertheless, according to Suyemoto (1998) there is a growing consensus that the incidence of self-mutilation is on the rise. The available data also indicate that the incidence of self-injurious behavior in psychiatric populations is considerably higher than in the normative population, ranging from 4.3% to 20%. For instance, Briere and Gil (1998) reported a self-injurious behavior prevalence of 4% in a community sample of 927 individuals, and 21% in a clinical sample of 321.

1.3.1.2. Prevalence of Specific Topographies
Klonsky et al. (2003) reviewed the recent literature on the prevalence of *deliberate* self-injurious behavior in clinical and non-clinical samples that included several studies

Table 1.5: Prevalence estimates of common topographies of self-mutilation in the intellectually typical population

	Klonsky et al. (2003)[a]	Rodham et al. (2004)[b]
Self-cutting	70+	65
Self-burning	15–35	–
Self-hitting, -banging, self-battery	21–44	4
Interference with wound healing	22	–
Self-poisoning	–	31
Recreational drug use	–	4
Hanging or strangulating	–	1
Ingestion of non-edible substance or object	–	<1
Electrocution	–	<1

[a] Self-injurious behavior in various clinical and non-clinical samples.
[b] Direct and non-direct self-injurious behavior in a sample of 15 to 16 year olds.

(Herpetz, 1995; Briere & Gil, 1998; Gratz, 2001; Favazza & Conterio, 1988; Langbehn & Pfohl, 1993; Nijman, Dautzenberg, & Merkelbach, 1999). As Table 1.5 shows, it appears as if the most common forms of direct self-injury in the intellectually non-disabled population are self-cutting, burning, self-hitting or banging, and interference with wound healing.

Rodham et al. (2004) surveyed in a sample of 15–16 year olds looking at *direct* as well as *non-direct* forms of self-injurious behavior. Topographies surveyed were direct forms of self-injurious behavior (self-cutting and self-hitting) and the indirect forms (self-poisoning, recreational drug use, self-hanging or strangulating, the ingestion of non-edible substances or objects, and self-electrocution). Again, the most common form of self-injurious behavior was self-cutting. The most common form of indirect self-injurious behavior in young adolescents seems to be self-overdosing.

1.3.1.3. Self-Injurious Behavior and Gender
Prevalence of self-injurious behavior in the non-intellectually disabled population is one-and-a-half to three times higher among women than in men (Yates, 2004). Suyemoto (1998) summarized her review of the literature by stating that the majority of individuals who engage in self-mutilation are single females.

1.3.2. Epidemiology in Persons with Intellectual Disabilities

Before we discuss the extant literature on the epidemiology of self-injurious behavior in people with intellectual disabilities, it is important to lower the readers' expectations from the start. The state of the art in the epidemiology of intellectual disabilities in general is woeful due to a lack of standardized research methods and widely varying definitions of the targeted behavior (Roeleveld, Zielhuis, & Gabreëls, 1997).

This problem is compounded when it comes to self-injurious behavior in this population. A table in the Appendix systematically describes key characteristics as well as the ascertained results of published surveys and epidemiological studies on self-injurious behavior in people with intellectual disabilities since 1966. Not included in that review were epidemiological studies on specific genetic syndromes, which will be discussed later.

1.3.2.1. Self-Injurious Behavior Prevalence
Among the reviewed surveys it was the exception to find inclusion or exclusion criteria of the types of behaviors that were considered self-injurious behavior. Most of the surveys reported some form of point prevalence. *Point* prevalence rate refers to the proportion of cases within a reference population in which the cases are identified at a given point in time (Kiley & Lubin, 1983). The term is also used for prevalence estimates that allow for a relatively narrow time window, such as two months during which the respective behavior must have been observed. Such a provision is necessary for clinically severe, but relatively rare behaviors. Most prevalence estimates come from cross-sectional studies.

Considering the variety of different reference populations, sampling strategies, settings, and assessment methods, it is not surprising that self-injurious behavior prevalence rates varied greatly across different epidemiological studies. Large-scale studies from the U.S. and some European countries that surveyed the whole intellectual spectrum of individuals of all ages in both the community and in institutions found self-injurious behavior prevalence rates to range between 4% and 9% (Table 1.6).

If we dare to accept these numbers as ballpark estimates, disregarding the numerous problems that impinge on each one of them, we can make cautious projections. If we are assuming that the U.S. population is 300 million, that the prevalence of individuals with intellectual disabilities is 1.4% (Larson, Lakin, & Anderson, 2001), and that the self-injurious behavior prevalence is 4%, the following figures emerge: there are approximately 168,000 individuals with intellectual disabilities and self-injurious behavior in this country. If we accept the self-injurious behavior prevalence to be 10% and all other assumptions remaining equal, there would be 420,000 individuals with intellectual disabilities and self-injurious behavior in the U.S.

1.3.2.2. Self-Injurious Behavior Incidence
Incidence refers to the number of newly emerging cases within a specified time period (Kiley & Lubin, 1983). Incidence data are best obtained with longitudinal studies,

Table 1.6: Self-injurious behavior prevalence in intellectual disabilities from large scale surveys

4.2%	Kebbon and Windahl (1985)	Sweden
8.0%	Rojahn et al. (1993)	California and New York
9.3%	Borthwick-Duffy (1994)	California
4.0%	Emerson et al. (2001)	UK
4.4%	Holden and Gitselen (2006)	Norway
5.3%	Lowe, Allen, & Jones (2007)	Wales

which tend to be much more expensive than cross-sectional studies. Therefore, it is not surprising that to this date no large-scale incidence studies of self-injurious behavior have been reported.

Perhaps the only study that established something approaching incidence estimates of self-injurious behavior, albeit for a temporally limited time period of 18 months, was conducted by Murphy, Hall, Oliver, and Kissi-Debra (1999). The main purpose of that study was to examine potential risk markers for newly developing self-injurious behavior in young children. The investigators followed two cohorts of children, one that was described as being at risk for self-injurious behavior, while the other one was not. For a period of 18 months, each child was evaluated every three months with multiple rating scales and direct observations. They estimated that among 614 children 10 years old or younger with severe intellectual disability, 3% of new self-injurious behavior cases emerged within three months.

Other sources that shed some indirect light on incidence data are cross-sectional prevalence data across age distributions (see further below).

1.3.2.3. Prevalence of Specific Topographies

Table 1.7 illustrates the lack of a consensus among researchers as to what specific self-injurious behavior topographies should be included or excluded under the term "self-injurious behavior." Nevertheless, some similarities can be observed across studies as well. All studies in Table 1.7, for instance, included some form of hitting. However, comparing prevalence rates for hitting behaviors across studies is not a straightforward matter, because alternative terms that may or may not be synonymous have been used (e.g., banging, butting, striking, slapping). To complicate matters, some researchers distinguished between different hitting behaviors even further by specifying the body part that is likely to be injured (arm, body, face, head), and the object that was used in the act (hands, objects). A similar problem exists with the semantic similarities between digging, gouging, poking, and stuffing. It is thus difficult to draw any firm conclusions about the relative prevalence of different self-injurious behavior topographies.

Self-biting was reported as the most prevalent form of self-injurious behavior in six different studies, yet only 10 of the 14 studies even surveyed self-biting. The relative prevalence rate of biting ranged from 12% to 93%. Other frequently represented and relatively high rate behaviors were scratching (reported in eight studies, relative prevalence rate ranging from 4% to 42%), hair pulling, rumination, and different types of gouging.

Until researchers begin to adopt standard survey instruments it will remain difficult to get a good sense of the prevalence of SIB in general and of specific topographies in particular.

1.3.2.4. Self-Injurious Behavior and Gender

As mentioned previously, in the intellectually typical population self-injurious behavior has been found that self-injurious behavior is much more prevalent in women than in men (e.g., Favazza, 1999).

Table 1.7: Prevalence of self-injurious behavior topographies in percent of the self-injurious behavior samples across studies

	Studies											
	A	B	C	D	E	F	G	H	I	J	K	L
Head banging with body part	23	18	9	45	37	42	36		29		47	18
Head banging with/against objects	57	26	9	30	29	30	28	57	13		42	
Body hitting with body part			9	31	14	20	10			22	35	9
Body hitting with object			4	17		17	10			16	27	
Throwing self to floor, wall, furniture	x		3						7	21		
Biting self (including lip chewing)	66		13	45	39	46	38	42	37	27		16
Scratching	26		13	42	26	24			16	6	20	13
Pinching	46		<1	19		19	4					3
Fingers in body cavities, gouging	x	x	5	16	10	15	8	54		1	12	6
Hair pulling		8	4	15	6	15	8				11	3
Pica (including eating feces)			5	15	13	7		24	10		19	10
Self-induced (ruminative) vomiting		x	<1	8	5	10		9			4	4
Pulling out nails, flesh, teeth			5							6		1
Digging in wounds			4				1					
Inserting objects in body cavities			1	4								1
Rubbing	x		1							6		6
Teeth grinding			4	14		14					7	6
Excessive masturbation		x	3									
Burning			2									
Cutting			2				2					
Mouthing					15	12						
Air swallowing				4			39				1	1
Excessive drinking		19		11		11	2				11	1
Skin picking									16			
Tool banging												
Self-choking, strangling		x	<1									
Stopping blood circulation			2									

x = for prevalence rates lower than 10% no exact number are provided.

Sources: (A) Smeets, 1971; (B) Singh, 1977; (C) Maurice & Trudel, 1986; (D) Rojahn, 1986; (E) Griffin et al., 1986; (F) Griffin et al., 1987; (G) Oliver et al., 1987; (H) Johnson et al., 1988; (I) Emerson & Walker, 1990; (J) Bodfish, Powell, Golden, & Lewis, 1995b; (K) Emerson et al., 2001; (L) Rojahn et al., 2001.

In the population with intellectual disabilities, however, no clear relationship between self-injurious behavior and gender has been discovered (except for x-linked genetic syndromes such as the Lesch–Nyhan syndrome). Table 1.8 presents a summary of studies that presented some information on gender and self-injurious behavior prevalence. Only two total population studies were found with clear gender-related information on the prevalence of self-injurious behavior, Borthwick, Meyers, and Eyman (1981) and Rojahn, Borthwick-Duffy, and Jacobson (1993). The mean prevalence in males and females was 9% and 7%, respectively. Given the large numbers of individuals in these two studies it is likely that the differences were statistically significant, but in the opposite direction compared with the intellectually typical population. However, we would caution to draw any conclusions about gender from these numbers, due to inherent weaknesses in those databases (both studies involved administrative rather than research data sets).

As the table in the Appendix shows, other studies presented data on gender in their respective self-injurious behavior samples as well. However, those data cannot be

Table 1.8: Prevalence rate of self-injurious behavior in percent as a function of sex

	Female	**Male**
Prevalence		
Borthwick et al. (1981)	9	10
Rojahn et al. (1999)	5	8
Mean	7	9
Range	5–9	8–10
Prevalence within SIB sample		
Collacott et al. (1998)	43	57
Emberson and Walker (1990)	50	50
Emerson et al. (2001) 1988 survey	35	65
Emerson et al. (2001) 1995 survey	31	69
Griffin et al. (1986)	44	56
Hillery and Mulcahy (1997)	42	58
Kebbon and Windahl (1985)	44	56
Maisto et al. (1978)	55	45
Oliver et al. (1987)	42	58
Rojahn (1984)	54	46
Rojahn (1986)	51	48
Schroeder et al. (1978) (mild SIB)	49	47
Schroeder et al. (1978) (severe SIB)	47	53
Singh (1977)	40	60
Smeets (1971)	40	60
Mean	47	53
Range	40–55	45–60

SIB – self-injurious behavior.

meaningfully interpreted because the gender composition of the reference population was not provided.

1.3.2.5. Self-Injurious Behavior and Level of Functioning

There is a strong and consistent trend across studies suggesting that the prevalence of self-injurious behavior increases with decreasing intellectual ability.[5] It is important to remember that the vast majority of individuals with intellectual disabilities have mild intellectual disability. The estimates vary from study to study and only rough estimates are available. Prevalence estimates of mild intellectual disability range from 85% to 90%, moderate between 7% and 10%, severe between 2% and 3%, and profound between 1% and 2%. To the extent to which we can rely on those data, the mean estimated percentage of SIB in people with mild intellectual disability is 4% (Table 1.9), 7% of those with moderate intellectual disability, 15.5% with severe and 25% with profound intellectual disability show self-injurious behavior.

1.3.2.6. Self-Injurious Behavior and Chronological Age

Only a handful of studies were designed to estimate prevalence across age groups of individuals with intellectual disabilities. Eyman and Call (1977) reported a prevalence rate of 15% before and after 12 years of age among almost 7,000 service recipients with intellectual disabilities from two regional centers in two Western states. Compared to earlier data we showed, this is a high estimate, but the composition of the reference population may have been skewed toward lower levels of functioning. Borthwick et al. (1981) later surveyed a sample similar to the one surveyed earlier by Evman and McCall's and reported that the self-injurious behavior prevalence in young children with intellectual disabilities from birth to 3 years was 6%, increased in children between the ages of 4–10 to 10%, then stabilized during the teen's ages 11–20 at 10%, and then dropped slightly in adults to 9%.

Figure 1.2 shows data published by Jacobson (1982) that were recalculated by the authors. In that data set it appears as if an interaction between age and level of intellectual disability occurred.[6] While the self-injurious behavior prevalence among the children and adolescent was 7% (0–21 years) and 7.5% in the adults (22–45 years), the prevalence in the mild and moderate group was similar and stable across age groups (approximately 2–3%), a reversed trend can be noticed in the moderate and the profound groups. While the prevalence in severe intellectual disability in the younger group (9%) was higher than the adults (6%), the opposite was true in the profound group; self-injurious behavior prevalence in the children and adolescent with profound intellectual disability was 14%, which increased to 18% among the adults.

Saloviita (2002) reported a curvilinear relationship between age and self-injurious behavior prevalence for a sample of hospital residents in Finland. For the youngest group (up to 17 years old) self-injurious behavior prevalence was 34%, for then for the young adults between 18 and 34 the prevalence increased to 47%, but then dropped in

---

[5] According to the definitions of intellectual disability in the DSM-IV and ICD-10.

[6] Since we did not have access to the raw data we were unable to test the differences statistically.

Table 1.9: Self-injurious behavior point prevalence in percent[a]

	Level of mental retardation			
	Mild	**Moderate**	**Severe**	**Profound**
Prevalence				
Ballinger (1971)	6	10	18	29
Ross (1972)	13	18	25	26
Borthwick et al. (1981)	4	7	15	25
Jacobson (1982) – ages 0–21	2	3	9	14
Jacobson (1982) – ages 22–45	3	3	6	18
Kebbon and Windahl (1985)	1	1	7	13
Rojahn et al. (1993)	4	7	16	25
Borthwick-Duffy (1994)	1	2	3	7
Miller, Canen, Roebel, and MacLean (2000)	27	37	49	60
Saloviita (2000)	19	31	35	53
Median	4	7	15.5	25
Range	1–27	1–37	3–49	7–60
Prevalence within self-injurious behavior sample				
Ballinger (1971)	9	16	28	45
Singh (1977)	8	36	48	8
Danford and Huber (1982)	2	4	17	78
Kebbon and Windahl (1985)	1	12	48	41
Griffin et al. (1986)	1	9	19	66
Rojahn (1986)	13	28	43	16
Hillery and Mulcahy (1997)	0	42	53	5
Median	2	16	43	41
Range	0–13	4–42	17–53	5–66

[a] Only studies that reported prevalence rates across all four MR levels separately are listed.

older adults to the young adult level (36%). Questions remain about the extent to which those age distribution data can be generalized.

1.3.2.7. Self-Injurious Behavior and the Living Environment

Table 1.10 summarizes the results of five studies conducted in the U.S. that addressed the prevalence of self-injurious behavior according to residential settings. The residential categories are roughly arranged along a restrictedness or "normalization" gradient of the environment, ranging from traditional institutions to independent living arrangements. The difficulty in tabulating data of this kind across studies in addition to all the problems that plague epidemiology of intellectual disability mentioned earlier is the heterogeneity of environments within the categories. One interesting finding is the

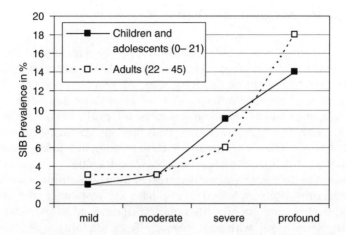

Figure 1.2: SIB Prevalence: Interaction between age and level of mental retardation (drawn by the authors from data published by Jacobson, 1982).

Table 1.10: Prevalence rate of self-injurious behavior in percent as a function of residential settings[a]

	Independent living	Parents/ Family	Community care	Intermediate care/ Nursing home/ Convalescent hospital	Institution
Borthwick-Duffy (1994)	<1	<1	6	5	12
Borthwick et al. (1981)	8	13	8	18	38
Hill and Bruininks (1984)		(11)[b]			22
Jacobson (1982) [ages 0–21]	0	7	9	(no data)	16
Jacobson (1982) [ages 22–45]	1	3	5	(no data)	15
Mean[c]	3	6	7	12	21
Range	<1–8	<1–13	5–9	5–18	12–38

[a] Only studies conducted in the United States were included.
[b] The authors of this study distinguished only between institutional and non-institutional residence.
[c] Means and ranges were calculated only across those studies that had separate values reported on each of the four levels of mental retardation.

decreasing trend in the prevalence of self-injurious behavior in segregated institutions from 38% (in Borthwick et al., 1981) to 12% (Borthwick-Duffy, 1994).[7] However, whether this discovery reflects actual changes in the true prevalence or just differences in survey methods remains unclear.

---

[7] The Borthwick et al. (1981) data were collected in 1979 in Arizona, California and Nevada, on a sample of 6,202 people who received services for individuals with developmental disabilities, while the Borthwick-Duffy paper was based on all individuals with developmental disabilities who received services in California ($n = 91,164$).

1.4. Effects on Parents and Care Takers

Caring for people with developmental disabilities can be difficult and demanding and create disruptions for families (e.g., Seltzer & Heller, 1997). But adding the burden of severe behavior problems can be daunting. Over 15 years ago the cost of care in the U.S. alone for people with intellectual disabilities who exhibit destructive behavior was estimated to exceed $3 billion (National Institutes of Health, 1991). This is a staggering amount of money. The big problem is that funding the acute service needs for challenging behaviors siphons off funds from less pressing but no less deserving service needs of individuals without conspicuous behavior difficulties.

But in addition to the mere fiscal burden created by self-injurious behavior and other destructive behaviors, problem behaviors also have a devastating and subverting effect on caretakers, parents, and families. Mossman, Hastings, and Brown (2002) conducted a control comparison study with staff members from schools for children with intellectual disabilities. Each one watched one of five videotapes depicting a student without self-injurious behavior, with self-injurious behavior maintained by positive reinforcement, self-injurious behavior maintained by negative reinforcement, and self-injurious behavior unrelated to social events. Those viewing the video without self-injurious behavior reported fewer negative emotional responses than did those watching self-injurious behavior videos. Interestingly, they also found an effect of behavioral function on the self-reported emotional responses of the mediators. In particular, self-injurious behavior maintained by negative reinforcement was associated with more self-reported negative emotion. Bailey, Hare, Hatton, and Limb (2006) also found evidence that direct-care staff that work with individuals with intellectual disabilities and problem behaviors experienced negative emotions such as sadness, hopelessness, helplessness, frustration, and guilt.

Many anecdotal reports and case studies indicate that self-injurious behavior contributes to parental stress and that it can be very disruptive to families (e.g., Stein, 2005). Baker et al. (2003) found that parenting stress was associated with behavior problems in children with developmental delays. In fact, parental stress was more strongly linked to behavior problems than to developmental delay. Similarly, Lecavalier, Leone, and Wiltz (2006) found that stress in parents and teachers of young people with autism spectrum disorders was related to behavior problems in general, and to self-injurious behavior in particular. Plant and Sanders (2007) reported similar findings.

In summary, self-injurious behavior is not only a problem due to its immediate deleterious effect on the physical health and well-being of the person who exhibits it. Although we do not have enough studies on the social side effects of severe self-injurious behavior, the ones that have been published clearly and unanimously reveal very negative emotional effects on others whether at home or in specialized care facilities. Caring for someone with incessant self-injurious behavior can be highly stressful and demoralizing for direct care workers and families alike.

Chapter 2

Etiology and Maintenance

2.1. Psychodynamic Models

Empirical evidence for the utility of psychodynamic theories or for the treatment of self-injurious behavior (SIB) in people with intellectual disabilities is weak at best. Nevertheless, in keeping a broad view of the topic, we will give a brief overview of some historical as well as contemporary, neo-psychodynamic theories of self-injurious behavior. None of them were developed explicitly with the intellectually disabled population in mind.

2.1.1. Traditional Psychoanalytic Interpretations

Based on Sigmund Freud's theory of the struggle between the death and life instinct, Menninger (1935) saw the root of self-injurious behavior in the conflict between the aggressive–destructive impulses, and the opposing will to live. The aggressive and destructive impulses, which are assisted by the superego, would drive us into suicide were it not for the opposing will to live. Self-injurious behavior, or partial suicide, can be seen as a compromise that avoids total suicide. Owing to the role of the superego, self-mutilation always implies some form of self-punishment, regardless of whether it occurs as part of religious practices, during puberty rites, or in psychotic behavior. Menninger also thought that self-mutilation can be the manifestation of some neurotic condition. In those cases, injury of some body part often symbolizes castration, which is performed to satisfy erotic and aggressive cravings and at the same time to gratify a need for self-punishment.

Cain (1961) disputed the indispensable role of the superego in self-injurious behavior. Since self-injurious behavior can be observed in animals and in children well before significant superego development, Cain concluded that SIB obviously can exist without a role of the super-ego. Therefore, and in contradiction to Menninger's position, SIB is not necessarily a self-punitive act. Cain drew a distinction between *auto-aggressive* and *self-aggressive* behavior, dependent on the degree of involvement of a developed "self." He also rejected the notion that turning inward of aggressive behavior is not necessarily an outlet when outwardly directed aggressive behavior has been blocked.

While classical psychodynamic theories are mostly of historical interest, neo-analytic theories hold much more promise in contributing to our practical understanding of risk factors of SIB in people with intellectual disabilities.

2.1.2. Neo-Analytic Interpretations

The common characteristics of traditional and neo-analytic theories of psychopathology that emerges later in life hold that internalized experiences of early social relationships contribute and shape later behavioral outcomes and emphasize the role of the caregiver. Since the theoretical contributions of neo-analytical schools of thought have as yet not had any noticeable impact on clinical research or treatment of self-injurious behavior among individuals with intellectual disabilities, we will provide only a short description of a few and refer the interested reader to cited primary and secondary sources. For the preparation of the following section, we owe much to Yates (2004) and her excellent review paper.

2.1.2.1. Object Relations Theory

Object relations theory is based on the works of Fairbairn (1952), Winnicott (1953, 1960) and others and postulates that the ego-self exists only in relation to other objects, external or internal. The internal objects are internalized versions of external objects and are primarily formed during early interactions with the parents. There are three fundamental "affects" that can exist between the self and the other – (1) attachment, (2) frustration, and (3) rejection. These affects are universal emotional states that are major building blocks of the personality. Traumatic early life experiences may lead to the development of a false sense of self. This false sense of self can produce and use self-injurious behavior as a strategy to protect the "true" self from harm (Yates, 2004).

2.1.2.2. Attachment Theory

Attachment theory, which originated in the work of Bowlby and Ainsworth, is concerned with the tendency of human beings to maintain proximity to an attachment figure. A healthy mother–infant relationship during first two to three years of life sets the stage for the child's later socio-emotional adaptation (Bowlby, 1969/1982, 1988). Socio-emotional development includes important components such as a sense of self, expectations of others, the ability to engage in reciprocal empathic relationships, and the capacity for arousal modulation. Ainsworth, Blehar, Waters, and Walls (1978) distinguished between three attachment styles[1]: (1) securely attached, (2) avoidant/insecurely attached, and (3) ambivalent/insecurely attached.

---

[1] To classify infant behavior, the "strange situation" procedure was developed to assess the effect of short-term maternal absence on the infant behavior upon reunion with the mother. Secure attachment is suggested when the infant greets and seeks attachment with the reappearing mother. Avoidant/insecure attachment is indicated when the infant rejects the mother. An ambivalent/insecure attachment is manifested by an alternation of anger and seeking attachment with the mother.

Insecure attachment can lead to negative self-expectations and pessimistic expectations of others and of the relationships one can have with others and may set the stage for a later development of self-injurious behavior. Yates (2004) assumes that a disorganized attachment may be an important mechanism by which a traumatic experience in the early caregiving environment can endanger healthy socio-emotional adaptation. Deficient socio-emotional adaptation can later become a contributing factor to the emergence of self-injurious behavior as a stress coping mechanism, especially when adaptive coping strategies are unavailable to the person and when relationships with others are not seen as a source of support.

Attachment theory finds some support by the early primate work of Harlow (1958) and other researchers that followed in his step over the years since that time (e.g., Kraemer & Clark, 1990). One of the key insights was that almost all rhesus monkeys that were raised in isolation, either without their mothers or without their peers later developed severe self-injurious behavior (Harlow, Harlow, & Suomi, 1971). Kraemer and Clark (1990) developed a comprehensive neurobiological model of self-injurious behavior in rhesus monkeys (discussed in more detail in Chapter 4).

2.1.2.3. Psychosomatic Theories

Psychosomatic theories view self-injurious behavior as a means to resolve body-based conflicts that are rooted in poorly developed, clear boundaries between self and non-self, between self and others. Unhealthy forms of caregiving, such as overly intrusive caregiving or emotional unavailability are said to disrupt the development of a cohesive mental representation of one's own body. People who lack secure body representation are forced to rely on external referents to establish a sense of their boundaries, identity, and self-worth. In such a scenario, self-injurious behavior may be a strategy to resolve body-based conflicts. As we can become more self-critical and self-depriving on a psychological level, so we also become physically self-destructive (Yates, 2004).

2.1.2.4. Anxiety–Hostility (Alexithymia) Model

Alexithymia, a condition that refers to deficiencies in recognizing, describing, and processing emotions has been linked to self-mutilation by several authors over the years (e.g., Evren & Evren, 2006; Zlotnick, Shea, & Pearlstein, 1996). The basic notion is that individuals who "have" alexithymia are not able to properly regulate emotions such as anger or hostility and may use self-injurious behavior as an emotion regulating strategy.

The premise of the *anxiety-reducing model* is that life stress can lead to tensions. If tensions build up and the person lacks proper means of resolving stressful situations, anxiety may occur which triggers self-injurious behavior, which then reduces the anxiety. In the *hostility-reducing model*, which is seen as an extension of the anxiety-reducing model, it is hypothesized that the individual resorts to self-injurious behavior because of the inability to overtly express anger and hostility. Increasing tension triggers self-injurious behavior, which leads to tension reduction and channels hostility and anger toward an "acceptable" source, namely, the self. Individuals who lack the ability to adequately express anger and hostility may choose self-injurious behavior as an expression of hostility.

Ross and Heath (2003) studied the validity of an anxiety- and a hostility-reducing model of self-injurious behavior in a community sample of 61 adolescents. Of 440 students who were screened, 61 responded affirmatively. A comparison group of 61 non-self-injuring students was added and the participants completed standardized rating scales and interviews. Overall, the authors found support for the hostility model of self-injurious behavior: Students with self-injurious behavior reported significantly more anxiety, intropunitive hostility, and extra-punitive hostility than the control group. In addition, prior to self-mutilation, feelings of both hostility and anxiety were described.

These two models imply a functional explanation of self-injurious behavior by suggesting that the behavior is maintained by negative reinforcement (reduction of tension, anxiety, and hostility). The question is how self-injurious behavior gets to the point to reduce those aversive emotions? In search of an answer to this question, Paivio and McCulloch (2004) conducted a questionnaire study with 100 female undergraduate students and found evidence for a link between childhood maltreatment and self-injurious behavior that was mediated by alexithymia. The question is then, what is alexithymia?

2.1.2.5. Developmental Psychopathology

Developmental psychopathology attempts better to understand mal-adaptation by contrasting typical development and successful adaptation with atypical development and unsuccessful adaptation (e.g., Luthar, Burack, Cicchetti, & Weisz, 1997). From the viewpoint of developmental psychopathology, self-injurious behavior is considered as a compensatory regulatory strategy in post-traumatic adaptation (Yates, 2004). Childhood traumata, especially in the form of abuse and maltreatment, can endanger the healthy maturation of essential regulatory and adaptive abilities such as motivational and emotional adjustment, and attitudinal, instrumental, and social interactive competence. The lack of healthy competencies leaves the child to resort to alternative compensatory strategies such as self-injurious behavior to cope with post-traumatic adaptation.

Based on empirical and theoretical foundations of psychoanalytic, neo-analytic, behavioral, and biological paradigms, Yates (2004) proposed a comprehensive developmental psychopathology model of *impulsive* self-injurious behavior (see Figure 2.1 for a schematic representation).

Yates' developmental psychopathology model was constructed specifically for the explanation of *impulsive* self-injurious behavior in Favazza's (1996) sense, and she does not claim its applicability to the type of self-injurious behavior commonly seen in individuals with intellectual disabilities.

Yates (2006) conducted a prospective study of self-injurious behavior in a low-income community sample, which was part of the Minnesota Longitudinal Study of Parents and Children. Study participants were 164 ($n = 83$ males, $n = 81$ females) 26-year-olds who were interviewed about non-suicidal, direct self-injurious behavior.

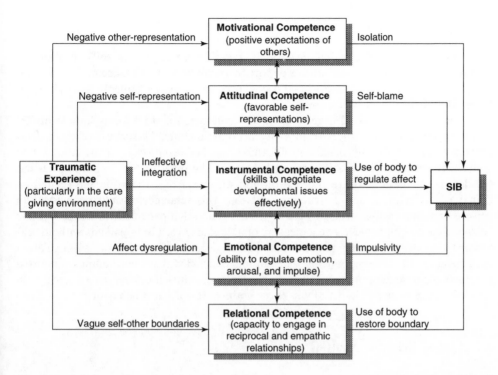

Figure 2.1: Schematic representation of the developmental psychopathology model of self-injurious behavior (SIB) (Yates, 2004).

Statistical analyses of the interview data, archival information of key developmental precursors of self-injurious behavior, and core developmental processes and difficult experiences in the caregiving situation and self-injurious behavior produced evidence that was consistent with a developmental psychopathology model of self-injurious behavior. Yates reported that child sexual abuse and neglect predicted severe self-injurious behavior, while child physical abuse appeared more predictive of mild self-injurious behavior. Dissociation and somatization were also associated with severe self-injurious behavior and made unique contributions to severe self-injurious behavior in addition to child maltreatment.

The disastrous natural experiments in Romanian orphanages during the post–WWII Ceausescu communist regime provide further evidence that untoward conditions during early childhood can lead to major psychological problems, including cognitive delays and problem behavior (e.g., Beckett et al., 2002).

The developmental psychopathology model of self-injurious behavior has much to offer, especially by pointing to the importance of negative early life experiences. It focuses exclusively on intra-psychic constructs and processes, however, and ignores the importance of the contingency-based learning that has been demonstrated to play an important role in the development and maintenance of self-injurious behavior, at least among individuals with intellectual disabilities.

2.1.3. Self-Regulation of Self-Esteem

According to some psychoanalytic models, people who engage in self-injurious behaviors have an unstable self and a disturbed regulation of self-esteem. This is sup-
posed to be especially the case with those who harm themselves openly as opposed to
those who harm themselves secretly.

To test this hypothesis, Fliege et al. (2003) conducted a study on a sample of 354
patients who received services from a psychosomatic clinic. Thirty-two of them demonstrated self-destructive behavior. Of these, 18 had exclusively overt and 6 had
exclusively covert types of self-harming behavior. The investigators hypothesized that
self-destructive patients have more profound disorders of narcissistic self-regulation
than patients without self-destruction and that this tendency should be evident in
persons with overt self-destructive behavior. They found that patients with self-destructive
behavior showed higher levels on a measure of a threatened self than patients without self-
harm. Overtly self-harming patients had higher degrees of narcissistic self-regulation
than covertly self-harming patients. The authors concluded that their findings supported
the theoretical assumptions of disturbed regulation of self-esteem in patients with
self-destructive behavior, especially in those with overt self-harm behavior.

2.2. Applied Behavior Analysis

Behavior analytic models of self-injurious behavior are based on the assumption that all
behavior, including self-injurious behavior, is learned. The origin of self-injurious behavior is a peculiar one, because it typically does not begin in full force. Instead, it
gradually evolves and eventually becomes a problem. Only then is the person referred for
assessment and treatment. Before the behavior has developed into problematic proportions, parents and other caretakers typically have little or no reason to pay attention to
it, and so the exact starting point of self-injurious behavior usually goes unnoticed.

Human behavior, whether problem behavior or otherwise, is presumed to be functionally related to other events in time and space. From a deterministic standpoint,
which is a core element of behaviorism, behavior does not spontaneously appear.
Instead, it has its origins in the environment and develops through its adaptation to
and interaction with those environmental events. As behavior is comprised of both the
movements a person performs and the relationships of those movements with the
environment (more specifically with antecedent, consequent, and co-occurring events
inside and outside the organism), contemplating the origin of any behavior requires a
consideration of conditions under which it first occurred.

2.2.1. Development of Self-Injurious Behavior

We can distinguish at least four possible behavior analytic models that could account
for the generation of self-injurious behavior (or most other behavior for that matter).

They include respondent behavior coming under operant control, transfer of control from one operant to another type of operant, contrived or inadvertent shaping of operant behavior, and evocative effects of various schedules of reinforcement that can produce adjunctive responding. We will briefly discuss each one of them.

2.2.1.1. Respondent Behavior Coming Under Operant Control

Respondent behavior is behavior that is controlled solely by its antecedents. An eye blink to a puff of air given during a glaucoma test is likely an unlearned reflex, as is a cough induced by a food bolus entering the trachea. Much of our emotional behavior also has respondent components. Feeling dread and a chill on hearing awful medical test results, feeling saddened on seeing one's child appearing distraught, or feeling excited on hearing that one has won a large prize likely have respondent components.

A large body of literature on self-injurious behavior exists that describes the role of operant (or instrumental conditioning); that is, self-injurious behavior that is maintained by its consequences. Likewise, there is a large body of operant literature describing antecedent control of self-injurious behavior. However, there is not much literature that describes respondent components of self-injurious behavior.

Yet, respondent behavior can be brought under operant control and thus it becomes operant behavior. For example, Hoch, Babbitt, Coe, Duncan, and Trusty (1995) described a procedure in which elicited (respondent) swallowing was brought under antecedent (operant) control of instructions and consequent control of positive reinforcers: Thus swallowing becomes an operant. In this study, the elicitation was eliminated, leaving swallowing under operant control. While respondent behavior can certainly evolve into operant behavior, through either contrived or naturally occurring contingencies, this phenomenon has not yet been documented with regard to self-injurious behavior.

2.2.1.2. Control Transfer from One Operant to Another Type of Operant

A response that is under control of one type of contingency can come under control of other contingencies. Thus, what once was one response, in fact becomes another. This principle has been documented, and, indeed programmed and utilized, especially in the verbal behavior training literature. There are numerous reports of response topographies that were initially being taught as mands, with stimulus control subsequently being modified so that the behavior occurs as a tact (Sundberg & Partington, 1998). Responses initially trained as echoics can subsequently be brought under mand, tact, sequelic, or other stimulus control, thereby coming to be another behavior (Barbera & Kubina, 2005; Sundberg & Partington, 1998).

In a self-injurious behavior analogue, should self-scratching that is initially evoked by an itch and followed by alleviation of the itch come to also be followed for instance by someone's attention, then scratching which initially occurred only when evoked by an itch can come to be evoked by lesser levels of attention and become maintained by positive social reinforcement. In other words, at first the person scratched the itch, but now the person scratches when he "itches" for attention.

2.2.1.3. Inadvertent Shaping of Operant Behavior

Other behaviors can be shaped either through planned successive approximation trials, or inadvertently by the course of naturally occurring events. Although it is unlikely that anyone would intentionally implement a shaping procedure to produce self-injurious behavior in a person, Lovaas and Simmons (1969) did just that in a demonstration of the awesome power of shaping in an early study. Similarly, Turp (2002) suggested that self-harm exists on a continuum of visibility, which ranges from highly visible forms of self-injury (such as cutting and burning), through a host of intermediary forms (sexual risk-taking, repetitive strain injury, and "invited" accidents), to virtually invisible ones (overwork and overexercise). It is more likely that the shaping of self-injurious behavior occurs inadvertently (Kennedy, 2002).

In a 12-month analysis of stereotypic and self-injurious behavior among 12 children, Richman and Lindauer (2005a, 2005b) found that existing self-injurious topographies continued to be controlled by the same variables over time, but that during the course of the study, new self-injurious behaviors evolved from previously existing stereotyped behaviors. Such precursors to self-injurious behavior, also called "proto self-injurious behaviors," have become a recent focus of research. Similarly, Shirley, Iwata, and Kahng (1999) found apparent, inadvertent shaping of maintenance of self-injurious behavior maintained by positive reinforcement while conducting a standard functional analysis. Whereas this behavior previously occurred for other reasons, it came to occur when there was an immediate deficiency in availability of particular objects, and produced access to those objects.

2.2.1.4. Self-Injurious Behavior as Adjunctive Behavior

Adjunctive or schedule-induced behavior can be described as behavior that – although typically controlled by its own controlling events – comes under indirect control by events that typically control another behavior (Foster, 1978). For instance, so-called self-stimulatory behaviors (or behaviors that are maintained by automatic reinforcement) can be induced by schedules of events. Behaviors that are typically maintained by automatic reinforcement are self-grooming, eating, drinking, smoking, or reading. These behaviors tend to occur during breaks in other behaviors that are maintained on other schedules of reinforcement and by other reinforcers. Consider, for example, the behavior of drivers in their cars while waiting at a red stoplight. Some may sip coffee, apply makeup, or check their hair – all automatically reinforced behaviors. When the light changes and driving resumes, many of these behaviors stop until the next red light is encountered. Sipping coffee under such conditions would be called adjunctive behavior.

The concept of adjunctive behavior seems underinvestigated and may hold promise for self-injurious behavior. Nevertheless, a few studies have appeared that hold some promise. Wieseler, Hanson, Chamberlain, and Thompson (1988) found that stereotyped behavior in three adults with profound intellectual disability became adjunctive or schedule-induced when response requirements to access reinforcers were lengthened. In another study, Emerson (1992) found schedule-induced stereotyped behavior in eight adults and children with severe and profound intellectual disabilities. Both of these findings are interesting, given more recent work documenting stereotyped behavior as proto behavior for self-injurious behavior, in some instances. Lerman, Iwata, Zarcone, and Ringdahl (1994) examined stereotyped behavior and self-injurious behavior in four participants who exhibited both behaviors. It appeared as if automatic reinforcement was driving stereotyped behavior in all four individuals, but self-injurious behavior seemed to be maintained by social negative reinforcement for two individuals or by nonsocial consequences for the other two. When the researchers delivered food on a variety of fixed time schedules, they found schedule-induced stereotyped behavior for one person, but no schedule-induced stereotyped behavior for the remaining participants, and no schedule-induced self-injurious behavior for any. While these particular findings may have been influenced by the response-independent (as opposed to response-dependent) schedules, they do suggest that adjunctive self-injurious behavior is unlikely when fixed time schedules are used. Additional research is needed regarding the possibility and potential parameters of adjunctive self-injurious behavior.

Discussion thus far has focused primarily on molecular contingencies surrounding behaviors (e.g., discrete antecedent and consequent events of particular response topographies). Molar contingencies and conditions (i.e., changes in sleep–wake cycles; nature, type, and availability of social interactions with others; general health; and general living conditions, for example) can also potentially influence development of self-injurious behavior.[2] Potential effects of such phenomena will be discussed later in this chapter. As mentioned earlier, one must bear in mind that the reason why a first instance of a behavior occurs is rarely the same reason why it continues over time (Skinner, 1968; Symons, Sperry, Dropick, & Bodfish, 2005). Discussion of etiology can be very useful from a standpoint of preventing evolution of self-injurious behavior in the repertoire of a person who does not already exhibit the behavior, or preventing inadvertent, iatrogenic shaping of self-injurious behavior from other topographies. As the events that initially brought about the behavior may well differ from those currently maintaining it, then maintenance of self-injurious behavior must also be discussed.

To determine what is maintaining self-injurious behavior, one must conduct functional assessment or a functional analysis. Functional analyses (also called experimental analyses or analogue analyses) are discussed in greater detail in Chapter 3 of this book. For present purposes, a functional analysis involves systematically varying antecedent conditions (such as discriminative stimuli and motivating operations) and consequent events (such as potential reinforcers) in the context of a single-subject experimental design, and examining changes in self-injurious behavior rates as a result of those manipulations. When rate of self-injurious behavior is reliably greater in one or more conditions than in other conditions, the contingencies exemplified by that (or those) condition(s) are said to be evoking and maintaining the behavior. Functional analyses can produce very precise demonstrations of the types of variables and contingencies currently maintaining self-injurious behavior.

---

[2] A theoretical discussion of the differences between the molecular and molar views in behavior analysis can be found in Baum (2002).

In contrast, functional assessment does not involve direct manipulation of antecedents and consequences. Instead, functional assessment involves observing the behavior in the natural environment and keeping track of the antecedent and consequent events. Functional assessments also typically include interviewing those people who are familiar with the person exhibiting the self-injurious behavior, and if possible the person her/himself, regarding possible relations between antecedent and consequent events. Functional rating scales can also assist in functional assessment and some of them will also be presented in Chapter 3. Although, perhaps, less reliable than a functional analysis, functional assessments can produce valid information from which effective action can be taken to remedy the problem behavior.

In the sections that follow, descriptions of maintaining contingencies, positive and negative reinforcement, will be mostly based on recently published studies involving functional analysis or functional assessment. Empirical evidence produced by functional analysis or assessment, however, does not necessarily account for all possible behavioral dynamics that may or may not influence the behavior. Therefore, we will discuss more complex hypothetical models that incorporate antecedents and consequences as well as respondent components of self-injurious behavior that go beyond what typically revealed by functional analyses and assessments. Behaviors such as self-injurious behavior have a long and complex history of learning and it is reasonable to assume that more may be influencing any given behavior than meets the eye. The purpose of these complex behavioral models is to remind us of dynamics that may be overlooked, and which may be at the root of those instances of failure, when even the most state-of-the-art behavior programs fail to eliminate self-injurious behavior altogether.

2.2.2. Maintenance of Self-Injurious Behavior

2.2.2.1. Positive Reinforcement
2.2.2.1.1. Positive External Reinforcement
Positive external reinforcement is typically divided into social reinforcers and tangible reinforcers. This distinction, however, is sometimes confounded since it is often the case that tangible reinforcers can only be obtained with the help of somebody else. Table 2.1 summarizes types of contingencies found to maintain self-injurious behavior and references for studies identifying them. These contingencies are described in greater detail in the sections that follow.

Social Positive Reinforcers When contingent social attention maintains self-injurious behavior, it is possible that a greater density of attention occurs during periods immediately following self-injurious behavior than when self-injurious behavior has not happened. For example, an otherwise occupied caregiver may attend to a child primarily when he hits his head, but may busy herself with other activities when the head hitting does not occurr.

In some instances, however, it is not simply contingent attention that is maintaining the self-injurious behavior, but instead recovering social attention that had been diverted (O'Reilly, Lancioni, King, Lally, & Dhomhnaill, 2000). In such an instance, a

Table 2.1: Examples of publications that address different functional properties of self-injurious behavior

Types of contingencies	Select references
Maintained by consequences	
Social positive reinforcement	Broussard and Northup (1997), Hanley et al. (2003), Iwata et al. (1994), Kurtz et al. (2003), Moore et al. (2002), Northup et al. (1995), O'Reilly et al. (2000), Richman and Hagopian (1999)
Positive reinforcement by access to tangibles	Day et al. (1994), Fischer et al. (1997), Hagopian et al. (2001), Hanley et al. (2003) Iwata et al. (1994), Kurtz et al. (2003), Lalli et al. (1997), Shirley et al. (1999), Vollmer and Vorndran (1998)
Non-socially mediated positive reinforcement	Deaver et al. (2001), Goh et al. (1995), Hanley et al. (2003), Healey et al. (2001), Iwata et al. (1982/1994), Iwata et al. (1994), Kennedy and Souza (1995), Kurtz et al. (2003), Lindberg et al. (2003), McKerchar et al. (2001), Moore et al. (2004), Patel et al. (2000), Piazza et al. (2000), Rapp et al. (1999), Roscoe et al. (1998), Shore et al. (1997)
Negative external reinforcement	Goh and Iwata (1994), Iwata et al. (1982/1994), Iwata et al. (1994), Kahng and Iwata (1998), Kurtz et al. (2003), Lalli et al. (1995), Lalli et al. (1999), Mace et al. (1999), Roberts et al. (1995), Smith et al. (1995a, 1995b), Steege et al. (1990), Vollmer et al. (1995a, 1995b), Zarcone et al. (1994)
Negative automatic reinforcement	Carr et al. (2003), O'Reilly et al. (1997)
Evoked by motivating operations	
Task relevant operations	Smith et al. (1995a, 1995b), Zarcone et al. (1994)
Sleep disturbance	Eshbaugh et al. (2004), Horrigan and Barnhill (1997), O'Reilly and Lancioni (2000), Sovner et al. (1993)
Physiological or other medical issues	Carr et al. (2003), O'Reilly (1997), Wacker et al. (1996)

mother may be attending to her child, but may then respond to a sibling or to a ringing telephone. If the child then bangs its head the mother may quickly return her attention to the child again. In other instances, quality of attention provided contingent on self-injurious behavior is important. Richman and Hagopian (1999), for example, found that it was not attention per se, but that it was exaggerated and somewhat emotional attention delivered after self-injurious behavior that maintained self-injurious behavior for two six-year-old study participants. Further, Broussard and Northup (1997) and

Northup et al. (1995) found that attention from other children, rather than adults, maintained disruptive behavior.

Attention delivered contingent on self-injurious behavior in functional analysis often takes the form of reprimands, occasionally along with brief physical contact to a shoulder or hand. Unfortunately, the exact way the contact occurs is often poorly described (Hanley, Iwata, & McCord, 2003). A detailed description of the conditions is particularly important since studies have shown that it is not always social attention per se that maintains a behavior, but the specific way in which social attention is given (Richman & Hagopian, 1999) and by whom (Broussard & Northup, 1997; Northup et al., 1995). Inadequate descriptions of the relevant components of a positive social reinforcer can lead to incorrect conclusions.

The social aspects involved in the delivery of nonsocial reinforcers can complicate matters (Iwata et al., 1994). They have to be carefully considered lest one draws the wrong conclusions. When it is reported, for example, that self-injurious behavior was maintained by reinforcers that consisted of pieces of popcorn, then the conclusion that the behavior was maintained by the popcorn rather than by the social aspect of delivery of the popcorn, would be misleading unless this possibility was experimentally controlled for (Moore, Mueller, Dubard, Roberts, & Sterling-Turner, 2002). It is for this reason that some researchers report separate data for maintenance by social positive reinforcement as well as social mediation of other consequences (Iwata et al., 1994; Kurtz et al., 2003).

Of course, not all social attention consists of spoken words. Consider, for example, the nature of contingent physical restraint or application of mechanical restraining devices as part of a behavioral treatment plan to suppress self-injurious behavior. By necessity, these procedures involve physical contact with the client. The physical contact may be more or less prolonged and may be accompanied by spoken words or signed communication, thereby increasing the overall social nature of the consequent event. Favell, McGimsey, and Jones (1978) demonstrated the positive reinforcement function of a physical restraint procedure – a form of social stimulation – for three participants. Therefore, it is important with socially involved procedures such as response-contingent physical restraint intended to suppress self-injurious behavior, to monitor carefully that the rate of self-injurious behavior is actually decelerating rather then accelerating.

Examining 152 functional analyses of self-injurious behavior conducted across a 11-year period, Iwata et al. (1994) found that 26.3% of cases involved self-injurious behavior maintained by social positive reinforcement. The authors point out that such reinforcement, however, not only involved social attention contingent on self-injurious behavior (23% of cases), but also the delivery of nonsocial reinforcers, such as leisure (2.0%) and food items (1.3%), as they required the intervention of another person to mediate their delivery. In a more recent study with 29 individuals who exhibited self-injurious behavior, Kurtz et al. (2003) reported that 1 individual (3.4%) exhibited self-injurious behavior that was maintained solely by social attention; 3 (10.3%) by tangible reinforcers that required social mediation; and 7 (24.1%) by attention and by social mediation. Hanley et al. (2003) surveyed 235 self-injurious behavior functional analysis datasets, and found 59 (25.1%) were maintained by attention.

Tangible Positive Reinforcers   With *tangibles* we mean the variety of different objects such as toys, tokens, or food that have been found to be effective reinforcers with some people, as well as access to preferred activities. Several different types of tangible reinforcers have been demonstrated to maintain self-injurious behavior including preferred objects, edibles, pieces of one's own clothing, and even self-restraint materials.

Different scenarios of how self-injurious behavior may produce access to tangibles include:

1. Presence of the tangible which is out of reach or otherwise inaccessible unless and until the self-injurious behavior occurs.
2. Prior to removal of the tangible, with self-injurious behavior producing re-accessing the tangible.
3. Ongoing access of the tangible, with notice that the tangible's removal is impending and with the self-injurious behavior producing continued access to the tangible, instead.
4. Absence of the tangible, without close prior temporal removal, but with self-injurious behavior producing access to the tangible, and others.

In many instances, however, the delivery of the tangible reinforcer itself is social in nature, and so it is possible that the self-injurious behavior is maintained solely by access (or continued access) to the tangible, jointly by access (or continued access) to the tangible and social mediation that produces it, or solely by the social mediation involved in tangible delivery (Iwata et al., 1994; Kurtz et al., 2003; Moore et al., 2002). It may be that the instances in which self-injurious behavior is maintained solely by access to particular tangibles may be considerably fewer than the instances in which the behavior is jointly maintained by access to tangibles and social positive reinforcement (Kurtz et al., 2003).

Aside from this problem in correctly identifying maintenance by tangible (or social) positive reinforcement, assessment procedures themselves may occasionally influence the contingencies such that self-injurious behavior that was not maintained by access to tangibles prior to assessment comes to be maintained in this way during the course of assessment (Shirley et al., 1999). For this reason, it is essential to design assessments that maximize internal validity and setting generality. Indirect assessment methods, such as interviews or checklists may be especially vulnerable to confounded tangible and social reinforcement because the responses of the person who is interviewed or is completing a checklist are based only on experiences where the two contingencies occur together. Functional analysis, conditional probability analysis, or direct observation and event recording may be better suited to disentangle the confounded social and nonsocial contingencies. This matter is discussed further in Chapter 3.

Based on functional analysis, Iwata et al. (1994) found that in only 3.3% of analyses was the behavior maintained by gaining access to tangibles. Kurtz et al. (2003), on the other hand reported that 3 of their 29 participants (10.1%) exhibited self-injurious behavior that was maintained by access to tangibles, and that 7 (24.1%) exhibited self-injurious behavior maintained jointly by attention and tangibles. Hanley et al. (2003) report 28 of 235 functional analyses (11.9%) indicating maintenance by access to tangibles.

2.2.2.1.2. Positive Internal ("Automatic") Reinforcement

Automatic, or sensory, or non-socially mediated reinforcement refers to hypothesized internal contingencies that are experienced by interoception but are invisible to others. In functional analyses and assessments, automatic reinforcement is often a default option, inferred when no external reinforcers could be identified. In other words, the identification of automatic reinforcement is essentially made by exclusion, when the rate of occurrence of the self-injurious behavior is unaffected by manipulations of response contingent tangibles, attention, or the termination of presumed undesirable assignments. Alternatively, non-socially mediated reinforcement is sometimes identified when self-injurious behavior occurs at higher rates in the absence of contingent or non-contingent antecedent social or material stimulation. Positive automatic or non-socially mediated reinforcement consists of occurrence, increase, or persistence of non-socially mediated stimulation, which would not occur if the behavior that produced it or accessed it did not occur first, and which maintains or accelerates the behavior that produces it.

Consider, for example, hand mouthing, which consists of placing one or more fingers or portions of one's fingers or hands into one's mouth. Although not as likely to produce tissue damage as rapidly as other forms of self-injurious behavior (such as eye poking or self-biting), chronic hand mouthing can produce maceration of one's hands, lips, and tissue surrounding one's lips, and other untoward sequelae, and so is considered self-injurious. The stimulation produced by this behavior (and accessed only by this behavior) is presumably a complex combination of perceptual stimulation occurring on the surfaces of the tongue, palate, inner cheeks, and other oral surfaces, simultaneous with warmth and moisture experienced through haptic and temperature perception on hand or fingers. Absent antecedent aversive stimulation such as hand dryness or oral discomfort that may be alleviated by this behavior, hand mouthing may well be a type of self-injurious behavior maintained by the unique sensory stimulation it produces. When this is so, the hand mouthing is maintained by automatic (or non-socially mediated) positive reinforcement.

The particular type of automatic reinforcement for self-injurious behavior is sometimes identified by way of stimuli that successfully substitute for the automatic reinforcement. For example, following a functional analysis that ruled out socially mediated and other external sources of reinforcement for a child's eye poking, Kennedy and Souza (1995) found that the behavior occurred far less frequently when the child was provided with non-contingent visual stimulation than with non-contingent auditory stimulation, suggesting that the behavior was maintained by the visual stimulation it produced. Shore, Iwata, DeLeon, Kahng, and Smith (1997) similarly found decreased rates of self-injurious behavior maintained by automatic reinforcement when participants were provided free access to individualized leisure items, also suggesting automatic positive reinforcement of the self-injurious behavior.

Hanley et al. (2003) report 55 of 235 functional analyses of self-injurious behavior (or 23.4%) indicated maintenance by automatic reinforcement: self-injurious behavior occurred at higher rates socially mediated antecedent and consequent events were absent than when those events were present. They report 13 of 235 functional analyses (5.5%) showed maintenance of self-injurious behavior by automatic reinforcement determined by high-rate self-injurious behavior irrespective of any externally provided stimulation. Kurtz et al. (2003) report 4 of 29 functional analyses of self-injurious behavior (13.8%) identifying automatic reinforcement as the maintaining variable when higher rates of self-injurious behavior were found in absence of socially mediated antecedents and consequences than in their presence, and 11 of 29 functional analyses (37.9%) suggesting automatic reinforcement when self-injurious behavior occurred at similar rates irrespective of assessment condition. Neither study, however, reports separate rates of maintenance by automatic positive or automatic negative reinforcement. In their epidemiological study of self-injurious behavior, Iwata et al. (1994) report a suspected 19.7% rate of maintenance by automatic positive reinforcement (as identified by higher rates of self-injurious behavior in the absence of alternative sources of stimulation), with 4.6% of additional analyses indicating high rates of self-injurious behavior irrespective of type of stimulation provided (or not provided), suggesting either automatic positive or negative reinforcement in those cases. These authors also report partial maintenance of self-injurious behavior by automatic positive reinforcement in an additional 2.6% of functional analyses examined.

Self-injurious topographies reported or suggested to be maintained by automatic positive reinforcement have included hair pulling (Rapp, Miltenberger, Galensky, Ellingson, & Long, 1999), hand mouthing (Goh et al., 1995; Piazza, Adelinis, Hanley, Goh, & Delia, 2000; Roscoe, Iwata, & Goh, 1998; Shore et al., 1997), eye poking (Kennedy & Souza, 1995), arm rubbing (Roscoe et al., 1998; Shore et al., 1997), hitting hands against objects or surfaces (Roscoe et al., 1998), skin picking (Roscoe et al., 1998), and others. Topographies reported or suggested to be maintained by automatic reinforcement, but without specification of maintenance by either positive or negative automatic reinforcement, have included hand hitting against objects or surfaces (Moore, Fisher, & Pennington, 2004), hand mouthing (Iwata, Dorsey, Slifer, Bauman, & Richman, 1982/1994; Lindberg, Iwata, Roscoe, Wordsell, & Hanley, 2003), arm rubbing (Lindberg et al., 2003), head hitting (Iwata et al., 1982/1994; Lindberg et al., 2003), head banging (Iwata et al., 1982/1994), self-choking (Iwata et al., 1982/1994), hair pulling (Iwata et al., 1982/1994), and others.

The exact type of sensory experience that functions as a positive reinforcer for self-injurious behavior cannot be determined, because this experience is a private event observable only by the person experiencing it. Instead, the nature of automatic positive reinforcement is surmised. This can be done, for instance by identifying stimuli which successfully compete with the hypothesized sensory reinforcers (Healey, Ahearn, Graff, & Libby, 2001; Patel, Carr, Kim, Robles, & Eastridge, 2000; Piazza et al., 2000). Another option is to provide stimuli which will provide only part of the stimulation presumably produced by the behavior. Examining the differential response rates to the various stimuli allows one to surmise which aspect the stimuli typically produced by the self-injurious behavior is the functionally effective one (Goh et al., 1995). Alternatively, the very nature of the stimulation that maintains self-injurious behavior may be hypothesized on the basis of blocking various sources of stimulation (i.e., blocking or lessening visual stimulation with goggles or a sleeping mask; blocking or masking auditory stimulation by altering surfaces struck, using sound-masking equipment, or noise canceling headphones; and in other ways), and examining rates of self-injurious behavior across different sensory conditions (McKerchar, Kahng, Casioppo, & Wilson, 2001).

Types of stimulation found or hypothesized, based on empirical examination, to maintain self-injurious behavior topographies have included stimulation to the hand maintaining hand mouthing (Goh et al., 1995; Piazza et al., 2000; Roscoe et al., 1998), oral stimulation maintaining hand mouthing (Piazza et al., 2000), manual stimulation maintaining hair twirling (Deaver, Miltenberger, & Stricker, 2001), auditory stimulation maintaining body rubbing (Roscoe et al., 1998), tactile stimulation to the hand maintaining body rubbing (Roscoe et al., 1998), tactile stimulation to the hand maintaining arm rubbing (Roscoe et al., 1998).

2.2.2.2. Negative Reinforcement
2.2.2.2.1. Negative External Reinforcement
There are two types of negative reinforcement scenarios: escape and avoidance. In the escape contingency, a stimulus is present and ongoing, and the behavior occurs and terminates or lessens the stimulation, which, in turn, accelerates or maintains that behavior. Consider, for example, Mr. M., who disassembles computers as part of a recycling crew at a vocational habilitation facility. When prompted to work, Mr. M. bangs his head on the worktable. The floor supervisor removes the work materials, and the head banging subsides. In this instance, head banging escaped the demands of work. In an avoidance contingency, in response to a stimulus that reliably precedes another aversive stimulus, the person engages in some behavior that both terminates the experienced stimulus and either prevents or prolongs the delay to the not-yet-experienced aversive stimulus. Consider again Mr. M., who begins head banging when he arrives at his empty work station (which reliably precedes work and the other stimuli associated with it), and who is subsequently escorted to the break room, resulting in termination of his head banging and where he can instead spend his day, thereby avoiding task demands.

Iwata et al. (1994) reported 38.1% of functional analyses of self-injurious behavior surveyed demonstrated maintenance by social negative reinforcement. Types of social negative reinforcement included termination of task demands (35.4%), termination of social interaction that did not involve task demands (1.3%), termination of physical contact (0.7%), and termination of ambient noise (0.7%). Kurtz et al. (2003) report only 1 of 29 participants (3.4%) exhibited self-injurious behavior maintained solely by negative reinforcement, that an additional 2 (7.0%) exhibited self-injurious behavior maintained jointly by either contingent attention or access to tangibles and negative reinforcement. Hanley et al. (2003) report 65 of 235 functional analyses examined (27.6%) indicated self-injurious behavior maintained by external negative reinforcement.

Topographies demonstrated to be maintained by external negative reinforcement have included hand mouthing (Lalli, Mace, Wohn, & Livezey, 1995), head banging (Goh & Iwata, 1994; Iwata et al., 1982/1994; Mace, Shapiro, & Mace, 1999; Smith, Iwata, Goh, & Shore, 1995a; Zarcone, Iwata, Mazaleski, & Smith, 1994), ear pulling or gouging (Iwata et al., 1982/1994), self-biting (Iwata et al., 1982/1994; Zarcone et al., 1994), face or head hitting (Goh & Iwata, 1994; Mace et al., 1988; Roberts, Mace, & Daggett, 1995; Smith, Klevstrand, & Lovaas, 1995b; Zarcone et al., 1994), self-biting

(Smith et al., 1995a, 1995b), body hitting (Smith et al., 1995a, 1995b), and hair pulling (Mace et al., 1988). Stimuli whose termination or lessening has been found to reinforce self-injurious behavior have included academic, vocational, or other task instructions (Goh & Iwata, 1994; Iwata et al., 1982/1994; Kahng & Iwata, 1998; Lalli et al. 1995; Lalli et al., 1999; Mace et al., 1988; Smith et al., 1995a, 1995b; Vollmer, Marcus, & Ringdahl, 1995a; Zarcone et al., 1994); grooming activities (Steege et al., 1990); and loud, ambient noises (Smith et al., 1995a, 1995b).

It is very likely that the range of stimuli that can function as negative reinforcers for self-injurious behavior is much larger, and that the range of empirically identified negative reinforcers for self-injurious behavior has been artificially constricted by typical experimental functional analysis methodology. Further, although quality of social attention functioning as positive reinforcement for self-injurious behavior has received attention (Richman & Hagopian, 1999), parameters of quality of social stimuli that serve as negative reinforcers for self-injurious behavior has not received adequate attention. For example, it is possible that task demands presented in different ways may produce differing quantities and qualities of self-injurious behavior, ranging from extremely frequent and severe to none at all.

2.2.2.2.2. Negative Internal ("Automatic") Reinforcement
In contrast to negative reinforcement by external events, automatic negative reinforcement involves the termination of aversive internal stimulation by self-injurious behavior. Consider, for example, scratching an itch. I feel my itch, I scratch, and the itch is alleviated. Another person can see neither my itch nor its termination, only the scratch.

To empirically identify automatic negative reinforcement, one first has to rule out that the behavior is maintained by socially mediated variables. Once that is established, indirect strategies can be considered that may serve in identifying the specifics of the negative reinforcement produced by the self-injurious behavior. In some cases, one could try to identify alternative sensory stimuli that can compete with the presumed reinforcer (Healey et al., 2001; Patel et al, 2000; Piazza et al., 2000), and in others one could try to block or alter the sensory input (McKerchar et al., 2001). In these cases one generally provides neutral or potentially enjoyable stimulation. In some cases one can also try to experience for oneself the sensations that may be involved. However, we can never be certain that we actually experience what the other person experiences.

The ethical dilemma in trying to identify automatic negative reinforcement mechanisms is that one cannot deliberately expose the individual to internal aversive stimulation. This may be the reason for the relative lack of empirical demonstrations of automatically negatively reinforced self-injurious behavior. Despite this, a number of studies have been published that describe procedures and findings suggesting that the self-injurious behavior was evoked by physiologically based aversive stimulation, and that the self-injurious behavior either attenuated this stimulation, or provided distracting or masking stimulation. Carr, Smith, Giacin, Whelan, and Pancari (2003) found self-injurious behavior to occur for four women predominantly during their menses, and found that the self-injurious behavior was alleviated when palliative measures were taken. O'Reilly (1997) found self-injurious behavior occurred in the context of otitis for a toddler with intellectual disability, and that the behavior remitted when the infection and its presumed pain were treated. Bosch, Van Dyke, Smith, and Poulton (1997) reported that on medical examination, 28% of participants in their study who exhibited self-injurious behavior were found to have previously undiagnosed medical difficulties, and that once those difficulties were treated, self-injurious behavior remitted for 86% of those participants. Pary and Khan (2002) suggested that cluster or migraine headaches may be an underdiagnosed and undertreated phenomenon in people with intellectual disabilities, and that episodic or cyclical self-injurious behavior may be indicative of such a malady.

Developers of some functional assessment instruments have understood the possibility that reducing or attenuating physical discomfort may maintain self-injurious behavior. For instance, the *Questions about Behavioral Function* (Vollmer & Matson, 1995) includes items asking the informant to indicate the extent to which the self-injurious behavior is believed to occur because the person is in pain or not feeling well, or more often when she/he is ill or when something is bothering her/him physically, when she/he is uncomfortable. The *Functional Assessment Interview* developed by O'Neill et al. (1997) includes a number of questions pertaining to medical difficulties and physical discomfort. The *Behavioral Diagnostic Interview* (Pyles, Muniz, Cade, & Silva, 1997) inquires about possible allergy symptoms and other maladies.

There is possibility that in some instances where social reinforcement seems to maintain self-injurious behavior, it may, in fact, be automatic negative reinforcement that controls it. For example, hand and arm banging evoked by one's having gotten out of proper positioning in one's wheelchair, thereby producing much physical discomfort, may well result both in gaining social attention in the form of sympathizing and physical contact while also potentially gaining repositioning, thereby alleviating the discomfort. Should this behavior come to occur reliably under this set of antecedent and consequent circumstances, it would be partially a mand reinforced by termination of physical discomfort.

2.2.2.3. Multiply Maintaining Contingencies

Iwata et al. (1982/1994) found evidence that self-injurious behavior can be maintained by more than one type of contingency. For instance, functional analysis of three of their nine individuals with self-injurious behavior showed both social positive reinforcement and social negative reinforcement contingencies. In their 1994 review of 152 functional analyses of self-injurious behavior, Iwata et al. reported that the self-injurious behavior of eight individuals (5.3%) was maintenance by various multiple contingencies. In four cases (2.6%) self-injurious behavior was reported to be maintained by social positive and social negative reinforcement, in two (1.3%) by social positive and automatic positive reinforcement, and in two (1.3%) by social negative and automatic positive reinforcement. Hanley et al. (2003) reported that 6.4% of 235 functional analyses of self-injurious behavior indicates maintenance by multiple variables. Similarly, Kurtz et al. (2003) found 2 of 29 functional analyses of self-injurious behavior (6.9%) to indicate multiple maintaining variables. When one considers the social aspect of delivering tangibles and edibles contingent on self-injurious behavior and the paucity of research examining separate contributions of the tangibles and edibles themselves and the social behavior of the party delivering them, it is possible that the frequency with which self-injurious behavior is partially maintained by thus far obscured social positive reinforcement is higher than has been reported (Table 2.2).

2.2.2.4. Motivating Operations (MO)

Motivating operations are events that have two basic temporary effects on a given behavior: (1) they change the value of a reinforcer (also called *value* altering effect) and (2) they increase the probability of responses that have produced that reinforcer in the past (also referred to as *probability* altering effects).

As for value altering operations, we distinguish between *establishing* and *abolishing operations*. Establishing operations (EO) are those that temporarily increase the potency of a reinforcer, and so evoke behavior that is likely to be reinforced by presentation of a positive reinforcer or by escape from or avoidance of a negative reinforcer (Laraway, Snycerski, Michael, & Poling, 2003). Twelve hours of fluid deprivation combined with hard labor are likely to increase the potency of water as a positive reinforcer, and make behavior that attains it more likely. Similarly, a migraine headache is likely to increase the potency of visual stimulation and loud sounds as negative reinforcers, and to evoke behaviors that terminate or avoid them.

Abolishing operations (AO) are events that lessen the potency of a reinforcer or punisher, and so alter the probability of behavior that is typically followed by those consequences, correspondingly. For example, when disruptive behavior is found to be maintained by the attention it produces, providing attention irrespective of the disruption on a schedule more frequently than that for which it had been delivered

Table 2.2: Outcome of self-injurious behavior functional analyses ($n = 152$; Iwata et al., 1994)

Negative reinforcement (socially mediated)	38.1%
Demand termination	35.4%
Social interaction termination	1.3%
Physical exam termination	0.7%
Ambient noise termination	0.7%
Positive social reinforcement (socially mediated)	26.3%
Attention	23.0%
Access to materials	2.0%
Access to food	1.3%
Automatic or sensory reinforcement (suspected)	25.7%
Sensory positive reinforcement	19.7%
Sensory negative reinforcement	1.3%
Undifferentiated high responding	4.6%
Multiple controlling variables	5.3%
Uncontrolled	4.6%

contingent on disruption has the effect of decreasing the reinforcing potency of attention for disruption, and decreasing probability of disruption. Motivating operation is the overall term describing variables that temporarily alter reinforcer or punisher potency and so alter probability of behavior, with EOs and AOs being subsets of motivating operations.

Many demonstrations of maintenance of self-injurious behavior by social positive reinforcement or access to tangibles rely on prior arrangement of EOs. For example, in the functional analysis described by Iwata et al. (1982/1994), the social disapproval condition, which assessed possible maintenance by social positive reinforcement, involved the experimenter beginning a session by instructing the child to play with the available toys, the experimenter withdrawing to the other side of the room, providing attention only when the child engaged in self-injurious behavior. In this condition, it can be argued that absence of social interaction for any behavior other than self-injurious behavior could increase the potency of such interaction as a reinforcer for self-injurious behavior. Likewise, in the academic demand condition designed to test the escape/avoidance hypothesis, the experimenter provided instruction and physical prompts to perform an aversive task, ceasing the prompts immediately when self-injurious behavior started or when the task was completed. When self-injurious behavior was more frequent than task completion, it could be argued that the prompts themselves functioned as EOs that evoked self-injurious behavior, which in turn brought about the termination of the prompts (and hence making them negative reinforcers). When functional analyses are conducted in a fixed cycle format (described in Chapter 3), the conditions are arranged such that prior conditions could potentially serve as motivating operations for later conditions.

Events that function as negative reinforcers for self-injurious behavior are also EOs that *evoke* the behavior. That is, they are antecedent conditions that evoke a particular behavior, which then terminates (or avoids or escapes) as the very condition that evoked it. For instance, self-injurious behavior that is maintained by termination of instructions to work is evoked by those very instructions, and is maintained by their termination. Similarly, self-injurious behavior evoked by physical discomfort may lessen that discomfort, thereby contributing to its maintenance.

A growing body of literature demonstrates that manipulating motivating operations could potentially produce reductions in self-injurious behavior. When we can deliver the relevant reinforcer independently of the behavior occurrence and at a greater rate than they are naturally produced by the self-injurious behavior, we are likely to reduce self-injurious behavior essentially by satiation (Carr, Bailey, Ecott, Ducker, & Weil, 1998; Carr et al., 2000; Wilder, Fisher, Anders, Cercone, & Neidert, 2001). Making more of the reinforcer that maintains self-injurious behavior available than self-injurious behavior typically does, weakens the reinforcement contingency, and renders the self-injurious behavior inefficient and irrelevant.

The discussion in this chapter has thus far focused on molecular maintaining variables; that is, events that occur immediately before or immediately after self-injurious behavior that influence its occurrence. Discussion now turns to molar events that may be more distant in time from self-injurious behavior but which, nonetheless, may function as motivating operations.

2.2.2.4.1. Sleep Disturbance

Sleep problems are said to occur in 16% of children with intellectual disabilities (Didden, Korzilius, van Aperlo, van Overloop, & deVries, 2002), and primary insomnia in 17% of adults with intellectual disabilities (Gunning & Espie, 2003). An estimated 56–68% of children with autism experience sleep disturbances (Richdale, 1999). Children with Down syndrome are particularly susceptible to disrupted sleep due to obstructive sleep apnea (Shott, Amin, Chini, Heubi, Hotze, & Akers, 2006).

Disrupted sleep is positively correlated with self-injurious behavior and other behavioral difficulties in people with intellectual disabilities (Brylewski & Wiggs, 1999; Matson et al., 1997; Mikhail & King, 2001; Symons, Davis, & Thompson, 2000). Dykens and Smith (1998) found sleep disturbance to be the strongest predictor of self-injurious behavior and other behavioral difficulties in people with Smith–Magenis syndrome. It is conceivable, then, that improving sleep could produce collateral behavioral improvements, with reductions seen in self-injurious behavior. Sovner, Fox, Lowry, and Lowry (1993) found substantial reductions in frequency of self-injurious behavior for two women with severe intellectual disability when their sleep had improved through administration of fluoxetine. Similarly, Eshbaugh, Martin, Cunnigham, and Luiselli (2004) reported a near 50% reduction in frequency of self-injurious behavior when a man diagnosed with autism and severe intellectual disability experienced improved sleep through medication intervention. Horrigan and Barnhill (1997) report that adding risperidone to the treatment regimens of 11 boys and men diagnosed with autism who exhibited sleep difficulties and self-injurious behavior resulted in improvements in both the problems. Quality of sleep also affects probability of self-injurious behavior. Harvey and Kennedy (2002) found duration of rapid eye movement (REM) during sleep to be inversely correlated with degree of intellectual disability, with lesser durations of REM sleep correlated with increased probability of self-injurious behavior.

Whether disrupted sleep produces self-injurious behavior, the sleep difficulty and self-injurious behavior co-occur but are not causally related, or the sleep difficulty and self-injurious behavior are both related to a third variable may depend on a particular individual's behavioral history and biological constitution. Further, self-injurious behavior that occurs in the context of disrupted sleep is not immune to environmental influence. O'Reilly and Lancioni (2000) report conducting a functional analysis of self-injurious behavior for a four-year-old girl diagnosed with moderate intellectual disability who experienced varying sleep durations from night to night. These researchers found an inverse relation between amount of sleep during the night and the following day's frequency of self-injurious behavior.

2.2.2.4.2. Physiological and Medical Issues

A number of studies have identified particular medical issues as functionally related to individuals' self-injurious behavior. Carr et al. (2003) found that alleviating presumed menstrual discomfort resulted in reductions in self-injurious behavior in four women. O'Reilly (1997) concluded that self-injurious behavior was functionally related to otitis after the treatment of the infection resulted in the elimination of the self-injurious behavior. Bosch et al. (1997) found that treating previously undiagnosed medical problems resulted in reductions in self-injurious behavior in 86% of patients treated. Pary and Khan (2002) raised the possibility that some self-injurious behavior may be attributable to cluster or migraine headaches, and also that these may be underdiagnosed conditions in people with intellectual disabilities. Bowel obstruction, constipation, discomfort due to untreated respiratory allergies, orthopedic difficulties, and other discomfort may likewise evoke self-injurious behavior in people who are unable to describe their experiences and otherwise request medical attention. Food deprivation has been found to evoke self-injurious behavior, with the behavior diminishing when mealtimes and amounts of food provided were adjusted (Wacker et al., 1996). People with intellectual disabilities and with visual and/or hearing impairments are generally more likely to exhibit self-injurious behavior than those without such impairments (Wieseler, Hanson, & Nord, 1995).

Medications may function as motivating operations that affect self-injurious behavior. Hellings, Kelley, Gabrielli, Kilgore, and Shah (1996), for example, reported worsening of skin picking for one of nine individuals whose self-injurious behavior was treated with sertraline. Withdrawal syndromes associated with antipsychotics or other medications may include irritability or other sensations that increase the rates of self-injurious behavior. Lethargy that occurs as a side effect of various antiepileptic drugs, antihistamines, or other medications could potentially increase probability of self-injurious behavior in people who are otherwise disposed to self-injure in order to escape demands.

Psychiatric disorders may be motivating operations for self-injurious behavior in the sense that certain events have different functional properties during periods of exacerbation of the disorder than they do during periods of remission. Similarly, antecedent stimuli can become more or less evocative of self-injurious behavior, as their salience is affected by differing motivational, perceptual, and hedonic states of the individual during the various phases of the disorder (Baker, Blumberg, Freeman, & Wieseler, 2002).

2.2.2.4.3. Neglect, Deprivation, and Environmental Impoverishment

The devastating effects on the children who were raised in orphanages during developmentally critical periods in communist Romania have been mentioned earlier. Many fortunate ones were eventually adopted by parents in other countries, including the US and Europe. A number of studies in recent years have examined the behavioral development of children who were adopted from Eastern European orphanages. Pre-adoption living conditions of these children were described as tremendously impoverished. Twenty-four percent of children adopted from Romanian orphanages were found to exhibit self-injurious behavior at the time of adoption, 16% continuing to engage in self-injurious behavior at three months post-adoption, and 13% when reaching six years of age (Beckett et al., 2002). This study also found a positive correlation between length of time spent living at the orphanage and presence of self-injurious behavior at the time of adoption. In a functional analysis of two sisters adopted from a Romanian orphanage, O'Reilly, Lacey, and Lancioni (2001) found tantrums to be evoked by diverted attention, and to be maintained by re-accessing the diverted attention. After implementing treatment based on this analysis, tantrums were eliminated, with zero noted at six months' follow-up.

An impoverishment environment itself is likely to increase the chances of persons with intellectual disabilities who are already at risk of developing self-injurious behavior (Schroeder, Bickel, & Richmond, 1986). A number of studies (Lindauer, DeLeon, & Fisher, 1999; Stainback & Stainback, 1983) reported reductions in self-injurious behavior for some participants when living environments improved.

2.2.2.4.4. Physical or Sexual Abuse
It is known that typically developing children who have experienced physical abuse are more likely than non-abused children to exhibit self-injurious behavior (Finzi et al., 2001). Even when physical abuse has not yet happened, typically developing children living in situations in which physical abuse is more likely have a greater probability of exhibiting self-injurious behavior than children who do not (Kolko, Kazdin, Thomas, & Day, 1993). The extent to which these findings are applicable to children and adults with intellectual disabilities is not clear as this matter has received insufficient attention as a possible risk factor for self-injury in this population. The type, intensity, and duration of the abuse; the relationship to the perpetrator(s) and the age when the abuse occurred; and protective factors may all influence the likelihood of self-injurious behavior or other forms of maladaptive behavior to emerge.

Compared with the general population, people with intellectual disabilities are more likely to become victims of crime, including violent crime (Office for Victims of Crime, 2002). Despite this increased probability, in general, fewer law enforcement and legal resources are allocated to crimes involving victims with intellectual disabilities. These crimes tend to be far less frequently reported to authorities when the victim has an intellectual disability, and they are far less likely to be considered an assault (in a legal sense) and instead are more likely to be labeled abuse (a social/legal phenomenon) (Petersilia, 2001). Whether crimes, including violent crimes, perpetrated against people with or without people with intellectual disabilities by people with intellectual disabilities are less likely to be reported or prosecuted is not known.

Similarly, people with intellectual disabilities are more likely than others to become victims of sexual assault (Petersilia, 2001). Despite this, the role of sexual abuse as a risk factor for later self-injurious behavior is unclear (Sequeira & Hollins, 2003). As far as childhood sexual abuse in intellectually typical children is concerned, we know that adolescent boys are more likely than adolescent girls to exhibit self-injurious behavior (Martin, Bergen, Richardson, Roeger, & Allison, 2004). Adult survivors of childhood sexual abuse by women are more likely than adult survivors of abuse perpetrated by men to self-injure and exhibit depressive symptoms (Denov, 2004). We also know that people with intellectual disabilities who have been victims of sexual abuse are more likely to suffer from psychiatric disorders and problem behaviors than those who have not. There is a positive correlation between the extent of the abuse and the degree of psychiatric and behavioral problems (Sequeira, Howlin, & Hollins, 2003). Further, psychiatric and behavioral difficulties of sexual abuse victims with intellectual disabilities are similar to those exhibited by sexual abuse survivors who have no intellectual disabilities, save for increased rates of stereotyped behavior (Sequeira et al.,

2003). Children with intellectual disabilities who have been sexually abused and who subsequently exhibit self-injurious behavior seem to display symptoms that are consistent with post-traumatic stress disorder (Burke & Bedard, 1994). In general, the long-term effects of sexual abuse in people with intellectual disabilities are still poorly understood and underresearched (Sequeira & Hollins, 2003).

Given the similarities of behavioral and psychiatric long-term effects of sexual abuse in people with and without intellectual disabilities (Sequeira et al., 2003), variations of successful treatments that are effective for intellectually typical sexual abuse survivors may be appropriate for individuals with intellectual disabilities.

2.2.2.4.5. Bereavement

People with intellectual disabilities generally respond to bereavement and loss similarly to people without intellectual disabilities (McEvoy & Smith, 2005). However, people with intellectual disabilities are more likely to be excluded by their families from mourning rituals, and this exclusion may deprive them of support when it is most needed (Summers & Witts, 2003). Behavioral difficulties following the loss of a loved one may include crying, emotional lability, tantrums, and irritability (MacHale & Carey, 2002). One study found that up to 15% of people with intellectual disabilities who had experienced a recent loss of a close family member subsequently showed self-injurious behavior (Harper & Wadsworth, 1993). Stoddart, Burke, and Temple (2002) found that people with borderline intellectual functioning who had participated in a bereavement therapy group had fewer depressive symptoms than others who did not. However, these results must be viewed with caution because it was not clear whether these individuals had self-injurious behavior at other times.

In summary, the presented evidence seems to suggest that the loss of a loved one is a significant event for many people with intellectual disabilities and may under certain unknown circumstances enhance the risk of self-injurious behavior. From a behavior analytic perspective, such a loss may be conceptualized as an EO for self-injurious behavior, regardless of whether it contributes to the evolution of this behavior or merely evokes pre-existing self-injurious behavior. Consider, then, other losses that are so frequently encountered in the lives of people with intellectual disabilities, such as the side effects of changes in the living situation or vocational programs, the loss of the companionship of others who are moved to other homes or work sites, adjustments to others who move in, difficulties involved in transportation, and so forth. Possible contributions of disruptive life events like these on the emotional well-being in general and their potential contribution to self-injurious behavior in particular have yet to be thoroughly examined. Opportunities for greater self-sufficiency has been examined, to some extent, and the results generally show that people who live and actively participate under circumstances that promote greater independence in adaptive behaviors are less likely to engage in self-injurious behavior (Baghdadli, Pascal, Grisi, & Aussillox, 2003; Chadwick, Piroth, Walker, Bernard, & Taylor, 2000).

2.2.2.4.6. Other Potential Motivating Operations

From a behavior analytic point of view, self-injurious behavior is generally very efficient. That is to say, it requires little effort to produce the consequences that fuel it.

For example, visual stimulation that is produced by eye pressing requires all but a minimal force of pushing a finger against the eyeball. Alleviation of an itch requires only a scratch. One approach to change the balance and to increase the response cost is increasing the amount of effort required to engage in the behavior, thereby lessening its efficiency. This treatment concept has been demonstrated to result in some improvement, at least in some select cases. Van Houten (1993) presented a good example when he reduced face slapping by adding exercise weights to the person's wrists. Obviously, tying dumbbells around someone's wrists is not a viable long-term treatment option, but a demonstration of a potentially useful behavioral principle that may be a temporary step in getting certain behaviors under control.

It has also been shown repeatedly that the suppression of one self-injurious behavior topography can result in acceleration of another topography, especially if it is a member of the same response class (i.e., all behaviors that produce the same consequences). This phenomenon has been known as *behavioral contrast*. A recent illustration by Kahng, Abt, and Wilder (2001) showed that applying arm restraints to a client's hands decreased head slapping, but accelerated head banging against objects. Behavioral contrast is likely to occur when not all topographies of the same response class are addressed.

Finally, as mentioned previously, although stereotyped behavior and other behaviors have been demonstrated as adjunctive behaviors (Emerson, 1992; Wieseler et al., 1988), to date, self-injurious behavior has not (Lerman et al., 1994). Given findings, however, that stereotyped behavior may be proto-behavior for subsequently evolving self-injurious behavior (Richman & Lindauer, 2005a, 2005b) additional research is warranted to examine potential schedule inducement of self-injurious behavior.

2.3. Interaction of Operant and Respondent Mechanisms

A largely ignored 1986 book chapter by Romanczyk introduced an interesting conceptual model that brought into focus a potential interaction of respondent and operant principles that may operate in the maintenance and spiraling exacerbation of some forms of self-injurious behavior. The model expanded the strictly operant model, which to this day has been the predominant behavioral perspective. Figure 2.2[3] shows a schematic drawing of two basic scenarios of the traditional operant model.

Self-injurious behaviors often occur in bursts and in an escalating fashion, with each bout starting relatively benign, but getting gradually more severe until the functional outcome is achieved. Starting with a low-intensity behavior makes sense in behaviors with increasing response cost as a function of increasing response intensity. Romanczyk, Lockshin, and Connor (1992) and his colleagues argued that self-injurious

---

[3] Legend to Figures 4–8: S^D, discriminative stimulus; S^{R+}, positive unconditioned reinforcer; S^{R-}, negative unconditioned reinforcer; S^{r+}, positive conditioned reinforcer; S^{r-}, negative conditioned reinforcer; UEO, unconditioned establishing operation; CEO, conditioned establishing operation; UAO, unconditioned abolishing operation; CAO, conditioned abolishing operation; CS, conditioned stimulus; UR, unconditioned reflex; and CR, conditioned reflex.

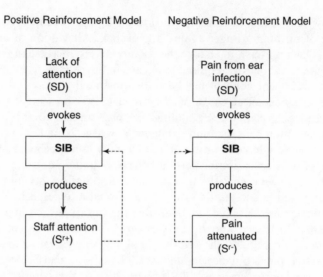

Figure 2.2: Examples of basic operant conditioning models of self-injurious behavior. The dotted lines symbolize the strengthening effect of the consequences of self-injurious behavior on its future probability of occurrence.

behavior of a certain intensity can be painful, which therefore triggers aversive arousal and agitation, which means that self-injurious behavior elicits unconditioned physiological and neurochemical reflexes (respondent mechanism). However, those physiological and neurochemical reflexes also function as discriminative stimuli (S^D) for self-injurious behavior.

Such a scenario is possible, for instance, in the context of contingent physical restraint procedures. The flow chart in Figure 2.3 is a schematic presentation of this dynamic. If the self-injurious behavior bout is terminated by physical restraint, pain, and arousal stop, which functions as negative reinforcement for self-injurious behavior (operant mechanism). However, if the bout is not terminated by physical restraint, self-injurious behavior escalates to a new level of intensity, which then functions as a S^D for a new bout of self-injurious behavior with higher intensity. This account, for instance, could help explain the driven and panicky nature of some forms of self-injurious behavior and the escalation of self-injurious behavior intensity and frequency in certain situations. A vicious cycle can be set in motion if, for example, therapists implement a treatment plan that involves contingent physical restraint upon the occurrence of self-injurious behavior. Let us assume the following scenario: A young man with severe intellectual disability and a history of self-injurious behavior starts to mildly bang his head. According to his behavioral treatment plan, the staff member ignores the mild self-injurious behavior. However, head striking becomes stronger and the young man gets visibly agitated. The staff member determines that self-injurious behavior is still not harmful enough to intervene and continues to ignore the head banging. At the point at which the young man is very agitated and anxious and his blows become vicious, the staff person can no longer ignore and opts to intervene. According to

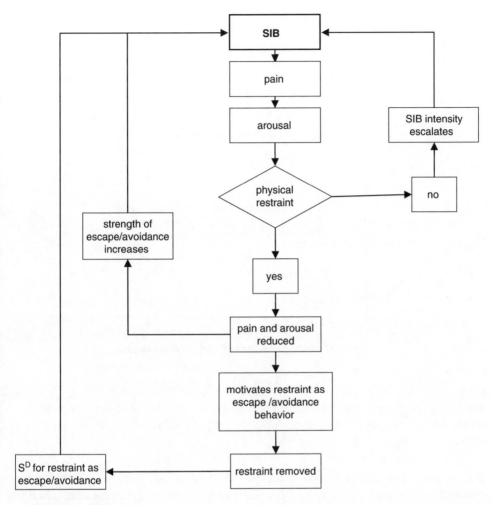

Figure 2.3: Romanczyk's operant-respondent model of physical restrain and self-injurious behavior (Romanczyk, 1986).

the treatment plan, a physical restraint procedure is implemented, which stops head banging. After a preset time and after the client has "calmed down" physical restraint is released. If the client is still anxious at the time of release from the restraint, he will engage in self-injurious behavior, because it had been successful in the past in reducing anxiety. Thus, a vicious cycle has been set in motion.

This model is intriguing. However, it has some shortcomings, which are in part a function of the time when it was published. First, the model does adequately account for the reason self-injurious behavior is exhibited to begin with. Secondly, in the past 20 years since the publication, the model we have come to better understand neurochemical processes involves self-injurious behavior. Thompson, Symons, Delaney, and England (1995) revisited and extended Romanczyk (1986) model by

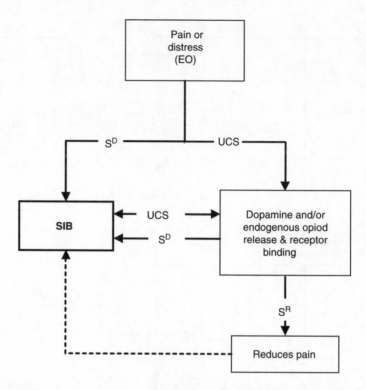

Figure 2.4: Pain or distress as establishing operations (EO) evoking self-injurious behavior and eliciting neurochemical release (based on Thompson et al., 1995). The dotted line symbolizes the strengthening effect of pain reduction on the probability of future occurrence of SIB.

adding neurochemical processes associated with distress, pain, and self-injurious behavior and by incorporating EOs (or *setting conditions* as they were then called by Thompson et al. (1995) that account for the events that trigger self-injurious behavior.

Figure 2.4 illustrates how pain and psychological distress operationalized as EO can evoke self-injurious behavior as an operant behavior, and as unconditioned stimuli (UCS) in eliciting internal biological events such as dopamine and endogenous opiods release (as unconditioned reflexes). Endogenous opiods have analgesic properties and we can therefore surmise that their release serves to attenuate the pain inflicted by self-injurious behavior. In addition, once dopamine and endogenous opiods are released, they bind to their postsynaptic receptors, a process which in itself is known to have reinforcing effects (Thompson et al., 1995).

The role of internal events that are produced by the release of dopamine, endogenous opiods, or both as S^D for self-injurious behavior is illustrated in Figure 2.5. Once self-injurious behavior has occurred, it continues to have social functions. In addition, self-injurious behavior induces pain, which eventually comes to serve as a conditioned reinforcer.

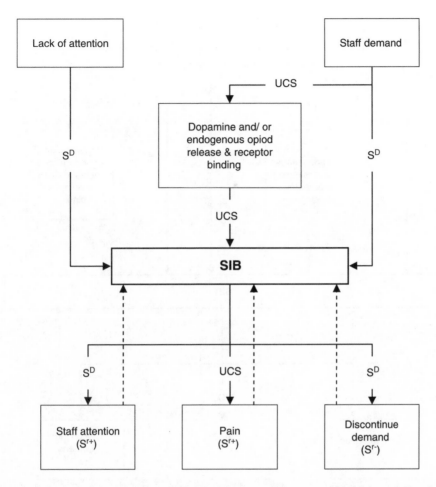

Figure 2.5: Conditioned interoceptive stimulus control over self-injurious behavior and the role of pain as a conditioned reinforcer (based on Thompson et al., 1995). The dotted line symbolizes the strengthening effects of three sources of reinforcement on the probability of future occurrence of SIB.

Figure 2.6 describes how internal neurochemical and external social events of self can interact into a complex dynamic system of injurious behavior that would suggest a combination of applied behavior analysis and psychopharmacology to be most effective.

We will discuss other important aspects of the Thompson et al.'s model in the chapter on bio-behavioral models of self-injurious behavior. The interaction between operant and respondent conditioning has not yet fully penetrated into intervention research on self-injurious behavior in individuals with intellectual disabilities are not clear. Nevertheless, we believe that this conceptual extension is important to enrich our understanding and the treatment of self-injurious behavior.

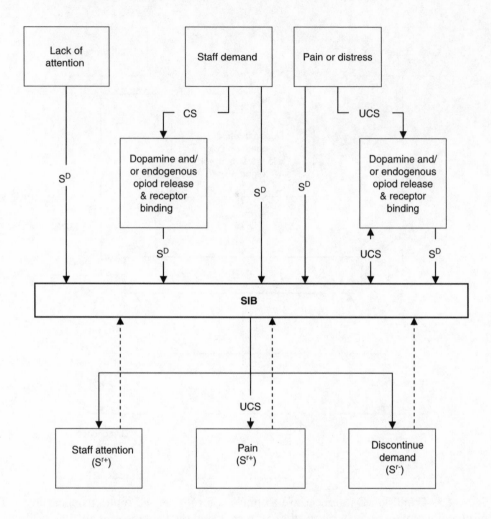

Figure 2.6: Combined neurochemical and social mediation of self-injurious behavior (based on Thompson et al., 1995). The dotted line symbolizes the strengthening effects of three sources of reinforcement on the probability of future occurrence of SIB.

Having introduced the notion of biological or bio-behavioral variables in self-injurious behavior, a more comprehensive discussion of these variables follows next.

2.4. Biological Models

When exploring the contribution of biological and bio-behavioral variables to the selection of self-injurious behavior by people with intellectual and developmental

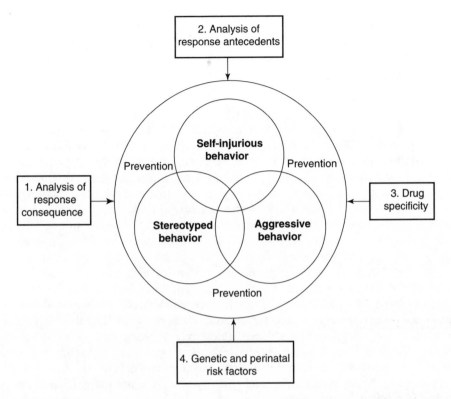

Figure 2.7: Antecedent analysis of chronic aberrant behavior – Multiple entry points.

disabilities, it is important to remember that self-injurious behavior is a heterogeneous response class which is multiply caused and multiply affected (Schroeder et al., 1980). And as we have mentioned earlier, there are many different topographies that do not fit neatly into one taxonomic scheme (see also Rojahn, 1994; Rojahn & Esbensen, 2002).

One can distinguish primarily between three groups of problem behavior in individuals with intellectual disabilities that tend to overlap: Self-injurious behavior, aggressive behavior, and stereotyped behavior. There are four critical points of entry to investigate them: (1) the analysis of response consequences; (2) the analysis of stimulus evokers; (3) the selective effects of pharmacological treatments; and (4) the study of genetic and neurobiological risk factors in humans and in animal models (Figure 2.7).

Self-injurious behavior often develops as a result of a combination of a complex set of behavioral and biological variables (Cataldo & Harris, 1982). Cataldo and colleagues (DeLeon, Rodriguez-Catter, & Cataldo, 2002) have given a useful scheme for classifying the resulting conceptual approaches which emerge from these sets of variables, which is consistent with the models proposed by Thompson et al. (1995).

		E	→	SIB	(see also Figure 2.4)
		B	→	SIB	(see also Figure 2.6)
		BE	→	SIB	(see also Figures 2.7 and 2.8)
B	→	E	→	SIB	
E	→	B	→	SIB	

In the first two equations, either environmental (E) or biological (B) processes independently evoke self-injurious behavior and are changed relatively independently. In the latter three equations, there is an interaction of environmental and biological variables. In the third case, both environmental and biological variables are contributing factors to developing and maintaining self-injurious behavior (e.g., self-injurious behavior maintained by automatic reinforcement). In the fourth case, biological variables, (e.g., dopaminergic supersensitivity, otitis media, sleep disorders, etc.) may create environmental circumstances, which lead to self-injurious behavior, which ordinarily would not be the case if they were absent. In the fifth case environmental variables, e.g., stressful events might induce release of high blood cortisol levels, a biological variable that would increase the likelihood of self-injurious behavior.

Bodfish and Lewis (2002) have given an excellent analysis of comorbidity of the symptoms from a variety of genetic disorders, neurological disorders, psychiatric disorders, and developmental disorders, which may be associated with self-injurious behavior. Many of these disorders have overlapping symptoms, including stereotyped behavior, compulsions, tics, motor disorders, and cognitive deficits. Bodfish and Lewis (2002) propose that a specific neurobiological system underlies the pattern of behavioral and movement disorders associated with self-injurious behavior in a wide variety of clinical conditions. These repetitive movement disorders are part of the symptomatology for a significant subset (about one-third) of people with self-injurious behavior. The chief neurobiological malfunctions appear to be in the brain circuitry of the basal ganglia. We will examine this hypothesis further as we treat each of these disorders in subsequent sections of this chapter. In the final analysis, self-injurious behavior appears to be a function of a number of neurodevelopmental disorders in which a variety of risk factors are involved.

Biological causes of self-injurious behavior are usually explored in a step-down algorithm in which all previously known biomedical antecedents are reviewed and ruled out until likely causal candidates are found, tested, and treated (Gualtieri, 1989). We will call these probable causes risk factors and explore them in the next section.

2.4.1. Genetic Risk Factors

2.4.1.1. Genetic Methodology
Is there a single gene for self-injurious behavior? The answer is that it is highly unlikely, but we do not know for sure. Since it is a heterogeneous response class, it likely has a variety of genetic polymorphisms responsible for its expression in certain

neurodevelopmental disorders. There are probably many genes for self-injurious behavior. First, we need to have an overview of the genetic work that has been done on self-injurious behavior. There are six types of genetics studies that provide evidence for genetic inheritance. We will use as examples two genetic disorders with a higher than usual incidence of self-injurious behavior: Lesch–Nyhan Syndrome, a single gene disorder, and autism, a polygenic disorder, to illustrate. We will then discuss each in more detail as behavioral phenotypes in a subsequent section.

2.4.1.2. Family Studies
This type of study simply asks, "Does self-injurious behavior run in families?" In the case of Lesch–Nyhan Syndrome, the answer is yes. The gene has been identified as an X-linked autosomal recessive gene carried by the mother and not by the father, which causes a deficiency in the enzyme Hypoxanthine-guanine phosphoribosyl transferase (HPRT) (Nyhan, 1967a). Other members of the family may carry Lesch–Nyhan variants, i.e., they do not carry the full dose of the HPRT deficiency and therefore, do not exhibit self-injurious behavior. Thus, we know that carrying this gene runs in families and raises the risk of self-injurious behavior. In families with autism, we know that having one child with autism increases the risk of siblings with autism in the family by a factor of 10 (Simonoff, 1998). Autism is a developmental disability with a higher than usual incidence of self-injurious behavior relative to similar comparison groups (Bodfish, Symons, Parker, & Lewis, 2000).

2.4.1.3. Twin and Adoption Studies
Twin and adoption studies ask the question, "Is this disorder inherited?" Because Lesch–Nyhan Syndrome is so rare, there are no twin-versus-adoption studies of it. But for autism, there are. The classic study by Folstein and Rutter (1978) showed that there was over 90% concordance for autism among identical twins, whereas concordance for dizygotic twins was about 9%, which is slightly greater than siblings in general (Smalley, Asarnow, & Spence, 1988).

2.4.1.4. Studies of High-Risk Populations
This type of study asks, "What is inherited? What non-genetic factors influence risk?" For instance, the study of the behavioral phenotypes of different syndromes may allow discovery of the relative influence of various gene mutations, as well as their expression as a function of environmental conditions. For example, the HPRT deficiency in Lesch–Nyhan Syndrome results in dopamine deficiency in the basal ganglia, which is thought to precipitate the tendency to self-injurious behavior. In the case of autism, it is thought that the symptoms in the third cluster of the Diagnostic and Statistical Manual of Mental Disorders (DSM-IV) (American Psychiatric Association, 1994) diagnostic criteria for autism, e.g., compulsive rituals and restricted repetitive behaviors, predispose autistic children to a higher rate of self-injurious behavior.

2.4.1.5. Segregation Analysis and Pedigree Analysis

This type of study asks, "How is the disorder inherited?" By studying parents, siblings, uncles, aunts, and cousins, one can explore how the trait is distributed in the family genealogy. This has been an especially fruitful strategy in researching the broader autism phenotype among family members who have a milder dose of the disorder and who do not qualify for a diagnosis of autism. This helps to search for *candidate genes* in polygenetic disorders like autism.

2.4.1.6. Linkage Analysis

This type of study asks, "Where are the abnormal genes?" Mendel's second law states that genetic loci, discrete regions of the deoxyribonucleic acid (DNA), are inherited independently of each other. This holds except when two or more gene loci are very close to one another. During meiosis such genes may exchange DNA among themselves (cross-over) and tend to be inherited together, i.e., they become linked. The closer two genes are physically, the more crossover occurs, the tighter they are linked, and the more likely they will be inherited together. Linkage studies offer the hope that, by studying the genetics of behavioral phenotypes, which also have a high incidence of self-injurious behavior, it will be possible to find genes co-localized with the disorder that may affect the expression of self-injurious behavior. For instance, Sandman, Spence, and Smith (1999) showed that a self-injurious behavior case that responded well to naltrexone treatment had a mutation of the pro-opiomelanocortin (POMC) gene in the opioid region. This suggests a genetic defect in the opioid system for self-injurious behavior cases that are naltrexone responders.

2.4.1.7. Molecular Genetic Analysis

Very sophisticated technology has now been developed to identify these linkage sites on genes, e.g., restricted fragment length polymorphisms (RFLPs) and, more recently, single nucleotide polymorphisms (SNPs). Because this work is so time-consuming to search the whole genome, computer technology has developed systems (e.g., the Affymatrix System) to the point where one chip can scan for 100,000+ SNPs simultaneously, thereby reducing the time and cost for whole-genome scans. This technology is now moving beyond linkage analysis to genomics analysis, where searches of the entire genome for candidate genes for a particular disorder can be done routinely.

2.4.2. Behavioral Phenotypes

The term "behavioral phenotype" was introduced by Nyhan (1972) to describe an observable behavior pattern so characteristic of a person with a genetic disorder, that its presence suggests an underlying genetic condition and structural deficits in the central nervous system (CNS). Over the past 35 years the study of such specific behavioral patterns characteristic of single-gene and polygenic developmental disorders has become increasingly important (Dykens, 1995). We will review briefly those with a higher incidence of self-injurious behavior relative to similar comparison groups. Each of these behavioral phenotypes has a distinctive pattern of self-injurious behavior topographies, which may be related to their particular underlying genetic, metabolic, and neuropathology.

2.4.2.1. Lesch–Nyhan Syndrome

Lesch–Nyhan Syndrome (Lesch & Nyhan, 1964) is the most distinctive genetic disorder with a behavioral phenotype in which almost 100% of the cases show a predisposition to severe, compulsive self-biting. It is a sex-linked recessive disorder of purine metabolism caused by the absence of the enzyme HPRT in the purine salvage pathway. Other features are hyperuricemia, cerebral palsy, choreoathetosis, spasticity, dystonia, dysarthric speech, and intellectual disabilities. Because people with Lesch–Nyhan syndrome are difficult to test, it may be that their intelligence is underestimated (Anderson, Ernst, & Davis, 1992). Because it is so rare, perhaps 1 in 100,000 (Crawhall, Henderson, & Kelley, 1972), there are only a few study groups of more than 50 cases in the U.S. Given these difficulties there are wide variations in prevalence estimates.

The characteristic forms of self-injurious behavior are biting of the lips, tongue, fingers, arms, and shoulders as well as head banging, arching and head snapping, eye poking, and getting fingers and toes caught in one's wheelchair (Nyhan, 1967a). The biting is often fierce and disfiguring, and apparently very difficult to inhibit. The person shows signs of pain and often begs for restraints when he is at risk. Sometimes, aggressive hitting and insulting the caregiver, then apologizing for being out of control, follow such begging.

No psychotropic medications or replacement therapies (e.g., enzyme therapy, gene therapy) have been very successful for Lesch–Nyhan syndrome as yet, although many have been tried (Nyhan, 1994). Lasting behavioral interventions have been successful under restricted conditions among milder cases, but not among severe cases. Perhaps this is because self-injurious behavior in Lesch–Nyhan disease is the result of an interaction of an X-linked genetic predisposition, maturational variables, and environmental variables. For an environmental intervention alone to have much effect, it might have to be very comprehensive, intensive, and extensive over infancy and childhood, and targeted toward the specific neurobiological dysfunctions related to self-injurious behavior.

A considerable amount is known about the neurobiology of self-injurious behavior in Lesch–Nyhan Syndrome (see Nyhan, 2002 for an excellent review). The metabolic abnormality is a genetic deficiency of the enzyme HPRT, resulting in excessive uric acid and gout unless it is treated with allopurinol. This treatment does not affect self-injurious behavior, however. It is believed that disruption of the neurotransmitter dopamine in the basal ganglia is the cause of the self-injurious behavior. Postmortem studies of Lesch–Nyhan cases by Lloyd et al. (1981) showed a significant loss of dopamine neurons in nigrostriatal and mesolimbic dopamine terminal areas in the basal ganglia. Wong et al. (1996) found similar results using in vivo Positron emission tomography (PET) scanning. Furthermore, the depletion was larger for the D1 dopamine receptor subtype than for other dopamine receptors. This is partial confirmation of results found in a rodent model for Lesch–Nyhan, self-biting in rats by Breese and his colleagues (for a review see Breese et al., 2005).

The Breese rat model of self-injurious behavior has been a useful heuristic model for examining the causes of self-biting in Lesch–Nyhan Syndrome and perhaps other forms of self-injurious behavior. First, it suggests that some self-injurious behavior may be primarily mediated by D1 dopamine receptor dysfunction. Therefore, D1 dopamine modulating drugs, e.g., primarily atypical antipsychotics such as clozapine, may be more efficacious in decreasing self-injurious behavior. Secondly, it suggests that, in cases where early (neonatal or perinatal) depletion of dopamine is related to the onset of self-injurious behavior, early intervention with self-injurious behavior is very important for later modulation of self-injurious behavior. Self-injurious behavior may be more readily preventable if intervention is begun earlier rather than if it is begun later in childhood.

There is also a mouse model for HPRT deficiency in Lesch–Nyhan Syndrome; however, these animals show no motor deficiencies or self-injurious behavior (Breese et al., 1995; Kasim, Kahn, & Jinnah, 2002). Despite this, these animals will be valuable in studying the neurodegenerative process in Lesch–Nyhan Syndrome.

Harris, Wong, Jinnah, Schretlin, and Parker (2002) have published an interesting series of neuroimaging studies comparing Lesch–Nyhan variants and classic cases with the full syndrome, which have added substantially to our knowledge of the potential mechanism for self-injurious behavior in Lesch–Nyhan Syndrome. They found that cases with higher levels of HPRT (1.5–8%) in intact cells had the neurological motor symptoms of Lesch–Nyhan syndrome, but no self-injurious behavior. Only cases with less than that had self-injurious behavior. Magnetic resonance imaging (MRI) showed that, in classic cases, there was a 31% decrease in volume of the caudate and putamen in the basal ganglia. In variants, there was a 1.8–20% reduction in these areas.

It appears that HPRT deficiency involves not only basal ganglia motor circuitry, but also cognitive circuitry in the lateral prefrontal area of the cortex. PET scans showed a reduction in presynaptic dopamine receptors for both classic cases and variants, so reduced dopamine receptor density in the basal ganglia is related to the movement disorder, but it is not a sufficient explanation for self-injurious behavior. MRS (magnetic resonance spectroscopy) studies essentially confirmed the PET scanning results but found also abnormalities in the lateral prefrontal cortex and in the limbic system. Self-injurious behavior in Lesch–Nyhan syndrome thus may involve a combination of deficiencies in the basal ganglia, the limbic system, and the frontal cortex. These results bear replication and further exploration also using other bio-behavioral methods in addition to brain imaging. It appears that self-injurious behavior in Lesch–Nyhan syndrome cannot be explained as simply a repetitive movement disorder.

2.4.2.2. Smith–Magenis Syndrome

Smith–Magenis Syndrome (SMS) is a complex multiple congenital anomaly associated with an interstitial deletion of the long arm of chromosome 17 located at region 17p11.2 (Smith et al., 1986). Prevalence is estimated at 1 in 25,000, but it may be underdiagnosed because it has only recently been discovered. At least 10 genes within the SMS region of the chromosome have been identified, but it is as yet not known how they affect the phenotype. It is postulated to be a contiguous deletion syndrome. There are over 100 studies in the biomedical literature analyzing this and other possibilities (see Chen, Potocki, & Lupski, 1996, for a review).

SMS has many clinical features. Chen et al. (1996) list 36 abnormalities: 9 craniofacial, 4 skeletal, 8 ophthalmic, 3 otolaryngology, 2 visceral, 1 thyroid, 1 immunoglobulin level, and 6 neurobehavioral. Some of the easily recognizable features are a flat mid-face; flat head shape; broad nasal bridge; curved upper lip; short stature; short, small hands; ear anomalies; a deep, hoarse voice; and a tendency to self-hug reflexively. Cognitive disabilities range from mild to profound (Dykens & Smith, 1998).

Dykens and Smith (1998) and Dykens, Hodapp, and Finucane (2000) have listed 15 salient maladaptive behaviors in a cohort of 35 cases of SMS aged 4–20 years (mean = 9.6): (1) demands a lot of attention; (2) disobedient; (3) hyperactive; (4) sleep disorders; (5) temper tantrums; (6) emotional lability; (7) lack of concentration; (8) destruction; (9) impulsivity; (10) bed-wetting; (11) argumentativeness; (12) assault; (13) bowel movement outside toilet; (14) stereotyped behavior; and (15) self-injurious behavior. Stereotyped behavior and self-injurious behavior were present in over 90% of the cases.

Finucane, Dirrigl, and Simon (2001) replicated and extended the self-injurious behavior results of the Dykens and Smith (1998) study in a cohort of 29 cases with a broader age range (1.78–49.04 years, mean = 15.43). All but 1 (96%) displayed several forms of self-injurious behavior (mean 4.5). In the order of frequency, they were: hand/wrist biting, 93%; head banging, 55%; skin picking, 52%; hair pulling, 34%; slapping self, 62%; yanking out fingernails, 48%; yanking out toenails, 34%; sticking foreign objects in ears, 31%; sticking foreign objects in nose, 17%; sticking foreign objects in rectum, 4%; sticking foreign objects in vagina, 21%. These behaviors were worse in the older group, but they were not inversely related to cognitive ability as has usually been found in other self-injurious behavior cohorts. This result may be due to the small sample size. Severity may worsen with age, especially with extremities and bodily orifices, because peripheral neuropathy sets in at a later age in SMS (Chen et al., 1996). Longitudinal research on SMS would help to answer this question.

SMS is a serious developmental disability that deserves much more study because of its distinctive behavior phenotype with a very high incidence of multiple self-injurious behavior topographies. Unlike Lesch–Nyhan syndrome, it is a polygenic disorder involving many genes, and it probably is more like a wide variety of self-injurious behavior cases whose etiology is currently unknown.

2.4.2.3. Cornelia de Lange Syndrome

Cornelia de Lange Syndrome (also called "Brachmann–de Lange Syndrome") is an autosomal dominant disorder with no distinctive biochemical or chromosomal markers. Discovered in 1933 (de Lange, 1933), the initial clinical features noted were dwarfism, distinctive faces, hirsutism, microcephaly, short forearms, abnormal hands and feet, severe feeding disorders, hearing loss, vision problems, sleep problems, seizures, severe growth, and intellectual disabilities (IQ range, 30–85).

The behavioral phenotype of Cornelia de Lange Syndrome includes limited speech, avoidance of being held, stereotyped movements, e.g., whirling, which has an autistic-like feature, and retarded social development. Surveys of parents' associations in Denmark (Beck, 1987), Germany (Sarimski, 1997), and the U.S. (Gualtieri, 1991; Hawley, Jackson, & Kurnit, 1985) suggest a prevalence between 1:50,000 and 1:100,000 live births.

Although the majority of Cornelia de Lange cases are placid and good-natured, a significant number show irritability, aggressive behavior, destructiveness, and self-injurious behavior. In the above-cited surveys self-injurious behavior was noted in 17% (Beck, 1987), 40% (Sarimski, 1997), and 64% (Gualtieri, 1991) of the cases. The Beck study surveyed 36 families; Sarimski, 27 families; and Gualtieri; 700 families of the Cornelia de Lange Foundation who reside mostly in the U.S. and other English-speaking countries. So differences in prevalence estimates may be related to sampling procedures.

According to Gualtieri (1991) who conducted the most in-depth surveys to date, antecedents for self-injurious behavior in Cornelia de Lange Syndrome appear to reflect immature patterns of social development, i.e., it occurred when the person was angry, frustrated, sick, in pain, or for attention, or in response to unreasonable demands. The most common topographies were self-biting, hitting, slapping, hair pulling, head banging, picking, scratching, and gouging, sometimes resulting in mild injuries. But the uncontrollable, fierce self-biting seen in Lesch–Nyhan Syndrome did not occur. Parents reported self-injurious behavior beginning at ages 2, 3, and 4 and worsening into later childhood and early adulthood and decreasing thereafter. This time course parallels that of most self-injurious behavior cases without a known genetic syndrome. Gualtieri's (1991) view is that their self-injurious behavior mainly grows out of immature behavior patterns, a temperamental nature, and sensitivity to aversive stimuli. No particular psychotropic medication has proven very successful in treating their self-injurious behavior, but few controlled case studies have addressed this issue.

2.4.2.4. Rett's Syndrome

Rett (1966) initially described this disorder in 22 girls. It consists of severe intellectual disability, stereotyped hand-wringing movement, dementia and autistic behavior, lack of facial expression, ataxic gait, cortical atrophy, seizures, and hyperammonemia. It only received international recognition after similar cases were noted in Sweden by Hagberg, Aicardi, Pias, and Ramos (1983).

Prevalence is estimated at 1:10,000 to 1:15,000. It occurs predominantly in females, as a result of mutation in the methyl CpG-binding protein 2 or MECP2 gene (see Zoghbi, 2002 for an exhaustive review). The prevailing hypothesis is that MECP2 mutations cause a partial or total loss of function of the protein that signals activation of genes at times when they should be repressed. As a result, the brain does not get the signals it needs for maturation of the autonomic nervous system and cortical regions responsible for numerous deficits, especially hand use and speech. Possibly, it is an autosomal dominant mutation that is lethal in males. At least two cases of monozygotic twins have been reported (Naidu, 1992). Two cases of families with several sisters have been reported. It is often misdiagnosed as autism. Some have argued that it is probably better classified not as a degenerative disorder but as a neurodevelopmental disorder (Hagberg, 2002).

From a developmental perspective, infants with Rett's Syndrome appear normal at birth, and then between 6 and 18 months there appears to be stagnation in growth followed by regression and deterioration until 36 months, a plateau in the school years, and further deterioration with spasticity and scoliosis in adulthood (Kerr, 1992). The Brain neurochemistry studies and post-mortem neuropathology studies have noted reduced levels of choline acetyltransferase (CHAT) and biogenic amines and metabolites (Wenk, Naidu, & Moser, 1989), low brain weight, small densely packed cells with limited dendritic branching in a variety of brain regions, suggesting arrested maturation (Bauman, 1991).

According to a survey completed by parents of children with Rett's Syndrome, (Sansom, Krishnan, Corbett, & Kerr, 1993) self-injurious behavior appears to arise out of anxiety, panic, agitation, and crying for no apparent reason. Mild self-injurious behavior by hand mouthing and biting occurred in 38% of cases. However, head banging and more serious self-injurious behavior also occur at much lower frequencies. The biting is not fierce and driven as in Lesch–Nyhan Syndrome.

Behavioral treatments aimed at self-injurious behavior in Rett's Syndrome have met with mixed success (Iwata, Pace, Willis, Gamache, & Hyman, 1986; Oliver, Murphy, Crayton, & Corbett, 1993; Smith et al., 1995a, 1995b). Treatments aimed at avoidance of anxiety attacks and agitation seem to work best at present. Psychotropic medications have not been selectively successful for self-injurious behavior in Rett's Syndrome (Harris, 1995).

2.4.2.5. Riley–Day Syndrome (Congenital Insensitivity to Pain)

Disorders involving congenital insensitivity to pain such as Riley–Day Syndrome (Riley, Day, Greeley, & Langford, 1949) may be associated with a subset of people who self-injure because pain perception is absent at birth over the entire body, while other sensory modalities are intact (Harris, 1992). Self-injurious behavior may be accidental or due to lack of caution. It does not follow the developmental syndromal pattern, as the previously discussed genetic disorders related to self-injurious behavior seem to do.

Riley–Day Syndrome is an autosomal recessive disorder estimated to occur in 1:10,000 to 1:20,000 live births. Intellectual disability occurs in about one-third of them. There appears to be a reduction in dopamine-B-hydroxylase, the enzyme that converts dopamine to epinephrine. The opioid system also seems to be involved. Dehen, Wilier, Boureau, and Cambier (1977) found that naloxone reduced the pain threshold and nociception reflex in these patients with congenital insensitivity to pain, but these results have not been replicated. This syndrome seems to be a natural one for studying the opioid system and self-injurious behavior, which is currently a topic of considerable interest (Sandman & Hetrick, 1995; Thompson et al., 1995).

It seems relevant to point out that a characteristic feature in persons with borderline personality disorder (BPD) is self-injurious behavior in conjunction with stress-induced reduction of pain perception. Reduced pain sensitivity has been experimentally confirmed in patients with BPD. In a recent study using blood oxygen level-dependent functional magnetic resonance imaging (fMRI), Schmahl, Bohus, and Esposito (2006) found that the interaction between an increased pain-induced response in the dorsolateral prefrontal cortex and the deactivation in the anterior cingulate and the amygdala in patients with BPD was associated with a pain-reducing mechanism.

2.4.2.6. Prader–Willi Syndrome

As described by Prader, Labhart, and Willi (1956), Prader–Willi syndrome is a congenital syndrome involving chromosomal translocations in the region of chromosome 15 in 80% of cases. A small percentage appears to have neither deletions nor disomy (Holm, 1996). There are nearly 30 diagnostic symptoms of which the major ones are neonatal and infantile hypotonia, feeding problems in infancy, excessive weight gain between 12 and 72 months of age, distinctive facial features, hypogonadism, developmental delay, hyperphagia, foraging, obsession with food, high pain threshold, and behavioral problems. It occurs in 1:10,000 to 1:20,000 live births.

Behavioral problems involve emotional lability, stubbornness, and tantrums often related to food seeking and gorging. Anxiety, aggressive behavior, and compulsive behavior are common (Stein, Keating, & Zar, 1993). In this survey of 369 cases Stein et al. (1993) also found that skin picking is the most common form of self-injurious behavior, occurring in 19.6% of cases. Other lower frequency self-injurious behavior topographies were nose picking, nail biting, lip biting, and hair pulling.

Treatment approaches involve behavior management, family interventions, and pharmacological interventions to control hoarding, overeating, weight gain, and psychiatric disorders. Stein et al. (1993) found that 17.5% were receiving serotonin reuptake inhibitors, 20.8% neuroleptics, and 25% stimulants. Recently, a few studies have successfully treated severe skin picking in Prader–Willi Syndrome with fluoxetine (Warnock & Kestenbaum, 1992; Tu, Hartridge, & Izawa, 1992) and sertraline (Hellings & Warnock, 1994). A comprehensive intervention program is needed to address all of the needs of these children.

2.4.2.7. Tourette's Syndrome

Although Tourette's syndrome may have been known in the 1600s, it was named in 1885 after Georges Gilles de la Tourette, who reported on nine people who exhibited this syndrome (Lees, Robertson, Trimble, & Murray, 1984). The main features were multiple frequent motor and verbal tics, involuntary movements, echolalia, and coprolalia (spontaneously spoken obscenities). Onset ranges usually between 2 and 15 years. Likely implication of genetic involvement comes from twin studies. It is probably an autosomal single dominant gene with incomplete penetrance (Van de Wetering, & Heutink, 1993). Its prevalence is estimated at 1:2,000.

Behavioral features are obsessive–compulsive behavior (OCD), hyperactivity (27%) attention deficit disorder, and learning disorders (24%). Sometimes it is accompanied by antisocial behavior, exhibitionism, inappropriate sexual behavior, and self-injurious behavior (13–53%). Severity of self-injurious behavior is related to severity of Tourette's symptoms. The wide range of prevalence estimates probably is due to referral bias to specialty clinics (see Robertson, 1992 for a review). Robertson, Trimble, and Lees (1989) did an in-depth study of an outpatient clinic cohort of 90 Tourette's cases, 33% of which did 23 topographies of self-injurious behavior similar to those observed among people with more severe intellectual disabilities, i.e., head banging, head-to-object hitting, self-biting, self-scratching, hair pulling, poking objects into bodily orifices, and a variety of less frequent topographies. The prevalence of self-injurious behavior in

Tourette's syndrome seems to be much higher than in other community psychiatric populations or among people with intellectual disabilities living in the community.

No consistent abnormalities in neuroanatomy, neuropharmacology, or neurochemistry have been found as yet, although hypotheses abound. Abnormalities of the dopamine system have received the most support (Singer, 1992). The treatment choice appears to be pharmacotherapy with dopamine antagonists, chief among which is haloperidol (Seignot, 1961), which has been known for over 35 years. The behavioral intervention literature for Tourette's syndrome is very limited.

2.4.2.8. Fragile X Syndrome

Fragile X Syndrome is a familial X-linked disorder first reported by Martin and Bell (1943). The fragile X intellectual disability 1 (FMR1) gene that contains the genetic information to synthesize the fragile X intellectual disability (FMRP) protein. Fragile X syndrome occurs when FMRP is missing. Recently, the gene FMR1 was cloned in DNA by Verkerk et al. (1991). Over the past 50 years, it has come to be recognized as the second most common form of heritable intellectual disabilities after Down syndrome (see Crnic & Hagerman, 2004 for a review). Its prevalence is estimated at 1:1,250 males and 1:2,500 females. Its primary clinical manifestations in males are: intellectual disability, abnormal facial features (long jaw and big ears), prominent forehead, macrorchidism, mitral valve prolapse, gaze aversions, and language delay. No specific neurochemical abnormalities have been found.

Behavioral problems in Fragile X Syndrome involve impulsivity, hyperactivity, autism (in 7% of cases), stereotyped behavior, aggressive behavior, and self-injurious behavior (Hagerman, 1990; Hagerman & Silverman, 1991). Hagerman, Jackson, Levitas, Rimland, and Braden (1986) found 66% hand flapping, 74% hand biting, and 84% unusual hand mannerisms in 50 males with Fragile X; but these figures have not been compared to a comparable group without Fragile X Syndrome. Symons, Clark, Hatton, Skinner, and Bailey (2003) reported similar results in a survey of 63 families in a longitudinal cohort study. Fifty-seven percent reported self-injurious behavior at some time in their lives. Mean age of onset was 31.2 months and 81% were still doing self-injurious behavior at the time of the survey. The most common type of self-injurious behavior was hand biting. Direct observations of stereotyped behaviors revealed a much lower rate (mean = 4%, range = 0–49%) than found in the Hagerman et al. (1986) survey study. The two main topographies were leg swinging and hand flapping. Behavioral and pharmacological interventions have not proven selectively more efficacious in the Fragile X population compared to the general population of people with intellectual disabilities (see Chapter 4 of this book for a review).

2.4.2.9. Autism

Autism is a brain disorder, the genetics and neurobiology of which is currently of intense research interest. Folstein and Rosen-Sheidley (2001) tabulated 60 candidate genes in the literature. By 2004, this number had grown to 90 candidate genes (Polleux & Lauder, 2004). No doubt this interest was fueled by a growing consensus on the behavioral phenotype of symptoms in three domains of symptom clusters specified in

DSM-IV (American Psychiatric Association, 1994): (1) socialization, (2) communication, and (3) restricted interests, compulsive rituals, and repetitive behaviors. Self-injurious behavior falls into the third symptom cluster.

It is therefore remarkable that there has been so little work on the behaviors of the third cluster, especially self-injurious behavior (Bodfish, 2004). The overwhelming share of the literature has been on the symptoms of socialization and communication. The only early study of self-injurious behavior prevalence was a parent survey by Bartak and Rutter (1976) of a group 36 autistic children in outpatient settings. They found that 71% of the cases had performed self-injurious behavior at some time in their lives, but only 6% were currently doing any. They were also the first to point out the inverse relationship of frequency and severity to IQ.

The best study of the frequency and severity of repetitive movement disorders, including self-injurious behavior and autism, was by Bodfish et al. (2000). In an institutionalized inpatient population they compared matched groups of adults with intellectual disabilities with ($n = 32$) or without autism ($n = 34$) using a battery of item-independent checklists that assessed stereotyped behavior, self-injurious behavior, compulsions, tics, akathisias, and dyskinesias, as well as other behavioral problems. The group with autism appeared to have a higher percentage of cases with self-injurious behavior (approximately 45%) compared to the matched group (approximately 25%), approaching statistical significance. The autistic group also had a greater number of topographies and higher severity of self-injurious behavior. However, the two groups did not differ in the distribution of self-injurious behavior topographies. So, autism does not appear to carry a distinctive self-injurious behavior phenotype, as has been observed in the other developmental disorders examined above. This work should be replicated in a larger outpatient population, because it carries many implications for the neurobiology of autism and self-injurious behavior, which we examine in a later section.

2.4.2.10. Other Syndromes
Other syndromes that have involved self-injurious behavior are Down syndrome, Cri-du-Chat syndrome, congenital rubella, prematurity, fetal alcohol syndrome, postnatal brain injury, 47XYY, and 49XXXXY chromosomal anomalies. Whether the incidence of self-injurious behavior is higher in these syndromes than in comparable groups without them is not known. Perhaps, they are related to mediating variables such as seizures and severity of intellectual disabilities, which are highly related to prevalence, and severity of self-injurious behavior.

2.4.3. Neurological Risk Factors

2.4.3.1. Seizures and Degenerative Neurological Conditions
Many of the previous genetic disorders involve a history of seizures and a degenerative neurological condition that may be related to a distinctive behavior phenotype for self-injurious behavior. Self-injurious behavior prevalence has also been found to be higher than that in the rest of the population with intellectual disabilities without a known genetic syndrome (Schroeder, Schroeder, Smith, & Dalldorf, 1978; Borthwick-Duffy,

1994; Bruininks, Olson, Larson, & Lakin, 1994; Jacobson, 1990; Rojahn, 1994). The association is related more to the severity than the type of the seizure or degenerative condition. In one study, Gedye (1989) argued that self-injurious behavior was caused by frontal lobe seizures; however, Coulter (1990) has disputed this view. Further study and replication is needed. The problem is that these self-injurious behavior cases with frontal lobe seizures are relatively rare, so that it is difficult to find a sufficient number to compare self-injurious behavior among people with different types of neurological disorders. Nevertheless one would expect from the literature on animal models for self-injurious behavior that focal lesions in the nigrostriatal and mesolimbic dopamine systems might be related to self-injurious behavior (see Breese et al., 2005 for a review).

2.4.3.2. Neuropathology of Pain and Self-Injurious Behavior

Not all forms of self-injurious behavior necessarily involve pain (e.g., pica or coprophagia). However, many of these behaviors would cause severe pain when inflicted to the average person. There is a variety of neurological, psychiatric, and developmental disorders associated with pain and self-injurious behavior. How much they overlap or how much they are cause and/or effect are still matters of speculation. Symons (2002) has provided an excellent integrative review of the human and animal work in all three areas. We will summarize only neuropathological pain in self-injurious behavior among people with developmental disabilities here, although these other areas need to be tracked and compared as knowledge accrues in this understudied area.

Self-injurious behavior and pain in developmental disabilities have been relatively neglected areas by self-injurious behavior researchers until recently (Symons & Thompson, 1997). Protracted high rates of intense self-injurious behavior, such as head banging resulting in permanent injury suggest disordered pain perception and pain mechanisms, but it is difficult to define or quantify in people who have limited capacity to report it (Barrera, Teodoro, Selmeci, & Madappuli, 1994). As we have pointed out in the earlier chapter, pain may be the cause and/or consequence of some forms self-injurious behavior. Better knowledge might lead to specific treatments for pain regulation and analgesia related to self-injurious behavior.

There are two basic neurological hypotheses posited for self-injurious behavior and pain regulation. The *dysesthesia* hypothesis suggests that some central or peripheral injury to the nervous system results in abnormal sensations leading to scratching, biting rubbing, etc., an affected area ("hot spot"), to relieve discomfort due some local neural dysfunction. The *anesthesia* (or *hypoesthesia*) hypothesis assumes that diminished pain perception of noxious stimuli results from an injury to the nervous system. Both scenarios are possible, depending upon the injury. A good example is compulsive skin picking in Prader–Willi syndrome, as noted in the previous section. Brandt and Rosen (1998) showed that sensory nerve action potentials for individuals with Prader–Willi syndrome are only 40–50% the size of the control subjects, suggesting peripheral neuropathy in their skin. In the latter case of acquired neurological disorders, such as brain injury, or in the case of congenital insensitivity to pain (Ishii, Kawaguchi, Miyakawa, & Nakajima, 1988), the onset is usually abrupt, intense, and is aimed at extremities, e.g., fingers and toes, leading to tissue damage. Pain perception appears to be absent.

Convincing corroborative evidence of altered pain mechanisms in self-injurious behavior of people with developmental disabilities comes from bio-behavioral measures known to be involved in neural pathways involved in the pain response (Melzack & Wall, 1983; Kandel, Schwartz, & Jessell, 1991). These include altered skin temperature at body sites associated with self-injurious behavior (Symons, Sutton, & Bodfish, 2001a); altered pattern of diurnal salivary Substance P (Symons, Sutton, Walker, & Bodfish, 2003); and abnormalities in epidermal nerve fibers at self-injurious behavior sites (Symons et al., 2005). This is new very promising work that needs to be expanded.

Potential mechanisms of pain in self-injurious behavior. The basic mechanisms accounting for the role of pain in self-injurious behavior of people with developmental disabilities are still largely speculative. Much more work is needed to explore the many biological and behavioral facets of pain and their interaction to affect self-injurious behavior. The two theories with the most evidence relevant to self-injurious behavior are the gating theory of pain (Melzack & Wall, 1983; Wall & Melzack, 1989) and the stress-induced analgesia theory of Sandman (1988).

In the *gating theory*, neural centers in the dorsal horn of the spinal cord act like a gate to increase or inhibit information from peripheral pain receptors in the skin as they travel up the spinal cord through thalamic relay stations to the cortical areas sensitive to perception of noxious stimuli. In the descending fibers of the spinal cord, the brain stem, and the midbrain, serotonergic and opioidergic fibers terminate in the gating centers to selectively inhibit and modulate the pain stimulus. Gating theory is often invoked to account for dysesthesias and anesthesias such as those that occur in Tourette's syndrome, Prader–Willi Syndrome, and other developmental disorders. These gates can sometimes be blocked by acupuncture (Pomerantz, 1987), transcutaneous low-intensity, high-frequency electrical stimulation administered via an apparatus called transcutaneous electric nerve stimulation (TENS) (Han, 1993), and stressful or strong noxious stimulation (Carlson, 1986). Symons and Thompson (1997) have shown that some forms of self-injurious behavior tend to be localized around acupuncture sites that vary according to the syndrome involved. TENS has been used effectively in some individual cases of self-injurious behavior (Linn, Rojahn, Helsel, & Dixon, 1988).

The *stress-induced analgesia theory* by Sandman (1988) asserts endogenous opioid-modulated analgesia during self-injurious behavior. It suggests that, in some cases of more severe and chronic self-injurious behavior, there is a congenital condition of permanently up-regulated opioid receptors and high circulating levels of endorphins in the brain which result in elevated thresholds to pain or lead to addictive responding to stimulate morphine receptors involved in endorphin release and pain regulation. This theory will be addressed in more detail as the Opioid Peptide Hypothesis in the section on Bio-behavioral Models of self-injurious behavior.

2.5. Mental Health Risk Factors

There are a number of studies showing a higher incidence of mental health disorders among people with self-injurious behavior (Borthwick-Duffy, 1994; Rojahn, Matson, Naglieri, & Mayville, 2004) than those without. Which is cause and which is effect is often difficult to determine because of the lack of overlap of standard psychiatric diagnoses and maladaptive behaviors, such as self-injurious behavior, as seen in the broader population of people with intellectual and/or developmental disabilities (Matson, 1986).

Prevalence estimates of overlap of self-injurious behavior in the dually diagnosed population vary greatly due to a variety of reasons: (1) lack of common definition of terms (Bodfish & Lewis, 2002); (2) different population samples, e.g., inpatient versus outpatient, developmental center, versus skilled nursing facility, versus community living versus home; (3) case ascertainment, e.g., convenience samples versus represent-ative stratified samples, inclusion/exclusion criteria, retrospective versus prospective sampling strategy, accounting for drop-out; (4) use of appropriate assessments validated on the population under study; (5) appropriate assessment of covariates, e.g., single versus multiple diagnoses, including all of the risk factors reviewed above; (6) proper statistical analyses, accounting for missing data, etc.; and (7) independent or blind assessments to assess reliability. It is difficult to study their interactions in a controlled way with a large enough sample population to allow sub-typing of mental health disorders in the developmental disabilities population. Research on people with dual diagnosis has been seriously underfunded by the Federal Government for over 30 years.

With the above caveats in mind, there are two classes of mental disorders in de-velopmental disabilities related to self-injurious behavior that have received substantial attention by researchers, i.e., mood disorders and compulsive disorders.

2.5.1. Mood Disorders and Self-Injurious Behavior

People with developmental disabilities show a full range of mood disorders, chief among which are depression and bipolar disorder (Reid, 1972; Sovner & Hurley, 1983; Charlot, Doucette, & Mezzacapa, 1993; Meins, 1996), but they may be difficult to diagnose. Patients often present with aggressive behavior, destruction, and self-injurious behavior. The history, mental status, and environmental factors have to be observed to make the diagnosis (see Hellings, 1999; Lowry, 1998 for reviews). Sovner and Lowry (1990) developed a methodology for diagnosing affective disorders in all people with developmental disabilities – even profound intellectual disabilities, but standardized measures designed for this population only became available later (e.g., Benavidez & Matson, 1993; Esbensen, Rojahn, Aman, & Ruedrich, 2003; Matson, 1998; Matson, Gardner, Coe, & Sovner, 1991).

Lowry and Sovner (1992) published a case report treating serious self-injurious behavior in a case with rapid cycling bipolar disorder. Reiss and Rojahn (1993) found that persons in an outpatient population with developmental disabilities and depres-sion were four-times as likely to show aggressive behavior as those without depression. The most thorough prospective study of the relationship between psychiatric condi-tions and behavioral problems among adults with intellectual and/or developmental disabilities was by Rojahn et al. (2004). They used two well-validated informant be-havior-rating instruments, the *Behavior Problems Inventory* (Rojahn et al., 2001), to assess self-injurious behavior, aggressive and destructive behavior, and stereotyped behavior, and the *Diagnostic Assessment for the Severely Handicapped* (Matson et al.,

1991). Both instruments will be discussed in Chapter 3. These researchers found that the presence of behavioral problems increased the likelihood of almost all psychiatric conditions, including mood disorders, up to three-fold. Self-injurious behavior and aggressive behavior tended to be more associated with impulse control and conduct problems, while stereotyped behavior was linked more to pervasive developmental disorders and schizophrenia.

2.5.2. Compulsions and Self-Injurious Behavior

In many cases of self-injurious behavior, there appears to be an involuntary compulsive component. Two neurobiological models of self-injurious behavior (King, 1993; Thompson et al., 1995), to be discussed in the section on bio-behavioral models of self-injurious behavior, attempt to describe the nature and extent of these compulsions. Bodfish and Lewis (2002) and Lewis and Bodfish (1998) provide good reviews of comorbidity of compulsions and other repetitive behaviors with self-injurious behavior. In 2002, Bodfish and Lewis reviewed studies on variety of syndromes associated with self-injurious behavior, and found that 11 of 15 contained compulsive behaviors, 10 of 15 contained stereotyped behaviors, 6 of 15 contained tics, and 10 of 15 contained motor disorders.

As was the case with mood disorders, until recently there were no appropriate assessment instruments designed to examine these repetitive behaviors in the self-injurious behavior population. Bodfish and colleagues have developed a whole series of validated item-independent scales of repetitive movement disorders to assess their comorbidity with self-injurious behavior. They have shown that, in a residential institutional population, persons with self-injurious behavior had a significantly increased prevalence (c. 70%) of stereotyped behavior (Bodfish et al., 1995a, 1995b), (c. 70%) of compulsions (Powell, Bodfish, Parker, Crawford, & Lewis, 1996), and (c. 20%) of tics (Bodfish & Lewis, 1997; Rosenquist, Bodfish, & Thompson, 1997) compared to a non-self-injurious behavior matched control group. These findings have been supported by other studies (Berkson & Davenport, 1962; Collacott, Cooper, Branford, & McGrother, 1998; Rojahn, 1986) in other intellectual disabilities and also in autistic populations (Bodfish et al., 2000).

These findings have strong clinical implications for treating self-injurious behavior. People who have self-injurious behavior should be examined for these other abnormal repetitive behaviors (e.g., tics, dyskinesia, dystonia, and stereotyped behavior). This information could be used to guide better-informed behavioral and pharmacological treatments (see the section on bio-behavioral models of self-injurious behavior and Chapter 4, the section on the psychopharmacology of self-injurious behavior).

2.6. General Medical Risk Factors

Several publications have provided evidence for the fact that medical conditions can precipitate self-injurious behavior among someone so inclined and which result in decreasing self-injurious behavior when removed (Bailey & Pyles, 1989; Bosch et al., 1997; Carr & Smith, 1995; Gardner & Sovner, 1994; Gualtieri, 1991; Reese, Hellings, & Schroeder, 2007). These include conditions that cause pain and discomfort, aversive emotional states, disease states, or metabolic disturbances (e.g., changes in blood sugar levels or electrolyte concentrations altering CNS function). Self-injurious behavior may be a nonspecific response to irritability, mood change, arousal, rage attacks, and disturbances in attention or supersensitivity-related psychotropic medication (e.g., withdrawal, anxiety, depression, akathisias, and dyskinesia). Adverse drug reactions may exacerbate existing self-injurious behavior tendencies (Gardner & Sovner, 1994). Most of the work that has been done is anecdotal and only a few experimental studies have been conducted.

2.6.1. Menses

Taylor, Rush, Hetrick, and Sandman (1993) examined the role of the endogenous opiate system in association with the menstrual cycles and self-injurious behavior of nine women with intellectual disabilities, residing at Fairview Hospital. They found that the highest frequency of self-injurious behavior occurred in the early follicular phase and late follicular phase rather than in the early or late luteal phases and was related to changing peripheral and central endorphin and pain threshold during the menstrual cycle.

2.6.2. Otitis Media

Several investigators have suggested a link between otitis media and periodic self-injurious behavior, such as ear banging (e.g., Gunsett, Mulick, Fernald, & Martin, 1989), but many of the existing reports are anecdotal. Luiselli, Cochran, and Huber (2005) observed unanticipated increases in self-injurious behavior that had been previously decreased by intervention in a five-year-old boy with autism. They found that the periods of elevated self-injurious behavior was linked to diagnosed otitis media. O'Reilly (1997) conducted a functional analysis with a 26-month-old girl with moderate developmental disabilities and discovered that self-injurious behavior occurred only during periods of acute otitis media.

2.7. Developmental Risk Factors

2.7.1. Chronological Age

Head banging and crib banging begins in typically developing children at around 6th month and is mostly gone by 60th month (de Lissavoy, 1961; Kravitz, Rosenthal, Teplitz, Murphy, & Lesser, 1960). Except for Lesch–Nyhan Syndrome and a few other genetic disorders, self-injurious behavior in people with intellectual disabilities is generally brought to the attention of clinicians around the age of two years or later (Borthwick-Duffy, 1994; Oliver et al., 1987; Rojahn, 1994), increasing into adulthood, then declining in the 1950s and 1960s. As Rojahn notes, it may be underreported during infancy and early childhood. As Schroeder et al. (1978) noted, early onset and chronicity tend to be correlated with severity of self-injurious behavior (see also the section on epidemiological research in Chapter 1 of thisbook).

2.7.2. Level of Intellectual Disability

There is a good agreement that frequency and severity of self-injurious behavior are generally positively related to severity of intellectual disability (Borthwick-Duffy, 1994; Jacobson, 1990; Maisto et al., 1978; Oliver et al., 1987; Rojahn, 1994; Schroeder et al., 1978; see also Chapter 1 of this book for epidemiological evidence concerning the relationship between level of intellectual disability and self-injurious behavior). This, however, does not necessarily hold for all the different genetic disorders associated with self-injurious behavior, which were examined in the previous section. The relation between level of intellectual disability and self-injurious behavior frequency and severity tends to differ somewhat for each syndrome. This fact suggests that level of intellectual disability may be a surrogate variable, which is multicollinear with several other disabling conditions like seizures, brain damage, and communication deficits.

2.7.3. Sensory and Communication Deficits

Visual, auditory, and language impairments were all found to be risk factors for self-injurious behavior by Schroeder et al. (1978). This result was replicated for lack of expressive communication associated with self-injurious behavior (e.g., Borthwick-Duffy, 1994; Griffin, Williams, Stark, Altmeyer, & Mason, 1986; Rojahn, 1994). Whether communication deficits in self-injurious behavior are collinear with level of intellectual disability is uncertain. Studying self-injurious behavior in syndromes where receptive or expressive language and intellectual disability level are less well-correlated, e.g., autism, William's Syndrome, Prader–Willi Syndrome, etc., would be of interest. There have been a number of studies showing that differential reinforcement of communication can decrease self-injurious behavior in some cases (see Carr et al., 1994, for a review); but there has not been a longitudinal developmental study showing that self-injurious behavior decreases as the capacity to communicate increases. This is an interesting question to study.

2.8. Bio-Behavioral Models

As we have discussed in Section 2.b. of this volume, there are numerous behavioral models for how self-injurious behavior is learned and how it develops. Many of these hypotheses are now testable by using functional analysis methodology and by confirming them on a case-by-case basis. There still remain, however, a number of severe chronic cases, perhaps 25–40%, who remain refractory to behavioral treatment alone and for whom bio-behavioral interventions need to be considered. These treatments usually involve rational pharmacotherapy alone or in combination with behavioral interventions based upon biological hypotheses related to biological causes for self-injurious behavior. We will review these bio-behavioral models for self-injurious behavior in this next section.

2.8.1. Physiological States Hypothesis

Physiological state conditions (e.g., arousal) have often been invoked as preventable conditions that may set the occasion for self-injurious behavior (see Schroeder et al., 1986 and Chapter 4, for reviews). Guess and Carr (1991) proposed a developmental model for self-injurious behavior based upon physiological states to explain the development of rhythmic stereotyped behavior and self-injurious behavior. The model has three levels. Level I consists of rhythmic behaviors, such as sleep, waking, and crying patterns, as internally regulated states common in normally developing infants, but abnormal or delayed in onset among children with handicapping conditions. Level II involves the development of self-regulation of arousal and homeostasis wherein stereotyped behavior and self-injurious behavior are viewed as adaptations to under- or over-stimulating environments. Level III represents stereotyped behavior and self-injurious behavior as learned behavioral tendencies that come to control the behavior of others. Behavior develops in a sequence from Level I to III. There are fluid transitions between levels. Delayed, abnormal, or arrested development represents a risk factor for pathology. Interventions that facilitate the transitions to age-appropriate levels are likely to prevent behavior problems. For instance, it may be that infants or children who are at Level I may not respond well to behavioral interventions. Premature inhibitory interventions of Level I behavior states may be counterproductive, until the child has the ability to respond appropriately.

The Guess and Carr model is a bio-behavioral descriptive model that attempts to integrate a variety of diverse findings about state conditions related to stereotyped behavior and self-injurious behavior. Although it has its critics (Lovaas & Smith, 1991; Mulick & Meinhold, 1991), it is the first attempt to show how self-injurious behavior *may develop* from rhythmic behavior states. Chaos theory (Guess & Sailor, 1993) is used to analyze phase changes and differentiation of behavior response classes. This is a very innovative but unproven idea. Thus far, Guess and colleagues (Guess et al., 1993) have concentrated on differentiating Level I state conditions among people with severe and profound intellectual disability. They have not as yet demonstrated the emergence of self-injurious behavior as implied by their theory, nor have they shown how the levels of state conditions interact to improve their prediction of selected forms of self-injurious behavior. This would be an important test of their theory and methodology.

Kennedy (2002) has described an account based on the Guess and Carr (1991) model of how self-injurious behavior might develop from stereotyped behavior through reinforcement and response differentiation. As yet there are no data to support this model over other models. The longitudinal work of Murphy et al. (1999) observing the development of self-injurious behavior of school children over an 18-month period and the work of Richman and Lindauer (2005a, 2005b), observing the development of self-injurious behavior of infants aged 18–32 months are consistent with the Guess and Carr (1991) description (see Chapter 4, section on prevention and early intervention for self-injurious behavior).

2.8.2. Compulsive Behavior Hypothesis

The compulsive behavior hypothesis holds that, for some individuals, self-injurious behavior is a compulsive behavior that occurs in the context of cerebral damage (Gedye, 1992; King, 1993). According to King (1993), the hypothesis is based on four observations. First, cerebral damage sometimes causes compulsive behavior. Second, severity of intellectual disability may reflect the degree of underlying cerebral impairment. Third, persons with susceptibility to self-injurious or to compulsive behavior both react similarly to stress, anxiety, and task demands. Fourth, some serotonergic drugs (e.g., clomipramine, fluoxetine, and buspirone) appear to ameliorate OCD and self-injurious behavior (Bodfish & Madison, 1993; Lewis, Bodfish, Powell, & Golden, 1995; Lewis, Bodfish, Powell, Parker, & Golden, 1996a).

The compulsive behavior hypothesis is almost entirely speculative and without conclusive empirical support. While it is interesting, like all other existing hypotheses of self-injurious behavior, it has had no disjunctive or exclusive test to prove its specificity. Nevertheless, it may be correct for a given subpopulation of self-injurious behavior cases. Several of the neurobiological and behavioral histories of OCD and self-injurious behavior may overlap in some cases. How and to what degree do they overlap are the big unanswered questions. Recently, Bodfish and his colleagues have set out to establish the existence of compulsive behaviors as an independent response class among people with intellectual disabilities (Bodfish & Madison, 1993; Bodfish et al., 1995a). In an institutional sample of 210 medically stable, ambulatory adults with severe or profound intellectual disabilities, they found considerable overlapping in the prevalence of stereotyped behavior (60.9%), self-injurious behavior (46.6%), and compulsive behaviors (40%). The instrument they used to assess compulsive behaviors was Gedye's (1992) Compulsive Behavior Checklist, a non-validated staff-rating instrument. Examples of items were: arranges objects, closes doors, and washes hand, taps floor, and licks objects. The stereotyped behavior checklist they used contained items from the Timed Stereotypies Rating Scale (Campbell, 1985). An adaptation of the self-injurious behavior questionnaire by Maurice and Trudel (1982) was used. None of these instruments had any formal validity study, yet the data are promising that compulsive behavior can be reliably identified in this population and may be associated with some self-injurious behavior cases.

King (1993) also cites as evidence the high incidence of self-injurious behavior and compulsive tics in Gilles de la Tourette's syndrome. We have discussed self-injurious behavior in Tourette's syndrome in a previous section. Research is needed to show how much overlap there is between these two self-injurious behavior populations and how similarly they respond to the same psychopharmacological and/or behavioral interventions. For instance, haloperidol, pimozide, and fluphenazine, the most effective drugs for treating motor and verbal tics in Tourette's disorder (Robertson, 1992) have had a much more inconsistent effect on self-injurious behavior in the intellectual disabilities population (Aman, 1993). Self-injurious behavior in Tourette's syndrome may represent a distinct subtype of self-injurious behavior.

2.8.3. Neonatal Dopamine Depletion Hypothesis

Breese et al. (2005) have recently published a comprehensive review of their self-injurious behavior model. Breese and Traylor (1970) found that injecting an adult rat with the neurotoxin 6-hydroxydopamine[4] (6-OHDA) in the corpus striatum created a selective lesion of dopamine neurons resulting in dopamine supersensitivity. If the rats were then challenged with a dopamine agonist such as L-DOPA or apomorphine, they became aggressive and hyperactive. If, however, these lesions were performed at age 5–15 days and then the rats as adults were challenged with a dopamine agonist such as L-DOPA or apomorphine, they also began biting themselves severely. Breese and Baumeister recognized this as a potential model for self-biting in Lesch–Nyhan syndrome (Breese et al., 1984a, 1984b). Examination of postmortem brain tissues of Lesch–Nyhan cases by Lloyd et al. (1981) showed indeed a large depletion of dopamine in the corpus striatum and elevated serotonin levels in the substantia nigra, as would be predicted by the Breese–Baumeister model. Similar results have been found in PET scanning studies with live Lesch–Nyhan patients (Wong et al., 1996).

The question then arose as to why dopamine blockers such as haloperidol and chlorpromazine do not decrease self-injurious behavior among humans very well (Aman, 1993). Breese posited that these drugs blocked primarily D_2 dopamine receptor subtypes, while self-injurious behavior is primarily a D_1 dopamine receptor phenomenon. Using the experimental drug SCH 23390, a specific D_1 receptor antagonist, he was able to block self-injurious behavior in neonatal dopamine depleted rats that had been challenged with apomorphine.

Unfortunately, there is no pure D_1 receptor antagonist available for clinical use as yet in the U.S. to test the neonatal dopamine depletion model in human self-injurious behavior cases. The dopamine system has been implicated in repetitive behavior disorders, such as self-injurious behavior (Bodfish et al., 1995b; Lewis, Schroeder, Aman, Gadow, & Thompson, 1996d). Clinical trials with D1 and D_2 receptor blockers fluphenazine (Gualtieri & Schroeder, 1989) and clozapine (see Schroeder et al., 1995 for a

---

[4] A neurotransmitter analogue that depletes noradrenergic stores in nerve endings and induces a reduction of dopamine levels in the brain.

review) have both been successful, but all these drugs have serious side effects. Clozapine also has an affinity for other dopamine (D_4) and serotonin receptors in addition to D_1 and D_2 dopamine receptors. These drugs are, therefore, not an unambiguous test of the neonatal dopamine depletion hypothesis, even though Criswell, Mueller, and Breese (1989) showed that clozapine at low doses was a relatively selective D_1 blocker in the Breese animal model. Nevertheless, this work points to atypical neuroleptic drugs such as clozapine, risperidone, olanzapine, and aripirazole as potentially efficacious for treating self-injurious behavior.

2.8.4. Serotonin Hypothesis

Serotonin is another major CNS neurotransmitter that often acts in a reciprocal relationship with dopamine. Mizuno and Yugari (1974) found that giving 5-hydroxtryptophan (5-HTP), a serotonin agonist, to four Lesch–Nyhan boys had a dramatic effect for a few weeks. Other investigators failed to replicate this finding until Nyhan, Johnson, Kaufman, and Jones (1980) gave 5-HTP along with carbidopa, and imipramine to prevent rapid excretion in the urine. They also found a dramatic effect, which disappeared after three months and could not be recovered.

More recently, there have been a number of serotonin reuptake inhibitors used in uncontrolled clinical trials that reduced self-injurious and aggressive behaviors in persons with intellectual disabilities. Examples of these drugs are fluoxetine, trazodone, buspirone, sertraline and related drugs (see Baumeister, Todd, & Sevin, 1993 for review). Since none of these studies was methodologically sound, they do not offer unequivocal support for the specificity of the serotonin hypothesis. But they do merit a closer examination in future research (Schroeder & Tessel, 1994). Lewis, Silva, and Gray-Silva (1995) found in a double-blind comparison with placebo that the serotonin uptake inhibitor, clomipramine, reduced stereotyped behavior, hyperactivity, self-injurious behavior, and irritability among people with severe and profound intellectual disabilities. Serotonin dysregulation also occurs in many psychiatric disorders in persons without intellectual disabilities.

Recent studies of risperidone for aggressive behavior and self-injurious behavior among people with intellectual disabilities (Van den Borre et al., 1993; Simon, Blubaugh, & Pippidis, 1996) suggest that drugs affecting serotonin and dopamine and their interactions might be very efficacious. Year-long in-patient and out-patient double-blind studies with risperidone by our group on 40 children and adults with intellectual disabilities and severe behavioral problems, including self-injurious behavior, aggressive behavior, and stereotyped behavior, have shown a marked reduction of destructive behaviors, i.e., 50%+ in 57% and 25%+ in 87% of cases (Hellings et al., 2006; Zarcone et al., 2001). Two short-term, double-blind studies found risperidone to be effective in autistic adults' repetitive behaviors, anxiety, depression, aggressive behavior, and irritability (McDougle et al., 1998a, 1998b) and for aggressive behavior, tantrums, and self-injurious behavior in autistic children (Research Units on Pediatric Psychopharmacology Autism Network, 2002). Other atypical antipsychotics, e.g., olanzapine (Bodfish, Mahorney, McKee, Sheitman, & Breese, 2001) and aripiprazole (Stigler, Posey, & McDougle, 2004) have also shown promise (see Chapter 4, section on psychopharmacology for more details).

2.8.5. Opioid Peptide Hypotheses

Two hypotheses by Sandman et al. (1983) are based on the clinical observation that some self-injurious behavior cases appear to be insensitive to pain or they even seem to seek painful stimuli. This raises the question as to whether pain regulatory system of these individuals is not working normally. Perhaps, stimulation of their pain receptors results in production of excessive amounts of opioid peptides, i.e., neurotransmitters involved in pain regulation.

The first hypothesis, *the pain hypothesis*, proposes that self-injurious behavior is a symptom of general sensory depression, including hypoalgesia, caused by chronic elevation of endogenous opiates. If a person has elevated pain threshold, self-injurious behavior might be a form of self-stimulation to reach it. Opiate blockers, such as naloxone and naltrexone, on the other hand, reduce the pain threshold and thereby lower self-stimulatory self-injurious behavior rate.

The second hypothesis, *the addiction hypothesis*, suggests that self-injurious behavior subjects are addicted to their opiate system and that they engage in self-injurious behavior to secure pain-induced release of opiates, producing a reinforcing opiate "high." Opiate blockers might attenuate self-injurious behavior by increasing pain and reducing the subsequent "high."

Sandman (1990/1991) reviewed 16 studies of naloxone and naltrexone involving 45 subjects, most of whom had autism and 28 of whom had self-injurious behavior. Of the self-injurious behavior cases, 24 had varied positive responses averaging about 50%. Symons, Thompson, and Rodriguez (2004) essentially replicated and extended this review with a meta-analysis of 27 research articles on 86 subjects with self-injurious behavior. Eighty percent improved during naltrexone administration and 47% had reduced their self-injurious behavior by 50% or more. These studies varied widely in methodological quality, and they will be discussed in detail in Chapter 4, in the section on psychopharmacology. Taken as a whole, however, they do offer support for the opioid peptide hypothesis, at least for naltrexone responders.

In order to improve the prediction of who will respond to naltrexone, Sandman has conducted a number of ingenious experiments. In the Sandman, Hetrick, Taylor, and Chicz-DeMet (1997) study, blood samples were collected from 10 self-injurious behavior adult cases with intellectual disabilities shortly after a self-injurious behavior act and also during self-injurious behavior-free periods in the mornings and afternoons. After self-injurious behavior episodes, β-endorphins, but not ACTH (adrenocorticotrophic hormone), were elevated in responders to naltrexone, suggesting dysfunctions of the pro-opiomelanocortin (POMC) system. The POMC system gives rise to β-endorphin, ACTH, and a host of other neuropeptides in the hypothalamic–pituitary–adrenal (HPA) axis. Dissociation of β-endorphin and ACTH, two neuropeptides that usually act together, may predict individuals' response to opiate blockers for self-injurious behavior. Sandman et al. (1999) found a mutation in the POMC gene region in a case with autism and self-injurious behavior. Sandman, Touchette, Marion, Lenjavi, and Chicz-DeMet (2002, 2003) replicated and extended their 1997 findings in nine more individuals. This time, they showed the uncoupling of β-endorphin and ACTH in morning baselines, thus supporting previous reports that the HPA axis is disturbed in some cases with self-injurious behavior. These tended to be the ones with "contagious" self-injurious behavior, i.e., the ones who engage in long bouts of severe self-hitting (Kroeker, Touchette, Engleman, & Sandman, 2004).

2.8.6. Endogenous Neurochemical Self-Administration

Thompson et al. (1995) published a new and compelling account of self-injurious behavior based upon the mechanisms of addiction and the commonalties in behavior patterns among persons who perform self-injurious behavior and among people addicted to cocaine and morphine. Citing the operant technology typically used to study drug addiction in animals, they draw many parallels between people performing self-injurious behavior and opiate self-administration and cocaine self-administration in animals in terms of (1) response requirements to maintain a constant blood level under a given schedule of reinforcement; (2) relationships between route of administration and unit dose; (3) availability of alternative reinforcers; (4) the primary reinforcing properties of dopamine and opioid ligand binding; (5) the role of stressful and painful events; (6) the interplay between social and neurochemical events (see Figures 2.4–2.6). They draw models to show how interoceptively conditioned and exteroceptively conditioned stimuli sometimes work together, sometimes against each other to reinforce and maintain self-injurious behavior. Some of the common denominators between self-injurious behavior, and opiate and cocaine self-administration are that

- they are mediated by dopamine binding in the nucleus accumbens and ventral tegmental area (VTA);
- they may come under control of the reinforcing properties of exogenous and endogenous neurochemical consequences; and
- they may be maintained in order to avoid withdrawal distress due to decrease in dopamine and opioid release.

The endogenous neurochemical self-administration hypothesis of self-injurious behavior is a plausible heuristic that begs for further study to test its validity and limits. As yet, there is little research in the self-injurious behavior literature, which is based directly on it except for the studies of the effects of naltrexone on self-injurious behavior and Symons' work on self-injurious behavior and disturbed pain mechanisms (see previous section on pain and self-injurious behavior). In many respects, this work is an extension of Sandman's two opioid peptide hypotheses.

2.8.7. Isolate-Rearing Model

Kraemer (1992) has posited a comprehensive psychobiological attachment theory (PAT) in which disruptions between the infant and its caretaker set the stage in the CNS for social dysfunction in later life. He summarized 25 years of research at the Harlow laboratories on isolate-rearing of infant rhesus monkeys. This research shows that, if an infant monkey is separated from its mother for the first 22 months of life and reared socially thereafter, c. 14% develop a variety of dysfunctional behaviors, e.g., abnormal stereotypic motor patterns, hyperphagia, hyper-responsivity to change, stereotyped rocking, self-injurious biting mostly of the digits and arms, head banging, and aggressive attacks when later confronted with normal monkeys (Kraemer & Clarke, 1990). These behaviors have been related to the decoupling in the brain of the "tuning" process affected by the norephinephrine (NE) system, of the "switching" processes by the dopamine (DA) system and by the "gate keeping" or "enabling" functions affected by the serotonin (5HT) system (Kraemer, Ebert, Schmidt, & McKinney, 1989; Kraemer, Schmidt, & Ebert, 1997). Social isolation is thought to produce cytoarchitectural changes in these brain biogenic amine systems that result in their dysregulation, such that the animal is not prepared to respond appropriately to normal social stimuli, but performs inappropriate behaviors instead.

PAT theory is also a persuasive heuristic, which attempts to integrate a wide variety of disparate findings from the animal literature and from human infant attachment theories Bowlby, 1969; Ainsworth, Blehar, Waters, & Walls, 1978. It also has many critics, as was evident from the open peer commentary following Kraemer's article. Probably the most controversial idea is that attachment systems alter neurobiological structures in the brain. This idea is supported only modestly by direct evidence. Most of it is indirect evidence inferred from assays of neurotransmitters, their precursors, and their metabolites in cerebrospinal fluid of live monkeys (Mason, 1992; Tiefenbacher, Novak, Jorgensen & Meyer, 2000). Nevertheless, Kraemer's approach begins to reflect the complexity of the effects of environmental and biological interactions on the development of stereotyped behavior, self-injurious behavior, and aggressive behavior, and points to future directions for research in terms of its neuroplasticity and the possibility of modifying it through behavioral and/or pharmacological intervention.

Novak, Crockett, and Sackett (2002), Lutz, Well, and Novak (2003), and Novak (2003) corroborated and extended Kraemer's results to the primate populations at both the Washington and the New England Regional Primate Centers (NERPC). At NERPC they also found similar results with macaque monkeys who had been reared socially, but were housed separately as adults. Therapies such as environmental enrichment and increasing cage size did not improve their behavior. When measuring self-injurious behavior monkeys' heart rate and blood cortisol levels in response to mild stress, i.e., placing them in a harness and sedating them, they were surprised to find a *lowering* of heart rate and cortisol levels instead of the expected elevated levels compared to non-self-injurious behavior controls. They concluded that self-injurious behavior monkeys have a disturbed HPA axis, a result similar to Sandman's et al. (2002) work on uncoupling of POMC and ACTH peptides in human self-injurious behavior cases.

Other work by Lewis, Gluck, Beauchamp, Keresztury, and Mailman (1990) and Martin, Spicer, Lewis, Gluck, and Cork (1991) at the Southwest Regional Primate Center showed that isolate-reared rhesus monkeys as older adults had abnormal anatomical brain features that were related to dopamine deficits in the striatum and striatal cortex. These primate models of stereotyped behavior and self-injurious behavior from four Regional Primate Centers agree in supporting the idea that there may be important abnormalities in neurochemistry and neuroanatomy of humans with stereotyped behavior and self-injurious behavior. These primates are an important population to study because of their detailed documented behavioral, genetic, and veterinary histories.

2.8.8. Dynamic Model of Self-Injurious, Stereotypic, and Aggressive Behavior

In their review of animal and human models of stereotyped behaviors, of which self-injurious behavior was viewed as a subset, Lewis and Baumeister (1982) put forth a cohesive view first posited for infants by Wolff (1967) that stereotyped movements are the behavioral expression of a central motor program controlled by neural pattern generators or oscillators to modulate stimulation. This hypothesis is an outgrowth of extensive biological research showing that the CNS does not need sensory feedback to generate sequenced rhythmic movements. Such a theory fits well some other regulatory theories of stereotyped behavior. For an excellent book on these theories, see Sprague and Newell (1996).

Support for the view comes from the dynamics of repetitive movements in stereotyped and self-injurious behavior.

- The regularity of number of bouts, bout length, and periodicity of much stereotyped body rocking, head weaving, etc.;
- Presence of ultradian rhythms in people who perform stereotyped behaviors;
- The apparent lack of discrete environmental stimulus control over stereotyped behavior;
- And the fact that, once triggered, stereotyped action patterns appear to run to completion independent of environmental stimulus control.

This holds not only for moment-to-moment fluctuations (Lewis et al., 1984) but also for longer periods of time (Lewis, MacLean, Johnson, & Baumeister, 1981). In fact, Lewis et al. (1995) have now extended this analysis to stereotyped self-injurious behavior, and aggressive behavior occurring over three- and five-month cycles in large institutional populations. Lewis interprets these rhythmic cycles as representing a shift from environmental stimulus control to internal self-regulation primarily under CNS control.

The presence of cyclicity in the occurrence of maladaptive behaviors is certainly noteworthy and important to caregivers. The theoretical explanations for the dynamics of cyclicity and intensity of stereotyped behavior and self-injurious behavior are still a matter of much speculation (Sprague & Newell, 1996; Newell & Bodfish, 2002). There have been no direct observations of neural pattern generators in the CNS. They must be inferred indirectly from behavioral or neurophysiological methods. The measurement devices for assessing movement in this area are very sophisticated. Force plates have been used to measure periodicity of stereotyped behavior (Newell & Bodfish, 2002), tics (Crosland, Zarcone, Schroeder, Zarcone, & Fowler, 2005), and kinematics and kinetics, to assess the speed and intensity of self-injurious behavior head hits (Newell et al., 1999). These are dimensions of self-injurious behavior that have received little attention but need elaboration in the future, in order to assess the variability and dangerousness of a given self-injurious behavior topography.

2.8.9. Genetic and Perinatal Risk Factors and Stress

Tessel and colleagues (Tessel, Schroeder, Loupe, & Stodgell, 1995a; Tessel, Schroeder, Stodgell, & Loupe, 1995b; Tessel et al., 1995a, 1995b; Loupe, Schroeder, & Tessel, 1995; Stodgell, Schroeder, Hyland, & Tessel, 1994) have combined the effects of isolate-rearing with three rodent models for stress-induced destructive behavior. They are

- a genetic model of aggressive behavior using the spontaneously hypertensive rat (SHR),
- a model of stereotyped behavior using methylazoxymethanol (MAM) injected prenatally to induce microcephaly in rat offspring, and
- a model of self-injurious behavior using the Breese–Baumeister neonatal dopamine depletion model in rats (6-ODHA).

Tessel and colleagues have found that, under conditions when rats were administered periodic unavoidable shock, members of the SHR group of rats initially demonstrated aggressive responses by biting the bars of the chamber; soon after, within the same session, SHR animals displayed marked increases in freezing behavior. MAM animals under the same conditions became hyperactive and engaged in stereotypic rearing behavior. No self-injurious behavior was observed in any group during shock sessions. However, when 6-OHDA animals that had experienced shock were exposed to apomorphine a nonselective dopamine receptor agonist, self-injurious biting did occur. Periodic food delivery to food-deprived animals induced non-rearing stereotypic behaviors among SHR animals and rearing and hyperactivity among both SHR and MAM animals. Together these data suggest that there are *specific behavior patterns* associated with the different models. Now the question occurs, will drug or other treatments serve to reduce the maladaptive behavior associated with the various models?

Another set of fascinating data derives from observations related to operant fixed ratio (FR) discrimination training. Initially subjects were taught to discriminate between FR-1 and FR-16 schedules. This procedure involved having subjects respond to a center lever and then when that lever was retracted and one of the two side levers was presented, the subjects responded to the left lever if the center lever had one ratio requirement, and to the right lever if the center lever had another ratio requirement. When the discrimination started with the easy FR-1 versus FR-16, discrimination and then gradually progressed to FR-8 versus FR-16, all groups learned the discriminations and their learning curves were essentially identical. However, when the discrimination was reversed, MAM rats reversed more slowly than the subjects of the other three groups. Moreover, when the fixed ratio discrimination started with the FR-8 versus FR-16 discrimination, MAM and SHR rats eventually learned the discrimination, but at a significantly slower rate than controls.

Analysis of brain structures and chemicals, however, yielded the most exciting findings. The 6-OHDA animals that had been given fixed ratio training showed a reversal of cerebral and striatal dopamine depletion. Similarly, MAM animals that had been given FR discrimination training showed a partial reversal of hippocampal hypoplasia (reversal of MAM-induced hippocampal weight and protein concentration reduction). These observations are the first to suggest the possibility that susceptibility to chronic maladaptive behavior and the presence of cognitive deficits may not only be amenable to prevention, they may be amenable to reversal. While changes in behavior must be associated with changes in the brain, no one has previously shown such specific and massive changes related to training. Moreover, the fact that changes were in the direction of normality for animals with specific lesions was totally unexpected.

These changes raise a number of important questions. First, are the changes related to a specific kind of training involving progressive increase in problem difficulty or would training on simple repetitive task result in the brain changes? Second, is such change restricted to rats or do they occur in other animals, including humans? Are these changes in brain structure and chemistry accompanied by more generalized changes in behavior? For example, do MAM animals who have been through fixed ratio discrimination training engage in less stereotyped rearing or do 6-OHDA animals no longer engage in self-biting when administered apomorphine and electric shock? Is it possible that such training will have a more generalized effect?

The combined approach of comparing conditions of isolate-rearing in different risk models may help to increase the specificity of these hypotheses related to animal models of the development of maladaptive behavior and subsequent intervention. This promises to be a fruitful line of research for the future. Almost all behavioral interventions in human self-injurious behavior studies have been aimed at modifying specific behaviors under specific conditions using operant techniques, but the present experiments suggest that regular engagement in structured operant training that is challenging, even if not specifically targeted at self-injurious behavior, may help to reduce self-injurious behavior.

We have reviewed the evidence for nine bio-behavioral hypotheses on multiple causes for self-injurious behavior. It is beyond the scope of this chapter to discuss in detail the neurobiological mechanisms underpinning these hypotheses. The interested reader is directed to an excellent review by Visser, Bar, and Jinnah (2000).

2.9. A Gene–Brain–Behavior Model of Self-Injurious Behavior

As shown in the preceding sections of this volume, several different theories have been put forward to explain the causes of self-injurious behavior and to describe mechanisms that maintain it. Although most of them have something to contribute, they are all somewhat restricted by the very heuristics on which they are based, in the sense that they use language best suited for their unit of analysis, but less so for conceptualizing alternative views (e.g., psychodynamic and developmental theories, behavior analysis, psychopharmacology, neuroscience, and genetics). Exploring a complex and heterogeneous behavioral phenomenon from different angles is useful, especially in the early stages. At some point, however, it becomes necessary to integrate those approaches that are promising, especially those that can be addressed and validated by empirical methods. Therefore, in the summary of Chapter 2, we are proposing a dynamic developmental model we call the *Gene–Brain–Behavior Model of Self-Injurious Behavior* that integrates several theoretical propositions (Figure 2.8).

The term has been borrowed from the recent book *Self-injurious behavior: Gene–brain–behavior relationships* by Schroeder, Oster-Granite, & Thompson (2002). It presents a generic framework that identifies key components that determine human behavior in general and self-injurious behavior in particular, and that assigns proper roles for various theories within a complex system. The intent is to integrate theories to explain self-injurious behavior of any kind, be it pathological or non-pathological, intentional or non-intentional, direct acting or cumulatively damaging, maintained by external or automatic, positive or negative reinforcement, and whether it occurs in people with profound intellectual disabilities, in psychiatric patients with acute psychosis or in teenage high school students.

The model is based on Skinner's (1974) assertion that human behavior can be explained as the interaction of the organism with its current environment, in acknowledgement of a two-level selection history.

1. The biological selection history, represents the natural selection of genetic information within a species, which determines an individual's genetic endowment. This *phylogenetic* history constitutes a person's biological predisposition.
2. The *ontogenic* history of the individual's behavior selections, which represents the current learning and the building of a person's response repertoire. The ontogenetic history of learning is embedded and influenced by cultural practices, traditions, and values of the social enviroment in which a person lives.

The molecular level can be conceptualized as the ongoing sequence of discrete trials of functional organism–environment interactions. Here, the acquisition of new behavior and the maintenace of operant and respondent behavior takes place. Behavior involves the entirety of human behavior, including motor behavior, emotional behavior, thoughts, language, neurochemical responses, etc. This continuous and ongoing process is symbolized in Figure 2.8 by cascading (symbolizing repeated trials) grey rectangles, each representing a discrete funtional organism–environment interaction. Learning is primarily characterized by interconnected classical and instrumental learning processes, as they were discussed earlier in more detail as represented in Figures 2.2–2.6.

Molecular learning is influenced by the accumulated or molar learned repertoire, which consists of (a) contingency-based learning, (b) rule-governed learning, and

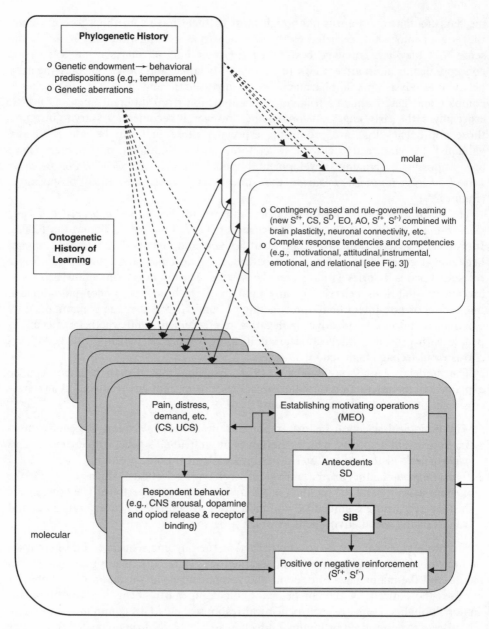

Figure 2.8: A Gene–Brain–Behavior Model of Self-Injurious Behavior.

(c) biological developments such as brain development and brain plasticity as a function of the exposure of the biological endowment with the envrionment. The molar repertoire represents acquired "meta-behaviors" or complex response tendencies ("personality," "traits"). For example, processes as described in the developmental psychopathology model of Yates (2004) fit here (e.g., "negative-other- and self-representation," "affect dysregulation"). The historical molar dynamic is symbolized in Figure 2.8 by cascading white rectangles.

Molecular and molar response repertoires are interactive, meaning that molecular learning influences the molar learning history and vice versa. This interactrive nature of molar and molecular processes is symbolized by solid bi-directional arrows, which represent the ontogenetic history of learning.

Learning on the molecular level is also determined by a person's phylogenetic history, which involves the (a) phylogenetic history of the species at large, (b) the specific genetic information passed on by the parents, (c) spontaneous gene mutations (i.e., genetic syndromes), and (d) prenatal and perinatal damage (e.g., fetal alcohol syndrome). The influence of the phylogenetic history on the molecular processes is symbolized by dotted one-directional arrows.

And finally, the accumulating molar level of learning with higher-level response tendencies is also influenced by the phylogenetic history. The one-directional influence of the phylogenetic history on the molar processes is symbolized by dotted arrows.

The main advantage of this model is that it allows one to incorporate various noteworthy contributions that were based on different theoretical approaches and that used to be fragmented and difficult to reconcile. For instance, it provides a conceptual basis for the integration neo-analytic theories, such as attachment theories or developmental psychopathology with the theory of learning. From that perspective it becomes clear that the primary contributions of attachment theory and developmental psychopathology (Yates, 2004) to our understanding of self-injurious behavior has been to the molar component of the ontogenetic history of learning, while much of the behavior analytic work and psychopharmacological research has focused on the molecular level. Neuroscience, genetics, and psychopharmacology are concerened with the biological components of the behavior. When all of the known facts about a given aspect of self-injurious behavior are in accordance across the molecular and molar levels, confidence in its validity is increased. Similarly, when findings at one level are at variance with facts at another level, caution is advised and reconciliation of the disparities is indicated. For instance, behavioral theories of self-injurious behavior which ignore its biological antecedents are likely to be incomplete and vice versa. The facts need to fit across levels. To restrict our view to only one of these components will give us an incomplete picture of self-injurious behavior.

Chapter 3

Assessment

3.1. Structural Assessment

Behavioral assessment includes several different steps and serves a number of different interrelated purposes. It includes (a) the identification of critical parameters of target behaviors, replacement behaviors, and unintended behavioral side effects of an intervention, (b) the detection of the functions that serve to maintain the behavior, and, finally, (c) monitoring and evaluating the effects of treatment. The first purpose can be described as the assessment of topographical or structural characteristics of behavior, such as the form, frequency, severity, and kinetic characteristics or the impact. This can be done for both behaviors that are to be weakened/eliminated or strengthened. The second purpose is referred to as functional assessment and analysis, which is vital in developing effective and individualized treatment programs. The third purpose includes assessment methods of the first and includes methods that are generally known as single-subject experimental design. This chapter will focus on the first two components of behavioral assessment of self-injurious behavior (SIB) and aggressive behavior. For more details about single-subject experimentation the reader is referred to Bailey and Burch (2002), Cooper, Heron and Heward (2007).

3.1.1. Direct Behavior Assessment

3.1.1.1. Systematic Behavior Observation
One of the hallmarks of applied behavior analysis is direct assessment of behavioral parameters (such as frequency and duration, intensity, response latency and inter-response time, sequential intra-behavioral response patterns, and inter-response sequences) through direct and systematic in vivo observation. Traditionally, behavior observation in behavior analytic research involved observers who, during predefined observation periods, recorded some parameter of one or two behaviors guided by operational definitions. Direct behavior observation is a scientific methodology, however, and cannot be discussed here in full detail. The interested reader is referred to other sources such as Bailey and Burch (2002), and Cooper et al. (2007), or Thompson, Felce, and Symons (2000). Rapid advances in affordable electronic equipment from multi-channel data input devices, video-recording and repeat display options,

digitization, analysis techniques, and data analysis computer software have revolutionized the observational technology.

A precursor of this development was a standardized observation system called the *Ecobehavioral Assessment Instrument* (Schroeder, Rojahn, & Mulick, 1978). This system was designed not only to capture the occurrence of a target behavior (such as self-injurious behavior and aggressive behavior), but also of collateral behavior of the person, as well as social interactive behavior, contingent, and non-contingent behavior of others directed toward the person with the problem behavior, and contextual events (number of staff and peers present, medication types and dosage, scheduled activities, etc.). Ecobehavioral observation was successfully implemented in a number of self-injurious behavior intervention studies (e.g., Mulick, Barbour, Schroeder, & Rojahn, 1980; Mulick, Hoyt, Rojahn, & Schroeder, 1978; Rojahn, Mulick, McCoy, & Schroeder; Schroeder, 1984; Schroeder & Gualtieri, 1985; Schroeder et al., 1982; Schroeder, Rojahn, & Mulick, 1978). As an assessment technology it was limited at the time by the low-tech interval recording method with its implicit errors. However, the basic assumptions underlying the ecobehavioral approach, namely the recognition of the importance of contextualized behavior analysis, which required more than the recording of a single-target behavior and the concurrent assessment of contextual events, which can provide rich information on a behavior's functions, are still relevant today. It also assumed that systematic manipulations of hypothesized controlling variables in combination with the assessment of behavior-antecedent and consequent events can reveal behavioral dynamics in the natural environment. In that sense, the *Ecobehavioral Assessment Instrument* can be seen as a methodological forerunner of functional and structural analyses and assessment, which will be discussed in detail in a later section of this chapter.

3.1.1.2. Behavioral Kinematic Analyses

Concerned with more basic research issues, Newell and Bodfish (2002) analyzed the temporal and force dynamics of self-injurious behavior. The assessment of *temporal dynamics* involved real time coding of self-injurious behavior to generate short-term (occurrence within a bout and within observation sessions) and long-term time series (across days, weeks, etc.). Thanks to readily available computer software, such data can be easily analyzed with linear (e.g., autocorrelations, ARIMA models, spectral analysis) and non-linear (e.g., approximate entropy) statistical procedures.

Force dynamics analysis, on the other hand, relies on classical mechanics and involves kinematics (describing the motions of the torso and limbs) and kinetics (characterizing the force produced over time). Kinematic analyses have been increasingly used to study stereotyped behavior and self-injurious behavior (e.g., Sprague & Newell, 1996; Newell et al., 1999). Newell et al. (1999), for instance, discovered that the head banging of an eight-year-old girl with profound intellectual disabilities and autistic disorder had a qualitatively highly consistent dynamic. In addition, the impact forces of her self-injurious behavior were similar to the low end of forces generated in boxing blows and karate hits.

3.1.2. Standardized Clinical Interviews

Most clinical assessment procedures start with interviews with parents, teachers, or care takers, and many clinicians follow their own script. For research purposes, however, interviews must be standardized to ensure consistency across participants and the ability to replicate methods across studies. Two such standardized interview protocols specifically geared to problem behavior research in intellectual disabilities will be described below.

3.1.2.1. Challenging Behavior Interview (CBI)

The CBI was developed by Oliver et al. (2003) in the U.K. as an assessment instrument for behavior problems, including self-injurious behavior and aggressive behavior. It consists of two parts. The first part identifies the occurrence of concrete forms of behavior problems during the past month, including self-injurious behavior, physical and verbal aggressive behavior, as well as disruption and destruction of property or the environment, and stereotyped behavior. Operational definitions are provided for the informant that characterize these behavior categories and distinguish them from one another. The second part assesses the seriousness of the problems. Fourteen scales measure the frequency and duration of the episodes, the effects the behavior had on the person and others, and the management strategies used by staff.

The authors have reported preliminary psychometric properties. For Chapter I, mean κ interrater reliability was .67 (range: .50–.80) and mean κ test–retest reliability was .86 (range: .70–.91). Pearson r mean interrater reliability was .48 (range: .02–.77) and mean test–retest reliability .76 (range: .66–.85). Concurrent validity was also assessed by Pearson r with the *Aberrant Behavior Checklist* (ABC) (described in more detail further below) and varied between .19 and .68. Content validity was assessed by comparing scores for each behavior on specific items relative to the relevant aspects of severity that would be expected depending on the behavior category.

To assess physical aggressive behavior and other behavior problems amongst a group of children with intellectual disabilities, Adams and Allen (2001) used a combined questionnaire and interview method. The questionnaire asked caregivers about 22 different types of aggressive behavior. Whenever a caregiver affirmed that a certain type of aggressive behavior occurred the following were asked in a structured-interview format: targets of the behavior, frequency of the behavior, severity of resulting injuries, management problems, intrusiveness of caregiver response, and efficacy of response. Davidson et al. (1999) used both observational data and one-on-one interviews with patients and caregivers to assess frequency, severity, and duration of problem behaviors such as aggressive behavior and self-injurious behavior.

3.1.2.2. Challenging Behavior Survey: Individual Schedule (CBS:IS)

The CBS:IS, a comprehensive semi-structured interview, was developed for a total population survey by Alborz, Bromley, Emerson, Kiernan, and Qureshi (1994). The interview has three major sections. The first section collects information on personal characteristics, such as age, gender, ethnic origin, residence, residential history, day service history and employment, education, and history of detention. In addition several questions are clustered around broad areas of adaptive functioning, such as level of physical functioning, self-care and domestic skills, communication skills, social skills, and stereotyped behaviors. The second section explores aggressive, self-injurious, and other serious disruptive or socially unacceptable behavior. The specific form of the behavior, frequency, circumstances, or functional properties, and the interventions required to deal with it are noted. Items are topographic descriptions of physical attacks on other people (8 items), self-injurious behavior (15 items), and stereotyped behaviors (5 items). These items are either identical or slightly modified versions of a precursor of the then unpublished Behavior Problems Inventory (BPI-01) (Rojahn et al., 2001). Items are scored on a categorical rating scale (1 = one of this person's most serious challenging behaviors; 2 = previously or potentially a challenge, but controlled in the setting; 3 = present, but a lesser challenge; 4 = not characteristic of person). In addition to the ratings of the topographic items, a number of detailed follow-up questions are provided to create a more comprehensive clinical picture. The third section of the CBS:IS deals with more general aspects of challenging behaviors, such as stress and the demands placed on staff, overall behavior consequences to the setting, required services, and treatments. No psychometric properties have been published for the CBS:IS.

Interviews have one important limitation. When interviewers ask informants about challenging behaviors they rely heavily on the caregiver's memory and subjective interpretations of behavior (Nottestad & Linaker, 2001).

3.1.3. Specialized Structural Behavior-Rating Scales

While interviews can provide important information about behavior problems, their utility in research is limited due to a general lack of objectivity and the generally unknown reliability and validity. Rating scales have the advantage of being strictly standardized and therefore are easier to evaluate in terms of its psychometric properties than interviews. The following will present three behavior-rating scales in alphabetical order that were developed with a narrow focus on the structural aspects of behavior disturbances such as self-injurious behavior and aggressive behavior.

3.1.3.1. Behavior Problems Inventory (BPI-01)
The BPI-01 is a 49-item behavior-rating instrument with 14 specific self-injurious behavior, 24 stereotypic behavior, and 11 aggressive/destructive behavior items. Each of the three problem behavior groups are preceded by a generic definition that applies to all items within the group. Items are scored on a five-point frequency scale (0 = never, 1 = monthly, 2 = weekly, 3 = daily, 4 = hourly) and a four-point degree-of-the-problem or severity scale (0 = no problem, 1 = a slight problem, 2 = a moderate problem, 3 = a severe problem). Only behaviors that have occurred at least once during the past two months are scored. For clinically significant behaviors that are not

captured by any of the 49 items, "other" categories are provided for each of the three behavior groups.

Rojahn et al. (2001) conducted a comprehensive psychometric study of the BPI-01 that involved 432 mostly low-functioning individuals with intellectual disabilities who lived in a developmental center. Four clinical psychology graduate students administered the BPI-01 via semi-structured interviews with direct-care staff. The frequency and severity scales correlated highly with one another (full-scale $r = .90$, self-injurious behavior subscale $= .93$, aggression/destruction subscale $= .87$). This study was replicated a few years later in the same residential faculty (González et al., in press).

For the frequency scale, Rojahn et al. (2001) reported *internal consistency* for self-injurious behavior subscales of Cronbach $\alpha = .61$ (stereotyped behavior and aggressive/destructive behavior subscales had alphas of .79, and .82, respectively). González et al. (in press) found a lower of Cronbach $\alpha = .48$ for the self-injurious behavior subscale. Sturmey, Sevin, and Williams (1995) reported relatively high internal consistency with Cronbach alpha for the self-injurious behavior scale ($\alpha = .71$) and for the aggression/destruction scale ($\alpha = .77$).

Test–retest reliability in the Rojahn et al. (2001) study for the frequency full-scale was r (Pearson) $= .76$ and for the self-injurious behavior subscale $= .71$. González et al. (in press) reported self-injurious behavior subscale test–retest reliability of $r = .65$ and .63. Sturmey, Fink, and Sevin (1993) reported a median Kappa coefficient across SIB items $\kappa = .68$ and a median percentage agreement of 96.0.

Interrater agreement was examined in a few studies. González et al. (in press) found $r = .67$ for the self-injurious behavior subscale and Sturmey et al. (1993) reported a median Kappa coefficient across SIB items $\kappa = .65$ and a median percentage agreement of 95%.

Criterion-related validity was explored in two other studies. Bodfish, Symons, and Lewis (1999) compared the self-injurious behavior and the stereotyped behavior scales of the *Repetitive Behavior Scale-Revised* (RBS-R, as described in more detail below) and the BPI-01 with 64 adults with intellectual disabilities, establishing criterion-oriented validity. The self-injurious behavior scales correlated at $r = .77$, and the stereotyped behavior scales correlated at $r = .68$. In another study, Rojahn, Aman, Matson, and Mayville (2003) compared the BPI-01 with the *Aberrant Behavior Checklist* (*ABC*). The two instruments produced largely consistent results in the sense that the data converged across subscales that have comparable content, and they diverged across subscales with little content relationship. In summary, criterion validity of the BPI-01 was promising. *Factor validity* of the BPI-01 subscales were established by combinations of confirmatory and exploratory factor analyses as well as by item total correlations within and across subscales and was satisfactory and that the three a priori BPI-01 subscales fit the data reasonably well (Rojahn et al., 2001; González et al., in press).

Most of the studies that generated psychometric evidence of BPI-01 were based on groups of individuals in the severe to profound range of intellectual disabilities who were residents of institutions. However, the BPI-01 was also found to be sensitive to drug effects in two studies of risperidone with community-based children with subaverage cognitive functioning (Aman, De Smedt, Derivan, Lyons, & Findling, 2002; Snyder et al., 2002).

The BPI-01 can be useful for epidemiological research, for administrative databases, and perhaps for repeated measurement of behavior problems. The instrument may also prove useful for longitudinal assessments for people who are at risk for behavior problems, as it permits monitoring changes in the frequency or intensity of existing behavior problems, the emergence of new behaviors, and the remission of others.

3.1.3.2. Repetitive Behavior Scale-Revised (RBS-R)

The RBS-R is an empirically derived behavior-rating instrument that was designed for the assessment of abnormal, repetitive behaviors in persons with a variety of conditions, including intellectual disabilities, psychiatric, neurological, and behavioral disorders (Bodfish et al., 1999; Bodfish et al., 2000). The scale was developed by compiling items from several existing behavior-rating scales that measured repetitive behaviors (Campbell, 1985; Maurice & Trudel, 1982; Gedye, 1992; Goodman, Price, & Rasmussen, 1989a, 1989b). The selected 43 items were assigned by clinical staff to one of six dimensions or subscales of repetitive behavior: (1) *Stereotyped behavior* (6 items), (2) *self-injurious behavior* (8 items), (3) *Compulsive behavior* (8 items), (4) *Ritualistic behavior* (6 items), (5) *Sameness behavior* (11 items), and (6) *Restricted behavior* (4 items). The first version of the instrument, the RSB, consisted only of the first three subscales (Bodfish et al., 1995) whereas the other three were later added. Items are evaluated on a four-point Likert scale (from 0 = behavior does not occur, to 3 = behavior occurs and is a severe problem). The scale has been used to measure repetitive behavior in people with intellectual disabilities and autism spectrum disorders.

Preliminary data reported by the authors (Bodfish et al., 1999) suggest good psychometric properties in general and for the self-injurious behavior subscale in particular. *Inter-rater agreement* of the severity scores was examined with a group of 114 adults with intellectual disabilities and/or autism. Overall inter-rater agreement for the overall RSB score was $r = .82$, and for the self-injurious behavior subscale $r = .93$ (Bodfish et al., 1999). *Test–retest* reliability in a sample of 30 adults with intellectual disabilities was $r = .71$ for the RSB overall score, and .69 for the self-injurious behavior subscale (Bodfish et al., 1999). Internal consistency and interrater reliability data were found to be good Lam (2005).

Diagnostic precision was estimated by comparing the RSB self-injurious behavior outcome with the target behaviors identified by clinicians. This was based on a sample of 210 adults with severe/profound intellectual disabilities. Diagnostic precision was found to be high, with only 1.9% false-positive rate of self-injurious behavior cases identified by the RSB as compared to the clinicians (i.e., proportion of cases identified by the RSB but not the clinicians) (Bodfish et al., 1999).

Bodfish et al. (1999) examined the extent to which the RSB subscales concurred with structured direct observations of behavior in samples of adults with severe/profound intellectual disabilities and repetitive behaviors. The resulting percent agreement for self-injurious behavior was 90.2% ($n = 41$). As mentioned earlier, Bodfish et al. (1999) established *criterion-oriented validity* by correlating the RBS and BPI-01 self-injurious behavior subscales in adults with intellectual disabilities ($r = .77$).

With an independent sample of participants, Lam (2005) conducted a survey with RBS-R involving 320 care providers recruited through an autism society. Factor analyses produced a clinically meaningful and statistically sound five-factor solution, one factor fewer than proposed in the original version (Bodfish et al., 1999). These factors were labeled "Ritualistic/Sameness Behavior," "Stereotypic Behavior," "Self-Injurious Behavior," "Compulsive Behavior," and "Restricted Interests."

3.1.3.3. Self-Injurious Behavior Questionnaire (SIB-Q)

Gualtieri and Schroeder (1989) developed a 25-item rating instrument with a five-point severity-rating scale (ranging from 0 = not a problem, to 4 = severe problem) intended for clinical research to evaluate the effect of psychotropic medication on problem behaviors. The items were grouped a priori into four areas. The first 5 items refer to a generic self-injurious behavior category (self-injurious behavior severity, self-injurious behavior frequency, whether restraints were used, whether self-inflicted bruises were present, whether wounds, or tissue damage was present). Items 6–14 assess common antisocial behavior problems (physical aggressive behavior, difficulty sleeping, stereotyped behavior, yelling, screaming, destruction, eating problems (pica), tantrums, peculiar behavior). Items 15 through 18 are concerned with attention and conduct problems. Finally, items 19 through 25 address emotional and mood problems. Schroeder, Rojahn, and Reese (1997) conducted an SIB-Q reliability study for self-injurious behavior and antisocial behavior problems and reported Pearson r inter-rater of .63 and .57, test–retest, .78 and .58, and internal consistency Cronbach, α .94 and .71, respectively. No information is available on the validity of the SIB-Q to date (e.g., factor structure, concurrent).

3.1.4. Psychopathology Assessment Instruments

Several broad-spectrum psychopathology instruments have been developed for individuals with intellectual disabilities. Given that self-injurious behavior and aggressive behavior comprise only a small portion of behavioral manifestations of psychopathology, such instruments contain only small number of items. By implication that means low reliability. Therefore, while broad-spectrum instruments may not be the instruments of choice for fine-grained analyses of specific types of behavior problems, select items may be used to screen for the occurrence of self-injurious behavior. The instruments will be introduced in alphabetical order. We will concentrate in our discussion primarily on aspects relevant to the assessment of self-injurious behavior. For a more comprehensive and discussion of rating scales see Lecavalier and Aman (2004).

3.1.4.1. Aberrant Behavior Checklist (ABC)

The ABC is one of the most widely used and psychometrically sound assessment instruments in research and clinical practice in developmental disabilities. It is an informant-oriented problem behavior-rating scale that was empirically derived by factor analysis based on a large sample in New Zealand (Aman, Singh, Stewart, & Field,

1985a). It consists of 58 items, each scored on a four-point scale (0 = not a problem, through 3 = problem is severe in degree). The items are divided into five subscales: (1) *Irritability, Agitation, Crying*, (2) *Lethargy, Social Withdrawal*, (3) *Stereotypic Behavior*, (4) *Hyperactivity, Non-Compliance*, and (5) *Inappropriate Speech*. Norms are available for adults and for children and adolescents (Aman & Singh, 1994; Aman et al., 1985a; Brown et al., 2002; Marshburn & Aman, 1992). Three nonspecific self-injurious behaviors are part of the *Irritability, Agitation, and Crying* subscale.

The factor structure of the ABC has been found to be stable across the age span (Brown, Aman, & Havercamp, 2002; Marshburn & Aman, 1992; Rojahn & Helsel, 1991) and a number of psychometric studies have confirmed that the *ABC* is a reliable and valid behavior-rating instrument (e.g., Aman, Singh, Stewart, & Field, 1985b; Aman, Singh, & Turbott, 1987; Bihm & Poindexter, 1991; Paclawskyj, Matson, Bamburg, & Baglio, 1997; see Aman, 2002 for summary). The ABC was primarily designed as an outcome measure for treatment evaluation (e.g., psychotropic medication, Aman, 1991), but has been more often employed as a general assessment tool. The ABC has also been found to be sensitive to pharmacological interventions and inter-individual comparisons (Aman, 2003).

3.1.4.2. Assessment of Dual Diagnosis (ADD)

The ADD (Matson, 1997) is a standardized psychopathology-screening tool for adults with mild and moderate intellectual disabilities, which is completed via interviews of direct-care staff by trained interviewers. Items are scored on a three-point Likert scale for the last month in terms of its frequency (0 = not at all, through 2 = more than 10 times), duration (0 = less than 1 month, through 2 = over 12 months), and severity (0 = no disruptions or damage, through 2 = caused property damage or injury). Seventy nine items fall into 13 subscales that were designed to reflect DSM-IV symptoms: (1) *Mania*, (2) *Depression*, (3) *Anxiety*, (4) *Post-Traumatic Stress Disorder*, (5) *Substance Abuse*, (6) *Somatoform Disorder*, (7) *Dementia*, (8) *Conduct Disorder*, (9) *Pervasive Developmental Disorder*, (10) *Schizophrenia*, (11) *Personality Disorders*, (12) *Eating Disorders*, and (13) *Sexual Disorders*. The only generic self-injurious behavior item is part of the Pervasive Developmental Disorder subscale.

Available data suggest that the ADD has good reliability. Matson and Bamburg (1998) examined the ratings obtained on a sample of 101 adults with intellectual disabilities. Internal consistency for the 13 subscales ranged from .77 to .95; interrater reliability for the 13 subscales, based on Spearman ranked correlations, ranged between .82 and 1.00, and test–retest reliability calculated with Pearson's product moment correlations for the 13 subscales after a two-week interval ranged from .82 to 1.00.

3.1.4.3. Developmental Behaviour Checklist (DBC)

The DBC is a standardized and normed assessment instrument that can be completed by non-professional informants to assess emotional and behavioral problems in children and adolescents with intellectual disabilities (Einfeld & Tonge, 1992, 2002). A parent and teacher version of the DBC is available. Raters use three-point scales that range from 0 (not true) to 2 (very true or often true). Ninety-six items (parent version) and ninety-three items (teacher version-three sleep disturbance items were removed from the teacher version) were assigned to one of five subscales: (1) *Disruptive/ Antisocial*, (2) *Self-Absorbed*, (3) *Communication Disturbance*, (4) *Anxiety*, and (5) *Social Relating*. Three self-injurious behavior items (bangs head, hits or bites self, scratches or picks skin) are imbedded in the disruptive/antisocial subscale. The DBC has excellent psychometric properties.

3.1.4.4. Diagnostic Assessment for the Severely Handicapped (DASH-II)

The DASH-II (Matson, 1995) is a multi-dimensional informant-based psychopathology-screening instrument for individuals with severe and profound intellectual disabilities. Like the ADD, the DASH-II was constructed to reflect major DSM categories that are assumed to be most relevant for this population. The DASH-II administered by interview. Forty-eight items are scored on three complementary three-point scales to capture the frequency (0 = not at all, 1 = 1 to 10 times, 2 = more than 10 times), the duration (0 = less than 1 month, 1 = 1 to 12 months, 2 = over 12 months), and the severity (0 = no disruption or damage, 1 = no injury or damage but interrupted others, 2 = property damage or injury). The DASH-II has 13 a priori subscales. Eight subscales represent major psychiatric conditions and five scales reflect behavior problems common for individuals with intellectual disabilities. The eight psychiatric condition subscales are (1) *Impulse Control*, (2) *Organic syndromes*, (3) *Anxiety*, (4) *Mood/ Depression*, (5) *Mania*, (6) *Pervasive Developmental Disorder/Autism*, (7) *Schizophrenia*, and (8) *Stereotypies/Tics*. In addition, the DASH-II has items for *Other Problem Behavior Noted*, including five self-injurious behavior items.

Factor analysis yielded six factors that were labeled emotional lability, aggressive Behavior/conduct disorder, language disorder/verbal aggressive behavior, social withdrawal/stereotyped behavior, eating disorder, and sleep disorder. Psychometric studies have produced adequate levels of test–retest, inter-rater reliability, and internal consistency (Matson, 1989; Matson et al., 1991; Sevin, Matson, Williams, & Kirkpatrick-Sanchez, 1995) and validity (e.g., Matson, 1989; Matson, Kiely, & Bamburg, 1997; Matson, Smiroldo, & Bamburg, 1998; Matson, Smiroldo, Hamilton, & Baglio, 1997; Matson, Smiroldo, & Hastings, 1998).

3.1.4.5. Nisonger Child Behavior-Rating Form (N-CBRF)

The Nisonger CBRF is another third-party rating scale for children and adolescents (Aman, Tassé, Rojahn, & Hammer, 1996; Tassé, Aman, Hammer, & Rojahn, 1996). The scale was adapted form of the Child Behavior-Rating Form (Edelbrock, 1985) by altering the instructions and adding new behavior problem items. The Nisonger CBRF has a teacher and a parent version with identical items. Both consist of a Social Competence and a Problem Behaviors section. The Social Competence section contains 10 items describing general adaptive/prosocial behaviors such as "Shared with or helped others" which are rated on a four-point Likert scale ranging from 0 (= not true) to 3 (= completely or always true). Factor analysis produced two subscales, which were labeled as Compliant/Calm and Adaptive Social. The 66-item Problem

Behaviors section contains 66 items that are rated on a four-point Likert scale reflecting a combination of rate and severity of the behavior. It ranges from 0 (= did not occur or was not a problem) to 3 (= occurred a lot or was a severe problem). Items are assigned to six subscales, (1) *Conduct Problem*, (2) *Insecure/Anxious*, (3) *Hyperactive*, (4) *Self-Injurious Behavior/Stereotypic*, (5) *Self-Isolated/Ritualistic*, and (6) *Overly Sensitive*. The N-CBRF contains six specific self-injurious behavior items that are part of the self-injurious behavior/stereotypic subscale (e.g., "Hits, slaps own head, neck, hand, or other body parts," "Harms self by scratching skin or pulling hair," "Gouges self, puts things in ears, nose, etc., or eats inedible things," "Repeatedly bites self hard enough to leave tooth marks or break skin").

The N-CBRF was found to be psychometrically sound with regard to factor structure (Lecavalier, Aman, Hammer, Stoica, & Mathews, 2004), test–retest reliability (Girouard, Morin, & Tassé, 1998), and interrater reliability and useful in assessing emotional and behavioral problems in children and adolescents with intellectual disabilities (Tassé & Lecavalier, 2000). It has also been shown to be sensitive to the effects of psychotropic medication in children with autism and in low-functioning children with comorbid conduct disorder (Aman, De Smedt, Derivan, Lyons, & Findling, 2002; Cohen, 2003; Snyder et al., 2002). The N-CBRF has age- and gender-based norms on a restricted sample of 369 children and adolescents between the ages of 3 and 16 years (Tassé et al., 1996).

3.1.4.6. PDD Behavior Inventory (PDDBI)

The PDDBI is an informant-based rating scale designed to assess children with a Pervasive Developmental Disorder (Cohen, 2003; Cohen, Schmidt-Lackner, Romanczyk, & Sudhalter, 2003). It has both a teacher and parent form. The parent form consists of a priori defined subscales, 10 for the parent form and eight for the teacher form. Both versions assess behavior along a maladaptive–adaptive continuum focusing on specific behaviors commonly associated with PDD. The maladaptive behavior subscales consist of (1) *Sensory/Perceptual Approach Behaviors*, (2) *Specific Fears*, (3) *Arousal Problems*, (4) *Aggressiveness/Behavior Problems* (assesses both self- and other-directed aggressive behavior), (5) *Social Pragmatic Problems*, and (6) *Semantic Pragmatic Problems*. The criterion-related validity of each subscale and the construct validity of the PDDBI have been demonstrated through regression and factor analytic techniques. It is important to note that the PDDBI is intended for use solely with persons with autism spectrum disorders, and was not designed for persons with a different diagnosis (e.g., intellectual disabilities).

3.1.4.7. Reiss Screen for Maladaptive Behavior (RSMB)

The RSMB is another screening instrument to facilitate the identification of concurrent psychopathology in adults with intellectual disabilities (Reiss, 1988). Thirty-eight items are scored on a three-point scale (0 = no problem, 1 = problem, 2 = major problem) that were assigned to eight subscales: (1) *Aggressive Behavior*, (2) *Autism*, (3) *Psychosis*, (4) *Paranoia*, (5) *Depression – behavioral signs*, (6) *Depression – physical signs*, (7) *Dependent Personality Disorder*, and (8) *Avoidant Personality Disorder*. The

RSMB contains only one self-injurious behavior item, namely "self-injurious behavior," which is further defined in the RSMB as "Repeatedly injures body on purpose. Examples: bites arm, hits self repeatedly, repeated hand-banging."

The RSMB may be a useful screening tool for aggressive behavior, however, it is probably not particularly useful for the assessment of self-injurious behavior.

3.1.5. Standardized Adaptive Behavior Scales

Standardized adaptive behavior scales play an important role in the diagnosis of intellectual disability and they can assist in establishing training goals and procedures for specific adaptive behaviors and in setting rehabilitation objectives. Most adaptive behavior scales also contain sections on maladaptive behavior, which typically include self-injurious behavior and aggressive behavior. The following discussion will introduce the instruments in alphabetical order.

3.1.5.1. AAMR Adaptive Behavior Scales

The *AAMR Adaptive Behavior Scales Second Edition, School* (ABS-S:2; Lambert, Nihira, & Leland, 1993) assesses personal independence and social skills in adults. It also includes maladaptive behavior domains, including a *Self Abusive Behavior* and a *Disturbing Interpersonal Behavior* domain. Measures of internal consistency and validity were high (exceeding .80). The *Adaptive Behavior Scales – Residential and Community* (ABS-RC:2; Nihira, Leland, & Lambert, 1993) was standardized for older individuals and psychometric properties that are comparable to the ABS-S:2.

3.1.5.2. Scales of Independent Behavior – Revised (SIB-R)

The SIB-R was developed for children and adults with developmental disabilities and other populations with needs for special assistance (Bruininks, Woodcock, Weatherman, & Hill, 1996) and was designed to determine the type and amount of special supports that people with disabilities may need. Norms were established on a sample of 2,182 individuals in 15 U.S. states, with ages ranging from 3 months to over 80 years. It contains four clusters of independence behavior (i.e., motor skills, social interaction and communication skills, personal living skills, and community living skills) and three clusters of problem behaviors (i.e., internalized, externalized, and asocial). The SIB-R can be administered either as a questionnaire or as a structured interview.

Only one self-injurious behavior item is included: "Hurtful to self." The item is further defined in more detail: "Does (name) injure his/her own body – for example by hitting self, banging head, scratching, cutting or puncturing, biting, rubbing skin, pulling out hair, picking on skin, biting nails, or pinching self?" If the answer is affirmative, the informant is then asked to rate the frequency (1 = less than once a month to 5 = one or more times an hour) and severity (0 = not serious, not a problem to 4 = extremely serious, a critical problem) of the self-injurious behavior.

3.1.5.3. Vineland Adaptive Behavior Scales, 2nd Edition

The Vineland Adaptive Behavior Scales, 2nd edition (VABS) is a measure of personal and social skills designed for a broad range of individuals, including individuals with intellectual disabilities, autism spectrum disorders, attention deficit/hyperactivity disorder, post-traumatic brain injury, hearing impairment, and dementia/Alzheimer's disease (Sparrow, Cicchetti, & Balla, 2005a, 2005b). It is the new edition of one of the most popular standardized assessment instruments for adaptive and maladaptive behavior. The VABS has four different forms, the *Survey Interview Form*, the *Parent/Caregiver-Rating Form*, the *Expanded Interview Form*, and the *Teacher-Rating Form*. The first three forms are normed from birth through 90 years of age and include an optional maladaptive behavior section. Maladaptive behaviors are rated on a three-point frequency scale (0 = never; 1 = sometimes; 2 = often) and a two-point severity scale (S = severe; M = moderate). They consist of 10 internalizing behaviors, 10 externalizing behaviors, 15 "other" behavior problems, and 14 "critical" items. One of the "critical items" addresses self-injurious behavior ("Displays behaviors that cause injury to self, for example bangs head, hits or bites self, tears skin, etc."). Whether the Vineland-II or any of the other scales with only one self-injurious behavior item are reliable screening tools for self-injurious behavior is unknown, because to our knowledge no sensitivity and specificity data are available for this specific purpose.

3.2. Functional Assessment and Analysis

Functional assessment and analysis are methods to identify factors that maintain a targeted behavior and to develop hypotheses regarding how those factors interplay with the behavior. Once such a hypothesis is established rational interventions can be designed that change, rearrange, or otherwise alter the relevant contingencies, thereby changing the behavior. The term functional assessment typically refers to information that has been gathered by direct and indirect assessment procedures such as naturalistic observations and rating scales. Functional analysis, on the other hand refers to the gathering of information that is based on the systematic manipulation of contingencies.

3.2.1. Organizing Functional Assessments or Analyses

A thorough functional analysis or assessment of self-injurious behavior considers motivating operations (MO) that evoke or inhibit the behavior and increase or decrease potency of the reinforcers maintaining the behavior, discriminative stimuli that occasion or inhibit the behavior, and the reinforcers that maintain the behavior. Beyond this, a wide range of other, systemic variables often need to be considered. Many of these systemic variables, of course, themselves can function as motivating operations. Three general methods of organizing functional assessment or functional analysis have been described as follows.

3.2.1.1. Behavioral Diagnostics

Bailey and Pyles (1989) developed a set of interview questions to consider at the outset of the assessment, encompassing a variety of important issues, such as the situations in which self-injurious behaviors occurs and those in which it does not occur, cyclical, chronic, acute, and iatrogenic physiological motivating operations; evocative social stimuli; maintaining social variables; and social and physiological effects produced by the behavior. Pyles et al. (1997) incorporated these questions into their comprehensive, cross-disciplinary assessment system also known as *behavioral diagnostics*, which requires transdisciplinary collaboration between behavioral and medical professionals on various aspects of the assessment. Behavioral diagnostic assessments involve a number of decision points. At the first point, psychiatric diagnoses are evaluated for those taking psychotropic medication, inaccurate diagnoses revised, direct observation data collection is begun on signs, symptoms, and behavioral equivalents, and medication efficacy is evaluated based on those data. Medications, dosages, or dosing schedules may be changed, or additional medical consultation sought. Should this medical evaluation and intervention guided by behavioral data produce improvement, medical intervention and behavioral data evaluation would continue. Should sufficiently efficacious improvement not be demonstrated, however, psychiatric or medical treatment is altered, or functional analysis or assessment requested. Those not taking psychotropic medication would enter at this point, with functional analysis or assessment being the first step. Functional analysis or assessment outcomes would result in the development and implementation of treatment procedures, either in concert with or independent of, medical or psychiatric intervention. Behavioral treatment efficacy, like that of the psychiatric or medical interventions, is assessed with direct observation data, and efficacious demonstrations result in maintaining the current treatment course, while demonstrations of inefficacy would result in altered behavioral treatment, or medical or psychiatric re-evaluation, or both. Data-based decision making in determining, evaluating, and altering the behavioral, psychiatric, and medical assessment and treatment is a defining feature of behavioral diagnostics. Evaluation and treatment are arranged in a cybernetic manner, such that evaluative information at every decision point provides feedback for determining the next step in assessment and treatment.

3.2.1.2. Three-Step Hierarchical Approach

O'Neill et al. (1997) developed a linear, three-step organizational structure for functional assessment or analysis. First, those who are familiar with the person who exhibits self-injurious behavior are interviewed about antecedents and consequences of the self-injurious behavior and about systemic variables such as the family, other caregivers, the school or vocational setting, medical information, etc. Second, this information then guides the development of systematic assessment strategies such as direct observation and measurement. Third, when the systematic data confirm the interview information hypotheses are developed about the functional contingencies, and treatment is derived to evaluate those hypotheses. Alternatively, should direct observation data conflict with informants' reports, or when direct observations confirm some or all of informants' reports, subsequent experimental analysis may be conducted prior to developing and implementing treatment.

3.2.1.3. Four-Step Hierarchical Approach

Carr et al. (2003) describe a four-step system that begins interviews of persons who have direct knowledge of and experience with the person who exhibits self-injurious behavior. Next, behavioral and medical records are reviewed to further guide hypothesis development. Information gathered in these first two steps then informs direct observation data collection, the third step. Finally, hypothesized contingencies are empirically assessed through systematic manipulation using an experimental functional analysis. Functional analysis determines the subsequent course of treatment.

3.2.2. Functional Analysis

Analogue functional analysis involves arranging and systematically varying antecedent and consequent conditions while measuring effects on the behavior of interest, to empirically identify contingencies maintaining that behavior. Although functional analyses had been conducted for other behaviors and their descriptions published in the behavior analytic literature prior to 1982, Iwata et al. (1982/1994) published the first demonstration of pre-treatment identification of maintaining contingencies for self-injurious behavior. In this study, nine children who exhibited various severe self-injurious topographies were exposed to four different experimental conditions, twice daily. These conditions varied antecedents (e.g., environment enriched with leisure materials versus devoid of leisure materials; regularly introduced task demands versus no or minimal task demands, presence or absence of an adult) and consequence conditions (e.g., no social interaction, non-contingent social interaction, or social interaction contingent on self-injurious behavior). More specifically, conditions were described as follows.

3.2.2.1. Social Positive Reinforcement Condition

This condition was designed to test the hypothesis that self-injurious behavior was maintained by socially mediated positive reinforcement in the form of contingent social and physical attention. The session began with the experimenter and leisure materials in the room together with the client. The experimenter instructed the client to play with the leisure materials, and then appeared to read a magazine. For the remainder of the session social attention by the experimenter was limited to expressing verbal disapproval (i.e., "don't do that") and to touching the child's hand or shoulder contingent on self-injurious behavior.

3.2.2.2. Socially Mediated Negative Reinforcement Condition

This condition was designed to test the hypothesis that negative reinforcement by demand termination maintained the client's self-injurious behavior. The sessions began with experimenter and client sitting at a table with task materials. The experimenter gave task-relevant instructions, and provided three-step guidance to ensure compliance. Following instructions by the client with or without prompting was followed by praise. Self-injurious behavior produced a 30-second interval during which no instructions were given (and during which the experimenter was turned away from the child), including a 30-second change over delay to prevent adventitious reinforcement of self-injurious behavior by praise.

3.2.2.3. Automatic Reinforcement Condition
This condition assessed whether self-injurious behavior was maintained by automatic, internal reinforcement. During these sessions, only the client was in the assessment room, without leisure materials. No antecedent or consequent social interaction was provided.

3.2.2.4. Control Condition
This condition was designed to control for presence of the experimenter, the availability of potentially stimulating materials, absence of demands, and delivery of social interaction. It was a control condition against which the data from other conditions could be compared. In this condition, also called *unstructured play sessions* the experimenter and the client were in the room together with leisure items. No instructions were given. A 30-second differential reinforcement schedule (DRO) was in effect, where the experimenter delivered praise and brief physical contact following every 30 seconds during which self-injurious behavior did not occur. No programmed consequences followed self-injurious behavior.

These conditions were repeated several times and alternated in a multi-element design, permitting rapid comparison of performances under the variety of contingencies, while simultaneously controlling for maturation and multiple treatment interference effects. Iwata et al. found maintenance by social negative reinforcement for two participants, positive social reinforcement for one, non-socially mediated (automatic) reinforcement for four, and undifferentiated performances for the remaining two participants.

Twelve years after the introduction of the original format of the experimental analysis Iwata et al. (1994) reported a retrospective review of 152 functional analyses conducted across an 11-year period. These involved the Attention, Demand, Alone, and Play conditions as labeled by Iwata et al. (1982/1994). In addition conditions that assessed social positive reinforcement that produced access to edibles (Social – Food) or leisure materials (Social – Materials) were added. Furthermore, conditions that assessed the role of negative reinforcement that terminated non-demand social interaction (Social Negative – Social Interaction) or medical examination (Social Negative – Medical) had been designed. Using his functional analysis methodology Iwata et al. (1994) found that self-injurious behavior was maintained by the following contingencies:

o Social positive reinforcement – 26.3%
  • attention – 23%
  • socially mediated access to materials – 2.0%
  • access to food – 1.3%

o Socially mediated negative reinforcement – 38.0%
  • demand termination – 35.4%
  • terminating social interactions – 1.3%
  • physical exam termination – 0.7%
  • ambient noise termination – 0.7%
o Automatic or sensory reinforcement – 25.7%
  • sensory positive reinforcement – 19.7%
  • sensory negative reinforcement – 1.3%
  • undifferentiated, high rate responding – 4.6%
o Multiple maintaining contingencies – 5.3%
  • attention and demand termination – 2.7%
  • attention and sensory positive reinforcement – 1.3%
  • demand termination and automatic positive reinforcement – 1.3%

Each person subsequently received function-relevant treatment, and the authors report 84.2% treatment effectiveness when antecedent interventions were used, 86.8% effectiveness when extinction was used, 82.5% effectiveness for differential reinforcement, and 88.2% for punishment. Only 12.3% of successful interventions involved punishment, whereas 87.7% did not.

3.2.2.5. Procedural Considerations with Functional Analyses

In planning a functional analysis several issues need to be considered. These include particular experimental design used to conduct the analysis, session duration, inter-session interval duration and activities, potential enhancements to discrimination between conditions, particular type and number of session conditions conducted, and others. These are described more fully below.

3.2.2.5.1. Experimental Design

Functional analyses can incorporate a variety of single-subject experimental designs, depending on specific circumstances in which the analysis is to be conducted. Multi-element designs are reported most often (Hanley et al., 2003), with pair-wise comparisons (Iwata et al., 1994) and withdrawal designs (Healey et al., 2001; Moore et al., 2004; Moore et al., 2002; Richman & Hagopian, 1999; Van Camp et al., 2000) often conducted following a multi-element design analysis to examine effects of varying parameters of identified maintaining variables on self-injurious behavior.

In a *pair-wise comparison design*, one test condition is alternated with the control (leisure or play) condition until stable responding is attained in each, and then a second test condition is introduced and the first retired. This procedure is described by Iwata et al. (1994), who presented illustrative data depicting attention and play conditions varying in the first phase, followed by demand and play in the second, and alone and play in the third. Play (control) data paths displayed near-zero rates of self-injurious behavior, and demand and alone data paths displayed low rates, while attention the attention data path was clearly elevated relative to the others.

In the *multi-element design*, test and control conditions are often randomly ordered without replacement to minimize multiple treatment interference effects. Alternatively, some order conditions in a fixed cycle to maximize prior conditions' establishing operation effects on subsequent conditions' responding (Iwata et al., 1994). For example, an alone condition may be conducted first, followed by a contingent attention condition, such that the attention deprivation in the alone condition could enhance acquisition of responding under control of the latter condition's contingencies.

Studies using *multi-element designs* have reported between one (Shore et al., 1997; Smith & Churchill, 2002) and eight (Iwata et al., 1994; Kahng & Iwata, 1999) functional analysis sessions conducted per day. Many studies, however, do not report number of sessions per day (see, for example, Borrero & Vollmer, 2002; Carr, Yarbrough, & Langdon, 1997). Whether number of sessions conducted in a single day influences functional analysis outcome has not been examined in the literature. Further, many studies report conducting functional analysis sessions on varying numbers of days per week (Kurtz et al., 2003; Lerman, Kelley, Vorndran, Kuhn, & LaRue, 2002, for example) or a constant number of days per week (Zarcone et al., 1993). To date, however, no study has examined whether frequency of session days per week, constant versus variable number of session days per week, or consecutive versus nonconsecutive session days influence response patterns.

3.2.2.5.2. Session Duration

Reported session durations have been 5 minutes (Harding, Wacker, Berg, Barretto, & Ringdahl, 2005; Kurtz et al., 2003; Northup, Kodak, Grow, Lee, & Coyne, 2004), 9 minutes (Healey, Ahearn, Graff, & Libby, 2001), 10 minutes (see, for example, Bergen, Holborn, & Scott-Huyghebaert, 2002 or Borrero & Vollmer, 2002; Borrero, Vollmer, Wright, Lerman, & Kelley, 2002), 15 minutes (see, for example, Carr, Yarbrough, & Langdon, 1997 or Cowdery, Iwata, & Pace, 1990), 20 minutes (Fisher, DeLeon, Rodrigues-Carter, & Keeney, 2004), or 30 minutes (Borrero et al., 2002). Some studies do not report session durations (Smith, Iwata, Goh, & Shore, 1995, Study 1). Ten-minute durations are reported most often (Hanley et al., 2003). Wallace and Iwata (1999) found that 5-, 10-, and 15-minute sessions produced essentially similar results, strongly suggesting that briefer sessions can enhance economy while preserving utility of analyses conducted with longer sessions. However, briefer sessions may preclude development of within-session response patterns that could differ from those seen in across-session comparisons. Further, shorter session durations may hamper acquisition of responding under control of condition contingencies (Kahng & Iwata, 1999).

3.2.2.5.3. Intersession Intervals

Intersession interval durations have been identified as approximately 5 minutes (Bergen et al., 2002), or 10–15 minutes (Zarcone et al., 1994; Zarcone, Iwata, Hughes, & Vollmer, 1993), but most often are not described. Since briefer intersession intervals increase probability of multiple treatment interference effects in multi-element designs (McGonigle, Rojahn, Dixon, & Strain, 1987), inconclusive analyses could potentially be clarified by continuing the analysis while lengthening the intersession interval. Alternatively, some functional analysis outcomes could potentially be artifacts of this type of confound. Continuing the analysis while altering intersession interval duration could rule out this confound, should overall data patterns remain unchanged.

Possible effects of intersession interval activities have not been well researched. Iwata et al. (1982/1994, p. 201) report only "within each series of conditions, experimenters were changed between sessions, and subjects were briefly removed from the room." Most studies do not comment on identified social conditions prior to functional analysis sessions as motivating operations producing idiosyncratic responding during sessions. Others have incorporated between session or pre-session motivating operation manipulations to enhance value of particular reinforcers during functional analysis conditions (Fisher et al., 2004; Kurtz et al., 2003). So, while some researchers explicitly describe conditions during some intersession intervals that are arranged to enhance session condition effects, most often intersession interval conditions are not described. Whether those conditions are held constant or permitted to vary, are explicitly programmed or happen haphazardly, and are of equal or unequal duration has generally not been described, and potential effects on functional analysis outcomes not examined.

3.2.2.5.4. Addition of Discriminative Stimuli

Various studies have incorporated procedures to enhance acquisition of responding under changing session conditions. McGonigle et al. (1987) paired different auditory (e.g., a low-tone buzzer or classical music) or tactile (e.g., a hand-held vibrator or a hand-held flashlight) stimuli with different conditions. Connors et al. (2000), Roscoe et al. (1998), Wordsell, Iwata, Hanley, Thompson, and Kahng (2000) conducted each type of functional analysis condition in its own room, with décor differing from room to room and condition to condition, and with a different experimenter assigned to each condition. Conversely, Iwata et al. (1982/1994) rotated therapists to prevent development of therapist-specific condition effects. The extent to which associating various extra-experimental stimuli with functional analysis conditions affects functional analysis outcome (other than by enhancing the rapidity with which condition-relevant responding is acquired under each condition) has not been adequately examined.

3.2.2.5.5. Required Time

Total time needed for an experimental analysis depends on the rate at which differential responding is attained under differing conditions, and cannot be determined prior to the analysis. Iwata et al. (1982/1994) reported number of days to complete a functional analysis averaged 8 (range = 4–11 days), and mean number of 15-minute sessions was 30 (range = 24–53 sessions), with mean in-session time being 7.5 hours (range = 6.0–13.25 hours). In an examination of 152 functional analyses, Iwata et al. (1994) reported number of sessions ranged from 8 to 66, and in-session time ranged from 2 to 16.5 hours. Certainly, session and intersession interval lengths, the number of sessions conducted per day, and the number of days per week during which sessions are conducted, could influence the total time needed to conduct a functional analysis.

3.2.2.5.6. Full versus Brief Functional Analyses

Full functional analyses are those with at least 3 sessions for each condition. Should differentiated data paths be obtained with only 3 sessions per condition, and with 5 conditions, then only 15 sessions would be needed for a full analysis. Northup et al.

(1991) described a brief functional analysis procedure, which could potentially max-imize economy while having the utility of a full analysis. In their procedure, 1 session of each of 2, 3, or 4 conditions (e.g., alone, escape, tangible, and attention) was conducted in a multi-element design. Sessions were 5 minutes long, and intersession intervals were 1–2 minutes. Each person exhibited different response rates under each condition, and condition contingencies producing highest response rates were said to reflect maintaining contingencies. Subsequent contingency reversals and brief-analysis derived treatment produced reductions in problem behaviors for all three participants (Northup et al., 1991).

Brief analyses sometimes do not produce differential response rates across condi-tions. For example, Vollmer, Marcus, Ringdahl, and Roane (1995b) report conducting brief analyses with 15 participants, but obtaining differentiated results for only 3. When this is the case, procedures to enhance discrimination between conditions (Connors et al., 2000; Roscoe et al., 1998; Wordsell et al., 2000) or subsequent full analyses could potentially produce differentiated results and identification of main-taining contingencies. Vollmer et al. (1995a, 1995b) conducted additional sessions in the play/leisure condition, and found high rate responding for 5 of the remaining 12 participants, suggesting automatic reinforcement in those cases. The remaining 7 par-ticipants were exposed to each condition in a withdrawal design, and differential re-sponding across conditions was found for 5. Only two functional analyses remained undifferentiated. Vollmer et al. (1995a, 1995b) report that total in-session time to complete brief analyses and brief analyses plus additional procedures ranged from 80 to 960 minutes.

Brief analyses may be more likely than full analyses to return false-positive results (Kahng & Iwata, 1999). To rule out false-positive findings, these authors recommend plotting end of session, rather than full session, data. Full session data may aggregate end of session response rates under condition contingency control with early in-session response rates, which may reflect a changeover from the prior session's (or intersession interval's) contingencies. Given this, Kahng and Iwata recommend longer rather than shorter (e.g., 15 rather than 5 minute) session durations in brief analyses.

3.2.2.5.7. *Type of Conditions*
Many published functional analyses have included attention, tangible, demand, alone, and play/leisure conditions. These conditions assess maintenance by various types of positive, negative, or automatic reinforcement contingencies, as well as motivating operation effects such as attention or tangible satiation or deprivation, should pre-session or intersession interval procedures arrange for the requisite motivating oper-ations. Other studies have assessed effects of person-specific variables, such as response to medication (Crosland et al., 2003; Mace, Blum, Sierp, Delaney, & Mauk, 2001), menses (Carr et al., 2003), otitis (O'Reilly, 1997), varying levels of sleep deprivation in people with sleep disturbances (O'Reilly & Lancioni, 2000), and having been in respite care versus having been at home (O'Reilly, 1996). In these instances, researchers maintained standard functional analysis procedures as extra-session establishing op-eration conditions changed, and were able to discern differential responding in some

functional analysis conditions when establishing operation conditions were and were not in effect.

Functional analyses need not include all standard test conditions. For example, English and Anderson (2004) determined through pre-analysis interview and scatterplot that only demand, tangible, and play conditions would likely be necessary. Functional analyses with only these conditions returned differentiated results for two children. Other person-specific conditions have been developed and conducted based on pre-functional analysis interview, observation, or other information gathering. When pre-functional analysis information suggested ambient noise functioned to evoke self-injurious behavior, McCord, Thompson, and Iwata (2001) compared a test condition characterized by contingent ambient noise termination with play and no interaction conditions (in which the noise was not present), and found that the self-injurious behavior functioned to escape ambient noise. Post-analysis information gathering can also lead to selecting or developing condition procedures when functional analyses have produced undifferentiated results. Given this situation, Harding et al. (2005) varied location (e.g., on floor or on sofa) and particular stimulus available (e.g., presence or absence) in additional play condition sessions, and found self-injurious behavior functioned to *mand* change in location, change in available stimuli, or both. Similarly, following undifferentiated standard functional analyses, and after consulting descriptive data, Fisher, Adelinis, Thompson, Wordsell, and Zarcone (1998a) examined rates of self-injurious behavior when participants were asked to stop or to begin engaging in an activity (termed "don't" and "do" instruction conditions, respectively), and found differential responding as a function of type of instruction given.

3.2.2.5.8. Safety Precautions and Caveats

Given that conducting a functional analysis requires that the self-injurious behavior be permitted to occur, a number of steps are often taken to ensure safety of the person and the therapists conducting the procedures. When the self-injurious behavior is sufficiently severe that conducting the functional analysis would pose greater risk than the person experiences in typical life events, medical personnel have been on hand to ensure the person's well-being, and therapists and medical personnel have developed termination criteria with which the overseeing medical personnel can terminate a session should serious injury occur or appear likely to occur (Iwata et al., 1982/1994). When the person wears protective equipment (i.e., helmets, arm splints, padding, etc.) to prevent injury due to self-injurious behavior, some investigators have conducted the analyses with the equipment in place and also with it removed. They have found different response patterns associated with presence or absence of the equipment (Le & Smith, 2002; Moore et al., 2004). In contrast, O'Reilly, Murray, Lancioni, Sigafoos, and Lacey (2003) report a functional analysis conducted for a 27-year old gentleman whose self-injurious behavior when not wearing his helmet and arm splints was sufficiently severe and high rate to preclude functional analysis without some or all of the protective equipment. Instead, they conducted the functional analysis while the client wore his protective equipment, and found the self-injurious behavior to be maintained by automatic positive reinforcement, thereby permitting its reduction when the client's splints were briefly removed at regular intervals per regulatory requirement by providing matched, non-contingent stimulation.

Many functional analyses have been conducted in specially designed and padded rooms to ensure the person's safety. Iwata et al. (1982/1994) provides a thorough description of such a room. Some have raised the possibility that functional analyses conducted in one setting may have poor setting generality; that is, were a functional analysis to be conducted in one setting, and then replicated in another, different results would be obtained (Anderson, Freeman, & Scotti, 1999). Indeed, one may consider pairing the room in which a particular functional analysis condition is conducted with various discriminative stimuli (e.g., room color, therapist conducting that type of session) for the sole purpose of establishing discriminative stimulus control of that location (and the contingencies implemented therein) over the person's responding, to prevent spillover of the person's response pattern to other locations (and conditions). Without explicitly programming to limit setting generality, Conroy, Fox, Crain, Jenkins, and Belcher (1996) found differences in contingencies found to maintain the participants' behavior in the context of the functional analysis and in the participants' naturally occurring environments. Despite this finding, Anderson et al. (1999) and Harding et al. (2005) found similar outcomes for functional analyses conducted across settings.

Functional analysis condition procedures themselves may produce iatrogenic results, threatening external validity and setting generality. Shirley et al. (1999) found that the manner by which self-injurious behavior produced access to tangibles differed substantially from the manner in which the person gained access to tangibles in her home, thereby producing high rate responding in the tangible condition. These researchers concluded that this difference in contingencies from natural to functional analysis setting resulted in a false-positive result. Similarly, when McKerchar et al. (2001) found high rate, undifferentiated responding across conditions, they altered alone condition procedure to more closely simulate the boy's more frequently encountered conditions. Data paths differentiated only after they made this procedural change, suggesting initial procedures obscured maintaining variables.

Temporal generality, or the reproducibility of results when functional analyses are repeated, may be questioned. Anderson et al. (1999) repeated identical functional analysis procedures, and Northup et al. (1991) compared brief and full functional analyses. Both reported that functional analyses conducted with the same condition procedures can have good temporal generality. This seems to be mostly true for scenarios in which the methodology of the initial and the repeated functional analyses were more or less unchanged. Studies in which the initial and the repeated functional analyses featured different procedures for the experimental conditions (Richman & Hagopian, 1999) or studies where the initial and the repeated functional analyses were conducted by different implementers (e.g., substituting parents or other caregivers for the therapists; English & Anderson, 1999) showed less reproducibility. However, these latter findings provide less evidence that functional analysis lack of reproducibility, but they reflect the effects of changes in the methodology.

Features to enhance setting and temporal generality can be designed into functional analysis. The analysis can incorporate stimuli or tasks similar to those the person typically encounters, or may be conducted in the person's natural settings if not contraindicated for safety reasons and when the analysis itself would not be compromised (Anderson et al., 1999; Fisher et al., 1998a, 1998b; Harding et al., 2005; Iwata et al., 1982/1994; Iwata et al., 1994). Parents, teachers, or other caregivers can be trained to implement functional analysis procedures (English & Anderson, 2004). But even when functional analyses were conducted in atypical settings with standard procedures they have resulted in development and implementation of procedures that have reduced or eliminated self-injurious behavior and promoted more beneficial behaviors (Anderson et al., 1999; English & Anderson, 2004).

When people exhibiting self-injurious behavior display more than one problem topography, it is essential to conduct separate analyses for self-injurious behavior and for the other topographies. Derby et al. (1994) conducted a functional analysis first on all maladaptive topographies exhibited by two participants, and then on each of the topographies separately. They found that the functional relations maintaining the self-injurious behavior differed from those maintaining the other topographies, and that this difference only became apparent when topographies were analyzed separately.

Sometimes self-injurious behavior occurs as part of a predictable sequence of behaviors, in which one or more other topography is reliably preceding the self-injurious behavior. The preceding behaviors, then, are indirectly maintained by the reinforcer(s) for the terminal, self-injurious behavior. Several studies (Lalli et al., 1995; Smith & Churchill, 2002) demonstrated that preceding behaviors were maintained by contingencies maintaining self-injurious behavior that occurred later in a reliable response sequence. Subsequently treating the preceding behavior reduced self-injurious behavior in both studies.

Functional analysis is complicated when days or weeks pass between bouts of a behavior. Functional analysis sessions conducted during that time would likely produce low, undifferentiated response rates (O'Reilly, 1996; O'Reilly, 1997). Tarbox, Wallace, Tarbox, Landaburu, and Williams (2004) conducted sessions only following sporadic self-injurious behavior, in what they termed a low-rate functional analysis. Their low-rate functional analysis outcomes revealed clearly differentiated response patterns, when previously conducted standard functional analyses did not.

Zarcone et al. (2004) discussed the drawbacks of using functional analysis in medication studies. They are very expensive and time-consuming. For instance it is difficult holding potentially intervening variables such as school and home programs constant during the functional analysis period; analyzing functional analysis data with low-frequency behaviors is difficult; early in the functional analysis honeymoon effects can occur; habituation effects may occur in later stages. Conducting the functional analysis in the subject's natural environment helps, but does not completely offset these problems.

3.2.2.6. Functional Diagnostics

The primary purpose of functional analysis is to identify contingencies maintaining behaviors, so that those contingencies can be changed or rearranged to improve the behavior for which help was sought. A recent development in applied behavior analysis and in behavioral pharmacology, functional diagnostics involves conducting functional analyses the context of psychoactive drug trials, to examine effects on the behavior of alternating behavioral contingencies, medication administration, both, or neither. Schroeder et al. (1995) conducted an experimental functional analysis with a 34-year-old woman with cerebral palsy, spastic diplegia, and a history of chronic self-injurious behavior (head and face hitting, and pressing the head against hard edges) to explore the role of medication (clozapine) on self-injurious behavior rate as a function of four-conditions (alone, demand, positive attention, negative attention). This single-blind placebo-controlled study revealed differential responding across the four experimental conditions, dependent on medication status. For instance, high rate of self-injurious maintained by negative reinforcement decreased almost completely during phase of active medication. This was plausible evidence for the role of clozapine as an establishing operation for the woman's self-injurious behavior. A few years later, Mace et al. (2001) conducted functional analyses and contingency-based treatment trials with 15 participants, some of whom received haloperidol and some of whom did not. Function-relevant treatments reduced frequency of self-injurious behavior for 83% of participants, whereas haloperidol reduced self-injurious behavior for only 25%. Similarly, in a double blind, placebo-controlled study, Crosland et al. (2003) conducted standard functional analysis conditions, examining rate of aggressive behavior and self-injurious behavior across varying dosages of risperidone. They found differential responding in functional analysis conditions for self-injurious behavior and aggressive behavior in response to presence or absence of risperidone. Moreover, they state "it appeared that risperidone had a differential effect across behavioral function, and (for one person), across behavioral topography." Examining medication response during functional analysis permits evaluation and comparison of medication and contingency-based treatment effects, alone and in concert, across both behavioral function and behavioral topography.

3.2.2.7. Conclusions – Functional Analysis

Functional analyses can identify relations between various antecedent and consequence events and self-injurious behavior. Research in the last two decades showed that functional analysis procedures are becoming more and more sophisticated and that the methods allow us to make very subtle discriminations. To take just one example, Patel, Carr, Kim, Robles, and Eastridge (2000) were able to determine particular sensations maintaining automatically reinforced behavior and, thereby, were able to reduce self-injurious behavior through non-contingent matched stimulation.

However, as we have pointed out, there are numerous procedural, clinical, and ethical issues that need to be considered and addressed carefully before and while conducting a functional analysis. Foremost, perhaps, is that in order to conduct a functional analysis of self-injury, generally one must permit the self-injury to occur. It is acknowledged that the self-injury also typically occurs in the course of everyday life for the person who is the focus of assessment, and permitting occurrence of the behavior in the circumscribed confines of the functional analysis session, with participation of appropriate medical personnel when indicated, could potentially lead to ascertainment of information that lessens the risk the behavior poses to the participant. Any risk posed by self-injury during a functional analysis can be reduced with proper oversight and by involving medical personnel, as is appropriate. A second risk is the possibility that the self-injury may come under control of contingencies that previously did not control it, during the course of the analysis. Although potentially a rare phenomenon, Shirley et al. (1999) reported just that. Functional analyses must, therefore, be conducted by parties with sufficient training in single-subject experimental design and related research and treatment methodology to prevent methodological confounds and potential iatrogenic problems. Third, functional analyses are typically more expensive in terms of time, resources, and personnel than are functional assessments. While useful results have been reported in as little as two hours or less in brief analyses (Northup et al., 1991), full analyses can take weeks or more to complete (O'Reilly, 1996). Finally, although setting generality may be a concern, work by Ellingson, Miltenberger, and Long (1999), Hanley et al. (2003), and Harding et al. (2005) indicates that functional analyses can be carried out and their findings found beneficial, in settings other than carefully controlled clinics.

3.2.3. Functional Assessment

3.2.3.1. Rating Scales
Time to conduct a functional analysis, albeit necessary (but not always sufficient) is, nonetheless, time during which treatment is delayed. Some advocate using specially constructed checklists to develop hypotheses regarding contingencies maintaining self-injurious behavior, as an alternative to functional analyses. These indirect assessment methods involve asking a standard set of questions of informants who are well acquainted with a person who exhibits self-injurious behavior. They also require sufficient interviewing skill to rephrase or reframe a question, if necessary, while preserving integrity of the question and of the instrument. Five such instruments are discussed next.

3.2.3.1.1. Contingency Analysis Questionnaire (CAQ)
This instrument, sometimes also referred to the *Motivation Analysis Rating Scale* (MARS) by Wieseler, Hanson, Chamberlain, and Thompson (1985), is one of the earliest instruments of its kind. It consists of 6 items that are scored on a five-point frequency of occurrence scale (ranging from "never" to "almost always"). The items represent four behavioral functions, social and tangible positive reinforcement, social and situational escape, and self-stimulation (Table 3.1). No psychometric properties were reported in the original paper and not much was heard of the CAQ since its introduction into the literature. Therefore, it is difficult to determine its value as an assessment instrument. While the small number of items may be an attractive feature as far as convenience and feasibility is concerned, it is probably also its weakness, in terms of its reliability.

3.2.3.1.2. Motivation Assessment Scale (MAS)
The MAS by Durand and Crimmins (1988) was one of the first instruments published to consider behavior from a functional, rather than structural, point of view

Table 3.1: Subscales for behavioral functions and number of items per subscale in various functional assessment rating scales (numbers refer to number of items)

Subscales	CAQ	MAS	QABF	FACT	FAST
	Wieseler et al. (1985)	Durand and Crimmins (1988)	Matson et al. (1995)	Matson et al. (2003)	Iwata and DeLeon (1995)
Positive social	1	4	5	14	4
Positive tangible	1	4	5	14	
Positive internal	2	4	5	14	4
Negative social or situational	1	4	5	14	4
Negative internal	–	–	5	14	4
Total number of items	6	16	25	35[a]	16

[a] Each item is a comparative statement contrasting two functions and, therefore, contributes to one of the two subscales

(Aman, 1991). Rather than classifying self-injurious behavior on the basis of its topography, this instrument was developed to explore the controlling variables. The MAS consists of 16 items on which informants rate the frequency with which the targeted behavior occurs to produce automatic reinforcement (e.g., *Sensory* scale), negative reinforcement (e.g., *Escape* scale), social positive reinforcement by attention (e.g., *Attention* scale), and social positive reinforcement by gaining access to tangibles (e.g., *Tangible* scale). The MAS uses a seven-point Likert scale (from 0 = never to 6 = always). Time required to complete the MAS is minimal.

Several investigators have examined the psychometric properties of the MAS. Unfortunately, the outcome is not very encouraging. While one study reported good internal consistency (Newton, 1991), interrater agreement (Conroy, Fox, Bucklin, & Good, 1996; Thomson & Emerson, 1995; Newton, 1991; Zarcone, Rodgers, Iwata, Rourke, & Dorsey, 1991), intra-rater agreement (Barton-Arwood, Wehby, Gunter, & Lane, 2003; Conroy et al., 1996; Thomson & Emerson, 1995), test–retest reliability (Conroy et al., 1996; cf.; Durand & Crimmins, 1988), and construct validity (Duker & Sigafoos, 1998) have been found to be poor. Behavioral frequency appears to influence the scale reliability with high-frequency behaviors generally producing greater reliability than low-frequency behaviors (Kearney, 1994).

3.2.3.1.3. Questions About Behavioral Function (QABF)
The QABF (Vollmer & Matson, 1995) is a 25-item questionnaire on which informants rate frequency with which self-injurious behavior occurs on a four-point Likert-type scale (e.g., zero indicating "never," one "rarely," two "some," and three "often"). The scale, which is still in a development stage, consists of five subscales, (1) social positive reinforcement via attention (e.g., *Attention* scale), (2) negative social reinforcement (e.g., *Escape* scale), (3) automatic positive or negative reinforcement (e.g., *Nonsocial* scale), (4) pain attenuation or physical discomfort reduction (e.g., *Physical* scale), and (5) socially mediated access to tangibles (e.g., *Tangible* scale).

Given that the QABF is a more recently published instrument than the MAS fewer psychometric studies have been published. Available research, however, suggests that the QABF has acceptable test–retest reliability, interrater agreement, and internal consistency (Paclawskyj, Matson, Rush, Smalls, & Vollmer, 2000). Matson, Bamburg, Cherry, and Paclawskyj (1999) compared outcomes of treatment derived from QABF outcome to treatment outcomes based on more standard, default procedures, and found a greater than three times reduction in self-injurious behavior over six months when treatment was derived from QABF outcome. Although these findings are promising, additional research is needed on this instrument's psychometric properties and utility.

3.2.3.1.4. Functional Assessment for Multiple Causality (FACT)
An interesting approach was taken in the development of the FACT (Matson et al., 2003). It was based on the observation that some self-injurious behaviors can be maintained by multiple functions. Therefore, it is necessary to prioritize the functions that determine the selection of intervention strategies. The FACT is an empirically developed informant-based scale with 35 forced-choice items. This means that each item juxtaposes two behavioral functions, from which the rater has to choose the one that applies better in a given case. Factor analysis produced five factors which was the basis for the scale's five subscales: (1) *Tangible*, which reflects that the target behavior has a history of producing tangible items; (2) *Physical*, which refers to behavior exhibited during physical discomfort; (3) *Attention*, behavior that attracts and is maintained by contingent attention from others; (4) *Escape*, referring to behavior used to escape disagreeable situations; and (5) *Nonsocial*, for behavior that appears to produce self-stimulation. The FACT subscales have excellent internal consistency (KR-20 coefficients ranging from .94 to .95). The scale shows great promise but more data on validity and reliability (interrater agreement and test–retest) will show its true potential.

3.2.3.1.5. Functional Analysis Screening Tool (FAST)
The FAST is an item informant-based rating scale developed according to general rules of scale construction (Iwata & DeLeon, 1995). The items were assigned into three sections or subscales: (1) *Social Influences on Behavior*, (2) *Social Reinforcement*, and (3) *Nonsocial (Automatic) Reinforcement*. B. A. Iwata (personal communication, May 2002) mentioned that the FAST interrater agreement was found to be only modest (around 67%). It is our understanding that the FAST continuous to be under development (I. DeLeon, personal communication, September, 2006).

3.2.3.1.6. Conclusion – Functional Analysis-Rating Scales
Rating scales can be completed in far less time than functional analyses. Less training is generally required for those administering rating scales, and fewer financial and other resources are needed (Paclawskyj et al., 2000; Vollmer & Matson, 1995). Further, unlike conducting a functional analysis, interviewing caretakers poses no health risk to the person, nor does it involve the unintended conditioning trials implicit in functional analyses.

However, interviewer skill in completing the questionnaire with the informant is a key determinant of the quality of the questionnaire data and actions subsequently taken on its basis (Sturmey, 1994). Likewise, repeated experience of the informant with the self-injurious behavior person's self-injurious behavior, in the situations in which the self-injurious behavior occurs is also important (Borgmeier & Horner, 2006; Sturmey, 1994). Although informant-provided questionnaire data could potentially lead to rapid treatment development and implementation (Floyd, Phaneuf, & Wilczynski, 2005; Paclawskyj et al., 2000), one must bear in mind that the informant's reports are based on recollections, judgments, and impressions of the focus person's self-injurious behavior and its circumstances, and that these may vary across potential informants and over time. Questionnaires may be very useful especially as part of a more complete assessment package, with complementary sources of information. Finally, interventions based on questionnaires should be considered as tests of those hypotheses (Vollmer & Matson, 1995), and be implemented in a limited manner with an eye toward confirming or disconfirming those hypotheses. Only when hypotheses are confirmed, should interventions be implemented on a broader scale.

3.2.3.2. Interviews
Most functional analyses or assessments involve some type of interview. Interviews can precede experimental functional analysis, and, in part, inform the selection of conditions (Harding et al., 2005). Post-analysis interviews can be conducted when functional analyses are undifferentiated, and can inform condition selection for re-analysis. Interviews can inform selection of targets for scatterplot analysis and interpretation of scatterplot data (Hoch, 2007; Touchette, MacDonald, & Langer, 1985).

3.2.3.2.1. Functional Assessment Interview (FAI)
O'Neill et al. (1997) developed very useful guidelines for structured interviews for their FAI, which is in part a comprehensive functional assessment system. These authors point out that the FAI is appropriately used to generate hypotheses regarding environmental variables that may influence self-injurious behavior or other problem behaviors, but caution that those hypotheses need to be tested through either functional analysis or direct observation prior to implementing treatment based on them. They recommend conducting the interview with more than one informant who has daily contact with the person, and suggest conducting the interview with the client to the extent possible. In the FAI the informant is asked to

- specifically identify the behaviors of concern;
- describe topographies and estimate behavioral frequency, duration, and intensity;
- determine whether any of those behaviors occur in a sequence, and, if so, to describe that sequence;
- list medications the client is taking and whether they appear to influence the client's behavior;
- list medical diagnoses, sleeping and eating patterns, and these may affect the person's behavior;
- describe events of a typical day, and indicate which events the person appears to enjoy and which ones are associated with problems; indicate how predictable the daily schedule is; describe social interactions, conditions, whether the client chooses

the events comprising her or his daily life, staffing and peer composition of the person's life, and the extent to which these influence the person's behavior;
- describe times of day, settings, people, and activities that are most and least likely to evoke the problem behavior;
- identify idiosyncratic situations that seem to evoke the behavior;
- describe how the client would behave if a difficult request was presented, a preferred event ended abruptly, an unexpected change occurred, if he/she wanted something but could not have something, or if she or he had no attention for 15 minutes;
- describe situations in which each of the problem behaviors occurs. Next, the informant describes what the person either receives or escapes or avoids contingent on those behaviors in those situations;
- rate the effort the target behavior requires in producing reinforcement (behavioral efficiency);
- list potential replacement behaviors in the client's repertoire;
- describe the client's expressive verbal behavior and motor imitation;
- indicate how to arrange for things to work out well, and what to avoid when working with the person;
- list preferences and potential reinforcers;
- provide a history of the behavior, including prior treatment procedures;
- develop hypotheses regarding possible maintaining contingencies.

Psychometric data are not available on the 1990 edition of the FAI (Sturmey, 1994), and appear unavailable for the 1997 edition. Several studies do report using the FAI for assessing functional relations maintaining self-injurious behavior. Sprague, Holland, and Thomas (1997) conducted FAIs to assess self-injurious behavior for two participants with intellectual disabilities. FAI-generated hypotheses were subsequently assessed and confirmed in functional analysis, and the resulting treatment substantially reduced self-injurious behavior for both participants. In contrast, English and Anderson (2004) compared hypotheses generated by the FAI with outcomes of experimental functional analyses for self-injurious behavior, and found that hypotheses developed on the basis of informants' reports (FAI) overestimated weak functional relations and underestimated strong ones. Despite this, if the instrument is used as recommended by the authors, and hypotheses are further assessed prior to developing and implementing treatment, the FAI appears to be a useful component of a comprehensive functional assessment and analysis.

3.2.3.3. Behavioral Diagnostics
Bailey and Pyles (1989) accumulated a set of important questions that could be administered in the form of interviews with knowledgeable caretakers. These questions encompassed the motivating operations, antecedents, contingencies, and the specific features of the targeted problem behavior. A few years later Pyles et al. (1997) incorporated these questions into a comprehensive, cross-disciplinary assessment system, which has come to be known as *behavioral diagnostics*.

3.2.3.3.1. Conclusion – Interviews

Certainly, much valuable information can be gained from well-conducted interviews such as those provided by O'Neill et al. (1997) and Bailey and Pyles (1989), especially when the informant is a knowledgeable and perceptive person who is intimately familiar with the client and his or her daily life. However, interviewing is a skill that requires clinical training. A recent survey by Ellingson et al. (1999) indicated that behavioral interviews are the most frequently used functional assessment technique. Unfortunately, they also discovered that interviewers often lack adequate training, which can easily obscure important clinical information and lead to wrong clinical conclusions. Therefore, interviews will be most beneficial if they are conducted by trained interviewers and knowledgeable informants and if the information is subsequently corroborated by more objective data.

3.2.3.4. Contingency (A-B-C) Event Recording

Bijou, Peterson, and Ault (1968) described a method for recording descriptions of behaviors of interest, and events that precede and follow them. This method, since called A-B-C recording, is an event-driven, observational data collection system (Figure 3.1).

Contingency (A-B-C) event recording typically involves constructing a recording form that includes columns for the date, time, and descriptions of antecedent events, behavior observed, and consequent events. Data utility can be enhanced by including columns to document location at which the behavior occurred (i.e., in the living room, at the day program, etc.), names of people present when the behavior occurred, and name or initials of the person making the data entry, should additional information be needed.

From these data entries, one can calculate the frequency with which the various recorded antecedent and consequent events precede and follow the targeted behavior, and these figures may suggest correlations between the behavior and environmental events, thereby suggesting possible functional relations. However, this method does not inform the user as to frequency with which those events occur irrespective of the behavior, thereby potentially producing inaccurate conclusions of contingency. Further, accuracy is compromised if observation and data collection is not continuous across the entire time frame for which the behavior could occur. For example, if one were recording A-B-C data of a student's self-injurious behavior during the school day, then observation and recording must take place across the entire school day, as missed time may result in potentially important overlooked information.

It is important to keep in mind that contingency event recording cannot by itself firmly establish functional relations because it does not allow one to distinguish between actual functional contingencies and mere contiguities. It does not separate relevant from irrelevant environmental events (Vollmer, Borrero, Wright, Van Camp, & Lalli, 2001). However, it can suggest the existence of functional relations, which then may or may not be corroborated with information from more objective sources. A-B-C recording could for instance be a useful starting point in determining experimental conditions for a functional analysis. Also, A-B-C data collection has been helpful in subsequent identification of maintaining contingencies when functional analysis outcomes were undifferentiated (Fisher et al., 1998a, 1998b).

ABC Event-Recording Chart

Name: _____

Date: _____

Time: _____

Informant: _____

General Setting	Immediate Antecedent Event	Target Behavior	Immediate Consequence

Figure 3.1: Example of an A-B-C Event-Recording chart.

3.2.3.5. Scatterplots

Some behaviors sometimes occur with temporal regularity, which may provide important clues about its maintaining conditions. Determining the days or the times of the day when self-injurious behavior is more and less likely to occur is a feature of a number of behavioral assessment interviews (see O'Neill et al., 1997). However information based on interview is subjective and can be biased or otherwise inaccurate. Stimulus control scatterplots, first reported by Touchette et al. (1985) can greatly aid discerning temporal behavioral patterns.

A scatterplot is a grid on which time of day runs along the vertical axis, and day of week along the horizontal axis. Depending on the nature of the data needed, records may be made around the clock, or during only certain hours, such as waking hours or during school hours only. Data may be recorded using partial interval sampling, whole interval sampling, or momentary interval sampling, depending on nature of the behavior and question to be answered by the scatterplot. Alternatively, frequency estimates can be recorded, or counts tallied.

To record data on the scatterplot, the observer makes a mark indicating occurrence or nonoccurrence (when using interval sampling), frequency estimate, or a tally of the behavior in the cell corresponding to the day and time on which the behavior happened. As such, recording can be relatively simple. Alternatively, data might be recorded in an A-B-C data collection system, and then the counts, frequency estimates, or records of occurrence can be transferred to the scatterplot at a later time.

Touchette et al. (1985) estimated self-injurious behavior frequencies for two participants with scatterplots featuring one-hour intervals along the vertical axis. When five or more instances of self-injurious behavior occurred within a given hour, a filled circle was recorded; one to four instances occurred, an open square was recorded. Hours with no self-injurious behavior were left blank. For one person, a pattern in which self-injurious behavior occurred almost exclusively during this residence's evening shift was apparent after five days. Beginning on the sixth day, staff that worked on day and evening shifts reversed shifts, and the temporal pattern of self-injurious behavior reversed. After two days, the staff again reversed shifts, and the temporal pattern again reversed. No treatment explicitly targeting self-injurious behavior was implemented, however, the man began spending day hours at an off-site work location, and only staff in whose presence self-injurious behavior did not occur worked during the evening.

For a second person, temporal pattern was less clear, with varying self-injurious behavior frequencies across all most waking hours and no discernable pattern of occurrence or nonoccurrence. Those working with the clients rated his daily activities on a five-point scale (ranging from 1 = least likely to produce self-injurious behavior to 5 = most likely to produce self-injurious behavior), and the schedule was altered to include only activities nominated as unlikely to produce self-injurious behavior beginning on the eleventh day. Most self-injurious behavior ceased, and a more regular temporal pattern emerged, with the behavior reliably occurring near noon and during evening half-hour intervals. Evening schedule was subsequently changed to consist of activities nominated as less likely to produce self-injurious behavior, and self-injurious behavior was virtually eliminated by the forty-second day (Touchette et al., 1985).

In both examples provided by Touchette et al. (1985) temporal patterns of self-injurious behavior occurrence became apparent, albeit with additional intervention in the second case. However, contingencies maintaining the self-injurious behavior (or promoting behaviors other than self-injurious behavior) were not suggested by the scatterplots, alone. No such contingencies were identified or addressed for the first person leaving the man vulnerable to recurrence of self-injurious behavior should he encounter a person with behavioral or other characteristics similar to those who had occasioned his self-injurious behavior. Observations and interviews suggested self-injurious behavior was related to various daily activities for the second person, but functional relations were not demonstrated. Despite this, altering day and evening schedules based on hypotheses generated from those observations and interviews resulted in substantial reduction in self-injurious behavior. Again, though, the person remained potentially vulnerable to recurrence of self-injurious behavior should the prior activity pattern be reintroduced without additional programming to carefully reintroduce those activities.

Although scatterplots have been used in functional assessment in some published reports on assessment and treatment of self-injurious behavior (Lalli, Browder, Mace, & Brown, 1993; Repp, Felce, & Barton, 1988), scatterplots themselves have rarely been published (Kahng et al., 1998). Scatterplots can become very lengthy when data are recorded across weeks or months, and recording in half-hour (or even hour) increments across the clock can possibly render a scatterplot illegible when reduced in size for publication.

A scatterplot may provide valuable data regarding temporal distribution of self-injurious behavior, but additional information and data from other sources would be needed for effective action toward behavioral improvement (Hoch, 2007). Kahng et al. (1998) examined utility of scatterplot analysis in functional assessment of self-injurious behavior and other problem behaviors for 20 participants living in residential care. Five datasets were unusable, given poor inter-observer agreement. The remaining scatterplots did not reveal discernable temporal patterns, and temporal distributions were only discerned when additional statistical procedures were applied. Kahng et al. concluded that, although such additional procedures may enhance utility of scatter-plots, other assessment methods may be more efficient, given the time required to aggregate sufficient data required for statistical analysis.

3.2.3.6. Conditional Probability Analysis
A main advantage of functional assessment over functional analyses is that the former poses practically no risk to the participant. Functional assessments may also be briefer and less expensive than a full functional analysis. However, functional assessment procedures are weaker in establishing a functional relationship between events and a targeted behavior. Functional assessment itself can only identify a temporal contiguity between the behavior and ongoing environmental events that precede and follow it. It cannot demonstrate whether the contiguity represents a functional relationship between the behavior and the events or a mere correlational relationship. Conditional probability analysis is a method to analyze observational data that does not involve manipulations of events.

For example, in conducting a conditional probability analysis to determine whether a given self-injurious behavior is maintained by access to attention or by termination of task demands the following steps would be taken. First, the behavior analyst observes the person in his or her natural environment, and scores (a) each instance of self-injurious behavior that is followed by someone else's attention, (b) each instance of self-injurious behavior that was followed by the termination of a demand, (c) each instance of self-injurious behavior that was followed by neither of these events, and (d) each instance of attention delivery and of demand termination that was not preceded by self-injurious behavior. Next, one would calculate probability of attention given self-injurious behavior as that proportion of instances of onset of attention delivery that was preceded by self-injurious behavior. For example, a client works in vocational rehabilitation setting on a task. The question is whether self-injurious behavior is maintained by positive social reinforcement or by socially mediated negative

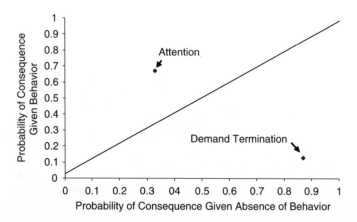

Figure 3.2: Sample dataset examining conditional probability of two potential consequence events given prior occurrence of SIB.

reinforcement (termination of the requirement to work on the assigned task). During a given observation period an observer records that staff members directed their attention to the client 15 times in a non-task related context; in 10 of those times staff attention was preceded by the client's self-injurious behavior; therefore, the conditional probability of attention given self-injurious behavior would be .67. By this logic, the conditional probability of attention without prior self-injurious behavior by the client would be .33. During the same period the observer records that a termination of task demand was terminated eight times, one of which was preceded by self-injurious behavior; the conditional probability of demand termination given self-injurious behavior would be .13, and conditional probability of demand termination given absence of self-injurious behavior would be .87. These figures are then plotted on axes, as illustrated in Figure 3.2, with probability of the consequence given the behavior running along the vertical axis, and probability of consequence given absence of the behavior running along the horizontal axis. The diagonal line indicates where the points would be were the consequence as likely to occur if preceded by the behavior as if not preceded by the behavior; that is, if prior occurrence of the behavior were irrelevant. Points above the line indicate the consequence is more likely to occur when preceded by the behavior; points below, less likely when preceded by the behavior. In this instance, the data suggest that the self-injurious behavior may be maintained by contingent attention (social positive reinforcement), but that it does not appear to be maintained by demand termination (social negative reinforcement).

Conditional probability analysis can also examine the potential degree of a relationship between antecedent events and behaviors. In this case, one would observe and calculate as described above, but would record occurrence of the potential antecedent when followed by the behavior, and occurrence of that event when not followed by the behavior, and adjust the calculations accordingly. Consider, for example, the possibility that academic instructions, physical proximity of another student (defined as that student being within 3 feet of the person), and having been asked to "stop" are suspected

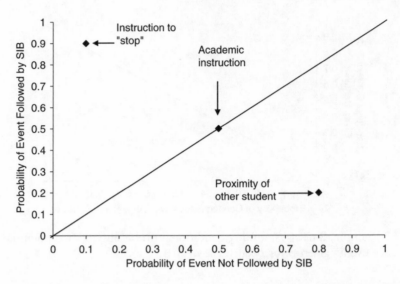

Figure 3.3: Sample dataset examining conditional probability of SIB given prior occurrence of antecedent events.

as potentially evoking self-injurious behavior. One would score occurrence of each of those events as being followed or not being followed by self-injurious behavior. Data indicate that 20 instructions were given, the other student was close by on 15 occasions, and the person was told "stop" on 30 occasions, and these were followed by self-injurious behavior on 10, 3, and 27 occasions, respectively. Conditional probability of self-injurious behavior given an instruction would be .50, and not given an instruction also .50; of self-injurious behavior given proximity of the other student .20, and given no proximity of the other student .80; and given having just been told "stop" .90, and given having not been told "stop" .10. Graphically, these would appear as in Figure 3.3. These data suggest no relation between academic instructions and self-injurious behavior, decreased probability of self-injurious behavior given presence of the other student, but greatly increased probability of self-injurious behavior following instructions to "stop."

Hagopian, Paclawskyj, and Kuhn (2005) examined the extent to which stereotypic behavior predicted self-injurious eye poking. In this study, they first calculated conditional probability of eye poking given prior stereotyped behavior, and then conditional probability of eye poking in the absence of prior eye poking. They next calculated overall probability of each of these behaviors as proportion of observation intervals in which each occurred, and then multiplied these two proportions to determine the probability of eye poking and stereotyped behavior occurring in the same interval by chance. Conditional probabilities of eye poking given prior stereotyped behavior and of eye poking given no prior eye poking were compared with the probability of co-occurrence by chance. Probability of eye poking following stereotyped behavior greatly exceeded chance probability, while probability of eye poking without prior stereotyped behavior was essentially similar to chance probability, suggesting that stereotyped behavior did, to some degree, predict eye poking. Subsequent treatment of stereotyped behavior resulted in collateral reduction in eye poking.

3.2.4. Comparison of Methods

Of all the methods discussed thus far, only functional analyses can demonstrate presence or absence of functional relations between behavior and other events, because it involves the systematic manipulation of independent variables according to an experimental design. However, highly trained and capable staff is an absolute necessity. These analyses are typically also time-consuming and resource intensive, as days to weeks (or longer) may be required to complete a thorough analysis. By necessity, they require that the person's self-injurious behavior be permitted to occur during session, and so some degree of risk is inherent. Potential health risk can be minimized by proper oversight. The risk for inadvertent conditioning of self-injurious behavior cannot be ruled out.

Conditional probability analyses can be less time and resource intensive. Observations are conducted in the person's natural environments, and environmental changes need not be contrived. The only risk involved is the risk the person encounters in a typical day. Although conditional probability analyses do provide useful and perhaps often sufficient evidence, they cannot *demonstrate* functional relations between behaviors and events, as functional analyses do.

Contingency (A-B-C) event recording does not require any modifications to the person's environment, and requires far less training and skill than do either analogue functional analyses or conditional probability analyses. They do require, however, that observation be conducted at all potential times of interest, and that all instances of the target behavior (and its antecedent and subsequent events) be documented clearly. Although one can conclude from A-B-C data the frequency with which antecedent and subsequent events precede or follow self-injurious behavior, A-B-C data provide no information about how frequently those events occur independently of the behavior or vice versa. Therefore, hypotheses derived from this method are likely to be less reliable than hypotheses derived from conditional probability analysis or functional analysis.

Scatterplots are also user-friendly in that they require minimal training and resources. This method is flexible with regard to type of data collected (e.g., occurrence or nonoccurrence versus frequency estimate) and method of data collection (e.g., whole or partial interval sampling, or momentary time sampling). Temporal behavioral patterns can be revealed by this method when they exist, but then further investigation would be needed to determine factors influencing occurrence of the behavior at those times (and influencing its nonoccurrence at other times) before further action can be taken. Further, continuous observation is needed if whole or partial interval sampling methods are used. So, while actual documentation potentially takes only as much time as is needed to record a single mark in a cell on a piece of paper, far more observation time is needed to determine which mark is made, and when. Functional relations cannot be determined by this method, and hypothesis development requires additional assessment.

Interviews are necessary components of any assessment or analysis and they can inform the development of functional analysis conditions, or guide the choice of functional assessment strategies. However, training and experience in clinical interviewing may be necessary. The targeted client who exhibits self-injurious behavior incurs no risk through the interview process itself. However, poorly conducted interviews can produce flawed hypotheses from which ill-suited and unsuccessful treatment may be developed. Even well-conducted interviews can be followed by incorrect presumption of contingency, thereby resulting in flawed hypotheses and poorly designed intervention strategies. Additional data are often needed to confirm or disconfirm the interview-based information.

Checklists are arguably the least expensive and quickest method of functional assessment, although additional research to improve their psychometric properties of some of these instruments is needed. Clinical interviewing skill is needed if the checklists are administered via interviews. As with unstructured or semi-structured interviews, the information one gathers from parents, staff, or other caretakers on a checklist easily renders biased or inaccurate results, as it is based on the informant's recollections and impressions about the person exhibiting the self-injurious behavior. Reliability can potentially be improved when more than one informant who is familiar with the client's behavior is interviewed.

3.3. Assessment of Target Sites, Trauma, and Pain

Inflicted trauma can be a type of behavioral outcome that could be of clinical and research interest, especially with dangerous self-injurious behavior. Two examples of self-injurious behavior produced trauma will be briefly introduced.

3.3.1. Self-Injurious Behavior Trauma (SIT) Scale

The SIT Scale developed by Iwata, Pace, Kissel, Nau, and Farber (1990) was modeled after injury measurement instruments used in emergency and trauma medicine. The scale classifies damage by

- Type of injury (abrasions/lacerations vs. contusions),
- Number of inflicted wounds rated on a three-point scale (1 = one wound; 2 = two to four; 3 = five or more),
- Severity of inflicted wounds; two kinds of injury severity are rated on three-point scales:
  - Severity of abrasions or lacerations (1 = area is red or irritated, with only spotted breaks in the skin; 2 = break in the skin is distinct but superficial, no avulsions; 3 = break in the skin is deep or extensive or avulsions present)
  - Severity of contusions (1 = local swelling only or discoloration without swelling; 2 = extensive swelling; 3 = disfigurement or tissue rupture),
- Injuries, which can occur on 21 specific body sites on the head, the upper and lower torso, and the extremities.

In addition to the summary data for the number and severity of wounds, the SIT also provides an algorithm to estimate the current risk that is based on the location and the severity of the trauma.

Inter-rater reliability was found to be very high when analyzed in a sample of 35 individuals with self-injurious behavior across five raters. The authors insist that the SIT is not an alternative to behavioral data or to medical screenings. Instead, they describe it mainly as a more systematic method to determine the extent of self-injurious behavior inflicted trauma. Several researchers have used the SIT scale, including McDonough, Hillery, and Kennedy (2000) who used it to document treatment progress in seven adults with intellectual disabilities and severe self-injurious behavior.

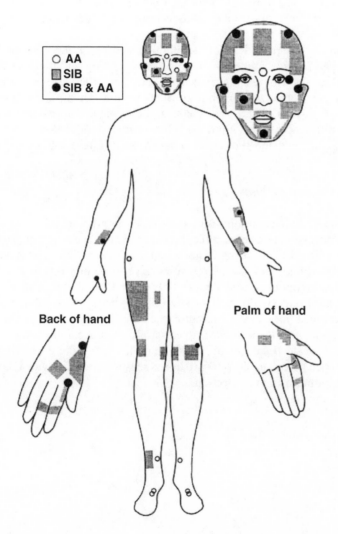

Figure 3.4: SIB Site Preference charts locating SIB injury sites (SIB) relative to acupuncture analgesia sites (AA) of the body (Symons & Thompson, 1997).

3.3.2. Self-Injurious Behavior Site Preference Charts

In an attempt to trace self-injurious behavior target sites relative to analgesia locations of the body, Symons and Thompson (1997) created a booklet with 14 schematic maps of body parts and of the entire human body with superimposed grids. To monitor preferred targets, squares on the grid that corresponded to the self-injurious behavior targeted site are shaded. A detailed system of inter-rater agreement indices was developed based on the records of 29 participants with daily self-injurious behavior occurrences, teaching staff agreed on 71% of the body areas toward which self-injurious behavior was directed. This analysis revealed that self-injurious behavior injury sites were disproportionately associated with acupuncture analgesia sites (Figure 3.4).

Wisely, Hare, and Fernandez-Ford (2002) followed up on the study by Symons and Thompson (1997) and examined the body site targeted by self-injurious behavior in a sample of 241 adults with self-injurious behavior. Using their assessment methodology Wisely et al. were able to corroborate Symons and Thompson's (1997) findings. Thompson and Caruso (2002) used the same body picture assessment technology to demonstrate differences in self-injurious behavior injury sites between individuals with Prader–Willi syndrome and those with other forms of intellectual disability.

3.3.3. Measurement of Pain

Pain measurement in the developmental disabilities population, especially among those who lack expressive language, is difficult. Experimental measures of pain with algometers, even when they are benign, are usually not permitted in this population by human subjects committees, so the measures have to be indirect. For example, LaChapelle, Hadjistavropoulos, and Craig (1999) and Oberlander, Gilbert, Chambers, O'Donnell, and Craig (1999) used facial coding schemes in combination with biobehavioral response measures to monitor pain during invasive medical procedures. Recently, Symons and Danov (2005) successfully used a combination of two rating scales, the SIT Scale (Iwata et al., 1990) and the Non-Communicating Children's Checklist-Revised (Breau et al., 2003), to assess self-injurious behavior-related pain in a child after a midbrain tumor resection.

Chapter 4

Prevention Management and Treatment

4.1. Prevention and Early Intervention

Infants, even Lesch–Nyhan syndrome babies, do not come from the womb biting themselves or banging their heads. Self-injurious behavior tends to begin later during infancy starting at about 6–10 months (de Lissavoy, 1961; Kelley & Wyngaarden, 1983; Kravitz & Boehm, 1971). Given the life-long serious consequences of self-injurious behavior, a research program on its early identification and prevention would seem to be a high priority. Yet, as an excellent recent review of the literature by Symons, Sperry, Dropik, and Bodfish (2005) has shown, only a small literature on this topic exists.

The following questions based on the literature of adult self-injurious behavior cases would be of interest for infants and young children:

1. Are there age-related risk factors that are related to age of onset and resistance to change of self-injurious behavior (e.g., choreoathetoid movements, HPRT deficiency, stereotyped behaviors, hand-to-mouth activity)?
2. Are there also non-age-related risk factors (e.g., severity of intellectual disability, central nervous system (CNS) damage, genetic defects, communication deficits, sensory handicaps such as blindness, deafness, and pain insensitivity) that increase the risk of self-injurious behavior?
3. Do behavioral treatments for infants and toddlers based on stimulating sensory reinforcement (e.g., sensory extinction) work better than other behavioral modification techniques (e.g., differential reinforcement of other behavior (DRO), time-out)?
4. Can successful early intervention, which has decreased acute self-injurious behavior, avert serious chronic self-injurious behavior in later life? Is it easier to reduce self-injurious behavior, the quicker it is discovered and treated?
5. Is it more difficult to decrease self-injurious behavior in older children who may have a more deeply ingrained "behavioral overlay," as postulated by Goldstein et al. (1986).

4.1.1. Significance of Early Identification

A large number of persons, representing a variety of diagnostic categories exhibit self-injurious behavior including autism, childhood schizophrenia, intellectual disability, visual impairment, emotional disturbance, and learning disabilities. In many cases, these behaviors are extremely severe and result in permanent injury, even death. Surveys conducted in typical pediatric practices reveal that 7%–20% of young children exhibit self-injurious behavior, but usually "grow out of it" by the age of 5 years. In the middle childhood and older developmentally disabled population self-injurious behavior is a life-long problem and is related to severity of intellectual disability, brain damage, communication deficits, early onset, chronicity, sensory impairment, and length of institutionalization (Schroeder, Reese, Hellings, Loupe, & Tessel, 1999).

What do primary and secondary prevention strategies have to offer self-injurious behavior cases at this time? They offer us the hope of developing rational theoretically sound neurobiological treatments, which can be used to enhance behavioral treatments for self-injurious behavior. Since self-injurious behavior appears to be a heterogeneous set of response classes reflecting several possible functional relationships with environmental setting factors, it is not surprising that it may also have several types of neurobiological antecedents, which set the occasion for a certain topography. In the case of Lesch–Nyhan syndrome, self-biting may be related to rather specific deficiencies in purine salvage pathways. With other more socially reinforced forms of self-injurious behavior, like head banging, biting, hair pulling, or gouging, the particular topography may be related to differential stimulus control or to neurobiologically mediated states such as depression, chronic hypertension, or to neurochemical factors following lesions in the extra-pyramidal system, as suggested by Breese and Baumeister, Frye, and Schroeder (1984). The particular topography may be related to: (1) the particular receptors affected, (2) age at which the lesion occurred, (3) environmentally arranged setting factors, or (4) a combination of all the above. Lesch–Nyhan patients may begin to bite themselves rather than head-bang when they get upset at the age of around 6 months to 2 years because of the combination of a lesion in their nigro-striatal pathway and the eruption of their teeth at about that same time. Once strongly reinforced, these behaviors may quickly become a permanent potent response in their repertoires. Thus, the study of Lesch–Nyhan syndrome, one of the few known genetic disorders with such a high incidence of a specific phenotype as severe self-biting, may be a neurobiological window for studying other self-injurious behaviors, too. Such a view would have several far-reaching implications. It also raises several important questions.

Another major question arises from the developmental hypothesis of Breese et al. (1984a, 1984b) that dopamine depletion in the basal ganglia at an early age is related to later production of self-injurious behavior. They found that if young rats (aged 5 days) were dopamine-depleted by administering the neurocytotoxin 6-hydroxydopamine (6-OHDA) into the substantia nigra, a later challenge with L-DOPA resulted in self-biting, whereas this did not occur with animals receiving the same lesion later in life. This result suggests that *later severe chronic self-injurious behavior may be related to early dopamine depletion.* Such an interpretation is supported indirectly by prevalence studies of self-injurious behavior (Baumeister & Rollings, 1976; Schroeder et al., 1978). Severe self-injurious behavior cases tend to have more severe intellectual disabilities, have more sensory and communication disabilities, be institutionalized longer, have a longer chronicity and a higher proportion of frank CNS damage (e.g., seizures, kernicterus, encephalitis, and meningitis) which might predispose them to more dopamine depletion than other severely and profoundly retarded clients have (Schroeder et al., 1980). However, these data come mostly from hospital records in which identification of early onset and patient histories are generally poor. As we have discussed in Chapter 2 of this book, there has not been adequate study on incidence of self-injurious behavior.

A developmental question of interest is whether there is a particular age-range during which pathological self-injurious behavior typically develops? Studies of crib-banging among infants suggest that it usually stops in the typically developing child by 12–18 months (Kravitz & Boehm, 1971) and is very rare beyond 5 years (de Lissavoy, 1961). Pathological self-biting in Lesch–Nyhan syndrome tends to begin not at birth but at about 6 months to 2 years of age (Kelley & Wyngaarden, 1983). Retrospective studies of self-injurious behavior (Schroeder et al., 1980) suggest that it is very difficult to trace self-injurious behavior before 3 years of age. A large cross–sectional study would be very important in identifying age of onset and possible risk factors related to dopamine depletion (e.g., abnormal extra-pyramidal movements).

Berkson and his colleagues (Berkson & Tupa, 2000, 2002; Berkson, Tupa, & Sherman, 2001) conducted longitudinal studies on the early development of stereotyped behavior, some of which appears to emerge into self-injurious behavior (proto-self-injurious). They followed 457 infants and toddlers aged 3–40 months with severe retardation who received services in Part C Birth-to-Three Programs in Chicago. Their observations suggest that the movements are often qualitatively different from the stereotyped movements of typically developing infants. Two groups were identified: self-injurious behavior that was mediated by social consequences, and self-injurious behavior that seemed to have no social consequences. A recent study by Richman and Lindauer (2005a, 2005b) in 12 infants and toddlers aged 12–32 months replicated and extended Berkson's findings using functional analysis procedures repeatedly over a year. Two patterns were delineated: one group simply increased the same form and function of their self-injurious behavior until it damaged tissue; a second group changed the form of their self-injurious behavior to other topographies related to their earlier stereotyped behavior as a function of social consequences. Studies that compared repetitive movements in older people with intellectual disability versus autism suggest that repetitive movements associated with intellectual disabilities tended to be qualitatively more stable than those in people with autism, but that they differ more in quantity and intensity (Bodfish et al., 2000).

Another group from the U.K. has been examining the onset of self-injurious behavior in school-aged children (Hall, Oliver, & Murphy, 2001; Murphy et al., 1999; Oliver, Hall, & Murphy, 2005). Murphy et al. (1999) screened children less than 11 years of age in London, Surrey, and Kent school districts. After ascertainment, 133 of 614 showed some form of self-injurious behavior. Of these, 17 index cases whose self-injurious behavior onset was less than three months and 14 controls of similar abilities but with no self-injurious behavior were chosen for the study. They were given a battery of tests plus naturalistic observations in their classrooms every three months for 18 months. The index group showed more potential self-injurious behavior than the control subjects. This was related to their mobility and developmental age but not to the degree of autism, sensory impairments, skill level, or problem behavior. Hall et al. (2001) followed up the same cohort, examining the relationship between early self-injurious behavior and environmental events. For four children whose self-injurious behavior escalated over the 18 months, there was a significant association between early self-injurious behavior and low levels of social contact across observation points. Oliver et al. (2005) confirmed this result using a conditional probability analysis to examine the distribution of the probability of social contact relative to bursts of self-injurious behavior and found that self-injurious behavior was followed by increased social attention by caregivers. Thus self-injurious behavior may have been maintained by mutual social reinforcement between child and caregiver.

A second major question is whether *early* intervention can attenuate self-injurious behavior in *later* life by secondary behavioral and pharmacological preventive measures. We have reviewed this literature (Schroeder et al., 1986). One set of behavioral procedures that might be acceptable in young children this age involves differential stimulus control procedures (Carr et al., 1994); another behavioral intervention involves the use of sensory extinction (Rincover, 1978).

An early intervention stimulation program comparing differential reinforcement of other behaviors with sensory extinction procedures, both standard behavioral intervention treatments for older self-injurious behavior children, would allow one to ask several questions: (1) Will stimulation which was initiated at earlier ages have a stronger effect than stimulation begun at a later age? (2) Will the effect be different for organic deficits more related to dopamine depletion a la Breese et al. (e.g., choreoathetoid movements, Parkinsonian symptoms, extra-pyramidal effects, etc.)? (3) Is selection of self-injurious behavior topography modality specific? For example, do hand-mouthing and teeth eruption lead to self-biting, while insensitivity to pain lead to head banging, neurodermatitis lead to scratching and gouging, organic conditions like gastrointestinal reflux and hiatal hernia lead to chronic ruminative vomiting or nutritional deficiencies lead to pica?

In the following pages, we will present analyses of different intervention methods for preventing self-injurious behavior and its devastating effects. There are few clear-cut examples of either primary, secondary, or tertiary prevention of self-injurious behavior. Rather, all these intervention procedures overlap considerably along a time continuum, which is marked by self-injurious behavior events (e.g., head hanging or gouging), which may result in self-injurious behavior. We only use this classification scheme as a tool to help us set goals and to establish priorities for intervention.

4.1.2. Neurobiological Importance of Early Identification

The more we learn about life earlier in development, the more precious do we find this period of development to be. For instance, early faulty embryonic development during neural tube closure may ultimately result in autism in some infants (Rodier, Ingram, Tisdale, Nelson, & Romano, 1996). But that there is developmental life beyond the embryo we know from Smotherman's (1995) exquisite work on later environmental influences during fetal life.

In the phases of a child's development of language, Locke (1994) points out that learning that leads to human speech begins in the last trimester of pregnancy. Long before they utter a word, infants are talking themselves into a language. It takes an infant about a year to start talking; but, on every day of that year, a variety of language-related mechanisms inch their way toward efficient action. This trajectory is shaped by the interplay of nature and nurture. One influences the other and vice versa in a social dance, as seen in Betty Hart and Todd Risley's (1995, 1999) books on the social world of the child beginning to talk. In fact, Thelen (1995) contends that the dynamic systems approach to development renders the nature–nurture controversy irrelevant. What is the neurobiological and neurobehavioral evidence that supports such a view? We would like to highlight briefly some of the research that we think illustrates the early developmental plasticity of brain–behavior relationships.

Brain maturation during the first months of life is an extremely critical period for our development. It is a period of rapid brain growth in myelination, affecting speed of neurotransmission; in synaptogenesis, affecting the density of neural networks; in brain metabolism, affecting the neurochemicals, which enable the neurochemical anatomy of the brain to emerge. Many of these functions continue to develop throughout life. *Early synaptogenesis* in the human cerebral cortex begins to appear by 15 weeks of gestation and continues after birth (Colnel, 1939/1963). Golgi preparations of human prefrontal cortex at postnatal ages from 1, 6, 24, and 48 months show that the number of dendritic spines on neurons increases with age. Spines are distributed along the dendritic shaft in a characteristic manner regardless of cortical region.

This organization is important to functional brain circuitry. Disorders of synaptogenesis and neuronal differentiation are often an associated feature of a wide variety of genetic, chromosomal, and toxic metabolic disturbances related to intellectual disability and seizures.

Later synaptogenesis appears to reflect nature's basic strategy of neuronal development, i.e., that synapses are overproduced early in development and selectively eliminated at a later time through a process called apoptosis, i.e., programmed cell death. This mechanism is a way of sculpting the neural circuitry in the developing CNS. The famous study published by Huttenlocher (1979) illustrated this phenomenon by counting the density of synapses in layer III of the middle frontal gyrus as a function of age, in postmortem studies of the brain. There was a sharp decline in synaptic density beginning around four years of age. By adolescence, synaptic density is about 60% of its maximum at two years of age. This suggests that the trajectory for cortical expansion is strongly affected by the rapid growth spurt during the first two years of life. From the work of Hubel and Wiesel (1970) on the development of responsivity to visual stimulation in newborns and from the work of Brown, Chapman, Kairiss, and Keenan (1988) on activity-dependent learning in the adult brain, referred to as *long-term potentiation*, we know that synaptogenesis is important to development.

Positron emission tomography (PET) now makes in vivo studies of brain development possible. In many ways PET studies have confirmed postmortem morphological studies and extended them in exploring this pattern of overproduction and subsequent pruning of neuronal processes over a protracted course of the brain's development. The process of transient exuberant connectivity as a general rule in brain development is believed to be biologically advantageous in reducing the genetic load that would otherwise be required for specifically programming the enormous numbers of synaptic contacts in the nervous system (Changeux & Danchin, 1976). Furthermore, fine-tuning of neuronal circuits based upon early exposure and environmental stimulation during these critical periods shapes the individual's unique neuronal networks.

PET scanning allows the noninvasive measurement of local chemical functions in different body organs. Since glucose and oxygen are the principal substrates used under normal circumstances for meeting the energy demands of the brain, the rates at which these substrates are utilized in various brain regions provide a measure of brain regional energy demands. The most common method is to use a radioactive tracer (14C-2-deoxyglucose or 2DG for short) to quantify local cerebral metabolic rates for glucose (LCMRglc) in the brain.

Using PET with the radioactive tracer FDG (flourodeoxyglucose) in children of various ages, Chugani and his colleagues have found that the pattern of brain glucose utilization in the human newborn differed markedly from that of normal young healthy adults. In the newborn, four brain regions showed the most prominent glucose metabolism: primary sensorimotor cortex, thalamic nuclei, brain stem, and cerebellar vermis (Chugani & Phelps, 1986; Chugani, Phelps, & Mazziotta, 1987; Chugani, 1994). More recent studies using higher resolution scanners indicate that the cingulate cortex, hippocampal region, and occasionally the basal ganglia also show a relatively high metabolic rate for glucose consumption in the newborn period. This pattern of glucose metabolism in the newborn, characterized by highest activity in phylogenetically old structures, is in keeping with the relatively limited behavioral repertoire of neonates. For example, it is likely that reflex behaviors, such as the Moro, root, and grasp responses present in newborns are mediated by these brain regions, which are functionally active during this period (Andre-Thomas & Saint-Anne Dargassies, 1960). More sophisticated activity, such as visuo–motor integration required in reaching out towards a target and other eye–hand coordination tasks, are at a relatively primitive level in the newborn (von Hofsten, 1982); this is not unexpected, judging from the relatively simple pattern of brain glucose metabolism.

Beyond the neonatal period, the ontogeny of glucose metabolism also follows a phylogenetic order, with functional maturation of older anatomical structures preceding that of newer areas (Chugani & Phelps, 1986; Chugani et al., 1987; Chugani, 1994, pp. 153–175). Moreover, the sequence of functional brain development as determined by regional glucose metabolism correlates well with the maturation of behavioral, neurophysiological and neuroanatomical events in the infant. As visuo-spatial and visuo-sensorimotor integrative functions are acquired in the second and third months of life (Bronson, 1974), and primitive reflexes become reorganized (Andre-Thomas et al., 1960; Parmelee & Sigman, 1983), increases in glucose metabolism are observed in parietal, temporal, and primary visual cortical regions, basal ganglia, and cerebellar hemispheres. Increasing glucose metabolism in cerebral cortex during the second and third months of life presumably reflects maturation of the cortex, and is consistent with the dramatic maturation of EEG activity seen during the same period (Kellaway, 1979).

Between six and eight months, the frontal cortex begins to show a maturational rise in glucose metabolism, at first in the lateral portion and subsequently also in the mesial and lastly in the dorsal prefrontal areas. Functional maturation of these frontal cortical regions coincides with the appearance of higher cortical and cognitive abilities. For example, the infant now shows more sophisticated interaction with its surroundings and exhibits the phenomenon of stranger anxiety (Kagan, 1972). Performance on the delayed response task, which is a commonly used neuropsychological paradigm for evaluating prefrontal lobe integrity (Fuster, 1984; Goldman-Rakic, 1984) markedly improves during this period of frontal lobe metabolic maturation. Neuroanatomical studies in human infants have shown that there is an expansion of dendritic fields (Schade & van Groenigen, 1961) and an increase in capillary density (Diemer, 1968) in frontal cortex during this stage of development. By one year of age, the overall pattern of brain glucose metabolism is similar to that seen in adults.

PET studies have shown that, although normal children reach a pattern of brain glucose metabolism similar to adults by about one year of age, dynamic changes of LCMRglc occur in a non-linear fashion whereby they exceed adult levels during much of the first two decades of life. These changes are most marked for the neocortex, show an intermediate magnitude for basal ganglia and thalamus, and are probably not present in brainstem and cerebellum. In other words, there appears to be a hierarchical ordering of structures in terms of the degree to which maturational increases in LCMRglc exceed adult values. The typically low neonatal values of LCMRglc, which are about 30% lower than adult rates, rapidly increase from birth and reach adult values by about the second year. Thereafter, LCMRglc values continue to increase and begin to exceed adult values during the third postnatal year. By about four years, a plateau is reached which extends until about 9–10 years; following this, there is a gradual decline in LCMRglc to reach adult values by about 16–18 years (Chugani et al., 1987; Chugani, 1994, pp. 153–175). The relative increase of LCMRglc over adult values, which is most pronounced in neocortical regions between 4 and 10 years, reaches a peak LCMRglc of over twice the LCMRglc levels seen in adults.

These studies replicate and expand upon earlier observations by (Kennedy & Sokoloff, 1957), who demonstrated that also the average global cerebral blood flow in nine normal children (aged 3–11 years) was approximately 1.8 times that of normal young adults. Similarly, average cerebral oxygen utilization was approximately 1.3 times higher in children than in adults. In other words, there appears to be a transient phase during development when the human brain requires more nutrients to support its activity.

4.1.3. Brain Neuroplasticity and Sensitive Periods of Development

Clinically, there also appears to be a relationship between diminishing brain plasticity in children and the gradual decline of LCMRglc with its onset between 8 and 10 years of age measured with PET (Chugani et al., 1987; Chugani, 1994). For example, in the human visual system, the decline of LCMRglc in visual cortex beginning at about 8–10 years coincides with a notable decrease in plasticity, as judged by the development of amblyopia (irreversible loss of vision from one eye) in the presence of monocular occlusion or certain kinds of strabismus (Awaya, 1978; Vaegan, 1979; Marg, 1982). In addition, patients with problems in depth perception enucleated prior to eight years of age perform better on depth-perception tasks than individuals whose enucleation occurs after eight years (Schwartz, Linberg, Tillman, & Odom, 1987).

It is also well known that compensatory reorganization of the brain following brain injury or radical surgery such as hemicerebrectomy for intractable seizures is greater in the developing nervous system compared to one that is fully mature (Kaas, 1991; Irle, 1987). The degree of plasticity following injury depends upon the species involved, the brain regions damaged, size of lesion, state of maturation at the time of injury, and other factors (Chugani, 1994). Chugani and Jacobs (1995) have shown that glucose metabolism in the basal ganglia following hemicerebrectomy recovers, signaling anatomical reorganization in the contralateral spared cortex.

Language acquisition and reorganization in response to dominant hemisphere damage in children are clearly most efficient during a critical period ending at about 10 years of age (Basser, 1962; Lenneberg, 1967; Curtiss, 1977). Children who have been isolated since birth in the wilderness away from all civilization and exposure to language, the so-called "feral" children, acquire language most successfully if intervention is initiated in early childhood prior to about 10 years of age (Curtiss, 1981). This is not to say that there is no language plasticity after 10 years, but clearly, there appears to be a "window of opportunity" during which the brain is particularly efficient in learning.[1]

How can environmental intervention modify brain function? How specific can it be? Is it spontaneous or is specific training required? Is there a dose/response function? Is there a critical period for neurobehavioral training? These are all questions the answers to which we would love to know. PET scanning, functional magnetic resonance imaging (fMRI) and newer noninvasive techniques will help us greatly to answer these questions in vivo with humans. Until then, however, we must rely on animal experimentation.

The animal modeling literature provides some cautiously optimistic directions to pursue, although we must beware of overgeneralizing across species.

Anatomical and biochemical changes in rodents associated with enriched environmental rearing conditions were noted over 30 years ago: greater cortical depth, increased cortical weight, more glial proliferation, more dendritic branching, increased acetylcholinesterase levels, increased complexity of the hippocampus (for reviews see Dong & Greenough, 2004; Greenough, 1976; Lewis, 2004; Rosenzweig & Bennett, 1976). This enrichment did not require long periods of exposure or extreme conditions in order to produce these anatomical and biochemical effects.

Recent studies have shown relatively specific dose effects of operant training on local recovery of brain tissue and neurotransmitters after localized brain lesions. For instance, Nudo, Wise, SiFuentes, and Milliken (1996) in a recent issue of *Science*, showed that, by mapping the motor cortex of the squirrel monkey before and after small ischemic lesions in the hand territory, the subsequent loss of hand representation around the lesion can be prevented by intensive operant retraining of hand skills if started five days after injury. Starting too soon or too late does not work and may

---

[1] With this in mind, one cannot help but wonder why second language is still taught in high school rather than prior to 10 years when it is best acquired.

worsen the damage. Highly stereotyped, repetitive training of the same movement is superior to conventional physiotherapy. The rhythmic proprioceptive and cutaneous input of repetitive training induces long-term potentiation in the sensorimotor cortex, a possible mechanism for motor learning.

Richard Tessel and colleagues (Loupe et al., 1995; Stodgell, Schroeder, & Tessel, 1996; Tessel et al., 1995a, 1995b) have also shown dose-effects of operant training-induced recovery of brain neurotransmitters following the lesioning in two rat models of intellectual disability (see also Chapter 2 for a review).

In the future, we hope to discover the pathways critical for the successful intervention with infants and toddlers with self-injurious behavior and developmental disabilities. In a recent paper (Schroeder, Loupe, & Tessel, 2006) we have shown that neonatally 6-OHDA-lesioned rats later trained on challenging operant discrimination tasks were more resistant to performing self-injurious behavior than untrained controls when challenged as adults with a dopamine agonist L-DOPA. Training-induced recovery restored dopamine that had been depleted by the 6-OHDA lesions and had a protective effect on self-injurious behavior. Could a program involving such a highly challenging and engaging training prevent the development of self-injurious behavior in young children?

4.1.4. Historical Overview of Preventive Intervention Studies

The vast majority of the early behavioral research on self-injurious behavior of people with developmental disabilities has to do with how to get rid of it, rather than why it occurs in the first place (Schroeder, Schroeder, Rojahn, & Mulick, 1982b). This approach probably reflects the historical fact that our technology for dealing with the consequences of behavior is much more developed than our technology for dealing with its antecedents (Sidman, 1978). Since the short-term mandate is to reduce the risk of injury and pain to the client, the social pressure is to opt for acute methods for decelerating self-injurious behavior. But, the question we want to explore is, whether this is the best strategy for managing self-injurious behavior. If self-injurious behavior is indeed the prepotent operant response in a person's repertoire, which must be maintained by strong reinforcers, should that response be suppressed without a plan to replace it with a more appropriate set of responses that will be maintained as long as possible?

Only a few longitudinal intervention studies of self-injurious behavior have looked at program maintenance beyond a year. From 1974 through 1977, we looked at incidence of self-injurious behavior in an entire population of a state residential facility for people with intellectual disabilities during a 3-year hospital improvement grant (Schroeder et al., 1978) and found some sobering results. Of those clients treated with behavior modification alone, 90% improved; of those treated with psychotropic drugs alone, 26% improved; of those treated with a combination of psychotropic drugs and behavior modification, 96% improved; and 21% remitted spontaneously without any treatment. However, there was a subset of 52 severely self-injurious clients whose behavior improved only temporarily. A 2-year follow-up (Schroeder et al., 1982a) showed that all but two of them had at least one serious relapse, which required an active behavior management program. Eight years later, all of them required a high-level behavioral management programs. So we were able to stifle but not eliminate the self-injurious behavior of these chronic severe cases. These results have sent us back to the drawing board to take a closer look at the forms and functions of antecedent factors, both behavioral and biological, which set the occasion for self-injurious behavior.

4.1.5. Is Self-Injurious Behavior Preventable?

It is useful just to consider what different treatment outcome possibilities there are for preventing self-injurious behavior successfully. In preventive medicine treatment outcomes can be organized into a hierarchy (Crocker & Nelson, 1983). It seems appropriate to cast treatment goals in terms of primary, secondary, and tertiary preventions, since the ultimate goal of all self-injurious behavior treatments is to reduce the risk of the client's injuring her/himself.

But are there risk factors, which, if averted, would decrease the probability of onset of self-injurious behavior? Both prevalence studies and stimulus control studies of self-injurious behavior suggest that there are. Prevalence of self-injurious behavior is positively associated with occurrence of severe schizophrenia, stereotyped behavior, aggressive behavior, communication deficits, neuropathology, early onset, length of institutionalization, and severity of intellectual disability (Baumeister & Rollings, 1976). Severity of self-injurious behavior is related to length of institutionalization, history of chronicity and number of organic disorders (Schroeder et al., 1980). In the following pages, we will present analyses of different intervention methods for preventing self-injurious behavior and its devastating effects.

4.1.6. Primary Prevention

Primary prevention refers to attempts to avoid the possibility of ever developing self-injurious behavior by treating another condition with which it is associated. Prototypic methodologies would be immunization, genetic counseling, and preventive education. Unfortunately, there is very little known about the primary prevention of self-injurious behavior that we can currently use in a clinical setting. This should not surprise us, since it is true for all forms of developmental handicap.

Genetic counseling strategies should be useful with developmental disorders like the Lesch–Nyhan syndrome, a genetic disorder of purine metabolism (Nyhan, 1967a), in which there is a very high incidence of self-injurious behavior. Pedigree studies (Nyhan, Pesek, Sweetman, Carpenter, & Carter, 1967b) show that it tends to run in families and therefore could be prevented by avoiding pregnancy. Prenatal genetic diagnosis and pre-implantation genetic diagnosis can also be very helpful in avoiding the genetic disorders with a high incidence of self-injurious behavior. Gene therapy is likely to be possible for single gene disorders like Lesch–Nyhan syndrome in the future (Moser, 1995), but not for multiple gene disorders.

There are a variety of animal models of neuropathological function in which self-injurious behavior can be produced or stopped by neuropharmacological intervention (Schroeder, 1984). For example, if a developing rat is given a high dose (100 mg) of 6-hydroxydopamine at the age of 5 days, he is made permanently hyperactive and aggressive. The same dose at any other developmental stage does not produce this effect (Shaywitz, Yager, & Klopper, 1976). Thus, it may be that certain drugs affecting neurotransmitter function, if given at a particular developmental age, create a lesion in the CNS, which increases the life-long risk of self-injurious behavior, which could have been avoided. We have discussed these models further in Chapter 2.

There is some evidence that sensory deprivation in an impoverished environment sets the occasion for self-injurious behavior (Berkson & Mason, 1964a, 1964b; Green, 1967) and that certain environments may be pathogenic for self-injurious behavior. From a primary prevention standpoint, it is difficult to study the onset of self-injurious behavior. If observed clinically in humans, there is strong ethical pressure to treat it. However, there is considerable support from primate research (Davenport & Berkson, 1963; Erwin, Mitchell, & Maple, 1973; Gluck & Sackett, 1974; Turner & Lewis, 2002) that maternal deprivation and isolate-rearing produce a syndrome of retarded development, depression, and stereotyped self-injurious behavior. Generalization from monkeys to humans, however, must be made with caution. For instance, selective breeding experiments in monkeys suggest that temperament of the caregiver and a predisposition on the part of the offspring may be setting conditions for such impoverishment to have a serious effect (Sackett, 1968). Such conditions could be prevented through preventive education of caregivers.

In summary, from prevalence studies we know of a number of risk factors, (i.e., psychosis, stereotyped behavior, communication deficits, neuropathology, severity of retardation, early onset, and length of institutionalization) which have a higher frequency among severe chronic self-injurious behavior cases. Yet we know very little about the onset (i.e., incidence) of self-injurious behavior. There are several models (mostly animal) available to study incidence, but the greatest push for new knowledge will have to come from the field of behavioral epidemiology. At this point in the study of self-injurious behavior, the behavioral epidemiology of the incidence of self-injurious behavior should be one of our top priorities.

4.1.7. Secondary Prevention

By secondary prevention we mean intervention by early screening, identification, and special support to avert risk of greater handicap later in life. Prototypical procedures would be newborn screening, early identification, and remediation of a deficit that has already occurred, so that resulting handicaps are avoided. A good example is newborn screening. For instance, there are now approximately 100,000,000 newborn babies screened for phenylketonuria (PKU) around the world. If the baby is not treated with special low phenylalanine diet, he or she will have intellectual disability later in life. If treated, the baby is likely to grow up with fairly normal intelligence. A good behavioral example is that it has been shown that babies who are born with a number of perinatal risk factors will likely grow up to be of normal intelligence if they are raised in nur-turant, middle socioeconomic status homes, but not if they are raised in impoverished lower socioeconomic status homes (Sameroff & Chandler, 1976). Early risk can often be changed through biological and environmental early intervention.

Whether early identification and intervention can head off later self-injurious be-havior is still largely a matter of speculation. One often hears the hope expressed by desperate parents and burnt out service providers that we ought to try to catch it early "before it becomes such an ingrained habit." Unfortunately, by the time it becomes a matter of intervention, it usually is a deeply ingrained habit, so we have not had the opportunity to observe whether development of self-injurious behavior follows a steep or flat learning curve. A variety of possibilities exist. Parents, when interviewed, often relate its onset to a traumatic incident (e.g., high temperature or a grand mal seizure) that happened early in life and "everything was down hill after that." Whether these descriptions culled from long-term memories are merely coincidental is impossible to determine. However, there are a variety of biological and behavioral antecedents, which, if manipulated, reduce the incidence of self-injurious behavior.

There are three classes of biological conditions, which, if treated, tend to reduce the probability of self-injurious behavior: physiological state conditions, sensory integra-tion, and neurochemical imbalance. They therefore could be high-priority targets for prevention of self-injurious behavior.

4.1.7.1. Physiologic State Conditions

There is evidence that in some self-injurious behavior clients, reduction of physiological arousal (Guess & Carr, 1991; Freeman, Horner, & Reichle, 2002; Romanczyk, Gordon, Crimmins, Wenzel, & Kistner, 1980, 1982), hypertension, and endogenous depression are correlated with a marked decrease in self-injurious behavior. The issue of mental illness among persons with intellectual disability is currently a topic of great interest. Clearly, there is much to be learned from combining these approaches for self-injurious behavior clients. While they may not fully account for the development and persistence of a particular self-injurious behavior topography, it is very likely that they can be strong setting factors for someone who is already inclined to perform self-injurious behavior.

4.1.7.2. Sensory Integration

There has been considerable interest in the application of Ayres' (1979) sensory inte-gration theory to decreasing the motivation for self-injurious behavior (Lemke & Mitchell, 1972). The relevance of Ayres' theory seems to lie in the emphasis on the development of the kinesthetic sense through vestibular stimulation. In this context, self-injurious behavior is a subset of stereotyped motor behaviors such as those seen in normal infants (Kravitz, Rosenthal, Teplitz, Murphy, & Lesser, 1960; Thelen, 1979), which presumably are superseded by normal motor development and tend to disappear by age 5 (de Lissavoy, 1961). The persistence of such movements in persons with intellectual disabilities reflects delayed development of integrated motor movements, which might be remediated by controlled vestibular stimulation. There is substantial evidence that vestibular stimulation enhances motor development of preambulatory normally developing and developmentally delayed children (Chee, Kreutzberg, & Clark, 1978; Clark, Kreutzberg, & Chee, 1977; Kantner, Clark, Allen, & Chase, 1976). In a well-controlled study MacLean and Baumeister (1981) did a clinical trial of vestibular stimulation in a motorized chair with four preambulatory severely developmentally delayed boys aged 17–41 months who had high rate stereotyped behaviors. They found large gains in motor and reflex development, but these gains were not necessarily correlated with a decrease in stereotyped behavior. One boy showed a substantial decrease and the others did not. So there is only weak support for the hypothesis. MacLean and Baumeister (1981) suggest that their results might have been confounded with other covariant organic conditions, like hydrocephalus, Down syndrome, etc. Nevertheless, to the extent that some self-injurious behavior overlaps with stereotyped behavior, there is substantial theoretical support for the notion that vestibular stimulation promotes motor coordination, kinesthesis, and therefore, modulation of sensory input, which may be the discriminative stimulus for self-injurious behavior.

A related notion is that self-injurious stereotyped behaviors are maintained by the sensory reinforcement resulting from performing self-injurious behavior (e.g., head banging). The technique of sensory extinction (Rincover, 1978) is based on the assumption that removing the source of sensory reinforcement (e.g., by using a padded surface) would prevent head banging from occurring. This technique has been successful in a number of experiments (Ornitz, Brown, Sorosky, Ritvo, & Dietrich, 1970; Rincover, Newsom, & Carr, 1979; Rincover, Cook, Peoples, & Packard, 1979) and should be examined further. In particular, it would be helpful to clarify the operational definition and variables related to sensory reinforcement of self-injurious behavior. Also, the main findings have not been widely replicated. This procedure definitely needs to be investigated in younger children at risk for self-injurious behavior, because it is one of the most frequently but inconsistently used methods because of its non-invasive nature.

4.1.7.3. Neurochemical Models Related to Early Development

The study of the neurochemical correlates of self-injurious behavior is one of the most exciting areas of research in this field. We have reviewed this work frequently (Baumeister et al., 1984; Schroeder, 1984; Schroeder, Breese, & Mueller, 1990; Schroeder & Tessel, 1994; Schroeder et al., 1999; and Chapter 2, this book). In the following sections, we will only touch upon three neurochemical models of self-injurious behavior on which there are some human data: (1) the dopamine receptor super-sensitivity model, (2) the Lesch–Nyhan syndrome, and (3) the opioid peptide blockade model.

The few autopsies that have been done have revealed no morphological differences (e.g., lesions, missing parts, etc.) between the brains of self-injurious behavior cases and those of other people who had not had a history of chronic self-injurious behavior. However, Lloyd et al. (1981) in a postmortem examination of the brains of three Lesch–Nyhan patients found a large loss of dopamine receptors in the basal ganglia that subcortical part of the brain thought to be responsible for the coordination and modulation of integrated motor activity. A malfunction of the receptors serving these areas of the brain might be the occasion for aberrant movements such as self-injurious be-havior. So, self-injurious behavior may be the result of faulty neurotransmitter function at receptor sites on the synapses of neurons in these mesolimbic areas of the brain.

4.1.7.3.1. Dopaminergic Super-Sensitivity Model

The dopaminergic super-sensitivity model was proposed by Lewis and Baumeister (1982) for stereotyped behavior, some of which is self-injurious. The basic idea is that, if synaptic transmission of dopamine is blocked for a time either through disuse or by denervation of postsynaptic receptor sites, an imbalance occurs such that an exagger-ated response results when synaptic transmission finally does occur. Most of this work has been done in animals as one might expect. However, there are two types of human analogue research on self-injurious behavior that may prove fruitful (1) studies of self-injurious behavior clients who are receiving chronic doses of neuroleptic medications and (2) studies on the effects of exercise on self-injurious behavior. It is well known that neuroleptic drugs, i.e., major tranquilizers such as thioridazine (Mellaril), haloperidol (Haldol), and chlorpromazine (Thorazine), inhibit the release of dopamine in the me-solimbic system in the basal ganglia. A major current concern over chronic admin-istration is that it causes tardive dyskinesia and a number of other movement disorders (Gualtieri, Quade, Hicks, Mayo, & Schroeder, 1984). However, it may also cause a behavioral super-sensitivity (Schroeder & Gualtieri, 1985) that may exacerbate the performance of stereotyped self-injurious behavior when situational demands are made on the client. These effects may be seen after prolonged use of the drug or when drug holidays are given. However, in the early neuroleptic withdrawal studies we have performed (Schroeder, 1984), we have seen multiple effects involving (a) withdrawal symptoms like nausea, vomiting, sleeplessness, and irritability; (b) tardive dyskinesia in about one-third of the clients; and (c) either an increase or decrease in self-injurious behavior of the clients. At present we are not sure whether these are rate-dependent effects or whether they are related to dose. It may be that there is a therapeutic window in which self-injurious behavior is increased at low doses and suppressed at high doses. The converse may occur when chronic doses of the drug are withdrawn.

In a system as complex as the brain where all subsystems are interconnected, it is difficult to isolate a selective effect on self-injurious behavior. But if there is any evidence for selective effects of neuroleptics on human behavior of persons with de-velopmental disabilities, it is on voluntary movements and stereotyped behaviors of which self-injurious behavior may sometimes be a subset (Davis, Sprague, & Werry, 1969; Heistad & Zimmermann, 1979; Hollis, 1968; Hollis & St. Omer, 1972; Singh & Aman, 1981; Zimmermann & Heistad, 1982). If there prove to be more reliable effects with atypical antipsychotics (Aman & Madrid, 1999), they are likely to be complex interactions with other neurotransmitter functions and environmental events.

4.1.7.3.2. The Serotonin Model

Serotonergic mechanisms in Lesch–Nyhan syndrome is another neurochemical model of significance (Nyhan et al., 1980). Nyhan et al. (1980) suggest that the disruption in balance between functions of serotonin, dopamine, and acetycholine may account for some of the choreathetoid movements observed in the self-injurious behavior of

Lesch–Nyhan patients. The autopsy studies by Lloyd et al. (1981), which we previously cited, support such a notion. The case of Lesch–Nyhan syndrome is interesting, in that, like PKU, we know that the biochemical defect is failure to produce an enzyme (HPRT) which results in an overproduction of uric acid and its excess accumulation in body fluids. But, unlike PKU, attempts to block the effect by reducing uric acid levels with allopurinol, does not prevent intellectual disability, cerebral palsy, choreoathetosis, or self-injurious behavior that occurs in Lesch–Nyhan syndrome. Giving clients L-5hydroxytryptophan (L-5-HTP) might prevent the CNS dysfunction in serotonin regulation related to self-injurious behavior. Unfortunately, human studies in which this was tried (Mizuno & Yugari, 1974, 1975; Nyhan et al., 1980) have shown only temporary effects. Other investigators have failed to find any effect of L-5-HTP treatment (Ciaranello, Anders, Barchas, Berger, & Cann, 1976). The relation of serotonin to self-injurious behavior in Lesch–Nyhan syndrome is currently an area of intense interest among animal researchers, and we should be seeing some clearer results in the near future.

4.1.7.3.3. Opiod Peptide Model

A third neurochemical model for self-injurious behavior is based on the possibility that a disturbed endogenous opiate system characterized by increased levels of β-endorphin creates a condition which could mediate and/or maintain self-injurious behavior (i.e., by elevating the threshold for pain or by increasing the tolerance for self-injurious behavior in an addictive sense). Many neurons in the mesolimbic dopamine pathway also contain these opioid peptide receptors. Naloxone (or its orally administered counterpart Naltrexone), a drug that inhibits release of β-endorphin, should prevent this tolerance for self-injurious behavior. So far there is some evidence for this hypothesis from controlled clinical trials and some evidence against it. Sandman et al. (1983) also noted that the strongest responders to naltrexone did not show a response to other analgesics, such as morphine. Thus, paradoxical responders to analgesics may form a subset of self-injurious behavior cases with an abnormal opioid peptide system, which might place them at risk for self-injurious behavior. Naltrexone might prevent self-injurious behavior by inhibiting this system. This is certainly a tempting hypothesis, since naltrexone is a short-acting drug with few side effects. For the present, the support in human research for the opioid peptide blockade model for self-injurious behavior is still growing, but promising. For an excellent analytic review of the efficacy of naltrexone treatment, see Symons et al. (2004).

4.1.8. Tertiary (Behaviorally Based) Prevention

We have performed several reviews of the behavioral interventions used to prevent tissue damage resulting from self-injurious behavior, and we have conducted many empirical studies of older children and adults in this area. Almost all of these studies are based on secondary and tertiary prevention strategies. Very few are aimed at trying to prevent self-injurious behavior from developing into a serious chronic condition. In a brief summary, these behavioral studies suggest that nearly every behavioral modification technique tried can be effective in subduing self-injurious behavior. But few studies have shown generalization and maintenance of effects beyond a year. It seems likely that, as our current review shows, there are chronic biological risk factors which, when combined with environmental setting factors, can predispose an infant/child to develop self-injurious behavior.

There are only three published controlled studies of functional communication training as an early intervention for self-injurious behavior, aggressive behavior, and destructive behavior exhibited by birth-to-three children with developmental disabilities ([381]Kurtz et al., 2003; Richman, Teichman, & Kolb, 2006; Wacker et al., 1998). The first by Wacker et al. (1998) conducted functional analyses and long-term functional communication training (FCT) for maladaptive behavior displayed by young children with disabilities. Parents of 28 children with developmental disabilities were trained to conduct functional analyses and functional communication treatment for their child's maladaptive behavior. Children ranged in age from 23 to 64 months, and home treatments lasted from 3 to 13 months. Most problem behaviors exhibited by this population were maintained by social consequences. Of this sample, parents implemented FCT for up to one year. FCT consisted of teaching the children to make requests for the same type of social consequences that were found to maintain their problem behavior. Treatment resulted in an 87% reduction in maladaptive behaviors across participants, and appropriate social behaviors (e.g., toy play, positive social collateral behavior such as smiling) increased by 69%. Parents also rated the assessment and treatment procedures as highly acceptable.

Similarly, Kurtz et al. (2003) studied 30 young children aged 10–48 months with varying degrees of intellectual abilities (i.e., no developmental delays to profound developmental delays). Results of the functional analyses indicated that a source of reinforcement for self-injurious behavior was identified for 62.1% of the children (positive reinforcement = 37.8%; negative reinforcement = 3.4%; positive and negative reinforcement = 7%, non-socially mediated = 13.8%). The remaining children (37.9%) demonstrated an undifferentiated pattern of responding during the functional analysis. This result suggested that the children failed to discriminate the contingencies tested in the assessment conditions, or that these behaviors were also non-socially mediated. FCT was prescribed for 17 of the 24 participants who completed the treatment analysis phase of the study. Once again, FCT was found to be a highly effective treatment for socially mediated self-injurious behavior, with an average 95% reduction of self-injurious behavior from baseline rates. Collectively, these studies support the effectiveness of FCT for treatment of socially mediated problem behavior in young children. Given these findings, along with the finding that the majority of self-injurious behavior is maintained by social functions in school-aged children and adults with developmental disabilities, it makes intuitive sense to study whether early intensive FCT can prevent the development of socially mediated self-injurious behavior.

A recent follow-up study by Wacker, Berg, and Harding (2006) suggests that the children in their study are still doing well. Hopefully the authors will continue to follow up on these children later in life.

Richman et al. (2006) published a preliminary report of an ongoing project on six children (mean age of 22 months) with developmental disabilities who exhibited non-socially mediated proto-self-injurious behavior. The treatment package consisted of response blocking of self-injurious behavior, redirecting behavior in an enriched environment, and increasing the person's response repertoire for requesting socially reinforcing consequences via early augmentative FCT. A 71% reduction (range 39–98%) in self-injurious behavior from baseline levels occurred in all participants. All of them quickly learned to mand during FCT. These children are now undergoing follow-up observations, but the data appear promising.

4.1.9. Summary – Prevention and Early Intervention

The area of early identification and intervention with self-injurious behavior is in its infancy. This area is likely to be one of the most important domains for future research and development, both for humanitarian and economic reasons. Preventive techniques for averting self-injurious behavior or preventing its development would avoid much human suffering and be much more cost-effective than current methods. We have reviewed a wealth of evidence, neurobiological, bio-behavioral, and behavioral, which supports these assertions. Yet there are only a few controlled studies that have been performed. This is one area of self-injurious behavior that is likely to grow substantially in the next decade.

4.2. Management and Treatment

4.2.1. Historical Overview

The treatment of self-injurious behavior historically played a significant role in the development of all treatments for people with developmental disabilities. Thompson and Caruso (2002) give an interesting account of early treatments going back to the 1700s. The modern era for research on the experimental psychology of intellectual and developmental disabilities dates back to the late 1940s at the end of World War II (Routh & Schroeder, 2003), which is where we will begin. Psychology of intellectual disabilities at that time was mostly concentrated on basic research characterizing the conditions.

The subfield of Behavior Analysis led by Bijou and colleagues (Bijou, 1966) based at Rainier School in Washington, by Sidman (Sidman & Stoddard, 1966) at Fernald School in Boston, and by Spradlin (1963) at the Parsons State Hospital and Training Center in Kansas focused not only on basic research, but also on treatment. In addition, there were several trends from different fields that converged to revolutionize the treatment of people with intellectual and developmental disabilities, including their self-injurious behavior.

4.2.1.1. Background
In the late 1940s and 1950s, the prevailing approach to treating people with intellectual and developmental disabilities was custodial care in large congregate facilities, often called State Institutions. People were removed from society and frequently their care

was deplorable. Hoyt and Spradlin (2006) give a graphic account of what it was like trying to build treatment programs in such pathogenic environments in that era. It was an uphill battle, even with federal grant funding. One of the first federal grants to fund such research came from the National Institute of Mental Health (NIMH) to the University of Kansas in 1958, to develop a language and communication training program for people with severe intellectual disabilities.

At that time, it was not widely believed that such people could learn skills systematically or could be trained to communicate effectively or to care for themselves independently. Ayllon and Michael (1959) had published the effective use of a token economy in managing a ward for people with mental illness at Anna State Hospital. Mimosa Cottage at Parsons State Hospital in Kansas (Girardeau & Spradlin, 1964) and the token economy at Murdoch Center in North Carolina (Birnbrauer & Lawler, 1964) were two of the first databased demonstrations of teaching basic self-help skills to severely and profoundly retarded people. These were break-throughs that gave great optimism to some people of even "curing" intellectual disability, and they were the supporting evidence for the deinstitutionalization movement later.

The first functional analysis of self-injurious behavior is usually attributed to Skinner (1953, pp. 366–367) in *Science and Human Behavior*, in which he explained how self-injurious behavior could become a discriminative stimulus for positive reinforcement. One of the first demonstrations of operant control of self-injurious behavior among people with intellectual and developmental disabilities was by Lovaas et al. (1965), published in the *Journal of Experimental Child Psychology*. Lovaas was a graduate of Bijou's Rainier Group who had moved to University of California, Los Angeles (UCLA), to start a center for treating autism. This heuristic paper contained the analysis of several functions of self-injurious behavior which would be precursors to the development of later procedures for treating it: (1) the effects of presentation and withdrawal of positive reinforcement contingent upon self-injurious behavior; (2) the effects of ignoring it (extinction); (3) the effects of differential stimulus control procedures; (4) the effects of differentially reinforcing of other and of incompatible behaviors; and (5) the effects of punishment on self-injurious behavior. A year later Tate and Baroff (1966) published in *Behavior Research and Therapy* a dramatic demonstration of suppression of self-injurious behavior in a severe case using a hand-held electric shock device. As mentioned earlier, they are frequently credited with the most often-used definition of self-injurious behaviors, i.e., acts directed toward one's self that result in tissue damage. It became clear that much of self-injurious behavior could be modified through a variety of behavioral interventions.

Many procedural refinements followed in the next decade and during the 1970s. These and other experiments gave rise to the first analytic review by Bachman (1972) of the functions of self-injurious behavior and their relationship to treatment effectiveness. Bachman's analysis was elaborated by Carr (1977), one of Lovaas' students, in an influential paper published in the *Psychological Bulletin*, entitled, "The Motivation of Self-Injurious Behavior," which pulled all of these previous behavioral studies into a cohesive rationale. It laid the groundwork for Iwata's approach to functional analysis of self-injurious behavior (Iwata, Dorsey, Slifer, Bauman, & Richman, 1982), which is treated in detail in the next section (4.2.2.).

4.2.1.2. Emerging Trends

The post–WWII war era also gave rise to several other trends that deeply influenced the treatment of people with intellectual disabilities in general and those with self-injurious behavior in particular.

4.2.1.2.1. Parent Advocacy and Legal Rights

Parent and professional coalitions, like the *National Association for Retarded Children* (later renamed ARC-US) and the *American Association on Mental Deficiency* (renamed in 2006 the American Association on Intellectual Developmental Disabilities), began to fight for community programs as well as for the right to treatment and education based upon the results they saw coming from behavioral research. The first and most influential of these advocacy efforts was Wyatt v. Stickney (1972), a class action suit against the State of Alabama, which articulated the right to treatment and freedom from restraints for people with developmental and intellectual disabilities. A rash of similar lawsuits quickly spread to almost every State in the U.S. after that.

Another very influential such class action suit was Haldeman v. Pennhurst State School and Hospital (1977), a State Institution in Philadelphia, Pennsylvania, in which the judge upheld the plaintiffs' view that the restrictedness of institutional environments was unconstitutional. This judgment led to a flood of reviews of many institutions in the U.S. by the Department of Justice and then led to their subsequent closure. Since that time, institutional populations for intellectual and developmental disabilities in the U.S. have decreased by more than 70% (Lakin et al., 2004). Their residents, including severe cases of self-injurious behavior, are being served in the community. This circumstance led to rethinking how effective behavioral procedures for treating self-injurious behavior which are also socially acceptable to local communities, can be implemented in a less-controlled environment. It was one of the main reasons for development of the *Positive Behavior Support Movement*, as we shall see below.

4.2.1.2.2. Behavioral Intervention in State Residential Facilities

Much of the early behavior analytic research on a variety of procedures for treating self-injurious behavior occurred in State residential facilities and in group homes in the community. Given the chaotic nature of some of these environments, the tendency was to develop specialized units where the ecology could be arranged suitably and treatment fidelity could be monitored. One of the authors (S. R. Schroeder) together with James A. Mulick and later J. Rojahn developed such a program on a Hospital Improvement Grant to Murdoch Center from 1974 to 1977. Much useful research came from this Self-Injurious Behavior Unit, which adapted procedures developed by Wahler, House, and Stambaugh (1976) and others, called ecobehavioral analysis (see Rogers-Warren & Warren, 1977, for an extensive review). Examples of such studies were exploration of the effects of toy availability on effectiveness of time-out for self-injurious behavior (Solnick, Rincover, & Peterson, 1977) and the relative effectiveness of differential reinforcement of incompatible versus other behaviors (DRI vs. DRO) on self-injurious behavior (Tarpley & Schroeder, 1979; Mulick, Schroeder, & Rojahn, 1980). Some of the first published antecedent-based treatments for self-injurious behavior were developed in this self-injurious behavior unit: the effects of self-protective devices on clients with self-injurious behavior and their caregivers (Rojahn, Mulick, McCoy, & Schroeder, 1978), and assessing a variety of environmental antecedents that affect management and maintenance of self-injurious behavior (Schroeder et al., 1982a, 1982b). It also included early research on the utility of replacement behavior, namely reducing self-injurious behavior by increasing toy play (Mulick et al., 1978).

Functional analysis methodology at that time was mainly modeled after that of Bijou et al. (1968). The Center for the Study of Self-Injury at the Kennedy Center at Johns Hopkins University, to which Iwata moved from Western Michigan University in 1978, evolved from the work in the Murdoch Self-Injurious Behavior Unit and other such self-injurious behavior units across the country. Our research on the severe problems with generalization and maintenance of our self-injurious behavior programs led us to discourage the formation of specialized units in the future and to integrate our treatments into the general population.

4.2.1.2.3. Behavioral and Bio-Behavioral Research Professions

The 1960s began an era of tremendous growth and expansion. During the Kennedy Administration, the President's Committee on Intellectual disability (PCMR), the National Institute for Child Health and Human Development (NICHD), the University Affiliated Programs (renamed AUCD in 2000) were founded. Intellectual disability research centers were funded by NICHD. Later the Bureau of Education of the Handicapped was started in the Department of Education. Thus, funding of research and training programs in developmental and intellectual disabilities became available.

Important professional organizations were founded to accommodate the influx of professionals into the field. Two important behavioral organizations were: the *Association for Behavioral Analysis* (ABA), with a strictly operant behavioral ideology and methodology, formalized in 1972, with its two lead journals, the *Journal of the Experimental Analysis of Behavior* (JEAB), an outlet for basic research, and the *Journal of Applied Behavior Analysis* (JABA), the latter first published in 1968. Another major professional behavioral organization is the *American Association for Behavior Therapy* (AABT), with its lead journal, *Behavior Research and Therapy* (BRAT), first published in 1962. AABT has a broader audience with more eclectic interests, including psychometric, physiological, interview-based measures, as well as direct observations of behavior, which accept both group- and single-subject methodologies. Since that time, many other journals, such as *Research in Developmental Disabilities* and handbooks on behavioral assessment and intervention have been published to assist the growth and development of the behavioral profession. This has been a major factor in the treatment of self-injurious behavior.

Behavioral Assessment really developed as a formal field within AABT as a reaction to traditional psychodynamic methods of assessment. Hans Eysenck, the first editor of BRAT, championed this new empirically based approach, which has been a significant contribution to the field, including self-injurious behavior research. There now exist a variety of validated instruments for assessing the functions of different self-injurious behavior behavioral phenotypes (see Chapter 3, this book), which have helped to guide treatment.

The early days of behavior analysis and intervention were spent on many methodological issues, e.g., appropriate methods for calculating observer reliability, effects of observer presence on intervention, laboratory analogue studies versus naturalistic setting studies, effects of treatment packages versus reductionistic analyses of single independent variables. With respect to self-injurious behavior, Thorndike's Law of Effect was replicated repeatedly in many different settings, and the variety of innovative procedures to suppress self-injurious behavior, especially punishment, proliferated. Pressure to leave the laboratory and go into the schools and home to conduct more socially valid work increased (Wolf, 1978; Kazdin & Matson, 1981). Attention to antecedents underlying the functions of self-injurious behavior, and Carr's (1977) analysis of the motivation of behavior continued to be ignored. Although Iwata et al. (1982) had published a structured analogue laboratory method to functionally analyze some of the major antecedents of self-injurious behavior and then to hypothesize a related appropriate in vivo intervention, this method did not really catch on until the early 1990s.

Bio-behavioral research on self-injurious behavior began to appear in the 1960s with the publication of Nyhan's research on Lesch–Nyhan syndrome (Lesch and Nyhan, 1964). It remained essentially biomedically oriented until the 1980s, when Sandman's first study appeared in 1981 at the Gatlinburg Conference on Research in Intellectual disability and Developmental Disabilities. He showed a dose effect of naloxone for treatment of self-injurious behavior. As discussed in Chapter 2, he proposed an addiction hypothesis and altered pain sensitivity hypothesis of self-injurious behavior (Sandman et al., 1983). Lewis and Baumeister (1982) published an important theoretical paper on dopamine super-sensitivity and repetitive self-injurious behavior, and suggested dopamine-blocking agents as a treatment. Animal models of self-injurious behavior began to be researched in earnest. Another concept paper by Cataldo and Harris (1982) summarized a variety of possible biological antecedents of self-injurious behavior. Since then, there has been a large increase in this work (see Schroeder et al., 2002 for an extensive review). Much of this information is summarized in Section 4.b.4. on psychopharmacology later in this chapter.

4.2.1.2.4. The Aversives Controversy

The counterintuitive nature of self-injurious behavior and its sources of motivation have raised ethical questions over the past three decades about legitimate methods to treat it. Since self-injurious behavior usually does not involve hurting others, although sometimes it can disrupt the immediate environment, the question arose at what point is it ethical to intervene and how intrusive should the permitted methods be? Some of the earliest demonstrations of the use of electric shock punishment procedures to suppress self-injurious behavior on extremely severe cases, though effective, also caused concern about their effects upon the therapists (e.g., Tate & Baroff, 1966; Baroff & Tate, 1968). Nevertheless, research on a variety of punishment procedures with different degrees of aversiveness, e.g., time-out, overcorrection, contingent restraint, proliferated during the 1970s and 1980s (see Sections A, B of this chapter).

By the 1980s, concerns about the social validity of many punishment procedures and about the dearth of research on positive reinforcement procedures raised ethical questions by some professional organizations, especially *The Association for the Severely*

Handicapped (TASH). The development of an automated head-mounted system to deliver shocks contingent upon self-injurious behavior at the Applied Physics Lab at Johns Hopkins University in 1982 was the proximate occasion for these organizations to mobilize in protest of all punishment procedures. For an excellent historical account of the development of the Self-Injurious Behavior Inhibiting System (SIBIS), see Iwata (1988). Behavior modification specialists were even accused of torturing their clients (Turnbull et al., 1986).

Several textbooks emerged contending that aversive procedures and ABA did not work and that "non-aversive" procedures alone were sufficient for treating self-injurious behavior effectively (e.g., LaVigna & Donnellan, 1986; Evans & Meyer, 1985). The evidence for this position was thin at this point in time, compared to the evidence for the effectiveness of punishment procedures. The argument became vitriolic, reaching a fever pitch by the end of the decade (Schroeder & Schroeder, 1989).

In late 1989, the NICHD convened a Consensus Development Conference in which a comprehensive review of all of the evidence was made. NICHD (1991) then published recommendations for future directions for research on intervention procedures on destructive behavior (aggressive behavior, self-injurious behavior, and property destruction). These were very contentious proceedings, which did not produce a consensus in the field, but the recommendation concerning the need for more research on effective positive intervention procedures was heeded. Also, Repp and Singh (1990) published a compendium of opposing opinions on the aversive controversy, which helped to clarify the issues. We will review some of these issues in Section 4.d. of this chapter.

In the 1990s, the use of non-aversive procedures was recast as "Positive Behavior Support" (PBS) (Horner et al., 1990; Koegel, Koegel, & Dunlap, 1996). This important move put the emphasis on developing appropriate research on positive intervention procedures that would be acceptable to consumers in all settings in the community. Since that time, the amount of research on positive behavior intervention procedures has increased substantially (Carr et al., 1999a; Marquis et al., 2000) and the use of positive behavioral procedures has largely replaced the use of aversive procedures in most self-injurious behavior cases (Kahng, Iwata, & Lewin, 2002).

PBS also implies the modification of the whole environmental ecology surrounding self-injurious behavior cases, in addition to specific behavioral intervention techniques. This is not an entirely new idea (Wahler et al., 1976; Rogers-Warren & Warren, 1977; Schroeder, Mulick, & Schroeder, 1979), but the broad scope and scale with which PBS researchers promoted the application of PBS is new. There are now systems-level PBS interventions in whole school systems (Anderson & Kincaid, 2005) and whole statewide service systems (Freeman et al., 2005), some of which are impressive.

Some investigators (e.g., Carr, 1997) hold that PBS is a distinct new discipline, which has replaced ABA as the procedure of choice, while other PBS devotees view it as an extension of ABA (Horner, 2000). There is still much controversy over the robustness of the effectiveness of PBS procedures when used alone (see Johnston, Foxx, Jacobson, Green, & Mulick, 2006 for an excellent critical review and analysis), whether it is a new science, or whether it is a just a broader extension of ABA to the service system (Wacker & Berg, 2002).

4.2.2. Applied Behavior Analysis

Several excellent articles giving a historical account of applied behavior analysis of self-injurious behavior have been published in recent years (Kahng et al., 2002; Pelios, Morren, Tesch, & Axelrod, 1999; Hanley et al., 2003). Although many other journals have published papers on applied behavior analysis, viewing its history with regard to the treatment of self-injurious behavior research through the prism of articles that appeared in the flagship *Journal of Applied Behavior Analysis* (JABA) may provide an interesting look at the birth of a field.

In the first JABA article on a behavioral treatment of self-injurious behavior Lovaas and Simmons (1969) reported self-injurious behavior by three children diagnosed with intellectual disabilities in response to various antecedent or consequent condition manipulations. Socially isolating two of the children for 90 min/day on consecutive days produced reduction in self-injurious behavior rates from nearly 900 to zero per day in 11 days for one child, and from 2,750 hits per day to nearly zero in 53 days for the second child. Next, during selected sessions interspersed among baseline conditions "painful" electric shock was applied contingent upon self-injurious behavior and immediate suppression of self-injurious behavior was seen for all three children. However, the effects were setting-specific, which necessitated the application of contingent shock in additional settings as well to generalize the effect. The authors also demonstrated that contingent social attention produced increases in rate of self-injurious behavior. The three experiments contained in this article might be considered to present a form of functional analysis rather than treatment (Lovaas & Simmons, 1969, p. 144).

The next self-injurious behavior JABA article examined a potential operant etiology and stimulus control in two rhesus monkeys (Schaefer, 1970). Also not a demonstration of treatment efficacy, this study showed differential response rates of self-injurious behavior in relation to differing stimulus conditions, with contingent attention producing the greatest rates of self-injurious behavior, and an attention satiation procedure producing rates approaching zero. Based on these findings, Schaefer (1970) suggested that attention given contingently on self-injurious behavior could potentially increase the rate of that behavior, and recommended that it is more advisable to use attention wisely in order to avoid the inadvertent strengthening of problem behavior.

Corte, Wolf, and Locke (1971) studied the effects of eliminating social consequences (social extinction), differential reinforcement of other behavior (DRO), and contingent electric shock contingent upon for self-injurious behavior in four children with intellectual disabilities. Their study did not include pre-intervention functional assessment. Contingent electric shock was found to be the most effective, while DRO produced only a moderate effect when pre-session deprivation of the putative reinforcer was in place (and no effect when no deprivation had been arranged). Social extinction produced no effect.

White, Nielsen, and Johnson (1972) conducted a dose study of varying isolation time-out durations on a group of problem behaviors (which included self-injurious behavior) in children diagnosed with intellectual disabilities. They counterbalanced 1, 15, and 30 min of contingent time-out, and interspersed baseline sessions for each of three groups of children. The authors found that longer time-out durations produced greater suppression than one-minute time-out for two groups, and all time-out durations produced suppression in the third group.

Repp and Deitz (1974) found that contingently saying "no" following self-injurious behavior in combination with a DRO procedure (i.e., candy was delivered following period without self-injurious behavior) significantly reduced the rates of self-injurious behavior to almost zero per minute. No pre-intervention identification of maintaining variables was reported.

Tanner and Zeiler (1975) used aromatic ammonia vapors contingent on the self-injurious behavior of a young woman diagnosed with autism, and found the behavior was rapidly suppressed to zero rates within treatment sessions. Generalization of the suppressive effects to her living area was accomplished only when the procedure was extended there as well. Griffin, Locke, and Landers (1975) report rapid cessation of self-injurious behavior in a person diagnosed with blindness and intellectual disability when contingent electric shock was applied directly following that behavior, maintained when intensity of shock was lessened, and maintained at three years follow-up after electric shock was applied across settings contingent on behaviors that were preceding self-injurious behavior. Again, neither of these studies reported pre-intervention functional assessment or evaluation.

Favell, McGimsey, and Jones (1978) commented on the frequency with which published reports of treatment for self-injurious behavior among people with intellectual disabilities predominately used punishment or time-out procedures. Their person was a 15-year-old girl diagnosed with profound intellectual disability whose self-injurious behavior had previously been suppressed with electrical shock, but was managed immediately prior to the study with near constant restraint. Staff members who were working with the client reported her only preferred situation was to be in restraints. This led the investigators to consider the possibility that restraint contingent on short periods without self-injurious behavior (combined with access to leisure items between restraint periods), might reduce the frequency of self-injurious behavior. They compared three conditions, (1) no treatment, (2) contingent lemon juice to the mouth, and (3) contingent lemon juice to the mouth combined with restraint contingent on self-injurious behavior-free periods and free access to leisure items. They found that the third condition produced the greatest reduction in self-injurious behavior. They later demonstrated restraint to function as a reinforcer for a prevocational task for this girl, a finding that, at the time, was remarkable given the widespread use of restraint to decelerate self-injurious behavior.

Kazdin (1980) also expressed concern about the nature of treatments reported for problem behavior. He asked 88 undergraduate students to rate the acceptability of differential reinforcement of incompatible behavior (DRI), isolated time-out, pharmacotherapy, and contingent electric shock for behavior problems exhibited by children. DRI was considered to be most acceptable, followed by isolated time-out, and pharmacotherapy. Contingent electric shock was rated least acceptable. The same order of acceptability was found when the procedure was repeated and descriptions of severity of problem behavior were provided. Although indicative of the growing unease with aversive or punitive procedures in the general population, one has to point out that this study did not reflect the views of affected families.

Seeking a more benign suppressor for self-injurious behavior, Dorsey, Iwata, Ong, and McSween (1980) compared a procedure involving "mild verbal punishment" (contingently saying "no") with a combination of the mild verbal punishment procedure with contingent water misting. The authors did not report pre-intervention functional assessment or analysis. Whereas the "mild verbal punishment" procedure did not reduce frequency of self-injurious behavior, the combination with contingent water misting produced near zero rates. (Interestingly, subsequent data collection suggested that saying "no," alone, without water misting, did reduce the rate of self-injurious behavior in settings other than the treatment setting, perhaps suggesting that saying "no" had become a conditioned punisher during the combined treatment.)

Given the failure of the mild verbal punishment used by Dorsey et al. (1980), Dorsey, Iwata, Reid, and Davis (1982) reported a study on the continuous and contingent use of protective, mechanical restraining devices to decelerate self-injurious behavior. Without reporting pre-intervention functional assessment, these researchers found that providing leisure items in a noncontingent fashion, toys and edibles contingent on 30 s of toy play in the absence of self-injurious behavior, and a forcefully spoken "no" contingent on self-injurious behavior resulted in little toy play and high percentages of intervals with self-injurious behavior. When contingent water misting was added, self-injurious behavior was reduced by more than 50%. However, the greatest reduction of self-injurious behavior and the highest elevation in toy play occurred when the mechanical restraints were applied contingently for a minimum of two minutes followed by their removal after 30 s without self-injurious behavior, combined with toy removal during that time produced. While continuous restraint produced the greatest reduction in self-injurious behavior it precluded toy play. The effects of contingent restraint, toy removal, and toy access in absence of self-injurious behavior package were replicated when the procedures were implemented by non-professionals, which suggested some form of automatic generality of the effects. The investigators concluded that carefully implemented contingent restraint could be part of an effective treatment package for some individuals who exhibit self-injurious behavior, and that it could be argued to be less restrictive or aversive than contingent electric shock or water mist.

The fourth issue of JABA published in 1986 included two articles detailing treatment of self-injurious behavior. Neither reported pre-intervention functional assessment or functional analysis. Pace, Iwata, Edwards, and McCosh (1986) accredited the protective benefit of continuous restraining devices, but also pointed out the untoward physiological and social effects of such restraint. Their study documented differential reinforcement, prompting, and restraint-fading procedures that produced rates of self-injurious behavior approaching zero for both participants, while producing greatly increased object engagement rates for the person for whom this behavior was also targeted. Later in that issue, Singh, Watson, and Winton (1986) compared potential suppressive effects on self-injurious behavior of contingent water mist, facial screening, and forced arm exercise, in an effort to determine whether either of the latter procedures would be an equally effective but potentially less intrusive form of punishment for self-injurious behavior. Facial screening and forced arm exercise were both found to suppress self-injurious behavior to a greater extent than water misting.

Repp, Felce, and Barton (1988) published the first instance of an explicit pre-intervention functional assessment or functional analysis for self-injurious behavior to appear in JABA in 1988. First, they recorded the effects the presence or absence of environmental events on self-injurious behavior. Then they developed hypotheses regarding the contingencies that might be maintaining the behavior (e.g., positive reinforcement, negative reinforcement, or automatic reinforcement). Based on those hypotheses they developed a treatment that was logically consistent with or matching the hypotheses, and another that was not. Hypothesis consistent treatment achieved a more rapid reduction in self-injurious behavior than the one that was hypotheses independent. The age of function-relevant treatment was dawning. What follows next are descriptions of function-relevant treatments for self-injurious behavior that is maintained by differing variables.

There are several ways in which one can develop treatments on the basis of the functional properties of a targeted behavior. Repp et al. (1988) implemented procedures that eliminated the reinforcers of self-injurious behavior (e.g., extinction implemented when the behavior was found to be maintained by positive or negative reinforcement), or they provided alternative, external stimulation when the behavior was assumed to be maintained by sensory stimulation. Similarly, Anderson et al. (1999) recommended a "contingency reversal" strategy: Target behavior that used to be reinforced by social attention, now should not produce attention any longer; behavior that used to be ignored is now to be attended to; behavior that used to produce escape now must fail to do so. When done in the context of an baseline, treatment, baseline, treatment (ABAB) design, with baseline conditions consisting of analogue functional analysis sessions, implementing contingency reversal can provide an empirical demonstration of treatment efficacy before asking others (e.g., parents, teachers, day care providers, etc.) to implement procedures. If only procedures that are previously demonstrated as effective for that behavior of a given person are implemented valuable time, effort, and resources could be saved.

Even before the Iwata et al. (1982) functional analysis methodology was published Matson and Kazdin (1981) recommended conducting clinical trials of treatment procedures before pursuing widespread use. O'Neill et al. (1997) describe a method they term the *Competing Behavior Model*, the goal of which is to identify and train an appropriate or desirable behavior that could replace the target behavior. This involves several critical steps

- Identify the contingencies that are currently maintaining the problem behavior.
- identify an alternative behavior that is already in the person's behavioral repertoire that produces the same consequence as the problem behavior (functional equivalence).
- identify a second alternative behavior that could potentially be taught or reinforced, but which is either functionally equivalent or can be maintained by a different but powerful consequence.
- Identify methods by which the establishing operations, antecedents, the behaviors, and the functional consequences could be altered, so that the problem behavior becomes irrelevant, ineffective, or inefficient.

4.2.2.1. Principles of Accelerating and Decelerating Operations

Operations that involve the manipulation of consequences can involve either presentation/addition or removal/disappearance of events or stimuli. As a result of these repeated operations, an increase in response rate or the maintenance of responding, a decrease in response rate, or no change in response rate can be seen, over time.

The response-consequent addition of events that lead to an increase in response rate or to the maintenance of responding is called *positive reinforcement*. When response rate increases or maintains as a function of response-subsequent lessening or removal of events, we speak of *negative reinforcement*. When response rate decreases due to response-subsequent addition or removal (or lessening) of stimulation, we have *positive* or *negative punishment*, respectively. The terms *positive* and *negative*, of course, are used in an algebraic sense, rather than in a social sense. When the response rate remains unchanged despite response-contingent addition or removal of stimulation, neither reinforcement nor punishment has occurred. What follows is discussion of function-relevant treatment for self-injurious behavior found to be maintained by various types of accelerating or decelerating operations.

4.2.2.2. Interventions for Behavior Maintained by Positive Reinforcement

Socially mediated positive reinforcement is an event, typically the behavior of another person that occurs after a behavior happens, that had not been ongoing prior to the behavior, and which results in an increase in rate (or maintenance) of that behavior over time. Alternatively, socially mediated positive reinforcement could result in a response-subsequent increase in the amount or quality of attention, rather than movement of an antecedent quantity of zero to a response-subsequent quantity greater than zero. Positive reinforcement by gaining access to tangibles (which are things, and which are not the behavior of another), can occur independent of another's behavior, but often these tangibles are delivered by another person, thereby adding a social component to tangible positive reinforcement. Given the similarities between the two types of reinforcements (which often intersect), they are discussed together.

When self-injurious behavior is maintained by gaining access to (or increasing quality or quantity of) attention or tangibles, several function-relevant treatment options are available.

4.2.2.2.1. Extinction

Contingent upon the self-injurious behavior attention or tangibles are withheld (or no change in quality or quantity of these events relative to the quality and quantity available prior to the behavior). However, it is important to realize that if the client had no (or few) opportunities to produce reinforcers other than with self-injurious behavior, extinction would not provide the person with an alternative strategy of attaining social stimulation or socially mediated tangibles.

4.2.2.2.2. Differential Reinforcement of Other Behavior (DRO)

DRO involves first determining the frequency with which the self-injury occurs, then the mean period of time between instances of the behavior (e.g., mean inter-response time), and then delivering either the reinforcer that maintains the problem behavior, or another reinforcer (that is unrelated to the problem behavior) after a little less than the mean inter-response time passes without the self-injurious behavior having occurred. Should the self-injury occur, the reinforcer is not delivered, and timing begins again. What one is reinforcing, essentially, is the person's engaging in any behavior at all except for the self-injury. DRO has also been known as *omission training*. Treatments for self-injurious behavior that consists of DRO only have met with mixed results at best (Corte et al.,1971; Repp & Deitz, 1974). However, DRO can be useful as a supplementary treatment element in a multi-component treatment package.

4.2.2.2.3. Differential Reinforcement of Alternative Behavior (DRA)

DRA involves determining the reinforcer maintaining the self-injury, selecting another behavior currently in the person's repertoire, and making the reinforcer available, following each instance of that alternative behavior while ensuring it no longer follows the self-injury. Success of such a procedure depends on a number of factors, including relative response effort to do the self-injury versus the alternative behavior; extent to which the self-injury goes unreinforced; and quality, quantity, and frequency with which the alternative behavior is reinforced. Functional communication training, described later in this chapter, often exemplifies DRA.

4.2.2.2.4. Differential Reinforcement of Incompatible Behavior (DRI)

DRI is very similar to DRA, but for specification that the alternative behavior that is reinforced be one that is physically incompatible (e.g., mutually exclusive) with the self-injury. For example, in a DRI procedure, one could potentially reinforce one's hands being in one's pockets and extinguish hand-to-head self-injury, given that one cannot simultaneously have one's hands in one's pockets and hit one's head with them.

4.2.2.2.5. Competing Behavior Training

Training competing behaviors involves the teaching of new or strengthening of existing alternative behaviors that produce to the same reinforcers that maintain the problem behavior, but in greater quantities, at greater quality, and with greater efficiency, thereby rendering self-injurious behavior irrelevant or ineffective and ultimately replacing it. For example, FCT, for instance, involves teaching manding through signing, speaking, or exchanging cards, for reinforcers that typically follow self-injury while simultaneously ensuring that those reinforcers do not follow the self-injury. Kern, Carberry, and Haidara, for example, found the self-injurious behavior exhibited by a 15-year-old girl diagnosed with autism and severe intellectual disability to be maintained by gaining access to preferred stimuli. When they combined mand training to produce access to the preferred stimuli with extinction for self-injurious behavior, they found increased manding accompanied by reductions in self-injurious behavior. Sigafoos and Meikle (1996), Braithwaite and Richdale (2000), and Neidert, Iwata, and Dozier (2005) reported similar findings.

4.2.2.2.6. Noncontingent Reinforcement[2]

Noncontingent reinforcement refers to the programmed, noncontingent delivery of a stimulus that can function as a reinforcer for the target behavior. This stimulus is delivered according to a schedule that is independent of the occurrence of the target behavior. *Response-independent reinforcement* is a term often used synonymously with noncontingent reinforcement, since the delivery of the reinforcer occurs independent of occurrence of the behavior, which it has been found to reinforce. Given the frequency with which the term noncontingent reinforcement is used in the current behavior analytic literature, this term will be used henceforth in this chapter. Fixed time schedules of reinforcement, which are response-independent schedules, are sometimes reported in noncontingent reinforcement procedures, such that the identified reinforcer is delivered following passage of identical, regularly occurring periods of time, irrespective of occurrence of any behavior.

Vollmer, Iwata, Zarcone, Smith, and Mazaleski (1993) identified social positive reinforcement of their participant's self-injury by the social attention that followed it. They compared effects of social attention delivered as part of a DRO procedure with social attention delivered on a fixed time schedule, and found self-injurious behavior to be substantially reduced by both procedures. Derby, Fisher, and Piazza (1996) and Persel, Persel, Ashley, and Krych (1997) report similar results, as do Marcus and Vollmer (1996) and Lalli, Casey, and Kates (1997), with the reinforcers provided on a fixed time schedule in the latter two studies being tangibles rather than social attention. Similarly, O'Reilly et al. (2001) found that tantrums (which included self-injurious behavior) exhibited by two children who had been adopted from Eastern European orphanages were evoked when their parents diverted their attention, and were maintained by regaining parental attention. The researchers coached the parents through delivering attention on a fixed time schedule at times when attention needed to be diverted, which resulted in the elimination of tantrums, an effect that was maintained six months later.

Fischer, Iwata, and Mazaleski (1997) found that empirically identified arbitrary reinforcers (e.g., stimuli that functioned as reinforcers, but which were not those that maintained the behavior of interest) delivered on a fixed time schedule were generally effective in reducing frequency of self-injurious behavior, even when the self-injurious behavior was followed by its customary (natural) reinforcers. These findings are important, given that naturally occurring reinforcers (i.e., the attention of other shoppers when self-injurious behavior occurs in the supermarket) cannot always be controlled, and that they demonstrate decreased rates of self-injurious behavior can be maintained on more economical (i.e., thinner) fixed time schedules.

Although not examining self-injurious behavior, Hagopian, Fisher, and Legacy (1994) examined effects of two fixed time schedules of attention delivery for four children whose destructive behavior was maintained by social positive reinforcement. These authors found a rapid reduction in destructive behavior for all four children

---

[2] The term "non-contingent reinforcement" is an oxymoron because "reinforcement," by definition, involves contingency (Poling & Normand, 1999). We will continue to use the term here in order to be consistent with the literature.

when attention was provided on a fixed time 10-second schedule, but also found that they were only able to produce a similar reduction with a fixed time 5-minute schedule when this schedule was preceded by a systematic schedule thinning procedure. The implication with regard to using noncontingent reinforcement to treat self-injurious behavior is clear; a leaner schedule will produce a more rapid reduction, but the schedule must be systematically thinned to improve economy.

4.2.2.3. Interventions for Behavior Maintained by External Negative Reinforcement

In functional analysis, maintenance by external negative reinforcement is typically assessed in the *demand* condition. In this condition, the person is presented with materials for and instructions to engage in tasks typically found in her/his natural environments (i.e., academic tasks and materials, prevocational tasks and materials, etc.). Should the person comply with the task relevant instructions, she/he is praised. Should the person not comply, three-step guidance is provided to complete the task, with brief praise given regardless of prompt level needed for completion. Should self-injurious behavior occur, however, instructions and prompting terminate and do not resume until a predetermined interval (30 s, for example) has elapsed without occurrence of self-injurious behavior. As described this way by Iwata et al. (1982/1994), this procedure assesses for negative reinforcement by termination of instructions (or task demands).

Other types of socially mediated negative reinforcement are possible, however. For example, if a therapist casually chats with a client, and consistently terminates his chatting for a short period of time whenever the client exhibits self-injurious behavior, and if the rate of self-injurious behavior increased over time by virtue of this "chat termination" procedure, then the self-injurious behavior can be said to have been maintained by socially mediated negative reinforcement; i.e., self-injurious behavior allows an escape from being talked to. Similarly, terminating the singing, physical proximity, physical touch, delivery of tangibles, and other socially mediated stimuli provided by another, resulting in an increase in rate of self-injurious behavior would also constitute socially mediated negative reinforcement of self-injurious behavior.

Reports of self-injurious behavior that is maintained by presumably innocuous or friendly social contact and that does not the termination of aversive demands are rare in the behavior analytic literature . Studies that showed self-injurious behavior being maintained by demand termination are much more common. This should not be taken to mean however, that the former is in fact rare. Rather, this may be an understudied phenomenon, which may be an artifact of standard functional analysis procedures. This having been said, most treatments reported in the paragraphs that follow are based on demonstrations of self-injurious behavior being maintained by demand termination.

4.2.2.3.1. Extinction

When self-injurious behavior is maintained by socially mediated and/or external negative reinforcement, one treatment option is to ensure that the stimulus that was previously terminated or attenuated by the behavior now continues at its pre-response frequency, intensity, and quality. In so doing, the contingency that used to occur and which used to reinforce the behavior now no longer does, thereby producing an extinction effect. Iwata, Pace, Kalsher, Cowdery, and Cataldo (1990) and Goh and Iwata (1994) report such a procedure. Functional analyses indicated that person's self-injurious behavior was maintained by termination of task demands. When the researchers arranged for the instructions to continue the task to persist despite self-injurious behavior, rate of self-injurious behavior declined substantially for all clients. Interestingly, extinction bursts, or initial increases in rate of responding in response to onset of the extinction procedure, were noted for several of the persons in the Iwata et al. (1990) study and for the person served by Goh and Iwata (1994). The matter of extinction bursts is discussed in more detail later in this chapter.

4.2.2.3.2. Noncontingent Negative Reinforcement

Noncontingent negative reinforcement involves delivering the reinforcer found to maintain the self-injurious behavior on a response-independent schedule. For example, Vollmer et al. (1995b) and Vollmer et al. (1995a) allowed breaks from work on a fixed time schedule for two participants with intellectual disabilities who exhibited self-injurious behavior. They found rapid reductions in self-injurious behavior to near zero frequencies for both individuals, with neither of them exhibiting an extinction burst, and with decreased rates maintaining when the fixed time schedule was thinned to a more manageable level. Despite promising results such as these, there are limitations to noncontingent negative reinforcement procedures. Tucker, Sigafoos, and Bushell (1998) point out that unless coupled with additional procedures, noncontingent negative reinforcement procedures do not promote a more acceptable replacement behavior, and may initially fill the person's time with consummatory behavior instead of the behavior from which the person had escaped.

4.2.2.3.3. Differential Negative Reinforcement (DNR)

A third option for treating self-injurious behavior maintained by socially mediated or external negative reinforcement is DNR. In such a procedure, the stimulus change identified as maintaining the self-injurious behavior might instead be delivered after elapsed periods of time during which the self-injurious behavior did not occur, which would be termed *differential negative reinforcement of other behavior*; delivered instead after a particular alternative behavior had been emitted, and so termed *differential reinforcement of alternative behavior*; or delivered instead after a specified behavior which is incompatible with the self-injurious behavior had been emitted, and which would be termed *differential negative reinforcement of incompatible behavior* (DNRI). Vollmer et al. (1995a, 1995b) compared negative reinforcement of other behavior with noncontingent negative reinforcement for one of their participants, and found them to produce similar effects. Roberts et al. (1995) compared negative reinforcement of other behavior (e.g., a 15-second break from bathing or toothbrushing occurring after 20s during which no self-injurious behavior had occurred elapsed) with differential negative reinforcement of alternative behavior (e.g., a 15-second break from bathing or toothbrushing occurring immediately on compliance with a bathing or toothbrushing instruction), and found generally more rapid and greater reductions in self-injurious behavior with DNR of alternative behavior than with negative reinforcement of other behavior. Steege et al. (1990) report short-term success of a DNRI procedure in which a brief break from grooming occurred after two children with disabilities manually activated a micro switch (which would say "stop"), but not after hand or arm biting, and that the reduction was maintained during follow-up for one of the children. Rather than reinforcing an incompatible behavior with escape from task, Lalli et al. (1999) delivered edibles found to function as reinforcers following compliance, while preventing and not preventing demand termination following self-injurious behavior for five participants diagnosed with a variety of intellectual disabilities. Interesting, and somewhat counterintuitive, was the finding that positively reinforcing the incompatible behavior, regardless of whether the self-injurious behavior was or was not simultaneously extinguished, produced reductions in self-injurious behavior to near zero rates, while producing substantial improvements in compliance.

4.2.2.3.4. Intervening Early in the Response Chain

Preceding behaviors are behaviors that regularly precede other behaviors (e.g., self-injurious behavior), and which are indirectly reinforced by the reinforcement for that other, terminal behavior. Lalli, Mace, Wohn, and Liverzy (1995) and Smith and Churchill (2002) identified behaviors that reliably preceded self-injurious behavior, and conducted functional analyses on both the preceding behaviors and the self-injurious behavior. In five out of six instances, they found both the preceding behaviors and self-injurious behavior to be maintained by the demand termination. The authors of both studies discussed the possibility of treating behaviors that regularly precede the onset of self-injurious behavior to reduce self-injurious behavior.

4.2.2.4. Interventions for Behavior Maintained by Automatic Reinforcement

Automatic reinforcement is a private operation that cannot be directly observed but only be deduced when no external contingencies can be ascertained. Behaviors that are said to be maintained by automatic reinforcement, sometimes also called "self-stimulatory behaviors," are believed to be reinforced by tactile sensations, arousal changes, a shift in nociception, or other privately experienced stimulation. Automatic reinforcement can be positive or negative. That is, it can involve response-subsequent addition or increase in stimulation (such as the visual stimulation one perceives when one gently presses on one's closed eyes), or response-subsequent termination or lessening of stimulation (such as what one experiences when shielding one's eyes from the sun with one's hand).

During a carefully conducted functional analysis, self-injurious behavior is typically surmised to be maintained by automatic reinforcement when there is no differential response across the analysis conditions; or when it occurs at high in the nonsocial condition, and at near zero rates in the conditions involving social interaction and environmental enrichment. Determining the type of perceptual stimulation maintaining the behavior often entails identifying stimuli that result in a decrease in self-injurious behavior when delivered noncontingently. For example, Sprague et al. (1997) first concluded that self-injurious behavior in two participants with severe intellectual disability and sensory impairments was maintained by sensory reinforcement on the basis of analogue functional analyses. Next, they tested effects of several types of noncontingent sensory stimulation. They found that noncontingent vibration, music, and a combination of both decreased self-injurious behavior for one person; but that for the second only the combined vibration and music reduced self-injurious behavior for the second. Similarly, O'Reilly et al. (2003) found noncontingent vibration and vibration and sound to reduce self-injurious behavior in a person, after having identified non-socially mediated reinforcement as the type maintaining the behavior. Rather than actually empirically identifying the type of stimulation maintaining the self-injurious behavior, practices such as these identify stimuli that successfully compete with, or substitute for the stimulation maintaining the self-injurious behavior (Sandler, 2001).

4.2.2.4.1. Noncontingent Delivery of Competing or Substitution Reinforcers

Treatment for non-socially mediated self-injurious behavior often involves noncontingent delivery of stimuli found to successfully compete with or substitute for perceptual stimuli presumed to maintain the self-injurious behavior. This involves first conducting a functional analysis to determine the nature of the maintaining variables and then, should automatic or non-socially mediated reinforcement be found, conducting empirical preference assessment and subsequently delivering empirically identified preferred stimuli in a noncontingent format while measuring rate of self-injurious behavior. Those stimuli found to decrease self-injurious behavior when delivered in a noncontingent fashion would then become part of the treatment procedure.

Healey, Ahearn, Graff, and Libby (2001), Kennedy and Souza (1995), Lindberg et al. (2003), and Piazza et al. (2000) identified external stimuli that successfully compete with or substitute for sensory reinforcers maintaining self-injurious behavior which, when applied noncontingently. Noncontingent access to matched stimuli, however, does not always produce reductions in self-injurious behavior. Carr, Dozier, Patel, Adams, and Martin (2002a), for example, found no reduction in self-injurious behavior under noncontingent access to matched stimuli conditions, until they added response blocking.

4.2.2.4.2. Sensory Extinction

Rapp et al. (1999) and Deaver et al. (2001) discovered that the stimulation to the hand was the reinforcer that maintained hair pulling and twirling in their clients. They subsequently implemented sensory extinction procedures, such that their clients wore either gloves or mittens, which changed the nature of the sensory stimulation to their hands when they engaged in hair pulling and twirling. In both studies self-injurious behavior rates approached zero when the sensory extinction procedure was implemented, although the effect did not generalize without implementation across additional settings (Deaver et al., 2001). Roscoe et al. (1998) compared effects of sensory extinction with effects of noncontingently delivered matched sensory stimulation for three participants with intellectual disabilities who exhibited self-injurious behavior, and found that both procedures effectively reduced self-injurious behavior, although noncontingent delivery of matched sensory stimuli did so more rapidly.

4.2.2.4.3. Differential Reinforcement

Differential reinforcement procedures have been used to decelerate self-injurious behavior maintained by sensory stimulation. Using a DRO procedure, Patel et al. (2000), for example, provided 5-second access to either of two types of sensory stimulation of the person's forehead contingent on 15 s without head hitting. Both stimuli were found to effectively reduce the rates of self-injurious behavior.

There are instances in which self-injurious behavior is so dangerous that protective equipment must be worn continuously to prevent serious injury (O'Reilly et al., 2003). In many cases, equipment must be removed for brief periods of time at regular intervals, whether to prevent untoward physiological (Luiselli, 1992) or social (Rojahn, Schroeder, & Mulick, 1980) effects associated with continuous use of restraints, or to satisfy regulatory requirements. Such periods can expose the person to a serious risk of injury. O'Reilly et al. (2003) conducted a functional analysis of their person's self-injurious behavior during periods when protective devices were removed, and found the behavior to be maintained by non-socially mediated reinforcement. On subsequent trials, they found that noncontingent access to vibration or to vibration coupled with sound resulted in decreased rates of self-injurious behavior. By virtue of subsequently providing free access to vibration and sound during periods of protective device removal, these researchers found their person exhibited zero instances of self-injurious behavior at six months' follow-up.

4.2.2.5. Extinction and Other Changes to Prevailing Schedules of Reinforcement

Earlier in this chapter, we discussed extinction procedures designed to decelerate self-injurious behavior that had been maintained either by external positive, external negative, or by automatic reinforcement.

Although extinction procedures can be considered as rather benign forms of intervention, one of the notorious problems associated with it are the so-called extinction bursts. Extinction bursts are temporary increases in the rate and intensity of problem behaviors shortly after the extinction procedure has been started, and before the behavior begins to extinguish. Self-injurious behavior extinction bursts have been reported in the literature (see Goh and Iwata, 1994, for example). However, the frequency of extinction bursts may be less than was presumed at one time (Lerman, Iwata, & Wallace, 1999). Lerman et al. (1999) examined 41 datasets for treatment of problem behavior involving extinction, and found 38% did not involve extinction bursts when extinction was the sole treatment, and only 15% involved extinction bursts when treatment packages including extinction were implemented. Further, these authors found that self-injurious behavior maintained by social negative reinforcement was more likely than either self-injurious behavior maintained by social positive reinforcement or automatic reinforcement to undergo a burst when extinction was initiated, with no instances of extinction burst found for extinction of automatically reinforced self-injurious behavior (Lerman et al., 1999). A number of studies have demonstrated reductions in self-injurious behavior without occurrence of extinction burst or extinction-induced self-injurious behavior when noncontingent reinforcement or noncontingent negative reinforcement, involving delivery of reinforcing stimuli on a fixed time schedule, is implemented, rather than a traditional extinction procedure (Hagopian et al., 1994; Marcus & Vollmer, 1996; Vollmer et al., 1998).

A related phenomenon is extinction-induced self-injurious behavior. This refers to the onset or the rate increase of self-injurious behavior due to implementation of an extinction schedule either for self-injurious itself or for another behavior. Extinction-induced self-injurious behavior is considered to be an extinction burst phenomenon (Vollmer et al., 1998).

Lerman, Iwata, Shore, and Kahng (1996) discussed implications with extinction procedures in treatment of problem behaviors maintained by intermittent reinforcement. They found that extinction of intermittently reinforced and of continuously reinforced problem behavior were both effective, but that extinction of continuously reinforced behavior was generally more rapid. Therefore, these authors argued that it may be beneficial to impose a continuous reinforcement schedule on a previously intermittently reinforced behavior to hasten subsequent extinction. Although not directly considering self-injurious behavior maintained by either positive or negative reinforcement, the implications of these findings on extinction of self-injurious behavior are clear. First, more rapid extinction with fewer responses occurring during the extinction procedure may be found for continuously reinforced, rather than intermittently reinforced self-injurious behavior. However, this means that the person whose behavior is found to be intermittently reinforced is potentially exposed to greater risk of injury at her/his own hand (often literally) during extinction, and so first exposing this person's self-injurious behavior to a continuous schedule of reinforcement, and then implementing an extinction procedure, may lessen risk of injury during the procedure.

4.2.2.6. Treatment Involving Punishment

Punishment can involve either contingent stimulus delivery, such as a stern "no," a disapproving look, water misting, or manual restraint delivered on self-injury, and resulting in a lessening in frequency of the behavior over time; or contingent stimulus removal, such as removal of one's preferred object following self-injury, resulting in a reduction in frequency of the self-injury over time. The former operation is called *positive punishment* as contingent application of stimulation produces the reduction in responding over time, and the latter operation *negative punishment* as contingent stimulus removal produces this behavioral change. The interested reader who is looking for in-depth and comprehensive discussion of punishment is referred to books by Axelrod and Apsche (1983), Matson and DiLorenzo (1984), a review by Matson and Kazdin (1981) and general applied behavior analysis textbooks such as Cooper et al. (2007) or Miltenberger (2007).

Applied behavioral research studies on punishment procedures to suppress self-injurious behavior in humans appear more rarely in the contemporary literature than they used to. As we have noted elsewhere in this book, by the 1980s, concerns about the social validity of many punishment procedures and about the dearth of research on positive reinforcement procedures raised ethical questions by some professional organizations, especially *The Association for the Severely Handicapped* (TASH). This led to a vitriolic debate and polarization within the community of applied behavior analysts, who as a group drew serious accusations from some others. Some even accused them of torturing their clients (Turnbull et al., 1986).

But even before this public *battle royal* the vast majority of behavior analysts were ethical and well-trained professionals and as such keenly aware of the ethical dilemmas and methodological drawbacks involved in punishment procedures for therapeutic purposes, especially with clients who often are unable to give consent, as evidenced by detailed guidelines to follow when considering use of punishment procedures by Matson and Kazdin (1981). The guidelines were as follows:

- Non-aversive methods have been proven ineffective for decelerating the behavior exhibited by the individual involved.
- The behavior selected for punishment must be sufficiently problematic to warrant treatment.
- The type of punishment to be used and the manner in which it is used must be consistent with legal, regulatory, and agency policies and practices.
- Adequate training must be provided in advance of the punishment procedure, and adequate oversight during its use, for those implementing the procedure.
- The particular procedure to be used must be acceptable to the recipient, her/his family, the agency, the community, etc.
- Personal experience of the punisher in all of its intended intensities and durations by all involved (including therapists, researchers, guardians, etc.), to ensure fully informed consent prior to implementing the procedure.
- Risk–benefit analysis has indicated that the self-injuring party is at greater risk without experiencing the punishment procedure than she/he would be, were the procedure to be implemented.
- A clinical trial demonstrating rapid deceleration of the self-injurious behavior when the punishment procedure is applied prior to implementing the procedure on a more widespread basis.

More recent ethical guidelines regarding the use of punishment were published by Bailey and Burch (2005) and by the *Behavior Analyst Certification Board* (2006).

However, besides ethical concerns, one also has to keep in mind that punishment as a teaching strategy has inherent shortcomings is often accompanied by intended negative side effects (Newsome, Favell, & Rincover, 1983). To name just a few:

o Punishment teaches what not to do, but not what to do.
o Punishment can generate avoidance behaviors – the therapist and all other environmental stimuli associated with the punishment procedure are likely to become a conditioned aversive stimulus (punisher).
o Due to its potential limited effectiveness, punishment can reinforce the punishing behavior of therapist.
o Punishment can result in modeling.
o Punishment can lead to retaliatory behavior.

Not all stimuli delivered as punishers are physically painful. For example, the sternly said "no" reported by Repp and Deitz (1974) and Dorsey et al. (1980) involved no physical contact between the parties involved. By definition, any stimulus whose response contingent presentation or removal is followed by a decrease in rate of responding in a punisher. This can include stimuli that not everyone would consider painful. An interesting example was given in the study by Fisher et al. (1998b) who used contingently activated *transcutaneous electric nerve stimulation* (TENS) to treat self-injurious behavior found to be maintained by automatic reinforcement. The gentleman participating engaged in sufficiently severe and intractable self-injurious behavior that it regularly produced serious tissue damage, even when the man wore protective equipment. Fisher et al. (1998a, 1998b) report that TENS delivered on a continuous schedule contingent on self-injurious behavior reduced frequency of self-injurious behavior, although not to a clinically significant extent. However, it is important to note, that it is likely that the suppressive effect that was observed could have been a function of an altered pain threshold rather than the TENS stimulation, which itself is not painful.

Rush, Crockett, and Hagopian (2001) worked with two clients who exhibited self-injurious behavior that seemed to be maintained by automatic reinforcement, and other problem behaviors that were socially mediated. The implementation of non-contingent attention and social extinction resulted in decreases in the other problem behaviors, but did not affect self-injurious behavior rate. The investigators then added a 30-second facial screening punishment procedure to the treatment package for both individuals, and found reduced self-injurious behavior. This procedure did not seem to have changed the positive effect in either one of the individuals, and the effects were maintained at three and six months' follow-up.

Punishment side effects have been discussed throughout the behavior analytic literature (see Cooper et al., 1987, for example). However, the exact nature of punishment side effects in humans is not quite clear and partly speculative, because much of that research has been conducted with non-human organisms (Matson & Kazdin, 1981). Punishment procedures in human patients are generally implemented only in combination with additional treatment procedures to accelerate alternative behaviors (Cooper et al., 1987; Bailey & Burch, 2005). Given this, effects produced by reinforcement or other additional treatment components may potentially attenuate side effects induced by punishment, and side effects, when they occur, may be very brief in duration (Matson & Kazdin, 1981).

Some side effects of punishment in humans have been discussed. Punishment-induced aggressive behavior has been reported (Thyer, 1987), but punishment-induced self-injurious behavior has not. This may mean that the latter phenomenon is either nonexistent, or underreported. Thompson, Games, and Koons (1967) found that punishment effects could potentially function as positive reinforcers for the punishing behavior of the agent delivering the punishers, thereby potentially increasing probability of punishment over time. This phenomenon certainly requires that proper training, supervision, and peer review is provided whenever punishment procedures are used.

A number of studies have considered variables that could affect punishment effectiveness. Thompson, Iwata, Connors, and Roscoe (1999) found that mild punishment of self-injurious behavior coupled with reinforcement for alternative behavior produced greater suppression of self-injurious behavior than did mild punishment for self-injurious behavior, alone. Lerman, Iwata, Shore, and DeLeon (1997) report intermittent schedules of punishment did not suppress self-injurious behavior for two individuals, regardless of whether it was preceded by systematic fading from continuous punishment, but that intermittent punishment preceded by systematic fading from continuous punishment did maintain low rates of self-injurious behavior among two other individuals, when self-injurious behavior for all was found to be maintained by non-socially mediated reinforcement. Finally, Toole et al. (2004) report that when empirically derived punishers are used, suppression by a single punisher or by multiple, varied punishers are essentially similar.

4.2.2.6.1. The Self-Injurious Behavior Inhibitory System (SIBIS)

The Self-Injurious Behavior Inhibitory System (SIBIS), although vilified by some, is a very special punishment device that has produced remarkably good results in extreme cases of self-injurious behavior. Several behavioral researchers in conjunction with the Johns Hopkins Applied Physics Laboratory, the American Foundation developed it for Autistic Citizens, the C. R. Bard Company, the Georgetown University School of Medicine and Child Development Center, Human Technologies, Inc., the Kennedy Institute (now Kennedy Krieger Institute), Kuehnert Homes, Oxford Medical Systems, Ltd., and Raytheon, Inc. (Linscheid, Iwata, Ricketts, Williams, & Griffin, 1990). This device was designed to be worn on the head, to detect self-injurious response occurrence and intensity, and to immediately deliver a tone and electrical stimulation (reported to range in intensity from imperceptible to similar to a rubber band snapping on one's arm) contingent on self-injurious response of sufficient intensity. This device was developed to automate response-contingent delivery of punishing stimuli, as reliance on human delivery would likely lead to variable implementation. Additionally, automated punisher delivery would avoid the situation in which a punishment mediator (who likely must also function as a teacher, therapist, or parent) would her/himself come to function as a conditioned punisher. In addition to delivering electrical stimulation, SIBIS could also be used as a switch to activate (or terminate) various forms of reinforcement via radio signal, to include a stereo, television, etc. (Linscheid et al., 1990)

Linscheid et al. (1990) reported the use of this device to treat self-injurious behavior exhibited by a 16-year-old girl diagnosed with profound intellectual disability. Although the person exhibited four discrete self-injurious behavioral topographies, the SIBIS was applied to only one. Rate of the targeted topography decreased rapidly from 19.8 responses per minute to 0.6, and collateral reductions occurred across the remaining three topographies. These authors report that the device was not activated during the last 20 days of the girl's inpatient treatment given the absence of self-injurious behavior, but also report that follow-up evaluation was not possible, as the girl's residential treatment provider had discontinued its use and replaced the SIBIS with a conventional helmet. These same authors also treated a 11-year-old boy diagnosed with autism and severe intellectual disability, whose baseline self-injurious behavior intensity exceeded 100 responses per hour, with near zero rate of self-injurious behavior achieved after only 13 SIBIS activations for a total of 1.04 seconds of electrical stimulation. Follow-up evaluation at four months posttreatment revealed that self-injurious behavior remained at lower than 1% of its baseline rate, with life-style improvements had taken place including moving from individual to small group supervision at school, leaving his classroom regularly for lunch and activities, taking field trips, and taking an airplane for a vacation. Linscheid et al. (1990) described similar SIBIS treatment outcomes for three additional individuals.

In a more recent study, Salvy, Mulick, Butter, Bartlett, and Linscheid (2004) used the SIBIS to reduce self-injurious behavior exhibited by a three-year-old girl diagnosed with significant intellectual disability, bilateral hearing loss, and visual impairment. The child had an 18-month history of self-injurious behavior, with baseline rates exceeding 100 per day. Simply wearing the SIBIS without activating the unit produced some reduction. When SIBIS was activated, however, a rapid and complete suppression of self-injurious behavior occurred, an effect that was maintained even when the device was deactivated, and generalized to home, and at 60 days following the complete discontinuation of the SIBIS.

4.2.2.7. Altering Discriminative Stimulus Control

There are three kinds of discriminative stimuli, S^D, S^Δ, and S^P. An S^D makes a behavior more likely to occur at any given moment because that behavior (or another that has been maintained by the same reinforcer) was positively reinforced in the presence of that stimulus in the past. An S^Δ, on the other hand, makes a behavior less likely to occur at any given time because that behavior had gone unreinforced in the presence of that stimulus in the past. Finally, the S^P makes a behavior less likely to occur when it is present because that behavior had been punished in the presence of that stimulus in the past. S^D's are said to occasion (or set the occasion for) behaviors, and S^Δ's and S^P's are said to inhibit behaviors.

Mace, Shapiro, and Mace (1999) worked with a seven-year-old girl who's SIB was jointly maintained by access to tangibles that were recently removed, and demand terminated. To address this problem, they began telling the child at 30-second intervals (beginning 2 min before changing activities) that the preferred tangibles would have to go away and the less-preferred task would begin. This antecedent stimulus manipulation, coupled with noncontingent reinforcement, decreased SIB more effectively than did extinction and noncontingent reinforcement.

Task difficulty, itself, can evoke SIB. When this is the case, adding discriminative stimuli such as prompts could result in task completion without SIB. When one adds prompts to achieve task completion, though, the task-completion behavior ends up being jointly under control of the task, the task instructions, and the additional prompts that have been given. Prompted versus unprompted task completion sets up two alternatives for the person completing the task: (1) complete the task with prompting (less effortful) or (2) complete the task without prompting (more effortful) (Kennedy, 1992). Choosing the more effortful option not only results in more work, but also likely in reinforcement delays. Should the prompts be delivered using a delayed prompting procedure (Touchette & Howard, 1984), one can not only lessen the probability that the needed task-completion behavior remains dependent on supplemental prompting, but also help ensure less effortful, more rapid access to reinforcement in the process.

In relation to reports involving manipulation of motivating operations, reports involving manipulation of immediate antecedents to decelerate self-injurious behavior have been relatively few. We turn now to consideration of motivating operations-based interventions.

4.2.2.8. Altering Motivating Operations

Interventions that are based on motivating operations (MO) can involve environmental enrichment, such that stimuli are provided that evoke particular behaviors incompatible or more probable than self-injurious behavior, and decrease the potency of reinforcers available for self-injurious behavior. Ringdahl, Vollmer, Marcus, and Roane (1997), for example, determined that self-injurious behavior was maintained for their three individuals by nonsocial reinforcement. They next gave individuals free access to a variety of stimuli, and measured time allocation to self-injurious behavior and to engagement with the stimuli. Those stimuli to which individuals devoted greater amounts of time than to self-injurious behavior were selected for the environmental enrichment phase, in which individuals had free access to a variety of these stimuli. Results indicated reductions in self-injurious behavior and increases in object engagement during the environmental enrichment phase. It is noteworthy, though, that this result was obtained after the environment was enriched with stimuli empirically demonstrated to successfully compete with the stimuli maintaining self-injurious behavior. Vollmer, Marcus, and LeBlanc (1994) described similar findings.

Some MO-based interventions can involve the modification of task or of task delivery. For example, novel tasks could potentially increase the rate of self-injurious behavior (Smith et al., 1995a, 1995b), and so this effect could be lessened through techniques such as *interspersal* training (i.e., interspersing familiar words during spelling instruction on new words, Neef, Iwata, & Page, 1980). Increasing instructional or task session durations could potentially increase the probability of self-injurious behavior (Smith et al., 1995a, 1995b), and so briefer sessions may lessen its probability. In some situations slow-paced tasks could increase the probability of self-injurious behavior to occur, compared to more rapid-paced tasks (Smith et al., 1995a, 1995b), and so increasing task pacing could, potentially reduce probability of self-injurious behavior. When presented with instructions to engage in a low probability (or disliked) behavior, probability of self-injurious behavior could be lessened, and the probability of compliance could be increased, if the task is presented as part of a high-probability task sequence (Zarcone et al., 1993; Zarcone et al., 1994).

MO-based interventions can include rescheduling events when it is hypothesized that the baseline event schedule is functionally related to self-injurious behavior. Indeed, Touchette et al. (1985) report only antecedent (and largely MO-based) interventions in treatment of problem behaviors exhibited by their two clients. Interventions included replacing events associated with self-injurious behavior with events that were not, and rescheduling presence of staff in whose presence self-injurious behavior was more likely to occur. Similarly, Wacker et al. (1996) report that rescheduling mealtimes and increasing quantity of food available at them lessened self-injurious behavior for both of their individuals.

Some MOs are physiologically based. For example, menstrual discomfort (Carr, Smith, Giacin, Whelan, & Pancari, 2003), otitis (O'Reilly, 1997), sleep deprivation (O'Reilly & Lancioni, 2000), and acute medical problems, in general (Bosch et al., 1997) have been demonstrated as MOs evoking self-injurious behavior in some individuals. Headaches (Pary & Khan, 2002) have been suggested as MOs sometimes functionally related to self-injurious behavior. Certain psychiatric conditions could also potentially be viewed as MOs, to the extent that they temporarily alter the valence of reinforcers and thereby altering evocative potency of various antecedent stimuli (Baker et al., 2002). And so can psychotropic or other medications if they alleviate pain or other symptoms to which self-injurious behavior is functionally related.

MOs, whether internal or external, cannot always be adjusted. For example, inclement weather, over which one has no control, may suddenly and unexpectedly strike, resulting in cancellation of the afternoon's planned activities. Another person's unexpected difficulties may divert staff attention away unexpectedly, thereby delaying delivering the activities originally planned for another individual. Horner, Day, and Day (1997) found that by inserting events, which they have termed *neutralizing routines* temporally between onset of an MO that would typically evoke self-injurious behavior or another problem behavior, and the immediate antecedent for that behavior, that they were able to reduce rate of problem behaviors (including self-injurious behavior). Neutralizing routines included 10 min of highly preferred, self-directed activity following delay in planned activity for one person; rescheduling the activity in a manner obvious to the involved party, and spending 10 min reviewing a preferred book after cancellation of a preferred activity for another person; and opportunity to take a 60 min nap when a third person had arrived at his program having had 5 h or less of sleep the night before.

Procedures that increase response effort required to achieve the customary magnitude of reinforcement for a particular response can be considered to be abolishing motivating operation (AO) interventions, because they diminish the value of the reinforcer relative to the new effort that is required to produce it.

Some researchers have altered the value of reinforcers for self-injurious behavior by increasing the effort that is required to access that reinforcement. Hanley, Piazza, Keeney, Blakeley-Smith, and Wordsell (1998), for example, examined the rates at which a six-year-old boy diagnosed with profound intellectual disability and multiple physical disabilities would engage in automatically reinforced self-injurious behavior, would operate microswitches which produced music and vibration or a recorded message inviting others to play with him, place a pacifier in his mouth, or would independently take bites of food while wearing 2-pound wrist weights on each arm. They found substantial reductions in self-injurious behavior to near zero rates, with increases in all adaptive behaviors measured, simply by virtue of increasing the response effort to engage in self-injurious behavior and providing the reinforcement that would naturally follow taking bites of food (e.g., food in mouth), inviting others to play (e.g., others coming to play), placing a pacifier in one's mouth (e.g., oral stimulation by the pacifier), and manual operation of a vibrating, musical switch (e.g., vibration to the hand

and auditory stimulation). Similarly, Irvin, Thompson, Turner, and Williams (1998) described an intervention where they first provide toys or other preferred leisure items together with prompts to interact with them. When this procedure failed to increase the rate of object engagement and did not decreasing the rate of hand mouthing, they used a method to increase response effort for self-injurious behavior. They applied arms splints of their clients, such that elbow flexion and functional arm use remained possible, but required greater effort. Substantial reduction in self-injurious behavior to near zero rates were the result, combined with increases in object manipulation in all individuals. Similar effects were described by Zhou, Goff, and Iwata (2000).

In this same way, noncontingent reinforcement and noncontingent negative reinforcement procedures are considered by some to be MO-based procedures that diminish the value of reinforcers otherwise produced by self-injurious behavior (Wilder & Carr, 1998). That is, when the stimulation that is typically produced by self-injurious behavior becomes available irrespective of that behavior, then greater effort is required to produce and consume that reinforcer by first engaging in the self-injurious behavior. This alteration of the potency of the reinforcer and subsequent abolishing operation effect with regard to evocative properties of the situation indicates that a MO mechanism, rather than an extinction mechanism, is responsible for the decrease in rate of responding. Like an extinction procedure, however, noncontingent reinforcement and noncontingent negative reinforcement disrupt the contingency maintaining self-injurious behavior.

4.2.2.9. Treatment by Promoting Alternative Behaviors
Some of the earliest articles in the behavior analytic literature addressing self-injurious behavior involved the attempts to influence self-injurious behavior indirectly by increasing alternative behaviors. Corte et al. (1971), for example, implemented a DRO procedure, but found it inferior to electric shock in reducing self-injurious behavior. Repp and Deitz (1974) implemented a DRO procedure along with a verbal reprimand for self-injurious behavior, and report that the combined treatment did reduce self-injurious behavior.

Vollmer and Iwata (1992) made practical recommendation to enhance the effectiveness of differential reinforcement procedures in reducing problem behaviors.

- The manner in which the initial interval is selected is critical and should be based on the mean inter-response time of the target behavior during baseline, and then backing up a bit. For example, were self-injurious behavior observed to occur 10 times in a 5-minute observation period, the mean inter-response time would be 30 s. Reinforcers should then be delivered after every 20 or 25 s during which any behavior other than self-injurious behavior occurred. The interval is reset following each instance of the target self-injurious behavior or reinforcer consumption.
- Target intervals could be increased systematically, such that what becomes implemented is a DRO with an escalating schedule of reinforcement. This increases the economy and decreases the response effort to maintain the procedure.
- Greater reduction of problem behavior may be achieved when functional, rather than arbitrary reinforcers are used.

Woods (1983) suggested that DRO and DRI were essentially identical procedures, with the difference being that DRO procedures are using ill-defined behavior which is incompatible with the problem behavior, while DRI selects occurrence of a very particular, incompatible behavior on which to base reinforcer delivery. Perhaps lack of precision of DRO and greater precision of DRI contribute to their differential effectiveness.

Many demonstrations of treatment of self-injurious behavior by promoting alternative behaviors involve what has come to be called *Functional Communication Training* (FCT) (Carr & Durand, 1985; Carr et al., 1994, 1999b). When self-injurious behavior is maintained by social positive reinforcement or access to tangibles, a differential reinforcement procedure may be put in place, which prevents reinforcement of self-injurious behavior and instead delivers reinforcement contingent on manding those reinforcers. Similarly, when self-injurious behavior is maintained by social negative reinforcement, demands or instructions persist despite self-injurious behavior, and are terminated only on task completion or (albeit temporarily) on manding a break.

Sigafoos and Meikle (1996) reduced self-injurious behavior of two boys with autism by reinforcing manding behavior. Self-injurious behavior was maintained by social attention and access to tangibles. Therefore, they trained manding and reinforced it with attention and tangibles, while extinguishing self-injurious behavior. Increases in manding and declines in self-injurious behavior were found. In a similar study, Kern, Carberry, and Haidara (1997) worked a 15-year-old girl with autism and severe intellectual disability who exhibited self-injurious behavior that was maintained by access to preferred stimuli. When they used the same preferred stimuli to reinforce manding, while putting extinction on self-injurious behavior, they found an increase in manding behavior and a concurrent decrease in self-injurious behavior. Cipani and Spooner (1997) describe how functional communication training might be used to replace self-injurious behavior (or other problem behavior) with manding. In their description, saying "no" or other forms of protest would be followed by activity or demand termination, while engaging in self-injurious behavior or other problem behavior would not. Alternatively, difficult tasks could be escaped by manding "help, please," while, again, self-injurious behavior would not produce task termination.

It is quite possible for self-injurious behavior to be maintained by more than one type of contingency. When Braithwaite and Richdale (2000) found the head banging and head hitting of a 7-year-old boy diagnosed with autism to be maintained by access to preferred items and by escape from difficult tasks, they first taught the child to mand using a mand frame (i.e., "I want —— please"). They observed a decrease in self-injurious behavior maintained by access to tangibles, but no change in self-injurious behavior to produce escape. When they extended mand training (teaching "I need help") to difficult tasks, a similar reduction was seen for negatively reinforced self-injurious behavior. They subsequently programmed delays to reinforcement for both types of mands, thereby rendering the FCT procedure more likely to be maintained, and found zero rates of self-injurious behavior after doing so.

FCT could, potentially, also be used to treat automatically reinforced behavior. In such a situation, the individual would be taught or prompted to verbally request the reinforcer upon which the matched sensory stimulation would be delivered. The extent to which such a procedure could effectively reduce self-injurious behavior depends on whether it is possible (a) to identify a stimulating event that is similar to the internally produced by given self-injurious behavior and (b) to be able to use it as a reinforcer for the specified mand, i.e., for properly requesting the reinforcer.

Quick transfer and other stimulus control transfer and shaping procedures described by Sundberg and Partington (1998) could be incorporated into some FCT programs to produce manding behavior in conventional topographies, or to produce manding under appropriate stimulus controls in an FCT procedure. The particular manner in which self-injurious behavior is addressed in FCT, however, has been the subject of some controversy. Durand and Merges (2001) recommend planned ignoring as the only suitable consequence operation for self-injurious behavior. This operation, social extinction, would potentially be effective when the self-injurious behavior is maintained by social attention and when manding is reinforced with social attention (and the self-injurious behavior is not too dangerous for the individual). However, it would not be functionally matched and therefore not very successful in cases where self-injurious behavior is maintained by other variables.

Other researchers, therefore, instead of using social extinction, implemented treatment components that were functionally matched with the operating maintaining reinforcers of the problem behavior. Fisher et al. (1993), for example, found FCT alone ineffective in reducing self-injurious behavior for a child with profound intellectual disability whose self-injurious behavior was maintained by tangibles. When FCT was combined with a punishment procedure (e.g., 30-second basket hold), however, rate of self-injurious behavior declined and the rate of manding exceeded the rate of self-injurious behavior.

As useful as FCT may be in many cases, it is important to note that it is not a panacea, and that in some cases it may contribute to the treatment of self-injurious behavior when combined with other methods. Hagopian, Fisher, Sullivan, Aquisto, and LeBlanc (1998) studied 10 individuals with self-injurious behavior, and found that in some of them the rate of self-injurious behavior actually doubled when FCT was administered alone. On the other hand, combinations of FCT with extinction or with punishment produced clinically relevant improvements in several cases.

4.2.2.10. Treatment Packages

It occurs very often that self-injurious behavior is evoked and/or maintained by multiple variables, which necessitates simultaneous implementation of more than one treatment procedure (O'Neill et al., 1997). Therefore, many treatment strategies for self-injurious behavior involve packages comprised of multiple intervention components.

In some cases, even self-injurious behavior that serves only one function may require a multi-component treatment package. Consider, for example, the individual who was served by McCord et al. (2001) whose self-injurious behavior was found to be maintained by avoidance of routine transition that required him to move from one setting to another. Providing advanced notice of upcoming transitions had no effect on self-injurious behavior and DRA produced only slight reduction in self-injurious behavior. Eventually, a DRA in combination with extinction and response blocking was necessary to decrease self-injurious behavior and to accomplish successful transitions from place to place. Similarly, Van Camp, Vollmer, and Daniel (2002) found a multi-component package consisting of environmental enrichment, response-effort manipulation, and inhibitory stimulus control, was necessary to reduce automatically reinforced self-injurious behavior exhibited by a 13-year-old boy with autism.

4.2.3. Behavior Therapy (Respondent Conditioning Methods)

It is somewhat surprising that the relationship between stress, anxiety, and arousal and self-injurious behavior has not received more attention from researchers in general and behavior analysts in particular and we argue that it is a woefully underexplored field of investigation. We have ample anecdotal evidence that some forms of self-injurious behavior in some individuals frequently occur within bouts of tantrums with obvious signs of distress. This seems to happen particularly often in individuals for whom contingent or noncontingent physical restraint procedures are in place. Nonetheless, little systematic research has been directed to explore the role that affective behavior may play within the contingencies of reinforcement of self-injurious behavior. Correspondingly, we have invested only very limited energies to explore the potential benefit of respondent conditioning interventions based on the principles of counter-conditioning and respondent extinction.

4.2.3.1. Relaxation Training

In one of the few studies in this realm, Schroeder, Peterson, and Solomon (1977) compared the effects of contingent restraint of two adolescents with severe intellectual disabilities who had a history of severe, high-rate head banging. They found that contingent restraint decreased self-injurious behavior. However, when contingent restraint was combined with electromyography (EMG) feedback taken from the right trapezius muscle in combination with verbal reinforcement of muscle relaxation, the procedure was even more effective. The authors concluded that the effectiveness of the combined intervention was based at least in part on the deep muscle relaxation, which is incompatible with the occurrence of self-injurious behavior and could present a treatment alternative for self-injurious behavior in non-verbal individuals. From an operant/instrumental perspective, contingent physical restraint functioned as a conditioned aversive event (S^{r-}), which suppressed the operant head banging (positive punishment). However, concurrent conditioned reflexes (muscle tension) are likely to influence the behavioral events in several ways, as a competing operant, a discriminative stimulus, or as a CEO. At this point, however, we can only speculate about the different effects such concurrent events may have and it may pay off to explore these complexities empirically.

Around the same time, Steen and Zuriff (1977) worked with a 21-year-old woman with profound intellectual disability and severe self-injurious behavior form whom noncontingent restraints were used to protect her from inflicting serious injury to herself. The investigators taught the woman to relax her hands and arms while she was still in full restraints. As she gradually learned to relax, the restraints were gradually removed. At the end of treatment, the woman had learned to relax when released from restraints with virtual elimination of her self-injurious behavior. Although Marholin and Luiselli (1979) later criticized Steen and Zuriff's account and argued that they had failed to demonstrate a clear cause–effect relationship between relaxation and the decrease of self-injurious behavior, the attempt to demonstrate the effect of relaxation training to control self-injurious behavior represented a novel and worthwhile approach, which remains yet to be replicated. The question is whether relaxation training is generally insufficient or altogether ineffective as an intervention for any kind of self-injurious behavior in people with intellectual disabilities. More, well-controlled research seems warranted.

4.2.3.2. Desensitization

Like with all exposure techniques, the theoretically effective principle of desensitization is assumed to be respondent extinction, which refers to the repeated confrontation of the individual with the conditioned aversive stimulus without experiencing the unconditioned aversive stimulus. Cunningham and Peltz (1982) used an in vivo desensitization procedure to control face slapping in a 10-year-old boy with moderate intellectual disability. Face slapping had increased with damaging intensity after a dental procedure and had to be prevented by the use of a hockey helmet. Attempts to remove the helmet resulted in increased agitation, self-injurious behavior, and the repeated efforts by the boy to replace the helmet, to self-restrain, or to prompt restraint from the adults. The authors introduced an in vivo desensitization procedure with increasingly extended periods of time without the helmet. Data were collected in four situations using a multiple baseline design. Self-injurious behavior was eliminated during active treatment. The boy also learned a self-control response, which consisted of putting on the helmet when agitated and removing it when relaxed. Continued improvement was reported at 6-, 9-, and 12-months follow-ups. At the 15-month follow-up, no self-injurious behavior was observed, and the use of the helmet was discontinued.

4.2.4. Psychopharmacology

4.2.4.1. History of Pharmacotherapy for Self-Injurious Behavior

Psychopharmacology of intellectual disabilities has come of age in the last 15 years (Schroeder et al., 1998). There are several textbooks, and whole-journal issues specifically reviewing this topic (e.g., Aman & Singh, 1990; Gadow & Poling, 1987; Gualtieri, 1991; Ratey, 1991; Reiss & Aman, 1998; Schroeder, 1999). There also now exist several practitioners' guides (e.g., Poling, Gadow, & Cleary, 1991; Werry & Aman, 2001), as well as several journal reviews, the most thorough and analytic of which are by Baumeister et al. (1993), Lewis et al. (1996d), and Thompson, Hackenberg, and Schaal (1991). Each of these reviews has different strengths and is worth reading each one of them carefully.

Reviews of the selective effects of pharmacotherapy for self-injurious behavior are much fewer (Aman, 1991; Baumeister et al., 1993; Singh & Millichamp, 1985; Singh,

Table 4.1: Drugs for which at least two valid self-injurious behavior studies were conducted

Antipsychotics	
Classical antipsychotics	
Phenothiazines	Chlorpromazine (Thorazine), Thioridazine, (Mellaril), Fluphenazine (Prolixin)
Butyrophenones	Haloperidol (Haldol)
Atypical antipsychotics	Clozapine (Clozaril), Risperidone (Risperdal), Olanzapine (Zyprexa), Quetiapine (Seroquel), Aripiprazole (Abilify)
Antidepressants	
Tricyclic antidepressants	Imipramine (Tofranil)
Serotonin reuptake inhibitors	Clomipramine (Anafranil)
Selective serotonin reuptake inhibitors	Fluoxetine (Prozac), Sertraline (Zoloft), Paroxetine, (Paxil), Fluvoxamine (Luvox), Citalopram (Celexa)
Atypical anxiolytics	Buspirone (Buspar)
α-adrenergic blockers	Clonidine (Catapres)
β-adrenergic blockers	Propanolol (Inderal)
Narcotic analgesics	Naloxone, Naltrexone
Mood stabilizers	Lithium Carbonate (Eskalith)
Anticonvulsants	Carbamazepine (Tegretol), Valproic acid (Depakote), Gabapentin (Neurontin), Lamotrigine (Lamictil), Topiramate (Topamax), Tiagabine (Gabatril)

Singh, & Ellis, 1992). From these four reviews and our own reading of the more recent literature, we constructed a summary table (Table 4.1) showing drugs for which there is some exploratory or confirmatory evidence, i.e., at least two well-conducted open-label or double-blind, placebo-controlled studies.

The research suggests mixed results of pharmacotherapy for self-injurious behavior compared to more consistent results of pharmacotherapy for aggressive behavior and for stereotyped behavior. The reasons for this are unclear at present, but it is likely that there are several reasons.

1. As mentioned in the beginning, the DSM-IV (American Psychiatric Association, 1994) treats self-injurious behavior as a subtype of Stereotyped Movement Disorder. The Psychiatric literature on self-injurious behavior also often lists self-injurious behavior as a subtype of aggressive behavior, i.e., aggressive behavior toward self as opposed to others, and lumps it together with self-mutilation (Favazza, 1996). This practice may or may not be legitimate. It is speculative, and it has not been empirically validated as yet. Thus, the diagnostic labels have been used inconsistently, as has been pointed out 20 years ago by Matson (1986) and more recently by Bodfish and Lewis (2002).
2. Until recently, many of the rating scales used to assess drug effects on self-injurious behavior (see Aman, 1991; Schroeder et al., 1997 for reviews), were not constructed

and validated as item-independent scales of self-injurious behavior, aggressive behavior, stereotyped behavior, and other repetitive movement disorders (Bodfish & Lewis, 2002). Assessment of selective effects of drugs on self-injurious behavior was often confounded with these other disorders (Williams & Saunders, 1997) unless they were corroborated by direct observations. Some researchers such as Sandman et al. (1999) oppose the use of rating scales as primary dependent measures and use primarily direct observations. Napolitano et al. (1999) have pointed out that both ratings and observations are useful, but they provide different information about drug efficacy.

3. There also has been disagreement in the field as to what are acceptable methodological designs for drug studies of self-injurious behavior.

4.2.4.2. Methodological Considerations

Many of the reviews of the 1970s (e.g., Sprague & Werry, 1971), 1980s, and 1990s (e.g., Aman, 1988, 1991; Baumeister et al., 1993; Singh & Millichamp, 1985; Singh et al., 1992), were very critical of uncontrolled, unmasked study designs in this area, suggesting that they tend to overestimate the positive effects of a drug. While this criticism was valid and useful in advancing more rigorous drug assessment technology in developmental disabilities, the tendency became prevalent to discount completely any study that lacked a randomized, double-blind, placebo-controlled design with large groups of individuals (e.g., Matson et al., 2000). This view often resulted in automatically excluding single-subject repeated-time series designs that may have been more clinically valid, but could not be totally blinded for ethical reasons (see Thompson, Hackenberg, & Schaal, 1991 for an excellent analysis). Some researchers (e.g., Sandman et al., 1993; Thompson, Hackenberg, Cerutti, Baker, & Axtell, 1994; Zarcone et al., 2001) compromised by conducting group studies using single-subject designs which could later be aggregated for analysis using group statistics, but this is a very time-consuming and costly proposition.

There is still not a consensus on the appropriateness of group versus single-subject designs for drug studies on self-injurious behavior. As Walkup, Labellarte, and Riddle (1998) have pointed out, much useful information can be gathered from open clinical trials which may be non-blind and unmasked, e.g., pilot data, unique adverse effects, clinical information about time course, pharmacokinetics, etc. They remain a staple in the field, therefore, as a predecessor and justification for larger, more expensive and intrusive randomized, placebo-controlled, double-blind studies, which remain the gold standard. In the present review, therefore, case reports and open-label studies will be viewed as providing exploratory, but not confirmatory findings.

The state-of-the-art methodological review of psychopharmacological research in developmental disabilities has been Sprague and Werry (1971) for many years. They list six minimum design requirements:

1. Placebo-control;
2. Random assignment of treatments and/or subjects;
3. Double-blind evaluation;

4. Multiple standardized doses;
5. Standardized valid and reliable assessment instruments; and
6. Appropriate statistical analyses.

These are stiff requirements to meet in the self-injurious behavior population where one must anticipate (1) lack of adequate sample size; (2) extreme heterogeneity of subjects; (3) subject attrition; (4) idiosyncratic all-or-none response by some subjects; (5) lack of specificity of effects of individual subjects; (6) ethics of using placebo or wait-list groups; and (7) difficulty of maintaining double-blind conditions. It is a rare study that does not have to compromise on at least some of these issues. Behavior intervention studies, by contrast, are rarely held to such rigorous standards.

It is true that no study in this area is without flaws. These flaws have been amply pointed out in previous reviews, especially Baumeister et al. (1993). Studies using potentially lethal drugs in this high-risk group of people who have limited ability to consent are extraordinarily difficult to conduct and require great caution. In most cases, tradeoffs between experimental rigor and the clinical welfare of the subject must be made. Never the less, our technology is improving; and, when it does, the results become clearer, as can be seen in the case of studies of naltrexone for self-injurious behavior discussed in Chapter 2.

Sheiner, Beal, and Sambol (1989)[3] conducted an extensive analysis of clinical dose-ranging drug-trials designs and have made a strong argument for single-subject dose escalation designs. There are many variations of this design, but they all start with baseline, placebo, and raising a dose by a fixed amount at a fixed interval until a clinical end point is reached. Each subject stops at his/her clinical end point within the dose-range studied. No dose reversals are permitted. Adverse responders are dropped. These single-subject design procedures also provide relatively unbiased data for least squares or weighted least squares group analysis. Sheiner et al. (1989) give an analysis of the various problems in different dose ranging study designs in Table 4.2.

The dose escalation designs are the most clinically valid, the most like normal clinical practice, and they have the fewest ethical problems. These and other drug-behavior intervention designs may need to be considered more generally in future studies of behavior problems in intellectual disabilities. Some new designs may be required to meet emerging research needs.

In summary, there is great hope in the future for a rational pharmacotherapy for people with intellectual disabilities and behavioral or psychiatric problems like self-injurious behavior. There is a distinct trend away from the trial-and-error methods of the past (Gualtieri, 1991). But, in order for this trend to succeed, several challenges will have to be met.

---

[3] The parallel dose design is a between-groups design in which each participant receives either drug or placebo throughout the trial. The crossover design is a within-groups design in which a participant receives drug and placebo treatments in counterbalanced order, so that treatment order and carryover effects can be controlled. In the dose escalation design, the drug dose is titrated up until a clinical effect, positive or adverse, is found. The titration is then stopped at the point for that individual participant. Group data imputation techniques are used to control for individuals' differing peak effective doses across the group (Sheiner et al., 1989).

Table 4.2: Potential problems for various dose-ranging study designs

Type of problem	Design type		
	Parallel-dose	**Crossover**	**Dose-escalation**
1 Ethical problems in study execution	+ +	+ + +	0
2 Number of patients (cost)	N	N/m	N/m
3 Time (cost)	1 unit	m units	m units
4 Need for many centers	+ +	+	+
5 Complexity of protocol, problems in study analysis	0	+ +	+ / + + +
6 Complexity, reliance on modeling	0	+	+
7 Assumptions	0	+	+ + +
8 Carryover effects	0	+ +	+
9 Period effects	0	+ +	+ +
10 Center effects	+ +	+	+
11 Few doses examined	+ +	+ +	0
12 Biased parameter estimates	+ + +	0	+
13 Poor/no estimates of variability	+ + +	+	+
14 Problems in extrapolation, not representative of individual response	+ + +	0	0
15 Not representative of clinical practice	+ +	+ + +	0
16 Not representative of patient group	+	+ + +	0

+, Mild problem; + +, moderate problem; + + +, severe problem. N, number of subjects. M, number of units (e.g., doses, time).
Source: Reprinted with permission from Sheiner, Beal, and Sambol, 1989.

1. Selectivity of drug response must be improved. Few drugs as yet can be shown to improve specific problem behaviors, without worsening learning or memory (Williams & Saunders, 1997) and with minimal side effects at a given dose in a given set of circumstances.
2. In order to succeed at this task: the screening and assessment technology and psychiatric diagnoses must improve so that they are reliable, sensitive, non-invasive, and ecologically valid.
3. As knowledge accumulates about drug–drug interactions and drug–behavior interactions, it will be possible to better distinguish between drug responders and non-responders.
4. At that point treatment acceptability on the part of the consumers will increase.
5. Finally, basic research on neurobiological and behavioral models of the causes of severe behavior problems in intellectual disabilities should eventually improve our prediction of a selective drug response, as it has for people with depression and schizophrenia.

Meeting these 12 challenges is a tall but necessary order for future researchers on the pharmacotherapy of self-injurious behavior.

4.2.4.3. Specific Drug Classes and Self-Injurious Behavior

One of the recent drug prevalence studies, which gives a breakdown of use by drug class, is Aman, Sarphare, and Burrow (1995b). This was a large survey of psychotropic drug use in group homes for developmental disabilities in the State of Ohio in a population relevant to our interest in self-injurious behavior. Percentage usage was as follows: neuroleptics, 21.2%; anti-Parkinsonian drugs, 5.1%; anticonvulsants, 5.4%; lithium carbonate, 5.2%; anxiolytics/hypnotics, 4.2%; antidepressants, 4.0%; β-blockers, 1.4%; naltrexone, 0.1%; clonidine, 0.4%; and methylphenidate, 0.4%. The most frequent reason for prescription was aggressive behavior; the second most frequent reason was self-injurious behavior. Thus, the psychopharmacology of self-injurious behavior clinically continues to be mostly a story about the antipsychotics.

4.2.4.3.1. Antipsychotics

This class of drugs is comprised of two subclasses, i.e., the classic antipsychotics and the atypical antipsychotics. Although the former are still in use, there has been a dramatic shift to the use of atypical antipsychotics for maladaptive behaviors of people with intellectual disabilities beginning in the early 1990s because of their decreased risk of drug-related movement disorders such as extra-pyramidal side effects (Aman & Madrid, 1999). We will cover the classic antipsychotics only in terms of their historical significance, and we will focus more on the atypical antipsychotics.

Classic Antipsychotics The modern era of psychopharmacology in developmental disabilities was ushered in by two classic reviews, one by Sprague and Werry (1971) and one by Lipman (1970). These two reviews drew attention to the overmedication of people with developmental disabilities with psychotropic drugs. The most prevalent drugs were primarily neuroleptics for aggressive behavior, destruction, self-injurious behavior, and hyperactivity. Sprague and Werry (1971) set a trend for reducing medications, minimum effective dose procedures, annual drug monitoring reviews, drug holidays, instruments for assessing side effects, State regulations, which improved clinical practice in psychopharmacology in developmental disabilities (see Valdovinos, Schroeder, & Kim, 2003, for an extensive recent review). Valdovinos et al. (2003) showed a decrease in prevalence in the use of psychotropic medications in the developmental disabilities population in the U.S. from 1970 to 2000 from 47.1% to 30.9%. A significant number, however, still receive them regularly for self-injurious behavior.

Two types of studies of classic neuroleptics for self-injurious behavior have been conducted, i.e., withdrawal studies and prospective studies (Schroeder, 1988). Neuroleptic withdrawal studies were conducted in the 1980s (Gualtieri, Hicks, Quade, & Schroeder, 1986; Heistad, Zimmermann, & Doebler, 1982; Schroeder & Gualtieri, 1985) and in the 1990s (Newell, Wszola, Sprague, Mahorney, & Bodfish, 2002) to assess the effects of long-term chronic neuroleptic medication on people with developmental disabilities. The outcome of these studies was that withdrawal of neuroleptics increased the risk of short-term withdrawal effects (apathy, drowsiness, lethargy, dry mouth, urinary retention and abdominal pain, and acute extra-pyramidal side effects such as akathisia, i.e., restlessness, dystonia, i.e., awkward movement, and pseudo-Parkinsonism), which usually remitted within three months. The main long-term side effects occurring in approximately one-third of patients were tardive dyskinesia, also an extra-pyramidal side effect characterized by a variable mix of involuntary movements of the face, mouth, tongue, upper and lower limbs, and, secondly, impaired postural control. These problems in motor control could last up to a year or might never remit. Withdrawal symptoms after reduction or discontinuation of neuroleptic treatment included nausea, anorexia, vomiting, diaphoresis, hyperactivity, and insomnia. These symptoms usually remitted within a month after neuroleptic withdrawal. This is a very troubling array of serious side effects that require a strong rationale for use of neuroleptics and then careful monitoring procedures when in use (see Kalachnik, 1999, for an excellent review).

Aman (1991, 1997) and Baumeister et al. (1993) are the three most thorough reviews of prospective studies of the specificity and efficacy of classic neuroleptics for self-injurious behavior. In summary, there is considerable evidence of suppression of stereotyped behavior, especially if it occurs at high rates, by phenothiazines such as chlorpromazine or thioridazine, and by butyrophenones such as haloperidol, but their effects on self-injurious behavior are mixed. If self-injurious behavior is stereotyped in form and function, classic neuroleptics may have an effect; but, if not, they do not seem to have a selective effect.

There was also a great deal of interest in the pharmacology of neuroleptics, in that their effectiveness in treating schizophrenia was attributed to their ability to modulate dopamine function in the brain. Extra-pyramidal side effects were viewed as a manifestation of too much blocking of dopamine function, i.e., "dopaminergic supersensitivity." Lewis and Baumeister (1982) made a strong case that repetitive movement disorders such as stereotyped behavior, of which self-injurious behavior was considered a subset, were the result of a similar dopaminergic supersensitivity in the nigrostriatal pathway of the basal ganglia. The Breese/Baumeister rat model for Lesch–Nyhan syndrome (see Chapter 2 for a review of the neonatal dopamine depletion hypothesis) posited that the depletion of D1 dopamine receptors led to the supersensitivity that resulted in self-biting in neonatally dopamine-depleted rats. This led to a possible explanation as to why classic neuroleptics, primarily D2 antagonists, did not suppress self-injurious behavior in humans consistently (see Schroeder et al., 1990 for a review). This led to a search for D1 dopamine antagonists for treating self-injurious behavior. There is none clinically approved for use in the U.S., although studies in Canada by Elie, Langlois, Cooper, Gravel, and Albert (1980) using an investigative drug, SCH-12679, primarily a D1 blocker, found it superior to thioridazine in suppressing aggressive behavior and self-injurious behavior among people with developmental disabilities. Gualtieri and Schroeder (1989) successfully used a D1 and D2 antagonist, fluphenazine, for self-injurious behavior, but the effect did not last, and the risk of classic neuroleptic extra-pyramidal side effects was high. We discontinued work on fluphenazine and turned our interest to the atypical antipsychotics, which carried a greatly reduced risk of neuroleptic side effects (Schroeder et al., 1995). While having only a weak effect on D1 dopamine receptors, the atypical antipsychotics clozapine, risperidone, and olanzapine, all inhibited agonist-induced self-injurious behavior in neonatally lesioned rats in the Breese/Baumeister model (Breese et al., 2005).

Atypical Antipsychotics Aman and Madrid (1999) published an excellent analytic review of the use of atypical antipsychotics in persons with developmental disabilities. They analyzed 21 studies on clozapine, risperidone, and olanzapine, mostly on self-injurious behavior and aggressive behaviors, performed in the 1990s. There have been a considerable number of studies since that time that involve these and other atypical psychotics which also add important information to the literature, supporting their efficacy for treatment of self-injurious behavior.

Clozapine. Clozapine (Clozaril) was the first atypical antipsychotic administered in the U.S. It was used as a last resort to treat chronic refractory schizophrenia. It is called an atypical antipsychotic because its neurochemical and neuroanatomical properties differ from classic antipsychotics, which have a high affinity for D2 dopamine receptors. Clozapine is a relatively potent D1, D3, and D4 antagonist and a less potent D2 antagonist (Jann, 1991). It also antagonizes alpha 2-adrenergic, muscarinic, cholinergic, H1-histaminic, and 5-HT serotonergic receptors (Meltzer, 1991). It does not cause tardive dyskinesia or other extra-pyramidal side effects. In fact, it has often been used as a remedy for it. Although rare, it can cause a blood disorder (dyscrasia) that results in a lowered white cell blood count, seizures, dysrhythmia, and agranulocytosis, which can be fatal if undetected. Alvir, Lieberman, and Safferman (1993) have shown that the risk is only 0.8%, if white cell count is monitored weekly.

Only a handful of clinical trials of clozapine have been conducted in the developmental disabilities population, probably because of the monitoring requirements, which call for weekly blood drawing. Most of them were open-label studies on people with schizophrenia, mild intellectual disability, who also exhibited aggressive behavior and self-injurious behavior (Ratey, Leveroni, Kilmer, Gutheil, & Swartz, 1993; Cohen & Underwood, 1994; Pary, 1994). To our knowledge, only three single- or double-blind, placebo-controlled studies specifically on the effects of clozapine on self-injurious behavior have been carried out (Hammock, Schroeder, & Levine, 1995; Schroeder et al., 1995; Hammock, Levine, & Schroeder, 2001). These were all single-subject, yearlong or more, repeated time-series, ABA reversal designs, using both direct observations and the *Aberrant Behavior Checklist* (Aman & Singh, 1986). Clozapine at steady-state low dose (200–300 mg/day) decreased self-injurious behavior and aggressive behavior by five-fold or more in three of four patients, but the effects on stereotyped behavior were mixed. Sedation, extra-pyramidal effects, and large weight gain did not increase significantly with clozapine. The effect was stronger in a leisure setting than a demand setting. So clozapine, while having a clinically significant effect on self-injurious behavior, did not have a selective effect relative to other problem behaviors. In one case, it was found to work for a risperidone non-responder. The results were consistent with but not confirmatory of the D1 dopamine hypothesis.

Risperidone. By far the most work on atypical antipsychotics has been performed on risperidone. Aman and Madrid (1999) list 16 studies most of which are targeted toward aggressive behavior among various developmental disabilities populations and only 3 of which are placebo-controlled double- or single-blind studies. Self-injurious behavior was included as a secondary measure in a few studies. One study they omitted was a positive open-label study of risperidone on self-injurious behavior in a Lesch–Nyhan syndrome case (Allen & Rice, 1996). All studies, however, showed a positive clinical response in 60–70% of the cases. We will only review the three placebo-controlled studies listed plus two more recent, more comprehensive studies, one by the Research Units For Pediatric Psychopharmacology group (RUPP group) published in 2002 (RUPP Autism Network, 2002) and the other series of studies by our group (Zarcone et al., 2001; Hellings, Zarcone, Crandall, Wallace, & Schroeder, 2001; McAdam, Zarcone, Hellings, Napolitano, & Schroeder, 2002; Valdovinos et al., 2002; Crosland et al., 2003; Zarcone et al., 2004; Hellings et al., 2006).

Vanden Borre et al. (1993) in a double-blind, placebo-controlled study on self-injurious behavior in the developmental disabilities population used 4–12 mg/day of risperidone as an add-on to preexisting pharmacotherapy for three weeks in 30 adults with developmental disabilities. The main outcome measures, *Clinical Global Impressions* (CGI) (National Institute of Mental Health, 1970) and the *Aberrant Behavior Checklist* (ABC) (Aman & Singh, 1986) total scores, both improved significantly without an increase in heart rate, blood pressure, or extra-pyramidal side effects.

McDougle et al. (1998b) also conducted a brief 12-week, placebo-controlled, double-blind parallel dose study of risperidone (1–6 mg/day) in 31 adults with autism or pervasive developmental disability and found a positive response in 57% of the risperidone group, with no increase in extra-pyramidal side effects. Of the measures relevant to self-injurious behavior which were used, the CGI, the *Yale–Brown Obsessive Compulsive Scale* (YBOCS, Goodman et al., 1989a, 1989b) and SIB-Q (Gualtieri & Schroeder, 1989), showed a significant decrease in repetitive behavior, compulsiveness, aggressive behavior, and self-injurious behavior with few side effects, except for mild transient sedation in the beginning weeks. Post hoc analysis showed the effects were not related to diagnosis, gender, setting, age, IQ, repetitive behavior, aggressive behavior, or dose in this range. This study is important because it was one of the first to attempt to find predictors of risperidone response, but it can be seen that the response, while positive, was not selective.

The Conduct Study Group reported on a brief six-week, multi-center, placebo-controlled, double-blind parallel groups designed study (0.02–0.06 mg/day) as add-on pharmacotherapy in 118 children with conduct disorder aged 5–12 years, ranging in IQ from 35–84 (Aman, De Smedt, Derivan, Lyons, & Findling, 2002; Snyder et al., 2002). Eighty percent had a comorbid diagnosis of Attention Deficit Hyperactivity Disorder (ADHD), Disruptive Behavior Disorder (DBD), and Oppositional Defiant Disorder (ODD). Concomitant medications allowed were psychostimulants, antihistamines, chloral hydrate, and melatonin. Since these two studies were both in good agreement, we report them here as one set. Of the measures relevant to self-injurious behavior and aggressive behavior, and stereotyped behavior, the *Nisonger Child Behavior Rating Scale* (Aman et al., 1996), the ABC (Aman, White, Vaithianathan, & Teehan, 1986), and the *Behavior Problems Inventory* (Rojahn et al., 2001) showed significant effects on aggressive behavior, but not on self-injurious behavior or stereotyped behavior. Direct observations were not used as measures. Transitory sedation was common, and weight gain, dyspepsia, and hyperprolactinemia (increased secretion of prolactin) were observed occasionally. It is important to point out that the participants in this study were not selected for their self-injurious behavior, so it is not surprising that their Behavior Problems Inventory (BPI) scores were low and that they did not show a selective drug effect on self-injurious behavior.

The RUPP Autism Network Study (2002) was a large multi-site outpatient study of autistic children 5–17 years of age, ranging in IQ from normal to severe intellectual disabilities. They had been referred for aggressive behavior, tantrums, or self-injurious behavior. Of the 270 screened, 101, 80% of whom were boys, were finally enrolled in a placebo-controlled, double-blind, parallel dose design[4] clinical trial of risperidone (1.0–4.0 mg/day) for eight weeks. Using the ABC (Aman et al., 1986) Irritability Subscale and CGI scale as the primary measures, 69% of the children decreased their scores by 25% or more. Significant ABC scores also occurred for the hyperactivity and stereotyped behavior subscales. No direct observation measures were used. Risperidone responders were then followed for 16 weeks in an open-label treatment of risperidone. The main side effects were increased appetite, weight gain, fatigue, and drowsiness, most of which were considered mild. In a second arm of the study, 38 of the 49 individuals in the risperidone group were enrolled in an 8-week, placebo-controlled discontinuation study. In the placebo group 63% reverted to their previous ABC scores, whereas only 13% in the group maintained on risperidone did so.

The above-cited studies, while very well conducted, were all relatively brief clinical trials on young developmental disabilities populations ranging in IQ from the severe to normal range, selected for autism, conduct disorder, or hyperactivity and not their self-injurious behavior. Their measures were confined to rating scales with no direct observations. In contrast, the study of risperidone by our group chose a wider age range (6–65 years) of persons ranging from mild to profound retardation with multiple psychiatric diagnoses and a high likelihood of chronic, severe self-injurious behavior, and aggressive behavior, and we followed them for a year or more. Inclusion criteria were: severe self-injurious behavior, aggressive behavior, property destruction, or stereotyped behavior for at least six months; aged 6–65 years; living in an appropriate habilitative environment; caregivers willing to participate; and baseline scores on the *Aberrant Behavior Checklist-Community* (ABC-C) (Aman, Burrow, & Wolford, 1995a) above the norm for age, gender, and setting. Exclusion criteria were: uncontrolled seizures within the past two years; acute illness; living in a pathological environment; degenerative disease; history of adverse reaction to risperidone. Measures included behavior-rating scales' ratings (ABC (Aman & Singh, 1986), SIB-Q (Gualtieri & Schroeder, 1989), NCBRF (Aman et al., 1996), DASH II (Matson, 1998)), behavioral observations (MOOSES (Tapp, Wehby, & Ellis, 1995)), biomedical measures (prolactin, hemoglobin A1c levels, lipid profile, weight), side effect measures (*The Dyskinesia Identification System* (DISCUS) Sprague, Kalachnik, & Slaw, 1989, *Neuroleptics Side Effects Checklist* (Gualtieri, 1984)), measures of cognition and learning (i.e., repeated acquisition of stimulus chains (Williams & Saunders, 1997; Yoo et al., 2003)), and social validity measures (McAdam et al., 2002).

---

[4] The parallel dose design is a between-groups design in which each participant receives either drug or placebo throughout the trial (Sheiner et al., 1989).

The placebo-controlled, double-blind, crossover design started with a 4-week wash-out baseline, followed by a 22-week, placebo-controlled, double-blind, crossover phase with two doses of risperidone ranging from 0.025 to 0.5 mg/kg, depending on age, followed by a reversal to placebo for 4 weeks, and then a 24-week open follow-up phase using the most effective dose for each risperidone responder.

Results of the study were that, of 343 patients screened, 50 met inclusion criteria and agreed to enroll in the study; 40 completed the trial. All, at entry to the study, had ABC-C scores above normal for age, gender, and setting. There were 21 children and adolescents (8–18 years) and 19 adults (22–56 years), 23 males, 28 with a DSM-IV (American Psychiatric Association, 1994) diagnosis of autism, 31 with self-injurious behavior and aggressive behavior, 4 with aggressive behavior only, and 5 with self-injurious behavior only. Eleven had mild, 9 moderate, 11 severe, and 9 profound intellectual disabilities. Nine were on medication that had controlled their seizures for at least a year and were left on them unchanged during the study.

Since there was a large placebo effect between baseline and placebo, covariance analysis was used for the main study comparing the drug effect of each person against his own placebo. Using the ABC *Irritability* subscale as the primary measure, there was a significant drug effect, but no significant dose effect for the range used, i.e., 2.0 mg/day (range 1.2–2.9 mg/day) for children and adolescents, and 3.6 mg/day (range 2.4–5.2 mg/day) for adults. Using 50% reduction in ABC *Irritability* subscore as a criterion, 57% showed a response; using a 25% reduction criterion, as in the RUPP studies, 85% showed a response (Hellings et al., 2006). The other rating scales showed similar significant effects, as did the direct behavior observational measures (Valdovinos et al., 2002; Zarcone et al., 2001; Crosland et al., 2003). Response was not related to psychiatric diagnosis, gender, mood, or the use of concomitant seizure medications, but was positively related to severity of intellectual disability and inversely related to chronological age.

McAdam et al. (2002), in a follow-up social validity study, showed that independent raters viewing videotaped segments of the individuals scrambled blindly, indicated that, when on medication, individuals displayed fewer maladaptive behaviors were less irritable, in a better mood, and were more responsive to the environment. Zarcone et al. (2004) conducted functional analysis diagnostics on 13 of the individuals. Of the 10 risperidone responders, 7 individuals showed undifferentiated response patterns across baseline and drug conditions; for 3 responders, a differentiated response pattern did occur during their baseline and risperidone treatment, producing function-specific reductions in their aggressive behavior and self-injurious behavior.

Eight of 29 side effects were significant: increased weight gain, increased appetite, drowsiness, tremor, being "too quiet" or "not themselves," lack of spontaneity, and nasal congestion. These were more persistent than those reported in the RUPP studies. Weight gain was a serious side effect (ranging from 12 kg to 9.6 kg). It occurred in 70% of individuals during the double-blind acute phase of the study, and it reversed during placebo (Hellings et al., 2001). The FDA has since issued a warning concerning the risks of weight gain from using risperidone. Care should be taken to manage weight gain if risperidone is administered chronically. Prolactin levels were also elevated while on risperidone (Hellings et al. 2005). This can also be a serious side effect if not monitored. Extra-pyramidal side effects were very low and few serious extra-pyramidal symptoms were observed. The overall severity of these side effects was moderate and manageable. Effects on cognitive performance at these low doses appeared to be slight (Yoo et al., 2003).

Taken as a whole, the research on risperidone at low doses showed a lasting positive response in 60–85% of cases in the developmental disabilities population with aggressive behavior, self-injurious behavior, and irritability. Main side effects were weight gain, increased appetite, and mild sedation. The effects were not shown to be selective for self-injurious behavior alone, however. In 2006, the Food and Drug Administration approved the use of risperidone for irritability among children and adolescents with Autism, so its use is expected to increase in the U.S.

From a pharmacological point of view, risperidone is of interest because it is a potent D2 dopamine blocker like haloperidol, but it does not cause extra-pyramidal effects. By design, it also exerts a serotonin 5HT2a postsynaptic receptor blocking effect that is approximately 50-times that of its D2 dopamine blocking effect (Meltzer, 1991). Serotonin measures are elevated in approximately 30% of people with autism. Serotonin reuptake inhibitors also seem to be effective in suppressing repetitive behaviors including self-injurious behavior, as we will see in the next section. So, it may be that risperidone's efficacy is a result of its modulation of serotonin–dopamine interactions in the brain. Nevertheless, the long-term effects (in terms of years) of chronic use of risperidone must still be evaluated, to assure its safe use.

Olanzapine. Only a few studies of olanzapine for aggressive behavior, self-injurious behavior, and stereotyped behavior, most of them open-label, have been conducted (Bodfish et al., 2001; McDonough et al., 2000; Potenza, Holmes, Kanes, & McDougle, 1999; Williams, Clarke, Bouras, Martin, & Holt, 2000). All of them showed a positive, but nonspecific, response on self-injurious behavior, with a side effects profile similar to that of risperidone.

Only one study (Bodfish et al., 2001) was conducted as a single-blind comparison of classic neuroleptics and olanzapine in a sample of 10 institutionalized adults with severe and profound intellectual disabilities. Direct observations and ABC *Irritability* scores were used as dependent measures. Patients receiving maintenance treatment with a classic neuroleptic received an initial four-week evaluation period, followed by a nine-week titration off of the classic neuroleptic and onto olanzapine, and then a final four-week evaluation period on olanzapine alone. Olanzapine produced a significant reduction in self-injurious behavior in 5 of 10 subjects, on the ABC, and on direct observations, with no extra-pyramidal side effects or overall side effects. Average weight gain was 4 lbs. There was also a significant reduction in prolactin levels.

Olanzapine is an interesting drug pharmacologically because it bears some structural similarities to clozapine, in that it blocks 5-HT1, 5HT2, D1, D2, D4, adrenergic, cholinergic, and histaminic receptors, but it does not cause blood dyscrasia, as clozapine does. There is not enough research to evaluate in detail the utility of olanzapine for self-injurious behavior as yet. Clinicians report that weight gain is a much a larger problem than described in the research so far. Weight gain is the main reason for discontinuation of olanzapine in the schizophrenic population.

Aripiprazole. This drug is also an atypical antipsychotic with an interesting pharmacological profile, in that it is a presynaptic dopamine auto receptor agonist with antagonism at postsynaptic D2 dopamine receptor sites. It is also a potent partial agonist at 5HT1a receptor sites, which may result in a favorable side effect profile. It has been proven effective in schizophrenia for almost a decade, but only one open-label study has been conducted in developmental disabilities so far, with results similar to risperidone (Stigler, Posey, & McDougle, 2004). It is believed that the side effects of weight gain with aripiprazole will be reduced in comparison to risperidone-induced weight gain.

4.2.4.3.2. Antidepressant Drugs

Antidepressant drugs include tricyclic antidepressants, monoamine oxidase inhibitors, serotonin uptake inhibitors, and serotonin 5HT1A agonists. They are widely prescribed to treat affective disorders such as major depressive disorder (MDD), obsessive–compulsive disorders (OCD), ADHD, nocturnal enuresis, anxiety disorders, and eating disorders. Antidepressants are used less frequently for people with developmental disabilities, five times less frequently than antipsychotics (Rinck, 1998), perhaps because of the difficulties in diagnosing depression in this population. When used, they often are prescribed for compulsive ritualistic behaviors, aggressive behavior, and self-injurious behavior (Sovner et al., 1998). There are very few studies of monoamine oxidase inhibitor (MAO) inhibitors and tricyclic antidepressants (TCDs). The only double-blind, placebo-controlled study of a TCD was by Aman et al. (1986) on imipramine in adults with profound intellectual disabilities in which the drug caused deterioration in depressive symptoms and increased acting-out behaviors, including self-injurious behavior. Since the emergence of the serotonin uptake inhibitors these drugs are rarely used today in the population with developmental disabilities.

Serotonin Uptake Inhibitors   Serotonin is a ubiquitous neurotransmitter in the CNS, which serves many functions, e.g., the treatment of depression, OCD, bulimia, social phobia, anxiety, and chronic pain. For self-injurious behavior, the most interesting one is its role in the treatment of affective disorders when manifested as aggressive behavior, ritualistic, stereotyped, or compulsive behaviors, of which some self-injurious behavior may be a subset.

Dietary studies of tryptophan, a metabolic precursor to serotonin, by McDougle, Naylor, Cohen, et al. (1996a, 1996b) suggest that there may be a relationship between tryptophan depletion in the diet and behavioral deterioration, including self-injurious behavior, in people with autism and developmental disabilities. Gedye (1990) has proposed a high-tryptophan diet for self-injurious behavior cases. The evidence for this treatment is slim, however; and her studies need replication by others.

The most thorough review of serotonergic agents and perseverative behavior, including self-injurious behavior, in people with developmental disabilities was published by Aman, Arnold, and Armstrong (1999). They reviewed 14 papers on the nonselective serotonin reuptake inhibitor, clomipramine; most of them were case reports and open-label studies, showing positive effects on compulsive behaviors, including self-injurious behavior. Probably the best study of clomipramine and self-injurious behavior was conducted by Lewis et al. (1996a). This was a 19-week, randomized, placebo-controlled, double-blind, crossover study of clomipramine as add-on treatment in eight institutionalized adults with severe or profound intellectual disabilities and with chronic severe self-injurious behavior. The individuals were observed in their day room and classroom using direct observations, the ABC and other rating scales. Other medications and behavioral interventions were held constant during the drug trial. Six of eight cases showed a 50% or more decrease in frequency and intensity in self-injurious behavior, and three of eight showed reduced ABC scores. Social validity studies showed that the staff needed to use fewer restraints while participants were on clomipramine, and five were returned to clomipramine treatment after the study was over. Eight treatment-limiting side effects were observed: constipation, increased appetite, heart pounding, increased frequency of urination, which were manageable, and treatment-emergent effects, i.e., tiredness, sedation, seizure (one case), mood worsening, agitation, and aggressive behavior with tachycardia (one case). Clomipramine response was not related to self-restraint for self-injurious behavior, but stereotyped behavior was also greatly reduced. Lewis et al. (1996a, 1996b, 1996c, 1996d) attributed clomipramine's efficacy to its ability to suppress compulsive and stereotyped behavior in people with developmental disabilities and autism, thus supporting King's (1993) compulsive behavior hypothesis of self-injurious behavior (see Chapter 3).

Serotonin Selective Reuptake Inhibitors (SSRIs)   These drugs act by inhibiting the reuptake of serotonin at the synaptic cleft by the presynaptic neuron, thereby making more serotonin available for use in synaptic transmission. The selective SSRIs (paroxetine, citalopram, fluvoxamine, sertraline, and fluoxetine) have minimal side effects in the CNS, whereas clomipramine, like other tricyclic antidepressants, also has significant side effects on dopaminergic, norepinephrinergic, cholinergic, and histaminergic neurotransmission. It thus has a broader spectrum of action.

SSRIs have been more attractive because of their milder side effects profile. Main side effects are: agitation, akathisia, irritability, gastrointestinal problems, and headache, which tend to be milder than with clomipramine (e.g., as in the Lewis et al., 1996a, 1996b, 1996c, 1996d study). There is less sedation, constipation, dry mouth, cardiotoxicity, or seizure activity with SSRIs.

Aman et al. (1999) cite 23 case reports and 9 studies on the positive effectiveness of SSRIs on behavior problems in approximately 60% of 192 cases with developmental disabilities. Only eight of these reports specified self-injurious behavior. Most studies used only rating scales and no direct observations. Two studies, one on fluvoxamine (McDougle et al., 1996a, 1996b), and another on sertraline (McDougle et al., 1998a, 1998b) were conducted on and over 70 participants with autistic disorders. There was a positive response in over 60% the adults and essentially a negative response in children. Several children had adverse effects in the latter case.

4.2.4.3.3. Serotonin 5HT1A Agonists

Several compounds, chief among which is buspirone, show a high affinity for the 5-HT1A serotonin receptor and efficacy for treating anxiety and depression. These drugs are considered atypical anxiolytics (Werry, 1999). Other drugs more typically used to control anxiety are general CNS depressants like alcohol, sedatives; selective CNS depressants like the benzodiazepines, antihistamine, and anticholinergics;

adrenolytics like alpha adrenergic agonists and β-adrenergic blockers; antidepressants like SSRIs; analgesics like opiates; and antipsychotics.

There are only a few open trials of buspirone for anxiety, aggressive, and self-injurious behavior in developmental disabilities (Ratey, Sovner, Mikkelson, & Chmielinski, 1989; Ratey, Sovner, Parks, & Rogentine, 1991; Ricketts et al., 1994). The Ratey et al. (1991) study was a placebo-controlled study of buspirone on anxiety, aggressive behavior, and self-injurious behavior. Four of six subjects had a reduction of aggressive behavior, but not anxiety or self-injurious behavior. There are no double-blind, placebo-controlled studies of buspirone on self-injurious behavior that we know of, although this drug is still used in clinical practice.

4.2.4.3.4. Alpha-Adrenergic Blockers

Clonidine hydrochloride reduces the release of norepinephrine in the brain. It was originally developed as an antihypertensive. Clinical indications in the developmental disabilities population are as secondary treatment for hyperactivity, irritability, and aggressive behavior in behavioral phenotypes such as Fragile X syndrome (Hagerman, Bregman, & Tirosh, 1998; Hagerman, 1999). We are unaware of any studies of clonidine on self-injurious behavior, although we have seen it prescribed clinically in some cases.

4.2.4.3.5. β-Adrenergic Blockers

This family of drugs was developed in the 1950s to treat cardiovascular disease, but now is also used for treatment of anxiety, aggressive behavior and other neuropsychiatric illnesses like neuroleptic-induced akathisia, anxiety, stress, and panic disorders (see Ruedrich & Erhardt, 1999, for a review). There is a large family of selective and non-selective β-blockers. The only one that has been researched extensively in the developmental disabilities population is propranolol (Tofranil), a non-selective β-blocker. There are 10 studies, 4 of which included assessments of self-injurious behavior (Ruedrich, Grush, & Wilson, 1990; Ratey et al., 1986; Ratey et al., 1992; Luchins & Dojka, 1989). A majority of patients (30 of 34) showed improvement on the drug. None of the studies was double-blind or placebo-controlled and several also gave propranolol as add-on to current medications, especially neuroleptics. Thus, a more comprehensive controlled clinical trial is needed to assess the therapeutic effects of β-blockers on self-injurious behavior.

4.2.4.3.6. Narcotic Analgesic Drugs

In Chapter 2, we reviewed the Sandman et al.'s (1983) two-opioid peptide hypotheses for self-injurious behavior: the pain hypothesis and the addiction hypothesis. We also reviewed Thompson et al.'s (1995) extension of the addiction hypothesis of self-injurious behavior to self-administered endogenous-reinforced opioid addiction regulated by self-injurious behavior. These two groups have developed the most elaborate theories for the selective response of a psychotropic drug for self-injurious behavior. Their research has focused almost entirely on the effects of an endorphin blocker, which blocks opioid receptors in the brain, which is responsible for blunting nociception. Naloxone, given as an injection, and naltrexone hydrochloride, its orally administered counterpart, was developed as an adjunct in treating opiate- and alcohol-dependent people. They have also been used in several studies on self-injurious behavior (see Symons et al., 2004 for an in-depth review). Symons et al. (2004) reviewed 48 studies, 27 of which were controlled, involving 86 participants. Eighty per cent of participants reduced their self-injurious behavior using a 5–49% criterion and 47% were improved using a 50–100% criterion. The population patients ranged in age from 3–67 years, primarily with severe or profound intellectual disabilities and mostly multiple forms of high rate self-injurious behavior involving severe head and body hitting or slapping and biting. The doses ranged from 12.5 mg to 200 mg/day.

There are several double-blind, placebo-controlled studies of naltrexone for self-injurious behavior, some with positive and some with no or negative effects. These results suggest that naltrexone works with a subpopulation of self-injurious behavior cases. We will review two of the most comprehensive of these controlled sets of studies, which used multimode measures and conducted both acute phases and long-term follow-up. All of them suggest that naltrexone reduces self-injurious behavior in a subgroup of the self-injurious behavior population of individuals with severe, high-rate head banging and self-biting.

Sandman et al. (1993) performed a 10-week double blind crossover study of naltrexone among 24 adults with self-injurious behavior and intellectual disability at Fairview Developmental Center. Out of the institutional population of 1,200 there were 129 self-injurious behavior cases out of which 24 with the highest self-injurious behavior rates were chosen. Other psychoactive medications (used in 43% of them) were kept constant during the trial. Different orders of weekly treatments of placebo, 0.5 mg/kg, 1.0 mg/kg, and 2.0 mg/kg of naltrexone were randomly assigned to the subjects. Videotaped observations, neurological examinations, ratings of adaptive and maladaptive behavior as well as a discrimination-learning task were conducted. Only the videotaped observations and the discrimination task yielded significantly positive results. There was a dose response effect of naltrexone on change scores of self-injurious behavior ranging from 10–90% reduction in 18 of 21 cases. The median was 50% reduction in self-injurious behavior at optimal naltrexone dose. There was also improvement on the discrimination task secondary to reduction of self-injurious behavior while on naltrexone. Use of change scores did not allow one to see the absolute baseline self-injurious behavior levels nor were potential drug–drug interactions between psychoactive medications, which subjects were using, studied. Nevertheless, this is an impressive study.

Sandman et al. (2000) replicated the above results with another placebo-controlled double-blind study lasting from 28–32 weeks and found a subgroup with long and persistent positive response to chronic treatment with naltrexone. However, another group of original naltrexone responders from their acute dose study increased their self-injurious behavior when they entered into the three-month long-term study of treatment with naltrexone. It may be that intermittent exposure to naltrexone, especially at lower doses, resulted in a long-lasting supersensitivity of opiate receptors in the brain. Patients with high baseline levels of endogenous opiates appeared to be the most responsive to chronic treatment with naltrexone.

An excellent double-blind crossover study of the effects of naltrexone on self-injurious behavior in eight adults with severe or profound intellectual disability was performed by Thompson et al. (1994). Five-minute behavioral samples were taken one per hour for 7 h each day over four 2-week phases (baseline, placebo, 50 mg, and 100 mg) in randomly assigned order. Half of the subjects also received 0.3 mg per day of clonidine along with naltrexone, in order to control for possible confounding due to opiate-like withdrawal symptoms that may accompany naltrexone administration. No psychotropic effects of clonidine were detected, but naltrexone significantly reduced high-intensity head banging and self-biting ranging from 23% to 100% in six of eight subjects. There was no improvement in eye-, nose-, or throat-poking or face slapping. The largest effects were on hand-to-head hitting and head-to-object hitting at acupuncture sites. Few physiological side effects (nausea, abdominal cramps, diarrhea, skin rash, and liver dysfunction) of naltrexone were observed. Form of the self-injurious behavior and the affected body location may be significant predictors of response to naltrexone. Sleep improved from 5.3 h to 6.7 h per night. Symons et al. (2001b) replicated and extended the Thompson et al.'s (1994) results using a double-blind, placebo-controlled ABAB single-subject experimental design, for four individuals with severe self-injurious behavior. Using sequential dependency analysis, they also showed that participants improved their contingent responsiveness to staff while on naltrexone, compared to placebo.

Taken together, these studies of naltrexone on self-injurious behavior show a highly consistent dose effect averaging about a 50% reduction in self-injurious behavior in 60–80% of cases, which is related to intensity, location, and topography of self-injurious behavior. This is the best-documented work on selective neuropharmacological hypotheses for some types of self-injurious behavior to date. The best summaries of their findings can be found in Sandman and Touchette (2002) and Thompson and Caruso (2002). See also Chapter 2, this book, for a brief summary of the opioid peptide hypotheses of self-injurious behavior and the evidence for them. As yet, a disjunctive test of the pain hypothesis versus the addiction hypothesis has not been conducted, so it is not clear whether they reflect distinct or compatible overlapping systems in the CNS. The work of Symons and colleagues on pain and self-injurious behavior (see Chapter 2) may help to clarify these issues.

4.2.4.3.7. Mood Stabilizers

The term "mood stabilizer" was first applied to lithium salts when given to patients with bipolar disorders to reduce their mood swings. It is used around the world (see Poindexter et al., 1998; Hellings, 1999, for reviews of mood stabilizers in developmental disabilities). Later it was found that some anticonvulsants were also effective mood stabilizers. The main ones were carbamazepine (CBZ) and valproic acid (VPA). More recently, other new anticonvulsants have also been used in this population: gabapentin (Neurontin), lamotrigine (Lamictil), topiramate (Topamax), and tiagabine (Gabatril) (Hellings, 1999). Their effects on aggressive behavior and self-injurious behavior are considered secondary to the patient's bipolar disorder. Most of them are case reports and open trials. There are only a few double-blind, placebo-controlled studies. These drugs are of interest, in that their CNS mechanisms of action involve neural transmitters, which act as CNS inhibitors.

Lithium Lithium is used clinically in the general and developmental disabilities population for mania, brain injury, or aggressive behavior (Poindexter et al., 1998; Rivinus

& Harmatz, 1979; Vanstraelen & Tyrer, 1999). In the developmental disabilities population, a small number of case reports suggest that lithium is effective for treating aggressive behavior and self-injurious behavior (Luchins & Dojka, 1989; Pary, 1991). There are no double-blind, placebo-controlled studies of lithium for self-injurious behavior of which we are aware. Lithium also has several adverse side effects, which can be toxic if blood levels are unmonitored, including polyuria, thirst, and gastrointestinal distress. This drug is used sparingly in developmental disabilities (Aman et al., 1995a, 1995b), and it should be used cautiously with appropriate monitoring guidelines (Pary, 1991).

Anticonvulsants Anticonvulsants have been used also for rapidly cycling patients or patients with mixed mania, irritability, aggressive behavior, self-injurious behavior, and hyperactivity in developmental disabilities. They seem to be better tolerated than lithium. While there are several positive case reports and open label studies, there are only a few double-blind, placebo-controlled studies.

In one study, carbamazepine prescribed for hyperactivity was not efficacious (Reid, Naylor, & Kay, 1981). Barrett, Payton, and Burkhart (1988) using a placebo-controlled double-blind, single-subject crossover design, demonstrated positive effects of 100–300 mg of carbamazepine in a girl with mild intellectual disability and a complex partial seizure disorder. Self-pinching and growling noises were completely suppressed at the high dose, while on-task behavior, nonsense speech, and foul language remained unaffected.

Several open-label studies (Sovner, 1989; Kastner, Finesmith, & Walsh, 1993) and case reports (Ruedrich, Swales, Fossaceca, Toliver, & Rutkowski, 1999) have shown that valproic acid (VPA) was helpful for improving mood-related symptoms and related aggressive and self-injurious behavior. However, the only double-blind, placebo-controlled study by Hellings et al. (2005) of VPA on aggressive behavior and self-injurious behavior in the developmental disabilities population of 30 children and adolescents aged 6–20 showed no significant effects on the ABC Irritability subscale (Aman et al., 1993) or the *Overt Aggression Scale* (Yudofsky et al., 1986). However, a subgroup of 10 VPA responders demonstrated a sustained response. Four of these responders later were tapered off the drug, but they relapsed significantly to their aggressive behavior. There may be a smaller subset of cases who do respond to VPA, but there is no evidence for a selective response on self-injurious behavior. VPA has been considered to have a mild side effects profile, although recently investigators have discovered risk for liver failure, pancreatitis, persistent abdominal pain, vomiting, and lethargy with long-term chronic use. Platelet count and hepatic enzymes should be monitored regularly (Hellings, 1999).

Topiramate is a new mood-stabilizing anti-seizure drug, which has a novel mechanism of action. It is a selective blocker of glutamate receptors and sodium channels and it potentiates GABA-ergic neural transmission in the brain. It inhibits CNS transmission in the basal ganglia circuitry involving dopamine and serotonin. It has also been used for weight control and suppression of binge eating in Prader–Willi syndrome (Smathers, Wilson, & Nigro, 2003). A recent open-label study by Shapira, Lessig, Lewis, Goodman, & Driscoll (2004), attempted to replicate this study in eight adults with Prader–Willi syndrome. The investigators failed to find an effect on weight control, but there was a significant reduction on aggressive behavior (ABC *Irritability* scores) and self-injurious behavior (*SIB Restraint Checklist*). Skin picking decreased and wound healing increased while on topiramate. Skin picking can be a very serious type of self-injurious behavior among Prader–Willi patients (Dykens, Cassidy, & King, 1999), which in the past has been controlled often by the use of SSRIs. Unfortunately, SSRIs can sometimes cause increase in weight, which, in the case of Prader–Willi syndrome, seems particularly counterproductive. This study should be replicated and expanded both for its practical and theoretical relevance to selective causes of self-injurious behavior.

4.2.4.4. Drug–Behavior Interaction Studies

We have performed two comprehensive reviews of drug–behavior interaction studies for people with developmental disabilities, one covering the period up to 1983 (Schroeder, Lewis, & Lipton, 1983) and one covering the period from 1983 to 1999 (Napolitano et al., 1999). There have been only a few studies in this area on self-injurious behavior. There are basically two types of studies: (1) studies, which evaluate pharmacotherapy alone or in combination with behavioral interventions and (2) studies of multiple effects of pharmacotherapy on different behaviors, e.g., learning versus social behavior or maladaptive behavior.

In treatment evaluation studies, group methodologies involve comparing effectiveness of a drug-alone group, a behavior intervention-alone group, a drug plus behavior intervention group, and a group with no treatment. The studies of this type have been almost exclusively on stimulant drugs and behavior intervention for hyperactivity. There are no group drug–behavior interaction treatment evaluation studies on self-injurious behavior of which we are aware. This is perhaps understandable, given ethical constraints on withholding treatment for serious self-injurious behavior cases. A few single-subject studies have been published comparing behavior intervention for self-injurious behavior alone or in combination with medication (Barrett et al., 1988; Grosset & Williams, 1995; Luiselli, 1986; Ryan et al., 1989), but they all are difficult to interpret because of confounding of order of treatment effects and the lack of adequate control treatment conditions.

Well-controlled studies of multiple effects of pharmacotherapy on self-injurious behavior are more common: (1) studies of drug effects on self-injurious behavior and cognition and attention; (2) studies on drug effects as a function of different behavioral contingencies, e.g., functional analysis studies; (3) studies of drug effects on staff behavior as well as on the target self-injurious behavior case; and (4) behavior pharmacological studies of dose response, reinforcement contingencies, e.g., schedule effects, stimulus factors, etc. We will consider each of these types of studies below.

4.2.4.4.1. Studies of Drug Effects on Cognition and Social Behavior

Studies of drug effects on cognition and social behavior have been in existence for over 30 years. A classic dose-response study by Sprague and Sleator (1977) of the effects of methylphenidate on hyperactivity in children showed that the peak effective dose for their attention was lower than that for their overactive behavior. This study has served as a model for subsequent research; but, as a review by Williams and Saunders (1997) has shown, analyzing such cognitive effects among people with developmental disabilities is a complex matter. Although there are several studies on stereotyped behavior and attention, memory, etc., (Napolitano et al., 1999), we will only examine two placebo-controlled double blind self-injurious behavior studies.

The Sandman et al. (1993) double-blind, crossover study of naltrexone for self-injurious behavior has been described previously in the section on narcotic analgesics. In addition to behavioral observations of self-injurious behavior, they measured learning with a paired associates task modified for people with severe and profound intellectual disability. The task required the subject to place an object in the correct tray using a Wisconsin General Test Apparatus procedure during drug and placebo conditions. Results indicated that learning improved and self-injurious behavior decreased during drug treatment phases (2 mg/kg).

Yoo et al. (2003) conducted a study of the cognitive effects of risperidone in the larger program study of risperidone on destructive behavior previously described in the section on atypical antipsychotics. The subject was a severe case of self-injurious behavior, aggressive behavior, screaming, and throwing objects. The cognitive task was a matching task adapted from the operant procedure of repeated acquisition of stimulus chains often used in animal behavior pharmacology. It has the advantage of simultaneously yielding scores of performance rate and accuracy, so that each learning session has its own control for performance. Results showed that the subject retained her matching accuracy under the reinforced drug condition, but not under the non-reinforced drug condition while on risperidone, even though her performance rate decreased. This suggests that reinforcement has a protective effect on the rate-decreasing effects of risperidone.

Taken together with results of studies on the suppressive effects of drugs on cognitive performance and stereotyped behavior (Napolitano et al., 1999), and the current studies on self-injurious behavior, it appears that they do not suppress cognitive function, as is often alleged, if their dose is adjusted properly. In some cases, accuracy might be improved by the drug. This is a promising area, which needs much more study.

4.2.4.4.2. Functional Analysis Studies of Drug Effects

Functional analysis studies of drug effects on self-injurious behavior have begun to appear only recently, although we have seen selective drug effects as a function of different environmental demands before (Schroeder & Gualtieri, 1985). Schaal and Hackenburg (1994) have labeled these "functional diagnostic" procedures.

The first published study of functional analysis of drug effects on self-injurious behavior was by Garcia and Smith (1999). They did a standard analogue functional analysis for 52 sessions during a double-blind, placebo-controlled trial of naltrexone in two individuals with serious self-injurious behavior and found a differential effect depending on the topography of self-injurious behavior and its functions across subjects. For one case, naltrexone decreased self-injurious behavior across all functional analysis conditions; for the other, it reduced head slapping, but not head banging, during the escape condition, and did not reduce self-injurious behavior in the other conditions. This is the first demonstration of function-specific and topography-specific effects of a drug on self-injurious behavior. The authors acknowledge some of the shortcomings of their data, but the study was nevertheless well conducted.

We have replicated results similar to those of Garcia and Smith (1999), i.e., function-specific effects for different self-injurious behavior topographies, functions, and subjects in three analogue functional analysis studies in our double-blind, crossover program study of risperidone for destructive behavior (Valdovinos et al., 2002; Crosland et al., 2003; Zarcone et al, 2004). In the latter study, 13 cases with self-injurious behavior, aggressive behavior, and disruptive behavior received weekly functional analysis sessions throughout the whole drug trial. Seven of 10 risperidone responders fell into the undifferentiated functional analysis category, whereas risperidone non-responders tended to show differentiated functional analysis response. Such information might be useful in predicting who will respond to a risperidone.

4.2.4.4.3. Drug Effects on Caregivers as well as the Target Cases
Schroeder and Gualtieri (1985) did a double-blind study of withdrawal of thioridazine in 23 individuals with severe self-injurious and aggressive behavior institutionalized adults severe and profound intellectual disabilities. Using direct observation al sampling, they showed that staff directed more positive attention to these people when they were withdrawn from the drug than when they were taking the drug irrespective of the persons' positive or negative behaviors.

The Lewis et al. (1996a, 1996b, 1996c, 1996d) double-blind, crossover study of clomipramine for self-injurious behavior has been described previously in the section on antidepressant drugs and self-injurious behavior. In addition to a significant decrease in self-injurious behavior, there was a 50% decrease in the need for staff intervention to stop self-injurious behavior.

Symons et al. (2001a, 2001b) in their replication of the Thompson et al. (1994) double-blind study of naltrexone for self-injurious behavior found that naltrexone responders became more responsive to their caregivers and vice versa.

4.2.4.4.4. Behavior Pharmacology Studies of Self-Injurious Behavior
Behavior pharmacology studies of self-injurious behavior have not as yet been conducted as far as we know, but parametric dose response studies comparing reinforcement contingencies would be very useful. Several studies previously cited have compared the effects of two or three fixed doses, but no dose-ranging studies have been conducted. Drug–behavior interaction studies of self-injurious behavior strongly support the concept of taking multiple levels of independent variables and multiple dependent measures of their effects on self-injurious behavior. Several self-injurious behavior drug studies have shown positive side effects as well as the usually cited negative side effects. Analysis of direct observational measures, such as the ones used in the Symons et al.'s (2001a, 2001b) study, appear to be useful to document such side effects in addition to the often-recommended more subjective social validity measures.

4.2.5. Conclusions – Psychopharmacological Research

In spite of the many difficulties in conducting high-risk psychopharmacological research in vulnerable populations such as those with intellectual disabilities and self-injurious behavior, remarkable advances have been made over the past two decades. With the help of the new genetics and advances in the neurobiology of self-injurious behavior, drugs can be prescribed much more effectively, with more specificity, and fewer serious side effects than ever before. Although much work remains to be done, we now have better diagnostic instruments to guide the selection of psychotropic drugs for the appropriate complex disorder related to self-injurious behavior. A small number of drug–behavior interaction studies exists by which we can assess bio-behavioral interactions with self-injurious behavior. Large-scale multisite studies are beginning to appear with larger numbers of participants. These are important for our ability to assess the core and the idiosyncratic features of the highly varied population of self-injurious behavior cases, so that, in the future, we will be able to better predict who will respond to a given drug and who will not. Clinical practice has traditionally used a trial-and-error approach. Hopefully, research will improve and become more theory-guided as our research on the psychopharmacology of self-injurious behavior improves and increases.

4.3. Other Treatments

Thus far, a variety of empirically supported, rational treatment procedures for self-injurious behavior have been discussed. What follows is discussion of some additional procedures that have appeared in the treatment literature on self-injurious behavior.

4.3.1. Noncontingent Restraint

When self-injurious behavior is of sufficient frequency and intensity that it would cause potentially serious damage, preventive continuous physical restraint is often a justified default strategy. Continuous restraint can involve use of mechanical restraining devices or protective equipment. While such devices can prevent injury due to self-injurious behavior by limiting body movement, they are ultimately undesirable for many reasons, including that fact that do not promote positive alternative behavior. Further, continuous use of restraints will not reduce the probability or severity of self-injurious behavior during periods when they are not worn.

Potential physiological and social untoward effects of noncontingent restraint use have been mentioned previously (Luiselli, 1992; Rojahn et al., 1980). Additionally, it is possible that restraint could function to reinforce the behavior that accesses it (Favell, McGimsey, & Schell, 1982). However, a risk–benefit analysis of noncontingent restraint use may indicate that the risks associated with restraint-free periods are lower than the risk of physiological and social side effects while being restrained. Regulatory or agency policy may require that the devices be removed for a minimum period of time within set intervals to permit range of motion exercise, air exposure of the skin, and so forth. These times, however, as we have seen in the example by Romanczyk (1986) may present particular danger for those for whom extreme self-injurious behavior has necessitated continuous restraint. The functional analysis and function-relevant treatment identification and delivery procedures developed by O'Reilly et al. (2003) and described earlier in this chapter could serve as a guide for determining procedures to implement during restraint-free periods.

Permanent, continuous restraint is not an acceptable form of intervention. Given the consultative expertise available from many practitioners, less invasive, function-relevant behavioral procedures could be developed that decelerate self-injurious behavior and reduce the reliance on restraint in many cases. Obi (1997) described a restraint fading procedure, combined with shaping, that effectively reduced self-injurious behavior while increasing social skills and positive work related behaviors in a 24-year-old man with Lesch–Nyhan syndrome. Similarly, Oliver, Hall, Hales, Murphy, and Watts (1998) implemented restraint fading combined with establishing inhibitory stimulus control, and maintained near zero rates of self-injurious behavior for three people with intellectual disabilities while permitting greater functional arm use.

4.3.2. Sensory Integration Therapy

Sensory integration is our ability to assimilate multiple types of sensory information (touch, movement, smell, taste, vision, and hearing), and to derive a coherent meaning from processing these stimuli, and to exercise motor and cognitive skills, while inhibiting inappropriate behavior and movements (Smith, Mruzek, & Mozingo, 2005). Sensory integration dysfunction can occur as a result of problems in the vestibular system (as indicated by poor posture or motor coordination), proprioceptive system (as indicated by stereotyped behavior), in the tactile system (as indicated by sensory over sensitivities or under sensitivities), or some combination of these. Sensory integration therapy is designed to remedy the underlying neurological problem that is producing the indicator response. Effective sensory integration therapy would indirectly produce improvements in attending, motor skills, social interaction, stereotyped behaviors, self-injurious behavior, or other indicator behaviors. Unfortunately, there is no evidence to date that supports the theory on which sensory integration is based (Smith et al., 2005). Likewise, there are no methods for assessing for and diagnosing sensory integration dysfunction that are empirically supported, and research on outcomes of the therapy itself has been characterized by methodological flaws, overstated results, negative results, or demonstrations of no effect (Smith et al., 2005).

Dura, Mulick, and Hammer (1988) examined rates of self-injurious behavior during 20-minute sensory integration therapy sessions and following those sessions, and reported reduced self-injurious behavior during the session, but rates at baseline levels by 15 min after the session. Mason and Iwata (1990) raise the possibility that improvements in self-injurious behavior sometimes seen after sensory integration therapy may depend on the relationship between the contingencies maintaining the behavior and the nature of the stimulation provided noncontingently during sensory integration therapy. Indeed, sensory integrative therapy has been shown to be followed by reductions in self-injurious behavior in some case (see Larrington, 1987). However, ignoring or denying presence of social and other environmental contingencies does not nullify their effect, and it remains possible that changes to these contingencies brought about in the confines of the sensory integration therapy session may well produce the behavioral changes occasionally seen. Perhaps conducting a conditional probabilities analysis of self-injurious behavior before, during, and after sensory integration sessions could answer this question.

4.3.3. Multisensory Environments

Sometimes called *Snoezelen rooms* (a neologism of the Dutch words for "snuffelen" (sniffing) and "doezelen" (dozing), multisensory environments have become popular in Europe and later also in the U.S. Snoezelen rooms are designed to be soothing and stimulating with lighting effects, colors, sounds, music, scents, different tactile materials, and various vestibular stimulations. Kwok, To, and Sung (2003) conducted a research project in a hospital that had built a multisensory environment. Thirty-one people with intellectual disability and psychiatric disorders received a four-week Snoezelen therapy, which consisted of using the multisensory room for one hour, once per week. After therapy, Snoezelen therapy was reported to have had a "marked effect" on 23% of the individuals, a "mild effect" for 36%, and "no effect" on 41%. The authors concluded that the multisensory environment used in this way was effective in reducing self-injurious behavior for more than half of the participants. However, the study is less than convincing due to methodological weaknesses: no pre-treatment or treatment accompanying assessment of self-injurious behavior was reported, no direct measurement of the behaviors was conducted, and no reliability data were collected.

Stadele and Malaney (2001) conducted a slightly better-controlled study with a 17-year-old boy and a 16-year-old girl, both diagnosed with autism. They directly measured the frequency of a variety of target behaviors including aggressive behavior, self-injurious behavior, noncompliance, and agitation, for a two-week period prior to the use of a multisensory environment, for two weeks during which the multisensory environment was used by each person individually for 20 min/day, and for two weeks after completing the two-week course of therapy. These authors report no discernable change in frequency of problem behavior from baseline to treatment to follow-up. Unfortunately, no reliability data were reported.

Lancioni, Cuvo, and O'Reilly (2002) reviewed 21 studies, 14 concerning people with developmental disabilities and 7 people with dementia. Of those studies, 14 reported positive within-session effects, 4 positive post-session effects, and 2 reported positive longer-term effects. In other words, there is no strong evidence to date that multisensory environments have a treatment effect on self-injurious behavior. To the extent that sensory integration, multisensory environments, and other empirically unsupported therapies do produce behavioral changes, a parsimonious explanation would be that they were the result of changes in the motivating operations.

4.4. Ethical Concerns in Treatment

The treatment of self-injurious behavior has raised many ethical concerns over the past three decades that culminate in the questions (a) at what point is it ethical to intervene and (b) how intrusive should the permitted methods be? As therapists, we are bound by professional ethical standards and guidelines have been developed by many professional organizations, state agencies, and private service providers for people with intellectual disabilities.

We have suggested a framework for judging the humaneness and effectiveness of treatments for self-injurious behavior (Schroeder, Oldenquist, & Rojahn, 1991), which we still think, is valid. We summarize it briefly.

4.4.1. Judging Humaneness of a Behavior Intervention Procedure

Judging humaneness of treatment involves guidance by some basic principles

1. Utilitarianism, which enjoins us to further the happiness of humanity.
2. Paternalism, which means caring for people for their own good although sometimes they might feel that their autonomy is restricted.
3. Dignity, which refers to the acknowledgment of people's worth as human beings;
4. Respecting the human rights of the individual. Rights also depend on our competencies, and our likelihood to harm ourselves and others. People have a right not to be treated cruelly. The Hippocratic oath holds that first we should do no harm. Harm implies mental or physical damage, and the justification of a therapy, painful or not, lies ultimately in diminishing harm.

A powerful test of the humaneness and acceptability of a treatment lies in reciprocity and role-reversal arguments: Is what you are recommending as therapy for others something you would accept being done to you? In the case of people with severe disabilities, the comparison is difficult, because one has to put oneself in that person's mindset. This is a hypothetical role reversal that must be done with care and sensitivity for each case, but it avoids theoretical questions about morality, religion, or ethical relativism. Calling specific treatments torture simply begs the question as to the appropriateness of their application. On the other hand, any procedure applied inappropriately or ineffectively offends the dignity of the individual and may be unethical.

4.4.2. Judging Treatment Effectiveness

Rush and Frances (2000) have published Expert Consensus Guidelines for the Treatment of Psychiatric and Behavioral Problems in Intellectual Disability, which is also a useful general guide for the selection of behavioral and psychopharmacological treatments of self-injurious behavior. However, in judging effectiveness in each specific case, we still need some specific criteria.

1. Sound methodology using either single-subject or group designs. The data must be recorded reliably and repeatedly, the procedures must be described in sufficient detail to permit replication, and the effects of the procedures must be replicated, to assess internal and external validity of the findings.
2. Measurement instrumentation must be valid and reliable.
3. Comparison of procedures must be done carefully. Two comparison strategies are (a) enumeration of positive results of different procedures across different experiments and (b) intra-subject comparisons of procedures within experiments.
4. Criteria for success must be comprehensive. Criteria for success have been a bone of contention for both behavioral and psychopharmacological treatments for self-injurious behavior. We have addressed criteria for success for psychopharmacological treatments in a previous section of this chapter, so we will concentrate only on the criteria for behavioral interventions here. First, we will consider traditional criteria for success in ABA studies; then we will discuss the PBS criteria for success proposed by Carr et al. (2002a, 2002b).

Behavior analytic criteria to judge effectiveness of treatment procedures have been agreed upon for several years (Baer, Wolf, & Risley, 1968). They are

1. degree and rapidity of change;
2. generalization to non-treatment settings, durability of change (maintenance);
3. favorable pattern of positive and negative side effects (covariation); and
4. social validity (Wolf, 1978; Kazdin & Matson, 1981), which can include the clinical significance of the treatment outcome (Risley, 1970), consumer satisfaction with the outcome (Holman, 1977), and community acceptance of the achieved goals (Kazdin, 1980).

With respect to rapidity and degree of change in self-injurious behavior, a recent review by Kahng et al. (2002) spanning the literature from 1964–2000 involving 396 studies and 706 subjects who met sound methodological inclusion criteria, a mean of 83.4% reduction in self-injurious behavior was achieved. The only change in results over 40 years was a reduction in variability in studies conducted from 1996–2000 compared to studies conducted from 1964–1995. So the technology seems to be improving. Practically, no studies with negative results and very few studies comparing different procedures were published, so a bias in publication practices toward accepting only positive results is likely to be present for this type of research.

With respect to generalization and maintenance, Kahng et al. (2002) reported that follow-up maintenance data were reported in only 13.7% of the studies reviewed, most of which were less than six months. Generalization data were reported in only 11%. The database on generalization and maintenance of behavioral interventions for self-injurious behavior is disappointingly small and does not seem to be increasing. There is no lack of analyses of generalization and maintenance (Stokes & Baer, 1977; Horner, Dunlap, & Koegel, 1988), but they have not led to an increase of this type of research on self-injurious behavior. It may be that some of these issues have been incorporated into the research methodology of PBS, e.g., conducting research in all target settings where the self-injurious behavior case resides. Such an approach might appear to mitigate the need for generalization training, but we doubt this.

The Kahng et al. (2002) review does not even report on covariation of side effects or social validity studies of behavioral intervention for self-injurious behavior. Carr et al. (1999a, 1999b) and our own review of the literature have yielded very few data-based studies (<10) in these areas. This is very disappointing, because most regulations calling for the use of behavior intervention procedures call for the replacement of self-injurious behavior with other more appropriate behaviors. However, as we pointed out already in 1988 (Schroeder & MacLean, 1987), the rules and models for substitution of self-injurious behavior behaviors in the repertoire are complex and not well understood. Johnston (2006) has made an excellent analysis of these problems and has called into question the therapeutic rationales and tactics that assume such a symptom substitution approach.

According to Carr et al. (2002b), PBS incorporates ABA techniques for reducing problem behaviors, but the realities of conducting research in natural and community settings necessitate changes in assessment methods, intervention strategies, and the definition of what constitutes successful outcome. Its critical features are comprehensive changes in life style, improvements in family life, jobs, community inclusion, supported living, expanding social relationships, and personal satisfaction, while de-emphasizing the focus on problem behavior. The important units of analysis are daily routines, schedules, and social interactions. Problem behavior is of note to the extent that it interferes with achieving positive results with respect to these molar variables. The primary intervention strategy involves rearranging the environment to improve the quality of life rather than reducing problem behavior.

Whether changing the context in which behavior interventions occur will be sufficient to decrease all self-injurious behavior remains to be seen. For some purely environmentally induced self-injurious behavior, changing the environment may be sufficient. However, the Kahng et al. (2002) review, and our own two-year follow-up data (Schroeder et al., 1978; Schroeder et al., 1982a) suggest that there is a core group of severe chronic cases, perhaps 25–40%, for which clear environmental reasons for their self-injurious behavior cannot be found and who will need more than environmental rearrangement to prevent their self-injurious behavior. We have discussed the bio-behavioral hypotheses for their self-injurious behavior in Chapter 2. These cases will likely need intensive ABA procedures, psychopharmacotherapy, long-term care, and surveillance regardless of their living environment.

Chapter 5

Summary and Future Directions

The research discussed in this volume offers considerable hope that approaches to diagnosis and treatment of self-injurious behavior are reaching a level of complexity and sophistication that will make possible a range of preventive strategies and clinically significant treatments resulting in lasting changes in this behavior. What is needed next is a plan for promoting these procedures on a large scale, so that they are available to all who need them. They must be socially valid and lasting for years, rather than for days, weeks, or months if parents and families are to accept them and demand them for their children.

Self-injurious behavior is a heterogeneous clinical phenomenon, currently best understood with a developmental bio-behavioral perspective.

It is certainly true that much of self-injurious behavior serves observable, external functions, such as gaining social attention or tangible reinforcers, and many of them are readily changed by altering social occasions for self-injurious behavior and the reinforcement contingencies that maintain it without necessarily addressing the biological conditions that set the occasion for it. Functional analyses have provided empirical evidence for the complex picture of the antecedents and consequences that maintain self-injurious behavior and improved assessment instruments have led to a richer and better set of treatments for individuals with self-injurious behavior.

There are also cases of self-injurious behavior, however, which may originally have been occasioned by social stimuli or contingencies but which, through extensive practice, have now altered interoceptive stimuli, e.g., dopamine and/or opioid release, whose functions must also be altered, in order to allow social contingencies to be effective in treating self-injurious behavior. In still other cases, e.g., Lesch–Nyhan syndrome, there may be a strong genetic or neurobiological predisposition toward self-injurious behavior where using social contingencies without considering neurochemical deficiencies and maturational variables is very unlikely to produce lasting effects.

The study of behavioral phenotypes in genetic syndromes associated with self-injurious behavior gives us hope that there are subtypes of self-injurious behavior, which, if considered sufficiently, will allow us to tune our algorithms in the treatment and prognosis for self-injurious behavior.

The bio-behavioral models for self-injurious behavior also give plausible accounts for the variety of forms and functions of self-injurious behavior. In some cases the independent variable is behavioral (e.g., isolate rearing or suboptimal parenting by parents who are overwhelmed with a special needs child). In other cases, it is biological (e.g., dopamine dysregulation). In still other cases, the model is mixed (e.g., as in the bio-behavioral state model by Guess & Carr, 1991). A given self-injurious behavior case might fit one or several of these models depending on the genetic disposition and on the neurobiological and behavioral history.

The tools we have for exploring the above risk factors continue to improve. We now have better rating scales. The various methods of functional analysis (e.g., *Journal of Applied Behavior Analysis*, *27*, 1994, issue 2) have been a major advance in our armamentarium. The study of genetic behavioral phenotypes with new genetic techniques such as linkage analysis (Dykens et al., 2000) and genomic analysis is another tool. The use of neurochemical assays of neurotransmitter functions, e.g., Lewis et al. (1996a, 1996b, 1996c, 1996d), may also aid in predicting who will respond best to which drug treatment. Together these tools will also help us with efforts to prevent self-injurious behavior.

Animal models of self-injurious behavior play a key role in discovering the biological causes and treatments for different types of self-injurious behavior. They are critical for our understanding the mechanisms by which adverse events cause self-injurious behavior and intellectual disability (Crnic & Nitkin, 1996). They permit us to experiment with therapies that would never be permitted on humans without such prior testing. Finally, we can check our behavioral findings with genetic and neurobiological techniques that are too invasive to be used on humans. To be sure, care must be used in comparing a particular animal phenotype with an appropriate homology in humans. But once homology is established, one can then experiment with the methods of producing, preventing, and curing the disorder. For instance, gene therapy for Lesch–Nyhan syndrome is a real possibility for the future, but currently it requires the study of the HPRT mouse model, in order to understand the purine salvage pathway in Lesch–Nyhan syndrome and how the genetic defect can be cured or prevented.

It is easy to forget that only 40 years ago the self-injurious behavior cases of the type discussed in this chapter were written off as hopeless, confined to physical and chemical restraints in highly restrictive environments. Today there are humane and effective interventions for *the majority* of self-injurious behavior cases in mostly unrestricted settings. That is a paradigm shift in treatment and prognosis that was brought about by the behavioral analytic revolution. We now think differently about and have different expectations for people with intellectual disabilities and self-injurious behavior.

It is only 20 years since our knowledge of the neurobiological causes of self-injurious behavior began to grow, and the rate of growth has been exponential ever since. We now have a few drugs based on a clear neurobiological rationale that selectively improve self-injurious behavior without serious side effects, e.g., naltrexone, the atypical antipsychotics, and the serotonin reuptake inhibitors. We now have behavior phenotypes whose self-injurious behavior is differentially affected by selected drugs. There are now drugs coming on the market, which are likely to work even better. There is even the prospect of gene therapy for certain self-injurious behavior-related genetic syndromes. Lastly, there is a prospect of non-invasive training-induced recovery from lesion-induced susceptibilities to self-injurious behavior. Truly we have come a long way with research on self-injurious behavior, but we still have a long way to go in order to address all of the aspects of this multiply caused and multiply-affected devastating disorder.

Appendix

Summary of Epidemiological Studies on Self-Injurious Behavior in Non-Specific Samples of Individuals with Intellectual Disabilities

Reference	Reference Population & Sampling	SIB Definition and Assessment	Results
1. Whitney (1966)[a]	*Reference Population* Residents of MR facility $n = 950$ *Age:* Unknown *Sex:* Unknown *MR Level:* Unknown *Sampling Method:* Unknown	*SIB Definition:* "Mutilated bodies to the extent to require restraint" *Assessment Tool:* Unknown	*Reference Population:* *Global SIB Prevalence* = 8.8% ($n = 84$) *By Age:* Unknown *By Sex:* Unknown *By MR Level:* Unknown *By SIB Topographies:* Unknown *SIB Target Population:* *Age:* Unknown *Sex:* Unknown *MR Level:* Unknown *SIB Topographies:* Unknown
2. Ballinger (1971)	*Reference Population* Patients in a hospital for individuals with MR in Scotland $n = 631$ *Age:* Unknown *Sex:* 44% f, 56% m *MR Level:* borderline = 8%; mild = 23%; moderate = 23%; severe 23%; profound 23% *Sampling Method:* Total population study	*SIB Definition:* "Any painful or destructive act, committed by the patient against his own body" SIB occurred within the previous month *Assessment Tool:* Unknown Individuals were examined by author	*Reference Population:* *Global SIB Prevalence* = 14.8% ($n = 93$) *By Age:* Unknown *By Sex:* Unknown *By MR Level:* Unknown *By SIB Topographies:* Unknown *By IQ:* 4% in 68 + 6% in 52–67 10% in 36–51 18% in 20–35 29% in 0–19

(Continued)

Reference	Reference Population & Sampling	SIB Definition and Assessment	Results
			SIB Target Population: *Age: Unknown* *Sex:* 55% f, 45% m *MR Level:* 2% = borderline 9% = mild 16% = moderate 28% = severe 45% = profound *SIB Topographies:* 38% = picking 22% = striking 20% = scratching 18% = banging 15% = biting
3. Smeets (1971)	*Reference Population* Residents in a private residential school for MR children and adults *n* = 400 *Age: Unknown* *Sex: Unknown* *MR Level: Unknown* *Sampling Method:* Total population study	*SIB Definition:* "Any behavior displayed by the individual, which can cause direct physical damage to himself, which may or may not be repetitious, rhythmical or stereotyped in nature, and which are not necessarily aversive to the individual himself but certainly would be aversive to 'normal' individuals" *Assessment Tool:* Unknown	*Reference Population:* *Global SIB Prevalence* = 8.8% (*n* = 35) *By Age: Unknown* *By Sex: Unknown* *By MR Level: Unknown* *By SIB Topographies: Unknown* *SIB Target Population:* *Age:* Mean f 19.9; mean m 16.3 *Sex:* 40% f, 60% m *MR Level: Unknown* *SIB Topographies:* 66% = biting 57% = head banging 46% = pinching 26% = scratching 23% = face slapping <7% = orifice gouging, severe skin rubbing, throwing self to the floor *Other Maladaptive behaviors:* 86% temper tantrums; 80% stereotyped behavior; 74% hyperactive behavior; 57% aggressive towards peers; 43% destructive behavior; 40% aggressive toward staff

4. Ross (1972)

Reference Population
State hospital residents with MR
$n = 11,139$
Age: Unknown
Sex: Unknown
MR Level: Unknown
Sampling Method: Total population study of a hospital population through the California census

SIB Definition:
"Self-destructive behavior"
Assessment Tool:
Census form

Reference Population:
 Global SIB Prevalence = 23% ($n = 2,562$)
 By Age: Unknown
 By Sex: Unknown
 By MR Level:
  13% in mild
  18% in moderate
  25% in severe
  26% in profound
 By SIB Topographies: Unknown
SIB Target Population:
 Age: Unknown
 Sex: Unknown
 MR Level: Unknown
 SIB Topographies: Unknown

5. MacKay, McDonald, and Morrissey (1974)

Reference Population
Inpatient population of a British hospital
$n = 600$
Age: Unknown
Sex: Unknown
MR Level: 33% moderate; 48% severe; 19% profound
Sampling Method: Unknown

SIB Definition:
"... painful or destructive act committed against own body" such as head banging, face slapping, skin picking, hair pull, regurgitation
Assessment Tool:
Questionnaire

Reference Population:
 Global SIB Prevalence = 19% ($n = 114$)
 By Age: Unknown
 By Sex: Unknown
 By MR Level: Unknown
 By SIB Topographies: Unknown
SIB Target Population:
 Age: Unknown
 Sex: Unknown
 MR Level: Unknown
 SIB Topographies: Unknown

6. Soule and O'Brien (1974)[a]

Reference Population
Residents of state MR facility
$n = 966$
Age: Unknown
Sex: Unknown
MR Level: Unknown
Sampling Method: Unknown

SIB Definition:
"Self injurious behavior such as biting and head banging"
Assessment Tool:
Unknown

Reference Population:
 Global Prevalence: 7.7% ($n = 74$)
 By Age: Unknown
 By Sex: Unknown
 By MR Level: Unknown
 By SIB Topographies: Unknown
SIB Target Population:
 Age: Unknown
 Sex: Unknown
 MR Level: Unknown
 SIB Topographies: Unknown

(Continued)

Reference	Reference Population & Sampling	SIB Definition and Assessment	Results
7. Eyman and Call (1977)	*Reference Population* Individuals with MR receiving services from two regional centers in California and Colorado community and institution centered services for MR and from the Nevada Division of Mental Hygiene and Mental Retardation n = 6,870 *Age:* 25% 0–12 years; 76% 13 or older *Sex:* 44% f, 56% m *MR Level:* 61% mild/mod; 21% severe; 18% profound *Sampling Method:* Total population study *Residential Setting:* 27% *institution;* 30% *community;* 43% *family*	*SIB Definition:* "Does physical violence to self" *Assessment Tool:* *Adaptive Behavior Scale* (Nihira et al., 1974) Ratings by direct-care personnel for the institutions and by social workers for the community placements	*Reference Population:* *Global SIB Prevalence* = 15% (n = 103) *By Age:* 15% in ages 0–12 15% in ages >12 *By Sex:* Unknown *By MR Level:* 8% in mild or moderate 20% in severe 36% in profound *By SIB Topographies:* Unknown *By Residential Setting:* 34% institution; 10% community facility; 8% family settings *SIB Target Population:* *Age:* Unknown *Sex:* Unknown *MR Level:* Unknown *SIB Topographies:* Unknown
8. Singh (1977)	*Reference Population* Patients in a hospital and training school for MR in New Zealand n = 368 *Age:* Unknown *Sex:* Unknown *MR Level:* Unknown *Sampling Method:* Total population study; all patients studied over 6 months	*SIB Definition:* "Self-inflicted behavior, which leads to lacerations, bruising, or abrasions of the patients own body" *Assessment Tool:* Unknown	*Reference Population:* *Global SIB Prevalence* = 22.8% (n = 84) *By Age:* Unknown *By Sex:* Unknown *By MR Level:* Unknown *By SIB Topographies:* Unknown *SIB Target Population:* *Age:* Unknown *Sex:* 40% f, 60% m *MR Level:* 8% = mild 36% = moderate 48% = severe 8% = profound *SIB Topographies:* 26% head banging 23% biting 19% skin picking 18% face slapping 8% hair pulling 43% other

9. Ando and Yoshimura (1978)

Reference Population
School for MR and autism in Japan
$n = 128$
Age: mean $= 10.6$; range, 6–14
Sex: 42% f, 58% m
MR Level: Unknown
Sampling Method: Total population study

SIB Definition:
"... compulsively and consciously destructive behavior against himself such as head banging or hand biting"
Assessment Tool:
Unknown
Teachers and aides evaluated children

Reference Population:
Global SIB Prevalence $= 5.5\%$ ($n = 7$)
By Age: Unknown
By Sex: Unknown
By MR Level: Unknown
By SIB Topographies: Unknown
SIB Target Population:
Age: Unknown
Sex: Unknown
MR Level: Mean IQ 31 ± 11
SIB Topographies: Unknown

---

10. Maisto, Baumeister, and Maisto (1978)

Reference Population
Individuals in a state residential training center
$n = 1,300$
Age: mean $= 33.5$; range, 10–70
Sex: 44% f, 56% m
MR Level: 5.2% mild; 8.7% moderate; 28.5% severe; 47.6% profound
Sampling Method: Total population study; personnel identified individuals who exhibited any type of SIB

SIB Definition:
"Repetitive acts by individuals directed towards themselves which results in physical harm or tissue damage"
Assessment Tool:
Unknown
Unit psychologists filled out measures

Reference Population:
Global SIB Prevalence $= 14.0\%$ ($n = 182$)
By Age: Unknown
By Sex: Unknown
By MR Level:
  0% in mild
  3% in moderate
  21% in severe/profound
  By SIB Topographies: Unknown
SIB Target Population:
Age: mean $= 28.3$; range, 10–62
Sex: 55% f, 45% m
MR Level:
  4% = moderate
  96% = severe/profound
  SIB Topographies: Unknown

---

11. Schroeder et al. (1978)

Reference Population
Residents of a developmental center for MR
Three repeated assessments: 1973, 1975, 1976
$n = 1,150$
Age: mean $= 25.6$; range, 5–85
Sex: 55% f, 45% m
MR Level: 4% mild; 11% moderate; 85% severe/profound
Sampling Method: Total population study; social workers referred cases with SIB

SIB Definition:
"Repetitive acts by individuals directed towards themselves which result in physical harm or tissue damage" (Tate & Baroff, 1966)
Assessment Tool:
Unknown
Social workers interviewed staff and conducted file searches

Reference Population:
Global SIB Prevalence $= 18.1\%$ over a three year period ($n = 208$)
approx. 10% for each annual survey
By Age: Unknown
By Sex: Unknown
By MR Level:
  2% in mild
  9% in moderate
  14% in severe/profound
  By SIB Topographies: Unknown
SIB Target Population:
Age: mean $= 22.3$
Sex:
  With mild SIB: f $= 49\%$, f $= 51\%$
  With severe SIB: f $= 47\%$, m $= 53\%$

(Continued)

Reference	Reference Population & Sampling	SIB Definition and Assessment	Results
			MR Level: Mild SIB: 1% = mild 8% = moderate 91% = severe/profound Severe SIB: 0% = mild 6% = moderate 94% = severe/profound *SIB Topographies:* Unknown *Maladaptive Behaviors:* 35% mild SIB (30% stereotypies); 37% severe SIB (25% stereotypies)
12. Borthwick et al. (1981)	*Reference Population* People receiving services for the developmentally disabled during 1979 in three states (AZ, CA, CO) $n = 6{,}202$ *Age:* Unknown *Sex:* Unknown *MR Level:* Unknown *Sampling Method:* Total population study – three states collect information from all clients receiving DD services in their state	*SIB Definition:* "Does physical violence to self" *(item from the Behavior Development Survey (BDS))* (Borthwick-Duffy, 1994; Borthwick et al., 1981) *Assessment Tool:* *Adaptive Behavior Scale* (Nihira et al., 1974), shortened version	*Reference Population:* *Global SIB Prevalence* = 19.8% ($n = 1{,}228$) *By Age:* 6% ages 0–3 10% ages 4–10 10% ages 11–20 9% ages 21+ *By Sex:* 9% f; 10% m *By MR Level:* 4% in mild 7% in moderate 15% in severe 25% in profound *By SIB Topographies:* Unknown *SIB Target Population:* *Age:* Unknown *Sex:* Unknown *MR Level:* Unknown *SIB Topographies:* Unknown *Dual Diagnoses:* 9% MR only; 16% dual diagnosis; 22% severe dual diagnosis *Residential Setting:* 38% institution; 18% convalescent; 8% boarding home; 13% family home; 8% own home *Maladaptive Behavior:* <1% SIB + aggression; 2% SIB + destruction; <1%

Individuals with MR in New York State

n = 30,578

(11.6% had a psychiatric disability and were excluded in this summary)

Age: 71% ages 21–44; 29% ages 5–20

Sex: 45% f, 55% m

MR Level:

Ages 0–21: 27% mild; 30%; moderate; 21% ; severe; 22% profound

Ages 22–45: 27% mild; 26%; moderate; 23% severe; 24% profound

Sampling Method: Total population study

"SIB which poses a serious impediment to independent functioning"

Assessment Tool:

Developmental Disabilities Information Survey (Jacobson, 1982)

Protocols were completed by clinical staff with DD experience

---

Global SIB Prevalence = 8.2% (n = 2,507)

By MR Level and Age:

Ages 0–21:

2% mild

3% moderate

9% severe

14% profound;

Ages 22–45

3% mild

3% moderate

6% severe

18% profound

By Sex: Unknown

By MR Level: Unknown

By SIB Topographies: Unknown

SIB Target Population:

Age: 8% in ages 0–21; 9% in ages 22 +

Sex: Unknown

MR Level: Unknown

SIB Topographies: Unknown

Residential Setting: Ages 0–21: 0% independent; 4% parents; 2% family care; 9% community; 16% dev. center; Ages 22–45: 1% independent; 2% with parents; 2% in family care; 5% in community; 15% in developmental center

---

14. Maurice and Trudel (1982)

Reference Population

Individuals residing in three institutions (two psychiatric, one MR) in Quebec

n = 2,858

Age = 45.8

Sex: 47% f, 53% m

MR Level: Unknown

Diagnosis: 43.7% MR; 48.5% psychotic

Sampling Method: Total population study – persons in charge of hospital wards identified residents with SIB

SIB Definition:

"Movement emitted voluntarily or involuntarily in a repetitive or stereotyped manner that contributed to a corporal damage to the person who emitted the movement" (SIB within last 2 years)

Assessment Tool:

Unknown

Interviews with direct care personnel

Reference Population:

Global SIB Prevalence = 14.1% (n = 403)

By Age: Unknown

By Sex: Unknown

By MR Level: Unknown

By SIB Topographies: Unknown

SIB Target Population:

Age: Unknown

Sex: Unknown

MR Level:

10% = mild

37% = moderate

53% = severe/profound

SIB Topographies:

13% = biting

13% = scratching

<10% = head banging, body hitting, pinching, gouging, hair pulling, pulling nails, digging wounds, etc.

Multiple SIB: 41% one SIB; 29% two SIB; 30% three+ SIB

(*Continued*)

Reference	Reference Population & Sampling	SIB Definition and Assessment	Results
15. Hill and Bruininks (1984)	*Reference Population* Residents in 236 public institutions and private community facilities throughout the US *n* = 2,271 *Age*: Unknown *Sex*: Unknown *MR Level*: Unknown *Sampling Method*: Random sampling of public institutions and private community facilities from entire 1977 list maintained by the National Association of Superintendents of Public Residential Facilities	*SIB Definition*: Unknown *Assessment Tool*: Interviews with direct care staff about major categories of maladaptive behavior: SIB, injuries to others, property damage and other disruptive behaviors	*Reference Population* *Global SIB Prevalence* = 14.2% (*n* = 323) *By Age*: Unknown *By Sex*: Unknown *By MR Level*: Unknown *By SIB Topographies*: Unknown *SIB Target Population*: *Age*: Unknown *Sex*: Unknown *MR Level*: Unknown *SIB Topographies*: Unknown *Residential Setting*: 11% community residential, 22% public residential
16. Reid, Ballinger, Heather, and Melvin (1984)	*Reference Population* Adults with severe and profound MR in a hospital in the UK *n* = 86 *Age*: mean = 41.3; range, 24–78 *Sex*: 57% f; 43% m *MR Level*: 52% severe; 48% profound *Sampling Method*: An original cohort of 100 residents was reexamined 6 years later	*SIB Definition*: "self injury" *Assessment Tool*: *Manifest Abnormalities Scale of the Clinical Interview Schedule* Nurses and psychiatrists rated subjects	*Reference Population*: *Global SIB Prevalence* = 19% nurses (n = 16) 7% psychiatrists (n = 6) *By Age*: Unknown *By Sex*: Unknown *By MR Level*: Unknown *By SIB Topographies*: Unknown *SIB Target Population*: *Age*: Unknown *Sex*: Unknown *MR Level*: Unknown *SIB Topographies*: Unknown
17. Rojahn (1984)	*Reference Population* Adults in a residential institution for people with severe and profound MR (Germany) *n* = 91 *Sex*: 46% f; 54% m *Age*: mean = 35; range, 19–49 *MR Level*: Unknown *Sampling Method*: Identification of lowest functioning people of the institution	*SIB Definition*: "Behavior which causes physical damage to the person's own body" (Tate & Baroff, 1966) *Assessment Tool*: German precursor of the *Behavior Problems Inventory-01* (Rojahn et al., 2001) Direct-care staff completed checklists on selected residents	*Reference Population*: *Global SIB Prevalence* = 65.9% (*n* = 60) *By Age*: Unknown *By Sex*: Unknown *By MR Level*: Unknown *By SIB Topographies*: Unknown *SIB Target Population*: *Age*: Unknown *Sex*: 54 f; 46% m *MR Level*: Unknown

SIB Topographies:
70% hitting
40% biting
25% scratching
17% pinching
15% mouthing & sucking
13% pica
12% Aerophagia
<10% gouging self, hair pulling, stuffing orifices, ruminative vomiting, coprophagia, polydipsia
Multiple SIB: 25% one SIB; 20% two SIB; 55% three + SIB

18. Kebbon and Windahl (1985)

Reference Population
Persons receiving services for MR in 22 of 25 counties in Sweden
n = 28,215
Age: Unknown
Sex: 44% f, 56% mf
MR Level: 24.7% mild; 34.6%; moderate; 28.6%; severe; 13.2% profound
Residential Setting: 26% institutions; 74% integrated settings
Sampling Method: Total population study

SIB Definition:
"Behavior including an overt motor component, one part of the body being moved against another or against objects in the individual's surroundings" (pica, vomiting and rumination excluded)

Assessment Tool:
Unknown
Informants were people assumed to know the daily living conditions of the individual

Reference Population:
Global SIB Prevalence = 4.2% (*n* = 1,198)
By Age: Unknown
By Sex: Unknown
By MR Level: Unknown
By SIB Topographies: Unknown
SIB Target Population
Age: Unknown
Sex: 44% f, 56% m
MR Level:
1% = mild
12% = moderate
48% = severe
41% = profound
SIB Topographies: Unknown
Residential Setting: 15% own home; 7% group home; 7% boarding school; 64% residential home; 8% special hospital

19. Griffin et al. (1986)

Reference Population
Clients in residential facilities or state schools for MR in Texas
n ~10,000
Age: mean = 32.2
Sex: 44% f, 56% m
Sampling Method: Total population study

SIB Definitions:
"Repetitive or isolated acts toward oneself that had resulted in physical harm during the preceding 12 months"
or
"Repetitive acts toward oneself during the preceding 12 months that were typically considered to represent a SIB response"
or
"Restrained or having received psychoactive medication during the preceding 12 months

Reference Population:
Global SIB Prevalence = 13.6% (*n* = 1,352)
By Age: Unknown
By Sex: Unknown
By MR Level: Unknown
By SIB Topographies: Unknown
Maladaptive Behaviors: 55% aggression; 47% personal aberrant behavior; 30% destruction of physical environment; 30% avoidance behavior; 51% motor idiosyncrasies; 17% sleep disturbances

(Continued)

Reference	Reference Population & Sampling	SIB Definition and Assessment	Results
		for causing or attempting to cause injury to oneself"	*SIB Target Population:*
			Age: mean = 29.5; range, 3–84
		Assessment Tool:	*Sex:* 44% f, 56% m
		Self-Injurious Behavior Identification Survey (Griffin et al., 1986; modeled after Schroeder et al., 1978)	*MR Level:*
			<1% = mild
			9% = moderate
		Surveys were completed by unit psychologists and reviewed by other members of clients interdisciplinary team	19% = severe
			66% = profound
			SIB Topographies:
			39% biting
			37% head hitting
			29% head banging
			26% scratching
			15% mouthing
			14% arm hitting
			13% pica
			10% orifice digging
			<10% hair pulling, eye gouging, ruminating, throat gouging
			Maladaptive Behaviors: 55% had other aberrant behavior
			Multiple SIB: 58% 1 SIB; 28% 2 SIB; 16% 3 SIB; 15% 3+ SIB
			Frequency: 5% every 30 min; 6% hourly; 55% daily; 26% weekly; 33% monthly or less
20. Mulick, Dura, Rasnake, and Callahan (1986)	*Reference Population*	*SIB Definition:*	*Reference Population:*
	Residents in a ICFMR for non-ambulatory with severe and profound MR	"Behavior which causes physical damage to the person's own body" (Tate & Baroff, 1966)	*Global SIB Prevalence* = 54% (*n* = 55)
			By Age: Unknown
	n = 102	*Assessment Tools:*	*By Sex:* Unknown
		Early version of the *Behavior Problems Inventor* (Rojahn et al., 2001)	*By MR Level:* Unknown
	Age: mean = 35; range, 21–68		*By SIB Topographies:* Unknown
	Sex: 47% f, 53% m	*Vineland Adaptive Behavior Scales* (Sparrow, Balla, & Cicchetti, 1984)	*SIB Target Population:*
	MR Level: Unknown		*Age:* Unknown
	Sampling Method: Total population study		*Sex:* Unknown
			MR Level: Unknown
			SIB Topographies:
			13% head hitting
			12% biting
			11% pica

21. Rojahn (1986)

Reference Population
Individuals with MR in Germany
n = 13,313
(from 134 participating facilities)
Age: Unknown
Sex: Unknown
MR Level: Unknown
Sampling Method: Nationwide mail survey of individuals registered in community day and residential programs of a large national service provider. Local societies distributed materials to local service facilities

SIB Definition:
"Behavior that causes, or at least has the potential to cause, manifest damage to the person's own body" (Tate & Baroff, 1966); SIB must have been observed within prior 2 weeks

Assessment Tools:
German precursor of the *Behavior Problems Inventory* (Rojahn et al., 2001)
Vineland Social Maturity Scale (Doll, 1935)
Staff completed the instruments

11% teeth grinding
<10% fingers in body orifices, scratching, rumination, hitting, hair pulling etc.
Multiple SIB: 51% one SIB; 31% two SIB; 18% three + SIB

Reference Population:
Global SIB Prevalence = 1.7% (*n* = 431)
By Age: Unknown
By Sex: Unknown
By MR Level: Unknown
By SIB Topographies: Unknown
By Setting:
8% in schools/training centers
3% in sheltered workshops
8% in group homes

SIB Target Population:
Age: Unknown
Sex: 48% f, 51% m
MR Level:
13% = mild
28% = moderate
43% = severe
16% = profound
SIB Topographies:
45% biting
45% head-body
42% scratching
31% body-body
30% head-object
19% pinching
17% body-object
16% fingers in cavities
15% hair pulling
15% pica
14% teeth grinding
11% extreme drinking
<10% rumination, objects in cavities, air swallowing
Residential Setting: 61% biological parents; 2% foster home; 34% group home; 3% other
Multiple SIB: 24% only one SIB

(Continued)

Reference	Reference Population & Sampling	SIB Definition and Assessment	Results
22. Griffin et al. (1987)	*Reference Population* Children and adolescents with DD in a metropolitan school district n = 2,663 *Age* = mean = 10.2; range, 2–20 *Sex:* 41% fm, 59% mf *MR Level:* 17.4% mild/mod 82.6% severe/profound Other treatments: 3.6% restraints; 0.7% psychotropic medication *Sampling Method:* Total population study. Surveys distributed within each school district to schools with reference population	*SIB Definitions:* "Repetitive or isolated acts toward oneself that had resulted in physical harm during the preceding 12 months" or "Repetitive acts toward oneself during the preceding 12 months that were typically considered to represent a SIB response" or "Restrained or having received psychoactive medication during the preceding 12 months for causing or attempting to cause injury to oneself" *Assessment Tool: Self-Injurious Behavior Identification Survey* (Griffin et al., 1987) Teachers with students identified as self-injurious completed the survey	*Reference Population:* Global SIB Prevalence = 2.6% (*n* = 69) *By Age:* Unknown *By Sex:* Unknown *By MR Level:* Unknown *By SIB Topographies:* Unknown *SIB Target Population:* *Age:* Unknown *Sex:* Unknown *MR Level:* Unknown *SIB Topographies:* 46% biting 42% head hitting 30% head banging 25% scratching 20% arm hitting 15% eye gouging 15% hair pulling 13% orifice digging 12% mouthing 10% ruminating <10% pica, throat gouging
23. Oliver et al. (1987)	*Reference Population* Residents with IQs <70 from Learning Disabilities service providers in a single Health Region in the UK (total population: 3.5 million) n = 616 *Age:* Unknown *Sex:* Unknown *MR Level:* Unknown	*SIB Definition:* "Repeated, self-inflicted, non-accidental injury, producing bruising, bleeding, or other temporary or permanent tissue damage. Also, any such behavior which would produce bruising, bleeding or tissue damage were it not for protective devices, restraints, specific medical or psychological interventions in use." (Individuals engaging in SIB in the past 4 months were referred to the project by professionals in the field.)	*Reference Population:* Global SIB Prevalence = Unknown *By Age:* Unknown *By Sex:* Unknown *By MR Level:* Unknown *By SIB Topographies:* Unknown
24. Murphy et al. (1993)	*Reference Population* *Sampling method:* Total population study; contacts with responsible health care and other service providers; letters sent to hospital wards asking if anyone exhibited SIB in past 4 months	*Assessment Tool:* Screening questionnaire Interviews with an individual who knew the subject well	*SIB Target Population:* *Age:* mean = 24.8; range, 2–88 *Sex:* 42% fm, 58% mf *MR Level:* 12% = mild 49% = moderate/severe 40% = profound

SIB Topographies:
39% skin picking
38% biting
36% head slapping
28% head banging
10% body banging
10% other SIB
Residential Setting: 51% MR hospitals; 28% hostels; 21% home; 12% within hospital
Multiple SIB: 54% had more than one SIB
Medication: 36% anti-psychotics; 4% sedatives-hypnotics; 10% anxiolytics; 20% CNS drugs

---

25. Johnson, Day, and Hassanian (1988)

Reference Population
"Trainable mentally retarded" (TMR)
$n = 857$
Age: Unknown
Sex: Unknown
MR Level: Unknown
Sampling Method: Total population study via mail survey to all school districts in Kansas
Other populations surveyed:
deaf/blind; severely multi-handicapped; personal and social adjustment problems; autism and other health impairment

SIB Definition:
"Chronic persistent, self-directed behaviors, frequently noted among (but not limited to) autistic and developmentally delayed children, which would be expected to cause pain in the average person, or which cause immediate or eventual tissue damage. Examples include, but are not limited to: hitting, scratching, or biting self; Self-injury may be either mild or severe in nature." (SIB must have been displayed within the past five months.)

Assessment Tool:
Survey instrument developed for the study (Johnson, Day, & Hassanian, 1988)

Reference Population:
Global SIB Prevalence $= 14\%$ $(n = 120)$
By Age: Unknown
By Sex: Unknown
By MR Level: Unknown
By SIB Topographies: Unknown
SIB Target Population:
Age: Unknown
Sex: Unknown
MR Level: Unknown
SIB Topographies:
58% striking
52% pinch, scratch, poke, pull
45% biting
17% pica
<1% vomiting

---

26. Fovel, Lash, Barron, and Roberts (1989)

Reference Population
Residents of a state-supported school for MR in Massachusetts in 1985 and 1988
$n = 669$
Age: mean $= 43$; range, 17–85
Sex: 46% f, 54% m
MR Level: 9% mild; 21% moderate; 40% severe; 29% profound
Sampling Method: Total population study of persons who self-restrain

SIB Definition:
"The occurrence of behavior(s) which produces redness, irritation, swelling, or bruising of one's own body *and* requires medical attention (e.g., cleaning or bandaging by a nurse and examination or treatment by a physician) at least once within the last year"

Assessment Tool:
Unknown author checklist

Reference Population:
Global SIB Prevalence $= 28.0\%$
$(n = 187)$
By Age: Unknown
By Sex: Unknown
By MR Level: Unknown
By SIB Topographies: Unknown
SIB Target Population:
Age: Unknown
Sex: Unknown
MR Level: Unknown
SIB Topographies: Unknown

(Continued)

Reference	Reference Population & Sampling	SIB Definition and Assessment	Results

27. Emberson and Walker (1990)	*Reference Population*
	Hospital residents for people with MR
	n = 525
	Age: mean = 43
	Sex: Unknown
	MR Level: Unknown
	Sampling Method: Total population study; contact letters sent to hospital wards asking if anyone exhibited SIB in past 4 months
	Obtained demographics, description of SIB, when it was first noticed and last displayed, and whether physical restraint was involved
		SIB Definition:
		"Repeated behavior which is self-inflicted, non-accidental injury producing bruising, bleeding or other temporary or permanent tissue damage"
		Assessment Tool:
		Unknown author checklist
		Direct care staff was interviewed
			Reference Population:
			Global SIB Prevalence = 31.0% (*n* = 163)
			By Age: Unknown
			By Sex: Unknown
			By MR Level: Unknown
			By SIB Topographies: Unknown
			SIB Target Population:
			Age: mean = 37
			Sex: 50% f, 50% m
			MR Level:
			   8% = mild/moderate
			   64% = severe
			   17% = profound
			SIB Topographies:
			   37% biting
			   29% face slapping
			   16% scratching
			   16% skin picking
			   13% head butting
			   12% scratching face
			   <10% head bang, hair pull, throw self
			Multiple SIB: 38% one SIB; 38% two SIB; 24% three+ SIB
			Frequency: 19% <once a week; 31% >once a week; 33% >once a day; 17% once per hour
			Medication: 53% anti-psychotic; 32% other meds; 26% anticonvulsants; 13% sedatives; 4% anxiolytics

28. Rojahn et al. (1993)	*Reference Population*
	n = 135,102
	California
	n = 89,419
	Age: 0–10 = 30%; 11–20 = 19%; 21–45 = 51%
	Sex: 57% f, 43% m
	MR Level: mild = 34%, moderate = 20%, severe = 20%, profound = 26%
		SIB Definition in California:
		"Behavior causing severe self-injury and requiring physician's immediate attention at least once per month and/or behavior causing minor self-injury and requiring first aid at least once per week"
		Assessment tool in California:
		Client Development Evaluation Report
		(Borthwick-Duffy, 1994; Borthwick et al., 1981)
			Reference Population:
			Global SIB Prevalence = 8.0% (*n* = 11,479)
			California: 7.9% (*n* = 7,866)
			New York: 8.0% (*n* = 3,613)
			By Age: Unknown
			By Sex:[b] 5% f; 8% m
			By MR Level:
			   4% in mild
			   7% in moderate
			   16% in severe
			   25% in profound

New York State
n = 45,683
Age: 0–10 = 2%; 11–20 = 6%; 21–45 = 98%
Sex: 56.8% f, 43.2% m
MR Level: mild = 42%, moderate = 28%, severe = 15%, profound = 15%
Sampling method: Total population studies involving the entire database of individuals who received DD services at the time

SIB Definition in New York:
"SIB which poses a serious impediment to independent functioning"
Assessment Tool in New York:
Developmental Disabilities Information Survey (Jacobson, 1982)

By SIB Topographies: Unknown
By Verbal expressiveness:
6% in verbal
18% in non-verbal
SIB Target Population:
Age: Unknown
Sex: Unknown
MR Level: *Unknown*
SIB Topographies: Unknown

29. Borthwick-Duffy (1994)

Reference Population
People served by California Department of Developmental Services in 1987
n = 91,164
Age: Unknown
Sex: Unknown
MR Level: Unknown
Sampling Method: Total population study

SIB Definition:
"Behavior causing severe self-injury and requiring physician's immediate attention at least once per month and/or behavior causing minor self-injury and requiring first aid at least once per week"
Assessment Tool:
Client Development Evaluation Report (Borthwick-Duffy, 1994; Borthwick et al., 1981)

Reference Population:
9.3% (*n* = 8,444) (at least once per week)
By Age: Unknown
By Sex: Unknown
By MR Level: Unknown
By SIB Topographies: Unknown
SIB Target Population:
Age: Unknown
Sex: Unknown
MR Level: Unknown
SIB Topographies: Unknown

30. Bodfish et al. (1995)

Reference Population
Residents with severe to profound MR living in a public residential facility
n = 210
Age: mean = 34.3; range, 18–26
Sex: 36% f, 64% m
MR Level: Unknown
Sampling Method: Total population study with a two-step screening process:
1. Subjects from total public residential facility for individuals with MR (*n* = 448) with severe/profound MR, ambulatory, and medical stability
2. Screened for target behaviors by caseload psychologists

SIB Definition:
"Repetitive movements that can cause tissue damage (e.g. hitting, slapping, biting self)"
Assessment Tool:
Self-Injury Checklist (Bodfish et al., 1999)
Rated by teachers

Reference Population:
Global SIB Prevalence = 46.6% (*n* = 98)
By Age: Unknown
By Sex: Unknown
By MR Level: Unknown
By SIB Topographies: Unknown
SIB Target Population:
Age: Unknown
Sex: Unknown
MR Level: Unknown
SIB Topographies:
27% biting
22% hits body parts
21% hits objects
16% hits with objects
<10% pulling, rubbing or scratching, poking
Multiple SIB: Mean = 2.9 SIB; 28% one SIB; 22% two SIB; 16% three SIB; 28% four SIB; 6% five SIB

(Continued)

Reference	Reference Population & Sampling	SIB Definition and Assessment	Results
31. Hillery and Mulcahy (1997)	*Reference Population* People in community care in Ireland n = 429 *Age:* mean = 25.7; range, 2–84 *Sex:* 46% f, 54% m *MR Level:* 73% moderate; 22% severe; 5% profound *Residential Setting:* 64% at home; 36% residential center *Sampling Method:* Total population study; all individuals with IQ<50, within geographical borders of a single community care area, were traced for one calendar month	*SIB Definition:* "Behavior which is self-injurious and non-accidental, producing bruising, bleeding, or other temporary or permanent tissue damage, or behavior which would produce bruising, bleeding or tissue damage were it not for the use of protective devices or restraints" *Assessment Tool:* Special recording sheet completed once a day, indicating if SIB occurred within a 24-hour time period, its type, and its severity Staff completed the recordings	*Reference Population:* *Global SIB Prevalence* = 14.4% (n = 62) *By Age:* Unknown *By Sex:* Unknown *By MR Level:* Unknown *By SIB Topographies:* Unknown *By Residential Setting:* Of those that lived at home 53% exhibited SIB *SIB Target Population:* *Age:* mean = 23.6, range 3–60 *Sex:* 42% f, 58% m *MR Level:* 42% = moderate 53% = severe 5% = profound *SIB Topographies:* (from most to least prevalent) biting, slapping, head banging, eye-poking
32. Collacott et al. (1998)	*Reference Population* Leicestershire Learning Disabilities Register, UK n = 2,277 *Age:* mean = 38.4; SD, 15.0 *Sex:* 43% f, 57% m *MR Level:* Unknown *Sampling method:* Total population study	*SIB Definition:* Specific topographies, e.g., head banging, picking at sores *Assessment Tool:* Unknown author checklist	*Reference Population:* *Global SIB Prevalence* = 17.4% (n = 365 estimated]) *By Age:* Unknown *By Sex:* Unknown *By MR Level:* Unknown *By SIB Topographies:* Unknown *SIB Target Population:* *Age:* mean = 33.6; SD, 12.7 *Sex:* 43% f, 57% m *MR Level:* Unknown *SIB Topographies:* Unknown Developmental level in SIB sample lower than in reference population SIB had higher rates of other maladaptive behaviors than reference population, including aggression, antisocial behavior, destructiveness, disturbing others at night, spiting, fecal smearing, etc. Logistic regression analysis identified age, developmental quotient, hearing status, immobility and number of autistic symptoms as predictors of SIB, with an 82.3%

33. Murphy et al. (1999)

Reference Population

Children with severe MR (learning disability) and/or autism in the UK. Selected students with potential for exhibiting SIB. Did not include students that were exhibiting SIB for more than 3 months

n = 614

Age: <11 years

Sex: Unknown

MR Level: Unknown

Sampling Method: Unknown

Prevalence and incidence study-students selected from schools for children with severe intellectual disabilities and/or autism listed in Education Authorities' Yearbook (1991)

Interviewed teachers who identified children. Families were contacted for consent

Matched control group: Children participating were matched (with help from teachers) with another child in their class without SIB, with similar age and adaptive level

SIB Definition:

"Behavior which causes physical damage to the person's own body" (Tate & Baroff, 1966)

Potential topographies were hitting head on objects, hitting objects to head, hitting body/ head or kicking body, self-biting, self-scratching, self-pinching, eye poking, hair pulling, inserting objects into orifices

Assessment Tools:

Vineland Adaptive Behavior Scales (Sparrow, Balla, & Cicchetti, 1984)

Childhood Autism Rating Scale (Schopler et al., 1980)

Aberrant Behavior Checklist (Aman & Singh, 1994)

Teacher Concern Scale (Murphy et al., 1999)

Naturalistic observations at 3 month intervals for 18 months

Reference Population:

Global SIB Prevalence = 25.1% (*n* = 154)

By Age: Unknown

By Sex: Unknown

By MR Level: Unknown

By SIB Topographies: Unknown

SIB Target Population:

Age: Unknown

Sex: Unknown

MR Level: Unknown

SIB Topographies: Unknown

Global SIB Incidence: 3% within 3 months; 22% SIB for longer than 3 months; 3% potential SIB

34. Saloviita (2000)

Reference Population

State hospital residents with MR, Finland

n = 421

Age: mean = 32; SD, 14

Sex: 45% f, 55% m

MR Level: Unknown

Sampling Method: Total population study

SIB Definition:

10 items that specified the type of SIB from the domain of "Self-abusive behavior"

Assessment Tool: AAMD Adaptive Behavior Scale-Part II (Nihira et al., 1974)

Reference Population:

Global SIB Prevalence = 40.6% (*n* = 171)

By Age:

  34% = 0–17

  47% = 18–34

  36%<34

By Sex: 44% f, 38% m

By MR Level:

  18.8% in mild

  30.6% in moderate

  35.1% in severe

  53.1% in profound

By SIB Topographies: Unknown

By Length of Institution:

Persons with frequent SIB had been longer in the institution than persons w/o SIB

(Continued)

Reference	Reference Population & Sampling	SIB Definition and Assessment	Results
			SIB Target Population: *Age:* Unknown *Sex:* Unknown *MR Level:* Unknown *SIB Topographies:* Self slapping, self-scratching, head banging, self biting, and self smearing were the most common forms, all >10%
35. Miller et al. (2000)	*Reference Population* Archival data from individuals with MR in Wyoming and South Dakota who received Medicaid Waiver services $n = 4,006$ *Age* = mean = 35.2; range, 3–96 *Sex:* 57% f, 43% m *MR Level:* 50% mild; 20% moderate; 12% severe; 18% profound Residential Setting 33.4% group home; 23.8% family; 22% independent; 9.9% semi-independent; 9.6% institution *Sampling Method:* Total population study *MR Level:* Unknown *SIB Topographies:* Unknown	*SIB Definition:* "Hurtful to self" *Assessment Tool:* Single item from the *Inventory for Client and Agency Planning* (Bruininks et al., 1986)	*Reference Population:* *Global SIB Prevalence* = 37.5% ($n = 1,502$) *By Age:* Unknown *By Sex:* Unknown *By MR Level:* 27% in mild 37% in moderate 49% in severe 60% in profound *By SIB Topographies:* Unknown *SIB Target Population:* *Age:* Unknown *Sex:* Unknown
36. Emerson et al. (2001)	*Reference Population* The Hester Adrian Research Center Challenging Behaviour Project *n:* Unknown *Age:* Unknown *Sex:* Unknown *MR Level:* Unknown 1988–7 District Health Authorities in UK 1995–2 District Health Authorities in UK *Sampling Method:* Total population study of individuals with "with challenging behavior which presented a serious management problem ..."	*SIB Definitions:* Operational definitions of 15 specific SIB topographies items from an early version of the Behavior Problems Inventory (Rojahn et al., 1998) *Assessment Tool:* *Individual Schedule* (Alborz et al., 1994)	*Reference Population:* *Global SIB Prevalence* = 4% (n = not reported) *By Age:* Unknown *By Sex:* Unknown *By MR Level:* Unknown *By SIB Topographies:* Unknown *SIB Target Population:* *Age:* Unknown *Sex:* 1988 = 35% f, 65% m 1995 = 31% f, 69% m *MR Level:* Unknown *SIB Topographies in 1995 survey:*

Stepwise sampling procedure:
1. All services for people with MR were identified (residential, day, respite, etc.)
2. Screening of each setting
3. Personal information on people with challenging behavior within the setting

35% hitting body with hand/body part
27% hitting body with/against objects
20% self-scratching; 19% self-pinching
19% pica
12% stuffing fingers in body openings
11% excessive drinking
11% hair pulling
<10% teeth grinding, self-induced vomiting, air swallowing

37. Rojahn et al. (2001)

Reference Population
Developmental center in Louisiana
n >650
Age: mean: 49.9; range, 14-91
Sex: 54%, f46% m
MR Level: 2% mild; 5% moderate; 20% severe; 72% profound
Sampling Method: Quasi random sample of residents

SIB Definition:
"Behavior that causes, or at least has the potential to cause, manifest damage to the person's own body"
Assessment Tool:
Behavior Problems Inventory-01 (Rojahn et al., 2001)

Reference Population:
Global SIB Prevalence = 43.3% (n = 317)
By Age: Unknown
By Sex: Unknown
By MR Level: Unknown
By SIB Topographies:
15.5 self-biting
18% head-hitting
13% self-scratching
10% pica
<10% body-hitting, poking, teeth grinding, vomiting, self-pinching, hair pulling, stuffing objects, nail pulling, aerophagia, drinking
SIB Target Population:
Age: Unknown
Sex: Unknown
MR Level: Unknown
SIB Topographies: Unknown

38. Wisely et al. (2002)

Reference Population
Survey of a community service and a residential housing service from urban settings in the UK
N: 241
Age: mean = 41.5 (SD = 12.5; range 19-25)
Sex: Unknown
MR-Level: Unknown

SIB Definition:
Unknown
Assessment Tool:
Structured interviews with service managers using the Challenging Behavior Scale (Harris, Humphreys, & Thomson, 1994)

Reference Population:
Global SIB Prevalence = 22% (n = 53)
By Age: Unknown
By Sex: Unknown
By MR Level: Unknown
By SIB Topographies: Unknown
SIB Target Population:
Age: Unknown
Sex: Unknown
MR Level: Unknown
SIB Topographies: Unknown

(Continued)

Reference	Reference Population & Sampling	SIB Definition and Assessment	Results
39. Holden and Gitlesen (2006)	*Reference Population* *n*: 904 *Age*: 0–9, 6.1%; 10–19, 13.2%; 20–29, 11.5%; 30–39, 17.2%; 40–49, 16.1%; 50–59, 20.6%; 60–69, 9.7%; 70–79, 3.9%; 80–89, 1.7% *Sex*: 45.3% f, 54.7% m *MR Level*: 28.3%, mild; 45.1%, moderate; 15.6%, severe; 10.9%, profound *Sampling Method*: All people, both children and adults, with administratively defined mental retardation, living in Hedmark Norway	*SIB Definition*: Unknown *Assessment Tool*: *Challenging Behavior Survey: Individual Schedule* (Alborez, Emerson, Kiernan, & Quershi, 1994)	*Reference Population*: *Global SIB Prevalence* = 4.4% (*n* = 36) *By Age*: Unknown *By Sex*: Unknown *By MR Level*: Unknown *By SIB Topographies*: Unknown *SIB Target Population*: *Age*: Unknown *Sex*: Unknown *MR Level*: Unknown *SIB Topographies*: Unknown
40. Lowe et al. (2007)	*Reference Population* All services providers in seven unitary authorities in the UK (South Wales) for people with intellectual disabilities were screened *n*: Unknown *Age*: mean = 36, range 5–93 *Sex*: 39% f, 61% m *MR Level*: Unknown *Sampling Method*: Stepwise sampling procedure: 1. Setting Questionnaire (Kiernan & Qureshi, 1986) administered to approximately 17,000 people with ID identify the target population of individuals with challenging behavior n = 1770 2. n = 901 remaining after attrition (e.g., no consent)	*SIB Definition*: Operational definitions of 15 specific SIB topographies items from an early version of the *Behavior Problems Inventory* (Rojahn et al., 1989) *Assessment Tool*: *Individual Schedule* (Alborz et al., 1994)	*Reference Population*: *Global SIB Prevalence* = 5.3% (Projected among approximately 17,000 individuals with ID) *n* = 902 *By Age*: Unknown *By Sex*: Unknown *By MR Level*: Unknown *By SIB Topographies*: Unknown *SIB Target Population*: *Age*: Unknown *Sex*: Unknown *MR Level*: Unknown *SIB Topographies*: Unknown

Note: Excluded were epidemiological studies of specific syndromes or conditions such as Lesch–Nyhan, Smith–Magenis, Autism, etc. The table is a modified and extended version of an earlier one published by Rojahn and Esbensen (2002).

[a] The data were extrapolated from Johnson and Day (1992, Table 2.3).

[b] These data were reported by Rojahn et al. (1999).

References

Adams, D., & Allen, D. (2001). Assessing the need for reactive behaviour management strategies in children with intellectual disability and severe challenging behaviour. *Journal of Intellectual Disability Research, 45,* 335–343.

Ainsworth, M. D. S., Blehar, M. C., Waters, E., & Walls, S. (1978). *Patterns of attachment: A psychological study of the strange situation.* Hillsdale, NJ: L. E. Erlbaum Associates.

Alborz, A., Bromley, J., Emerson, E., Kiernan, C., & Qureshi, H. (1994). *Challenging behaviour survey: Individual schedule.* Manchester: Hester Adrian Research Centre, University of Manchester.

Alvir, J. M., Lieberman, J. A., & Safferman, A. Z. (1993). Clozapine-induced agranulocytosis-incidence and risk factors in the United States. *New England Journal of Medicine, 324,* 162–167.

Aman, M. G. (1991). *Assessing psychopathology and behavior problems in persons with mental retardation: A review of available instruments.* Report prepared for the National Institute of Mental Health. Rockville, MD: U.S. Department of Health and Human Services, Public Health Service, Alcohol, Drug Abuse, and Mental Health Administration.

Aman, M. G. (1993). Efficacy of psychotropic drugs for reducing self-injurious behavior in developmental disabilities. *Annals of Clinical Psychiatry, 5,* 177–188.

Aman, M. G. (1997). Recent studies in the psychopharmacology of mental retardation. In N. W. Bray (ed.), *International review of research in mental retardation* (Vol. 21) (pp. 113–146). New York: Academic Press.

Aman, M. G. (2003). *Annotated bibliography on the aberrant behavior checklist (June 2003 update).* Columbus, OH: Ohio State University.

Aman, M. G., Arnold, L. E., & Armstrong, S. C. (1999). Review of serotonergic agents and perseverative behavior in patients with developmental disabilities. *Mental Retardation and Developmental Disabilities Research Reviews, 5,* 279–289.

Aman, M. G., Burrow, W. H., & Wolford, P. L. (1995a). The Aberrant Behavior Checklist-Community: Factor validity and effect of subject variables for adults in group homes. *American Journal on Mental Retardation, 100,* 283–292.

Aman, M. G., De Smedt, G., Derivan, A., Lyons, B., Findling, R. L., & the Risperidone Disruptive Behavior Study Group. (2002). Risperidone treatment of children with disruptive behavior disorders and subaverage IQ: A double-blind, placebo-controlled study. *American Journal of Psychiatry, 159,* 1337–1346.

Aman, M. G., & Madrid, A. (1999). Atypical antipsychotics in persons with developmental disabilities. *Mental Retardation and Developmental Disabilities Research Reviews, 5,* 253–263.

Aman, M. G., Sarphare, G., & Burrow, W. H. (1995b). Psychotropic drugs in group homes: Prevalence and relation to demographic/psychiatric variables. *American Journal on Mental Retardation, 99,* 500–509.

Aman, M. G., & Singh, N. N. (1986). *Aberrant Behavior Checklist manual*. East Aurora, NY: Slosson Educational Publications.

Aman, M. G., & Singh, N. N. (eds.) (1990). *Psychopharmacology of the developmental disabilities*. New York, NY: Springer-Verlag.

Aman, M. G., & Singh, N. N. (1994). *Aberrant Behavior Checklist-Community (Supplementary Manual)*. East Aurora, NY: Slosson Educational Publications.

Aman, M. G., Singh, N. N., Stewart, A. W., & Field, C. J. (1985a). The Aberrant Behavior Checklist: A behavior rating scale for the assessment of treatment effects. *American Journal of Mental Deficiency, 89*, 485–491.

Aman, M. G., Singh, N. N., Stewart, A. W., & Field, C. J. (1985b). Psychometric characteristics of the Aberrant Behavior Checklist. *American Journal of Mental Deficiency, 89*, 492–502.

Aman, M. G., Singh, N. N., & Turbott, S. H. (1987). Reliability of the Aberrant Behavior Checklist and the effect of variations in instructions. *American Journal on Mental Retardation, 92*, 237–240.

Aman, M. G., Tassé, M. J., Rojahn, J., & Hammer, D. (1996). The Nisonger CBRF: A child behavior rating form for children with developmental disabilities. *Research in Developmental Disabilities, 17*, 41–57.

Aman, M. G., White, A. J., Vaithianathan, C., & Teehan, D. J. (1986). Preliminary study of imipramine in profoundly retarded residents. *Journal of Autism and Developmental Disorders, 16*, 263–273.

American Psychiatric Association (1994). *Diagnostic and statistical manual of mental disorders, DSM IV*. Washington, DC: American Psychiatric Press.

American Psychiatric Association (2000). *Diagnostic and statistical manual of mental disorders*. Washington DC: Author.

Anderson, C. M., Freeman, K. A., & Scotti, J. R. (1999). Evaluation of the generalizability (reliability and validity) of analog functional assessment methodology. *Behavior Therapy, 30*, 31–50.

Anderson, C. M., & Kincaid, D. (2005). Applying behavior analysis to school violence and discipline problems: School wide positive behavior support. *The Behavior Analyst, 28*, 49–64.

Anderson, L. T., Ernst, M., & Davis, S. V. (1992). Cognitive abilities of patients with Lesch–Nyhan disease. *Journal of Autism and Developmental Disorders, 22*, 189–203.

Ando, H., & Yoshimura, I. (1978). Prevalence of maladaptive behavior in retarded children as a function of IQ and age. *Journal of Abnormal Child Psychology, 6*, 345–349.

Andre-Thomas, C. Y., & Saint-Anne Dargassies, S. (1960). *The neurological examination of the infant*. London: Medical Advisory Committee of the National Spastics Society.

Awaya, S. (1978). Stimulus vision deprivation amblyopia in humans. In R. D. Reinecke (ed.), *Strabismus* (pp. 31–44). New York: Grune and Stratton.

Axelrod, S., & Apsche, J. (eds.) (1983). *The effects of punishment on human behavior*. New York: Academic Press.

Ayllon, T., & Michael, J. L. (1959). The psychiatric nurse as a behavioral engineer. *Journal of the Experimental Analysis of Behavior, 3*, 123–142.

Ayres, A. J. (1979). *Sensory integration and the child*. Los Angeles, CA: Western Psychological Services.

Bachman, J. (1972). Self-injurious behavior: A behavioral analysis. *Journal of Abnormal Psychology, 80*, 211–224.

Baer, D. M., Wolf, M. M., & Risley, T. R. (1968). Some current dimensions of applied behavior analysis. *Journal of Applied Behavior Analysis, 1*, 91–97.

Baghdadli, A., Pascal, C., Grisi, S., & Aussillox, C. (2003). Risk factors for self-injury among 222 young children with autistic disorders. *Journal of Intellectual Disability Research, 4*, 622–627.

Bailey, B. A., Hare, D. J., Hatton, C., & Limb, K. (2006). The response to challenging behavior by care staff: Emotional responses, attributions of cause and observation practice. *Journal of Intellectual Disability Research, 50*, 199–211.

Bailey, J. S., & Burch, M. R. (2002). *Research methods in applied behavior analysis.* Thousand Oaks, CA: Sage Publications.

Bailey, J. S., & Burch, M. R. (2005). *Ethics for behavior analysts.* Mahwah, NJ: Lawrence Erlbaum Associates.

Bailey, J. S., & Pyles, D. A. M. (1989). Behavioral diagnostics. In E. Cipani, (ed.), *The treatment of severe behavior disorders. Monographs of the American Association on Mental Retardation.* (Vol. 12) (pp. 85–107). Washington, DC: The American Association on Mental Retardation.

Baker, B. L., McIntyre, L. L., Blacher, J., Crnic, K., Edelbrok, C., & Low, C. (2003). Pre-school children with and without developmental delay: Behaviour problems and parenting over time. *Journal of Intellectual Disabilities Research, 47*, 217–230.

Baker, D. J., Blumberg, E. R., Freeman, R., & Wieseler, N. A. (2002). Can psychiatric disorders be seen as establishing operations? Integrating applied behavior analysis and psychiatry. *Mental Health Aspects of Developmental Disabilities, 5*, 118–124.

Ballinger, B. R. (1971). Minor self-injury. *British Journal of Psychiatry, 118*, 535–538.

Barbera, M. L., & Kubina, R. M. (2005). Using transfer procedures to teach tacts to a child with autism. *Analysis of Verbal Behavior, 21*, 155–161.

Baroff, G., & Tate, B. (1968). The use of aversive stimulation in the treatment of chronic self-injurious behavior. *Journal of the American Academy of Psychiatry, 3*, 454–470.

Barrera, F. J., Teodoro, J. M., Selmeci, T., & Madappuli, A. (1994). Self-injury, pain, and the endorphin theory. *Journal of Developmental and Physical Disabilities, 6*, 169–192.

Barrett, R. P., Payton, J. B., & Burkhart, J. E. (1988). Treatment of self-injury and disruptive behavior with carbamazepine (Tegretol) and behavior therapy. *Journal of the Multihandicapped Person, 1*, 79–91.

Bartak, L., & Rutter, M. (1976). Differences between mentally retarded and normally intelligent autistic children. *Journal of Autism and Childhood Schizophrenia, 6*, 109–120.

Barton-Arwood, S. M., Wehby, J. H., Gunter, P. L., & Lane, K. L. (2003). Functional behavior assessment rating scales: Intrarater reliability with students with emotional or behavior disorders. *Behavioral Disorders, 28*, 386–400.

Basser, L. S. (1962). Hemiplegia of early onset and the faculty of speech with special reference to the effects of hemispherectomy. *Brain, 85*, 427–460.

Baum, W. M. (2002). From molecular to molar: A paradigm shift in behavior analysis. *Journal of the Experimental Analysis of Behavior, 78*, 95–116.

Bauman, M. (1991). *Neuropathology of Rett's syndrome.* Rett's syndrome symposium, Kennedy Institute, Baltimore, MD, June.

Baumeister, A. A., Frye, G., & Schroeder, S. R. (1984). Neurochemical correlates of self-injurious behavior. In J. A. Mulick, & B. L. Mallory (eds), *Transitions of mental retardation: Advocacy, technology and science.* Washington, DC: American Association on Mental Deficiency.

Baumeister, A. A., & Rollings, P. (1976). Self-injurious behavior. In N. R. Ellis (ed.), *International review of research in mental retardation* (Vol. 9) (pp. 1–34). New York: Academic Press.

Baumeister, A. A., Todd, M. E., & Sevin, J. A. (1993). Efficacy and specificity of pharmacological therapies for behavioral disorders of persons with mental retardation. *Clinical Neuropharmacology, 16*, 271–294.

Beck, B. (1987). Psycho-social assessment of 36 de Lange patients. *Journal of Mental Deficiency Research, 31*, 251–257.

Beckett, C., Bredenkamp, D., Castle, J., Groothues, C., O'Connor, T.G. & Rutter, M., & The English and Romanian Adoptees (ERA) Study Team (2002). Behavior patterns associated with institutional deprivation: A study of children adopted from Romania. *Journal of Developmental & Behavioral Pediatrics, 23*, 297–303.

Behavior Analyst Certification Board. (2006). *Guidelines for responsible conduct for behavior analysts.* Downloaded on October 16, 2006 from http://www.bacb.com/consum_frame.html

Benavidez, D. A., & Matson, J. L. (1993). Assessment of depression in mentally retarded persons. *Research in Developmental Disabilities, 14*, 179–188.

Bergen, A. E., Holborn, S. W., & Scott-Huyghebaert, V. C. (2002). Functional analysis of self-injurious behavior in an adult with Lesch–Nyhan Syndrome. *Behavior Modification, 26*, 187–204.

Berkson, G., & Davenport, R. K. (1962). Stereotyped movements in mental defectives: I. Initial survey. *American Journal on Mental Deficiency, 66*, 849–852.

Berkson, G., & Mason, W. A. (1964a). Stereotyped movements of mental defectives: III. Situational effects. *Perceptual and Motor Skills, 19*, 635–642.

Berkson, G., & Mason, W. A. (1964b). Stereotyped movements of mental defectives: IV. The effects of toys and the character of the acts. *American Journal of Mental Deficiency, 8*, 511–524.

Berkson, G., & Tupa, M. (2000). Early development of stereotyped and self-injurious behaviors. *Journal of Early Intervention, 23*, 1–19.

Berkson, G., & Tupa, M. (2002). Studies of the development of stereotyped and self-injurious behaviors in young children. In S. Schroeder, M. L. Oster-Granite, & T. Thompson (eds), *Self-injurious behavior: Gene–brain-behavior relationships* (pp. 145–150). Washington, DC: American Psychological Association.

Berkson, G., Tupa, M., & Sherman, L. (2001). Early development of stereotyped and self-injurious behaviors: I. Incidence. *American Journal on Mental Retardation, 106*, 539–547.

Bienstein, P., Smith, K., Rojahn, J., & Matson, J. L. (2006). *Differential functional properties profiles of chronic behavior problems in adults with severe and profound mental retardation.* Poster presented at the Annual Meeting of the American Psychological Association, New Orleans, August 10.

Bijou, S. W. (1966). Functional analysis of retarded development. In N. R. Ellis (ed.), *International review of research in mental retardation* (Vol. 1) (pp. 1–19). New York: Academic Press.

Bijou, S. W., Peterson, R. F., & Ault, M. H. (1968). A method to integrate descriptive and experimental field studies at the level of data and empirical concepts. *Journal of Applied Behavior Analysis, 1*, 175–191.

Bihm, E. M., & Poindexter, A. R. (1991). Cross-validation of the factor structure of the Aberrant Behavior Checklist for persons with mental retardation. *American Journal on Mental Retardation, 96*, 209–211.

Birnbrauer, J. S., & Lawler, J. (1964). Token reinforcement for learning. *Mental Retardation, 2*, 275–279.

Bodfish, J. W. (2004). Treating the core features of autism: Are we there yet? *Mental retardation and developmental disabilities research reviews, 10*, 318–326.

Bodfish, J. W., Crawford, T. W., Powell, S. B., Parker, D. E., Golden, R. N., & Lewis, M. H. (1995a). Compulsions in adults with mental retardation: Prevalence, phenomenology, and co-morbidity with stereotypy and self-injury. *American Journal on Mental Retardation, 100*, 183–192.

Bodfish, J. W., & Lewis, M. H. (1997). *Occurrence of tics, stereotypy, and self-injury in adults with mental retardation.* Proceedings of the 30th Annual Gatlinburg Conference on Research & Theory in Mental Retardation.

Bodfish, J. W., & Lewis, M. H. (2002). Self-injury and comorbid behaviors in developmental, neurological, psychiatric, and genetic disorders. In S. R. Schroeder, M. L. Oster-Granite, & T. Thompson (eds), *Self-injurious behavior: Gene–brain-behavior relationships* (pp. 23–39). Washington, DC: American Psychological Association.

Bodfish, J. W., & Madison, J. T. (1993). Diagnosis and treatment of compulsive behavior disorder of adults with mental retardation. *American Journal on Mental Retardation, 28,* 360–367.

Bodfish, J. W., Mahorney, S. L., McKee, J. R., Sheitman, B. B., & Breese, G. R. (2001). *A comparison of the atypical neuroleptic olanzapine to typical neuroleptics for the treatment of abnormal repetitive behavior.* Paper presented at the Annual Gatlinburg Conference on Research and Theory in Mental Retardation, Charleston, SC, March 15–18.

Bodfish, J. W., Powell, S. B., Golden, R. N., & Lewis, M. H. (1995b). Blink rate as an index of dopamine function in adults with mental retardation and repetitive behavior disorders. *American Journal on Mental Retardation, 99,* 334–335.

Bodfish, J. W., Symons, F. J., & Lewis, M. H. (1999). *Repetitive behavior scales.* Western Carolina Center Research Reports.

Bodfish, J. W., Symons, F. J., Parker, D. E., & Lewis, M. H. (2000). Varieties in repetitive behavior in autism: Comparisons to mental retardation. *Journal of Autism and Developmental Disorders, 30,* 237–243.

Bohus, M., Haaf, B., & Stiglmayr, C. (2000). Evaluation of inpatient dialectical-behavioral therapy for borderline personality disorder – a prospective study. *Behaviour Research and Therapy, 38,* 875–887.

Borgmeier, C., & Horner, R. H. (2006). An evaluation of the predictive validity of confidence ratings in identifying functional behavioral assessment hypothesis statements. *Journal of Positive Behavior Interventions, 8,* 100–105.

Borrero, J. C., & Vollmer, T. R. (2002). An application of the matching law to severe problem behavior. *Journal of Applied Behavior Analysis, 35,* 13–27.

Borrero, J. C., Vollmer, T. R., Wright, C. S., Lerman, D. C., & Kelley, M. E. (2002). Further evaluation of the role of protective equipment in the functional analysis of self-injurious behavior. *Journal of Applied Behavior Analysis, 35,* 69–72.

Borthwick, S.A., Meyers, C.E., & Eyman, R.K. (1981). Comparative adaptive and maladaptive behavior of mentally retarded clients of five residential settings in three western states. In: Bruininks, R.H., Meyers, C.E., Sigford, B.B., & Lakin, K.C. (eds), *Deinstitutionalization and community adjustment of mentally retarded people* (Monograph No. 4) (pp. 351–359). Washington, DC: American Association of Mental Deficiency.

Borthwick-Duffy, S. A. (1994). Prevalence of destructive behaviors: A study of aggression, self-injury, and property destruction. In T. Thompson, & D. B. Gray (eds), *Destructive behavior in developmental disabilities: Diagnosis and treatment* (pp. 3–23). Thousand Oaks, CA: Sage Publishing.

Bosch, J., Van Dyke, D. C., Smith, S. M., & Poulton, S. (1997). Role of medical conditions in the exacerbation of self-injurious behavior: An exploratory study. *Mental Retardation, 35,* 124–130.

Bowlby, J. (1969). *Attachment and loss: Separation, anxiety, and anger.* New York, NY: Basic Books.

Bowlby, J. (1969/1982). *Attachment.* London and New York: Hogarth Press, Basic Books.

Bowlby, J. (1988). *Secure base.* New York, NY: Basic Books.

Braithwaite, K. L., & Richdale, A. L. (2000). Functional communication training to replace challenging behaviors across two behavioral outcomes. *Behavioral Interventions, 15,* 21–36.

Brandt, B. R., & Rosen, I. (1998). Impaired peripheral somatosensory function in children with Prader–Willi syndrome. *Neuropediatrics, 29,* 124–126.

Breau, L. M., Camfield, C. S., Symons, F. J., Bodfish, J. W., MacKay, A., Finley, G. A., et al. (2003). Relation between pain and self-injurious behavior in nonverbal children with severe cognitive impairments. *Journal of Pediatrics, 142,* 498–503.

Breese, G. R., Baumeister, A. A., McCowan, T. J., Emerick, S., Frye, G. D., Crotty, K., et al. (1984a). Behavioral differences between neonatal- and adult-6-hydroxydopamine-treated rats to dopamine agonists: Relevance to neurological symptoms in clinical syndromes with reduced brain dopamine. *Journal of Pharmacology and Experimental Therapeutics, 231,* 343–354.

Breese, G. R., Baumeister, A. A., McCowan, T. J., Emerick, S., Frye, C. D., & Mueller, R. A. (1984b). Neonatal-6-hydroxydopamine treatment: Model of susceptibility for self-mutilation in the Lesch–Nyhan syndrome. *Pharmacology, Biochemistry and Behavior, 21,* 459–461.

Breese, G. R., Criswell, H. E., Duncan, G. E., Moy, S. S., Johnson, K. B., Wong, D. F., et al. (1995). Model for reduced dopamine in Lesch–Nyhan syndrome and the mentally retarded: Neurobiology of neonatal-6-hydroxydopamine-lesioned rats. *Mental Retardation and Developmental Disabilities Research Reviews, 1,* 111–119.

Breese, G. R., Knapp, D. J., Criswell, H. E., Moy, S. S., Papadeas, S. T., & Blake, B. L. (2005). The neonate-6-hydroxydopamine-lesioned rat: A model for clinical neuroscience and neuro-biological principles. *Brain Research Reviews, 48,* 57–73.

Breese, G. R., & Traylor, T. D. (1970). Effects of 6-hydroxydopamine on brain norepinephrine and dopamine: Evidence of selective degeneration of catecholamine neurons. *Journal of Pharmacology and Experimental Therapeutics, 174,* 413–420.

Briere, J., & Gil, E. (1998). Self-mutilation in clinical and general population samples: Prevalence, correlates, and functions. *American Journal of Orthopsychiatry, 68,* 609–620.

Bronson, G. (1974). The postnatal growth of visual capacity. *Child Development, 45,* 873–890.

Broussard, C., & Northup, J. (1997). The use of functional analysis to develop peer interventions for disruptive classroom behavior. *School Psychology Quarterly, 12,* 65–76.

Brown, E. C., Aman, M. G., & Havercamp, S. M. (2002). Factor analysis and norms for parent ratings on the Aberrant Behavior Checklist-Community for young people in special education. *Research in Developmental Disabilities, 23,* 45–60.

Brown, M. Z., Comtois, K. A., & Linehan, M. M. (2002). Reasons for suicide attempts and nonsuicidal self-injury in women with borderline personality disorder. *Journal of Abnormal Psychology, 111,* 198–202.

Brown, T., Chapman, P., Kairiss, E., & Keenan, C. (1988). Long-term synaptic potentiation. *Science, 242,* 724–728.

Bruininks, R. H., Hill, B. K., Weatherman, R. F., & Woodcock, R. W. (1986). *Inventory for client and agency planning.* Examiner's Manual. Chicago: Riverside.

Bruininks, R. H., Olson, K. M., Larson, S. A., & Lakin, C. (1994). Challenging behaviors among persons with mental retardation in residential settings: Implications for policy, research, and practice. In T. Thompson, & D. Gray (eds), *Destructive behavior in developmental disabilities* (pp. 24–48). Thousand Oaks, CA: Sage Publications.

Bruininks, R. H., Woodcock, R. W., Weatherman, R. F., & Hill, B. K. (1996). *Scales of independent behavior – revised.* Chicago, IL: Riverside.

Brylewski, J., & Wiggs, L. (1999). Sleep problems and challenging behaviour in a community-based sample of adults with intellectual disability. *Journal of Intellectual Disability Research*, *43*, 504–512.

Burke, L., & Bedard, C. (1994). Self-injury considered in association with sexual victimization in individuals with a developmental handicap. *Canadian Journal of Human Sexuality*, *3*, 253–262.

Cain, A. C. (1961). The presuperego turning-inward of aggression. *Psychoanalytic Quarterly*, *30*, 171–208.

California Department of Developmental Services (1979). *Client development evaluation report*. Sacramento: Author.

Campbell, M. (1985). Timed stereotypies rating scale. *Psychopharmacology Bulletin*, *21*, 1082–1085.

Cannella, H. I., O'Reilly, M. F., & Lancioni, G. E. (2006). Treatment of hand mouthing in individuals with severe to profound developmental disabilities: A review of the literature. *Research in Developmental Disabilities*, *27*, 529–544.

Carlson, N. R. (1986). *Foundations of physiological psychology*. Boston: Allyn & Bacon.

Carr, E. G. (1977). The motivation of self-injurious behavior. *Pychological Bulletin*, *84*, 800–816.

Carr, E. G. (1997). The evolution of applied behavior analysis into positive behavior support. *Journal of the Association of Persons with Severe Handicaps*, *22*, 208–209.

Carr, E. G., Dunlap, G., Horner, R. H., Koegel, R. L., Turnbull, A. P., Sailor, W., et al. (2002b). Positive behavior support: Evolution of an applied behavior science. *Journal of Positive Behavior Interventions*, *4*, 4–17.

Carr, E. G., & Durand, V. M. (1985). Reducing behavior problems through functional communication training. *Journal of Applied Behavior Analysis*, *18*, 111–126.

Carr, E. G., Horner, R. H., Turnbull, A. P., Marquis, J. G., McLaughlin, D. M., & McAtee, M. L., et al. (1999a). *Positive behavior support for people with developmental disabilities: A research synthesis*. Washington, DC: American Association on Mental Retardation.

Carr, E. G., Levin, L., McConnachie, G., Carlson, J. I., Kemp, D. C., & Smith, C. E. (1994). *Communication-based intervention for problem behavior: A user's guide for producing positive change*. Baltimore, MD: Paul H. Brookes.

Carr, E. G., Levin, L., McConnachie, G., Carlson, J. I., Kemp, D. C., Smith, C. E., et al. (1999b). Comprehensive multisituational intervention for problem behavior in the community: Long-term maintenance and social validation. *Journal of Positive Behavior Support*, *1*, 5–25.

Carr, E. G., & Smith, C. E. (1995). Biological setting events for self-injury. *Mental Retardation and Developmental Disabilities Research Reviews*, *1*, 94–98.

Carr, E. G., Smith, C. E., Giacin, T. A., Whelan, B. M., & Pancari, J. (2003). Menstrual discomfort as a biological setting event for severe problem behavior: Assessment and intervention. *American Journal on Mental Retardation*, *108*, 117–133.

Carr, E. G., Yarbrough, S. C., & Langdon, N. A. (1997). Effects of idiosyncratic stimulus variables on functional analysis outcomes. *Journal of Applied Behavior Analysis*, *30*, 673–685.

Carr, J. E., Bailey, J. S., Ecott, C. L., Ducker, K. D., & Weil, T. M. (1998). On the effects of noncontingent delivery of differing magnitudes of reinforcement. *Journal of Applied Behaivor Analysis*, *31*(3), 313–321.

Carr, J. E., Coriaty, S., Wilder, D. A., Gaunt, B. T., Dozier, C. L., Britton, L. N., et al. (2000). A review of "noncontingent" reinforcement as treatment for aberrant behavior of individuals with developmental disabilities. *Research in Developmental Disabilities*, *21*, 377–391.

Carr, J. E., Dozier, C. L., Patel, M. R., Adams, A. N., & Martin, N. (2002a). Treatment of automatically reinforced object mouthing with noncontingent reinforcement and response blocking: Experimental analysis and social validation. *Research in Developmental Disabilities, 23,* 37–44.

Cataldo, M. F., & Harris, J. C. (1982). The biological basis for self-injury in the mentally retarded. *Analysis and Intervention in Developmental Disabilities, 2,* 21–39.

Chadwick, O., Piroth, N., Walker, J., Bernard, S., & Taylor, E. (2000). Factors affecting the risk of behaviour problems in children with severe intellectual disability. *Journal of Intellectual Disability Research, 44,* 108–123.

Changeux, J. P., & Danchin, A. (1976). Selective stabilization of developing synapses as a mechanism for the specification of neuronal networks. *Nature, 264,* 705–712.

Charlot, L. R., Doucette, A. C., & Mezzacapa, E. (1993). Affective symptoms of institutionalized adults with mental retardation. *American Journal on Mental Retardation, 98,* 408–416.

Chee, F. K., Kreutzberg, J. R., & Clark, D. L. (1978). Semicircular canal stimulation in cerebral palsied children. *Physical Therapy, 58,* 1071–1075.

Chen, K. S., Potocki, L., & Lupski, J. R. (1996). The Smith-Magenis syndrome [del(17)p11.2]: Clinical review and molecular advances. *Mental Retardation and Developmental Disabilities Research Reviews, 2,* 122–129.

Chugani, H. T. (1994). Development of regional brain glucose metabolism in relation to behavior and plasticity. In G. Dawson, & K. W. Fischer (eds), *Human behavior and the developing brain* (pp. 153–175). New York: Guilford Publications, Inc.

Chugani, H. T., & Jacobs, B. (1995). Metabolic recovery in caudate nucleus of children following cerebral hemispherectomy. *Annals of Neurology, 36,* 794–797.

Chugani, H. T., & Phelps, M. E. (1986). Maturational changes in cerebral function in infants determined by 18pDG positron emission tomography. *Science, 231,* 840–843.

Chugani, H. T., Phelps, M. E., & Mazziotta, J. C. (1987). Positron emission tomography study of human brain functional development. *Annals of Neurology, 22,* 487–497.

Ciaranello, R., Anders, T., Barchas, J., Berger, P., & Cann, H. (1976). The use of 5hydro-xytryptophan in a child with Lesch–Nyhan syndrome. *Child Psychiatry and Human Development, 7,* 127–133.

Cipani, E., & Spooner, F. (1997). Treating problem behaviors maintained by negative reinforcement. *Research in Developmental Disabilities, 18,* 329–342.

Clark, D. L., Kreutzberg, J. R., & Chee, F. K. (1977). Vestibular stimulation influence on motor development in infants. *Science, 196,* 1228–1229.

Clark, L. A. (1996). *Schedule for nonadaptive and adaptive personality: Manual for administration, scoring and interpretation.* Minneapolis, MN: Minnesota University Press.

Cohen, E. (1969). Self-assault in psychiatric evaluation. *Archives of General Psychiatry, 21,* 64–67.

Cohen, I. L. (2003). Criterion-related validity of the PDD Behavior Inventory. *Journal of Autism and Developmental Disorders, 33,* 47–53.

Cohen, S. A., & Underwood, M. T. (1994). The use of clozapine in a mentally retarded and aggressive population. *Journal of Clinical Psychiatry, 55,* 440–444.

Cohen, I. L., Schmidt-Lackner, S., Romanczyk, R., & Sudhalter, V. (2003). The PDD behavior inventory: A rating scale for assessing response to intervention in children with pervasive developmental disorder. *Journal of Autism and Developmental Disorders, 33,* 31–45.

Collacott, R., Cooper, S.-A., Branford, D., & McGrother, C. (1998). Epidemiology of self-injurious behaviour in adults with learning disabilities. *The British Journal of Psychiatry, 171,* 428–432.

Colnel, L. (1939/1963). *Postnatal development of the human cerebral cortex.* Cambridge, MA: Harvard University Press.

Conroy, M., Fox, J., Crain, L., Jenkins, A., & Belcher, K. (1996). Evaluating the social and ecological validity of analog assessment procedures for challenging behaviors in young children. *Education and Treatment of Children, 19,* 233–256.

Conroy, M. A., Fox, J. J., Bucklin, A., & Good, W. (1996). An analysis of the reliability and stability of the motivation assessment scale in assessing the challenging behaviors of persons with developmental disabilities. *Education and Training in Mental Retardation and Developmental Disabilities, 31,* 243–250.

Connors, J., Iwata, B. A., Kahng, S. W., Hanley, G. P., Wordsell, A. S., & Thompson, R. H. (2000). Differential responding in the presence and absence of discriminative stimuli during multielement functional analyses. *Journal of Applied Behavior Analysis, 33,* 299–308.

Cooper, J. O., Heron, T. E., & Heward, W. L. (2007). *Applied behavior analysis* (2nd ed.). Upper Saddle River, NJ: Prentice Hall.

Corte, H. E., Wolf, M. W., & Locke, B. J. (1971). A comparison of procedures for elimination of self-injurious behavior of retarded adolescents. *Journal of Applied Behavior Analysis, 4,* 201–213.

Coulter, D. A. (1990). Frontal lobe seizures: No evidence of self-injury. *American Journal on Mental Retardation, 96,* 81–84.

Crawhall, J. C., Henderson, J. F., & Kelley, W. N. (1972). Diagnosis and treatment of Lesch–Nyhan syndrome. *Pediatric Research, 6,* 504–513.

Criswell, H. E., Mueller, R. A., & Breese, G. R. (1989). Clozapine antagonism of D-1 and D-2 dopamine receptor-mediated behaviors. *European Journal of Pharmacology, 159,* 141–147.

Crnic, L. S., & Hagerman, R., (eds) (2004). Fragile X syndrome: Frontiers of understanding gene–brain-behavior relationships. *Mental Retardation and Developmental Disabilities Research Reviews, 10,* 1–81.

Crnic, L. S., & Nitkin, R. M. (1996). Animal models of mental retardation: An overview. *Mental Retardation and Developmental Disabilities Research Reviews, 2,* 185–187.

Crocker, A., & Nelson, R. P. (1983). Major handicapping conditions: Mental retardation. In M. D. Levine, W. B. Carey, A. C. Crocker, & R. J. Gross (eds), *Developmental behavioral pediatrics* (pp. 756–769). Philadelphia: W.B. Saunders.

Crosland, K. A., Zarcone, J. R., Lindauer, S. E., Valdovinos, M. G., Zarcone, T. J., Hellings, J. A., et al. (2003). Use of functional analysis methodology in the evaluation of medication effects. *Journal of Autism and Developmental Disorders, 33,* 271–279.

Crosland, K. A., Zarcone, J. R., Schroeder, S. R., Zarcone, T., & Fowler, S. (2005). Use of antecedent analysis and a force-sensitive platform to compare stereotyped movements and motor tics. *American Journal on Mental Retardation, 110,* 181–192.

Cowdery, G. E., Iwata, B. A., & Pace, G. M. (1990). Effects and side effects of DRO as treatment for self-injury. *Journal of Applied Behavior Analysis, 24,* 497–506.

Cunningham, C. E., & Peltz, L. (1982). In vivo desensitization in the management of self-injurious behavior. *Journal of Behavior Therapy and Experimental Psychiatry, 13,* 135–140.

Curtiss, S. (1977). *Genie: A psycholinguistic study of a modern-day "wild child.".* New York: Academic Press.

Curtiss, S. (1981). Feral children. In J. Wortis (ed.), *Mental retardation and developmental disabilities,* (Vol. XXI) (pp. 129–161). New York: Brunner/Mazel.

Danford, D. E., & Huber, A. M. (1982). Pica among mentally retarded adults. *American Journal of Mental Deficiency, 87,* 141–146.

Davenport, R. K., & Berkson, G. (1963). Stereotyped movements of mental defectives: II. Effects of novel objects. *American Journal of Mental Deficiency, 67*, 879–882.

Davidson, P. D., Houser, K. D., Cain, N. N., Sloane-Reeves, J., Quijano, L., Matons, L., Giesow, V., & Ladrigan, P. M. (1999). Characteristics of older adults with intellectual disabilities referred for crisis intervention. *Journal of Intellectual Disability Research, 43*, 38–46.

Davis, K. V., Sprague, R. L., & Werry, J. S. (1969). Stereotyped behavior and activity level in severe retardates: The effect of drugs. *American Journal of Mental Deficiency, 73*, 721–727.

Day, M. M., Horner, R. H., & O'Neill, R. E. (1994). Multiple functions of problem behaviors: Assessment and intervention. *Journal of Applied Behavior Analysis, 27*, 279–289.

Deaver, C. M., Miltenberger, R. g., & Stricker, J. M. (2001). Functional analysis and treatment of hair twirling in a young child. *Journal of Applied Behavior Analysis, 34*, 535–538.

Dehen, H., Wilier, J. C., Boureau, F., & Cambier, J. (1977). Congenital insensitivity to pain, and endogenous morphine-like substances. *Lancet, 11*, 293–294.

de Lange, C. (1933). Sur un type nouveau dégénération (typus Amstelodamensis). *Archives de Médicine des Infants, 36*, 713–719.

DeLeon, I. G., Rodriguez-Catter, V., & Cataldo, M. F. (2002). Treatment: Current standards of care and their research implications. In S. Schroeder, M. L. Oster-Granite, & T. Thompson (eds), *Self-injurious behavior: Gene–brain–behavior relationships* (pp. 81–91). Washington, DC: American Psychological Association.

De Lissavoy, V. (1961). Head-banging in early childhood. *Journal of Pediatrics, 58*, 109–114.

Denov, M. S. (2004). The long-term effects of child sexual abuse by female perpetrators: A qualitative study of male and female victims. *Journal of Interpersonal Violence, 19*, 1137–1156.

Derby, K. M., Fisher, W. W., & Piazza, C. C. (1996). The effects of contingent and noncontingent attention on self-injury and self-restraint. *Journal of Applied Behavior Analysis, 29*, 107–110.

Derby, K. M., Wacker, D. P., Peck, S., Sasso, G., DeRaad, A., Berg, W., et al. (1994). Functional analysis of separate topographies of aberrant behavior. *Journal of Applied Behavior Analysis, 27*, 267–278.

Didden, R., Korzillius, H., van Aperlo, B., van Overlooop, C., & de Vries, M. (2002). Sleep problems and daytime problem behaviours in children with intellectual disability. *Journal of Intellectual Disability Research, 46*, 537–547.

Diemer, K. (1968). Capillarisation and oxygen supply of the brain. In D. W. Lubbers, U. C. Luft, G. Thews, & E. Witzleb (eds), *Oxygen transport in blood and tissue* (pp. 118–123). Stuttgart: Thieme, Inc.

Dong, W. K., & Greenough, W. T. (2004). Plasticity of nonneuronal brain tissue: Role in developmental disorders. *Mental Retardation and Developmental Disabilities Research Reviews, 10*, 85–90.

Dorsey, M. F., Iwata, B. A., Ong, P., & McSween, T. E. (1980). Treatment of self-injurious behavior using a water mist: Initial response suppression and generalization. *Journal of Applied Behavior Analysis, 13*, 343–353.

Dorsey, M. F., Iwata, B. A., Reid, D. H., & Davis, P. A. (1982). Protective equipment: Continuous and contingent application in the treatment of self-injurious behavior. *Journal of Applied Behavior Analysis, 15*, 217–230.

Duker, P. C., & Sigafoos, J. (1998). The Motivation Assessment Scale: Reliability and construct validity across three topographies of behavior. *Research in Developmental Disabilities, 19*, 131–141.

Dura, J. R., Mulick, J. A., & Hammer, D. (1988). Rapid clinical evaluation of sensory integrative therapy for self-injurious behavior. *Mental Retardation, 26*, 83–87.

Durand, V. M., & Crimmins, D. B. (1988). Identifying variables maintaining self-injurious behavior. *Journal of Autism and Developmental Disorders, 18,* 99–117.

Durand, V. M., & Merges, E. (2001). Functional communication training: A contemporary behavior analytic intervention for problem behaviors. *Focus on Autism and Other Developmental Disabilities, 16,* 110–119.

Dykens, E.M. (1995). Measuring behavioral phenotypes: Provocations from the "New Genetics", *American Journal on Mental Retardation, 99,* 522–532.

Dykens, E. M., Cassidy, S. B., & King, B. H. (1999). Maladaptive behavior differences in Prader–Wili syndrome due to paternal deletion versus maternal uniparental disomy. *American Journal on Mental Retardation, 104,* 67–77.

Dykens, E. M., Hodapp, R. M., & Finucane, B. M. (2000). *Genetic and mental retardation syndromes.* Baltimore, MD: Paul Brookes Publishing Co.

Dykens, E. M., & Smith, A. C. M. (1998). Distinctiveness and correlates of maladaptive behavior in children and adolescents with Smith–Magenis syndrome. *Journal of Intellectual Disability Research, 42,* 481–489.

Einfeld, S. L., & Tonge, B. J. (1992). *Manual for the Developmental Behaviour Checklist.* Clayton, Malbourne, and Sydney: Monash University Center for Developmental Psychiatry and School of Psychiatry, University of New South Wales.

Einfeld, S. L., & Tonge, B. J. (2002). *Manual for the Developmental Behaviour Checklist* (2nd ed.). Clayton, Malbourne, and Sydney: Monash University Center for Developmental Psychiatry and School of Psychiatry, University of New South Wales.

Elie, R., Langlois, Y., Cooper, S. F., Gravel, G., & Albert, J. M. (1980). Comparison of SCH-12679 and thioridazine in aggressive mental retardates. *Canadian Journal of Psychiatry, 25,* 484–491.

Ellingson, S. A., Miltenberger, R. G., & Long, E. S. (1999). A survey of the use of functional assessment procedures in agencies serving individuals with developmental disabilities. *Behavioral Interventions, 14,* 187–198.

Emberson, J., & Walker, E. (1990). Self-injurious behaviour in people with a mental handicap. *Nursing Times, 86,* 43–46.

Emerson, E. (1992). Schedule-induced stereotypy. *Research in Developmental Disabilities, 13,* 335–361.

Emerson, E., & Bromley, J. (1995). The form and function of challenging behaviors. *Journal of Intellectual Disability Research, 39,* 388–398.

Emerson, E., Kiernan, C., Alborz, A., Reeves, D., Mason, H., Swarbrick, R., et al. (2001). The prevalence of challenging behaviors: A total population study. *Research in Developmental Disabilities, 22,* 77–93.

English, C. L., & Anderson, C. M. (2004). Effects of familiar versus unfamiliar therapists on responding in the analog functional analysis. *Research in Developmental Disabilities, 25,* 39–55.

Erwin, J., Mitchell, G., & Maple, T. (1973). Abnormal behavior in non-isolate reared monkey. *Psychological Reports, 33,* 515–523.

Esbensen, A. J., Rojahn, J., Aman, M. G., & Ruedrich, S. (2003). The reliability and validity of an assessment instrument of anxiety, depression, and mood among individuals with mental retardation. *Journal of Autism and Developmental Disorders, 33,* 643–652.

Eshbaugh, B., Martin, W., Cunningham, K., & Luiselli, J. K. (2004). Evaluation of a bedtime medication regimen on daytime sleep and challenging behaviors of an adult with intellectual disability. *Mental Health Aspects of Developmental Disabilities, 7,* 21–25.

Evans, I. A., & Meyer, L. H. (1985). *An educative approach to behavior problems: A practical decision model for interventions with severely handicapped learners.* Baltimore: Paul Brookes Publishing Co.

Evren, C., & Evren, B. (2006). The relationship of suicide attempt history with childhood abuse and neglect, alexithymia and temperament and character dimensions of personality in substance dependents. *Nordic Journal of Psychiatry, 60,* 263–269.

Eyman, R. K., & Call, T. (1977). Maladaptive behavior and community placement of mentally retarded persons. *American Journal of Mental Deficiency, 82,* 137–144.

Fairbairn, W. R. D. (1952/1994). *Psychoanalytical Studies of the Personality.* Oxford, UK: Routledge.

Favazza, A. R. (1989). Why patients mutilate themselves. *Hospital and Community Psychiatry, 40,* 137–145.

Favazza, A. R. (1996). *Bodies under siege: Self-mutilation in culture and psychiatry* (2nd ed.). Baltimore: Johns Hopkins University Press.

Favazza, A. R. (1998). The coming of age of self-mutilation. *Journal of Nervous and Mental Disease, 186,* 259–268.

Favazza, A. R. (1999). Self-mutilation. In D. G. Jacobs (ed.), *The Harvard Medical School guide to suicide assessment and intervention.* San Francisco: Jossey-Bass.

Favazza, A. R., & Conterio, K. (1988). The plight of chronic self-mutilators. *Community Mental Health Journal, 24,* 22–30.

Favell, J. E., McGimsey, J. F., & Jones, M. L. (1978). The use of physical restraint in the treatment of self-injury and as positive reinforcement. *Journal of Applied Behavior Analysis, 11,* 225–241.

Favell, J. E., McGimsey, J. F., Jones, M. L., & Cannon, P. R. (1981). Physical restraint as positive reinforcement. *American Journal of Mental Deficiency, 85,* 425–432.

Finucane, B., Dirrigl, K. H., & Simon, E. W. (2001). Characterization of self-injurious behaviors in children and adults with Smith–Magenis syndrome. *American Journal on Mental Retardation, 106,* 52–58.

Finzi, R., Ram, A., Shnit, D., Har-Even, D., Tyano, S., & Weizman, A. (2001). Depressive symptoms and suicidality in physically abused children. *American Journal of Orthopsychiatry, 71,* 98–107.

Fischer, S. M., Iwata, B. A., & Mazaleski, J. L. (1997). Noncontingent delivery of arbitrary reinforcers as treatment for self-injurious behavior. *Journal of Applied Behavior Analysis, 30,* 239–249.

Fisher, W., Piazza, C., Cataldo, M., Harrell, R., Jefferson, G., & Conner, R. (1993). Functional communication training with and without extinction and punishment. *Journal of Applied Behavior Analysis, 26,* 23–36.

Fisher, W. W., Adelinis, J. D., Thompson, R. H., Wordsell, A. S., & Zarcone, J. R. (1998a). Functional analysis and treatment of destructive behavior maintained by termination of "don't" (and symmetrical "do") requests. *Journal of Applied Behavior Analysis, 31,* 339–356.

Fisher, W. W., Bowman, L. G., Thompson, R. H., Contrucci, S. A., Burd, L., & Alon, G. (1998b). Reductions in self-injury produced by transcutaneous electrical nerve stimulation. *Journal of Applied Behavior Analysis, 31,* 493–496.

Fisher, W. W., DeLeon, I. G., Rodrigues-Carter, V., & Keeney, K. M. (2004). Enhancing effects of extinction on attention-maintained behavior through noncontingent delivery of attention or stimuli identified via a competing stimulus assessment. *Journal of Applied Behavior Analysis, 37,* 171–184.

Fliege, H., Becker, J., Weber, C., Schoenreich, F., Klapp, B. F., & Rose, M. (2003). Störungen der Selbstwertregulation bei Patienten mit offenen versus heimlich selbstschädigendem Verhalten. *Zeitschrift für Psychosomatische Medizin und Psychotherapie, 49,* 151–163.

Fliege, H., Kocalevent, R.-D., Rose, M., Becker, J., Walter, M., & Klapp, B. F. (2004). Patients with overt or covert self-harm: Differences in optimism and self-efficacy. *Dermatology and Psychosomatics (Dermatologie und Psychosomatik)*, *5*, 54–60.

Floyd, R. G., Phaneuf, R. L., & Wilczynski, S. M. (2005). Measurement properties of indirect assessment methods for functional behavioral assessment: A review of research. *School Psychology Review*, *34*, 58–73.

Folstein, S., & Rosen-Sheidley (2001). Genetics of autism: Complex aetiology for a heterogeneous disorder. *Nature Reviews: Genetics*, *2*, 943–955.

Folstein, S., & Rutter, M. (1978). A twin study of individuals with autism. In M. Rutter, & E. Schopler (eds), *Autism: A reappraisal of concepts and treatment* (pp. 219–241). New York: Plenum Press.

Foster, W. S. (1978). Adjunctive behavior: An under-reported phenomenon in applied behavior analysis? *Journal of Applied Behavior Analysis*, *11*, 545–546.

Fovel, J. T., Lash, P. S., Barron, D. A., & Roberts, M. S. (1989). A survey of self-restraint, self-injury, and other maladaptive behaviors in an institutionalized retarded population. *Research in Developmental Disabilities*, *10*, 377–382.

Freeman, R., Horner, R. H., & Reichle, J. (2002). Functional assessment and self-restraint. In S. R. Schroeder, M. L. Oster-Granite, & T. Thompson (eds), *Self-injurious behavior: Gene–brain-behavior relationships* (pp. 105–118). Washington, DC: American Psychological Association.

Freeman, R. L., Smith, C., Zarcone, J., Kimbrough, P., Tieghi-Benet, M., Wickham, D., et al. (2005). Building a statewide plan for embedding positive behavior support in human service organizations. *Journal of Positive Behavior Interventions*, *7*, 109–119.

Freud, A. (1949). Aggression in relation to emotional development: Normal and pathological. In A. Freud, H. Hartmann, & E. Kris (eds), *The psychoanalytic study of the child* (Vol. 3/4), (pp. 37–42). Oxford, England: International University Press.

Fuster, J. M. (1984). Behavioral electrophysiology of the prefrontal cortex. *Trends in Neuroscience*, *1*, 408–414.

Gadow, K., & Poling, A. (1987). *Pharmacotherapy and mental retardation*. Boston, MA: Little, Brown, & Co.

Garcia, D., & Smith, R. G. (1999). Using analog baselines to assess the effects of naltrexone on self-injurious behavior. *Research in Developmental Disabilities*, *20*, 1–21.

Gardner, W. I., & Sovner, R. (1994). *Self-injurious behaviors*. Willow Street, PA: VIDA Publishing Co.

Gedye, A. (1989). Extreme self-injury attributed to frontal lobe seizures. *American Journal on Mental Retardation*, *94*, 20–26.

Gedye, A. (1990). Dietary increase in serotonin reduces self-injurious behaviour in a Down's syndrome adult. *Journal of Mental Deficiency Research*, *34*, 195–203.

Gedye, A. (1992). Recognizing obsessive-compulsive disorder in clients with developmental disabilities. *The Habilitative Mentalhealthcare Newsletter*, *11*, 73–77.

Girardeau, F. L., & Spradlin, J. E. (1964). Token rewards in a cottage program. *Mental Retardation*, *2*, 345–352.

Girouard, N., Morin, I. N., & Tassé, M. J. (1998). Étude de fidélité test-retest et accord interjuges de la Grille d'évaluation comportementale pour enfants Nisonger (GÉCEN). [Test-retest and interjudge reliability study of the Nisonger Child Behavior Rating Form.]. *Revue Francophone de la Déficience Intellectuelle*, *9*, 127–136.

Gluck, J., & Sackett, G. (1974). Frustration and self-aggression in social isolate rhesus monkey. *Journal of Abnormal Psychology*, *83*, 331–334.

Goh, H., Iwata, B. A., Shore, B. A., DeLeon, I. G., Lerman, D. C., Ulrich, S. M., et al. (1995). An analysis of the reinforcing properties of hand mouthing. *Journal of Applied Behavior Analysis, 28*, 269–283.

Goh, H. L., & Iwata, B. A. (1994). Behavioral persistence and variability during extinction of self-injury maintained by escape. *Journal of Applied Behavior Analysis, 27*, 173–174.

Goldman-Rakic, P. S. (1984). The frontal lobes: Uncharted provinces of the brain. *Trends in Neuroscience, 1*, 425–429.

Goldstein, M., Kuga, S., Kusano, N., Meller, E., Dancis, J., & Schwarcz, R. (1986). Dopamine agonist induced self-mutilative biting behavior in monkeys with unilateral ventral medial tegmental lesions of the brain stem: Possible pharmacological model for Lesch–Nyhan Syndrome. *Brain Research, 367*, 114–120.

González, M. L., Dixon, D. R., Esbensen, A., Rojahn, J., Matson, J. L., Terlonge, C., & Smith, K.R. (in press). Psychometric Evaluation of the Behavior Problems Inventory (BPI-01) in Institutionalized Adults with Intellectual Disabilities. *Journal of Applied Research in Intellectual Disabilities*.

Goodman, W. K., Price, L. H., & Rasmussen, S. A. (1989a). The Yale–Brown Obsessive Compulsive Scale: I. Development, use, and reliability. *Archives of General Psychiatry, 46*, 1006–1011.

Goodman, W. K., Price, L. H., & Rasmussen, S. A. (1989b). The Yale–Brown Obsessive Compulsive Scale: II. Validity. *Archives of General Psychiatry, 46*, 1012–1016.

Gratz, K. L. (2001). Measurement of deliberate self-harm: Preliminary data on the deliberate self-harm inventory. *Journal of Psychopathology and Behavioral Assessment, 23*, 253–263.

Green, A. H. (1967). Self-mutilation in schizophrenic children. *Archives of General Psychiatry, 7*, 234–244.

Greenough, W. T. (1976). Enduring brain effects of differential experience and training. In M. R. Rosenzweig, & E. L. Bennett (eds), *Neural mechanisms of learning and memory* (pp. 255–278). Cambridge, MA: M.L.T. Press.

Griffin, J. C., Locke, B. J., & Landers, W. F. (1975). Manipulation of potential punishment parameters in the treatment of self-injury. *Journal of Applied Behavior Analysis, 8*, 458.

Griffin, J. C., Ricketts, R. W., Williams, D. E., Locke, B. J., Altmeyer, B. K., & Stark, M. T. (1987). A community survey of self-injurious behavior among developmentally disabled children and adolescents. *Hospital and Community Psychiatry, 38*, 959–963.

Griffin, J. C., Williams, D. E., Stark, M. T., Altmeyer, B. K., & Mason, M. (1986). Self-injurious behavior: A state-wide prevalence survey of the extent and circumstances. *Applied Research in Mental Retardation, 7*, 105–116.

Grosset, D. L., & Williams, D. E. (1995). Effects of haloperidol, alone and combined with DRO, on self-injurious behavior in a woman with profound mental retardation and atypical psychosis. *Journal of Developmental and Physical Disabilities, 7*, 147–154.

Grossman, H. J. (1973). *Classification in mental retardation*. Washington, DC: American Association on Mental Deficiency.

Gualtieri, C. T. (1984). *The Neuroleptic Side Effects Checklist*. Unpublished Scale available from the author.

Gualtieri, C. T. (1989). The differential diagnosis of self-injurious behavior in mentally retarded people. *Psychopharmacology Bulletin, 25*, 358–363.

Gualtieri, C. T. (1991). *Neuropsychiatry and behavioral pharmacology*. New York, NY: Springer-Verlag.

Gualtieri, C. T., Quade, D., Hicks, R. E., Mayo, J. P., & Schroeder, S. R. (1984). Tardive dyskinesia and other consequences of neuroleptic treatment in children and adolescents. *American Journal of Psychiatry, 141*, 20–23.

Gualtieri, C. T., & Schroeder, S. R. (1989). Pharmacotherapy of self-injurious behavior: Preliminary tests of the D-1 hypothesis. *Psychopharmacology Bulletin*, *25*, 364–371.

Gualtieri, C. T., Schroeder, S. R., Hicks, R. E., & Quade, D. (1986). Tardive dyskinesia in young mentally retarded individuals. *Archives of General Psychiatry*, *43*, 335–340.

Guess, D., & Carr, E. (1991). Emergence and maintenance of stereotypy and self-injury. *American Journal on Mental Retardation*, *96*, 299–320.

Guess, D., Roberts, S., Siegel-Causey, E., Ault, M., Guy, B., & Thompson, B. (1993). Analysis of behavior state conditions and associated environmental variables among students with profound handicaps. *American Journal on Mental Retardation*, *97*, 634–653.

Guess, D., & Sailor, W. (1993). Chaos theory and the study of human behavior: Implications for special education and developmental disabilities. *The Journal of Special Education*, *27*, 16–34.

Gunning, M. J., & Espie, C. A. (2003). Psychological treatment of reported sleep disorder in adults with intellectual disability using a multiple baseline design. *Journal of Intellectual Disability Research*, *47*, 191–202.

Gunsett, R. P., Mulick, J. A., Fernald, W. B., & Martin, J. L. (1989). Brief report: Indications of medical screening prior to behavioral programming for severely and profoundly retarded clients. *Journal of Autism and Developmental Disorders*, *19*, 167–172.

Hagberg, B. (2002). Clinical manifestations and stages of Rett syndrome. *Mental Retardation and Developmental Disabilities Research Reviews*, *8*, 61–65.

Hagberg, B., Aicardi, J., Pias, K., & Ramos, D. (1983). A progressive syndrome of autism, dementia, ataxia, and loss of purposeful hand use in girls: Rett's syndrome – Report of 35 uses. *Annals of Neurology*, *14*, 471–479.

Hagerman, R. J. (1990). The association between autism and fragile X syndrome. *Brain Dysfunction*, *3*, 218–227.

Hagerman, R. J. (1999). Psychopharmacologic interventions in Fragile X syndrome, Fetal Alcohol syndrome, Prader–Willi syndrome, Angelman syndrome, Smith–Magenis syndrome, & Velocardiofacial syndrome. *Mental Retardation and Developmental Disabilities Research Reviews*, *5*, 305–313.

Hagerman, R. J., Bregman, J., & Tirosh, E. (1998). Clonidine. In S. Reiss, & M. G. Aman (eds), *Psychotropic medication and developmental disabilities: The international consensus handbook* (pp. 259–269). Columbus, OH: The Ohio State University.

Hagerman, R. J., Jackson, A. W., Levitas, A., Rimland, B., & Braden, M. (1986). An analysis of autism in fifty males with fragile X syndrome. *American Journal of Medical Genetics*, *23*, 359–374.

Hagerman, R. J., & Silverman, A. C. (eds.) (1991). *Fragile X syndrome: Diagnosis, treatment, and research*. Baltimore, MD: Johns Hopkins University Press.

Hagopian, L. P., Fisher, W. W., & Legacy, S. M. (1994). Schedule effects of noncontingent reinforcement on attention maintained destructive behavior in identical quadruplets. *Journal of Applied Behavior Analysis*, *27*, 317–325.

Hagopian, L. P., Fisher, W. W., Sullivan, M. T., Aquisto, J., & LeBlanc, L. (1998). Effectiveness of functional communication training with and without extinction and punishment: A summary of 21 inpatient cases. *Journal of Applied Behavior Analysis*, *31*, 211–235.

Hagopian, L. P., Paclawskyj, T. R., & Kuhn, S. C. (2005). The use of conditional probability analysis to identify a response chain leading to the occurrence of eye poking. *Research in Developmental Disabilities*, *26*, 393–397.

Hagopian, L. P., Wilson, D. M., & Wilder, D. A. (2001). Assessment and treatment of problem behavior maintained by escape from attention and access to tangible items. *Journal of Applied Behavior Analysis*, *34*, 229–232.

Haldeman v. Pennhurst State School and Hospital. (1977). 446 F. Supp. 1295 (E.D. Pa.).

Hall, S., Oliver, C., & Murphy, G. (2001). Early development of self-injurious behavior: An empirical study. *American Journal on Mental Retardation, 106*, 113–122.

Hammock, R. G., Levine, W. R., & Schroeder, S. R. (2001). Effect of clozapine on two risperidone non-responders with mental retardation. *Journal of Autism and Developmental Disorders, 31*, 109–113.

Hammock, R. G., Schroeder, S. R., & Levine, W. R. (1995). Effect of clozapine on self-injurious behavior. *Journal of Autism and Developmental Disorders, 25*, 611–627.

Han, J. S. (1993). Acupuncture and stimulation produced analgesia. In A. Herz (ed.), *Opioids II* (pp. 105–125). New York: Springer.

Hanley, G. P., Iwata, B. A., & McCord, B. E. (2003). Functional analysis of problem behavior: A review. *Journal of Applied Behavior Analysis, 36*, 147–185.

Hanley, G. P., Piazza, C. C., Keeney, K. M., Blakeley-Smith, A. B., & Wordsell, A. S. (1998). Effects of wrist weights on self-injurious and adaptive behaviors. *Journal of Applied Behavior Analysis, 31*, 307–310.

Harding, J., Wacker, D. P., Berg, W. K., Barretto, A., & Ringdahl, J. (2005). Evaluation of relations between specific antecedent stimuli and self-injury during functional analysis conditions. *American Journal on Mental Retardation, 110*, 205–215.

Harlow, H. F. (1958). *The nature of love.* Address of the President at the sixty-sixth Annual Convention of the American Psychological Association, Washington, DC, August 31, 1958. First published in *American Psychologist, 13*, 573–685.

Harlow, H. F., Harlow, M. K., & Suomi, S. J. (1971). From thought to therapy: Lessons from a primate laboratory. *American Scientist, 59*, 538–549.

Harris, J. C. (1992). Neurobiological factors in self-injurious behavior. In J. Luiselli, J. L. Matson, & N. Singh (eds), *Self injurious behavior: Analysis, assessment, and treatment* (pp. 59–92). New York, NY: Spring-Verlag.

Harris, J. C. (1995). *Developmental neuropsychiatry* (Vol. II),. New York: Oxford University Press.

Harris, J. C., Wong, D. F., Jinnah, H. A., Schretlin, D., & Parker, P. (2002). Neuroimaging studies in Lesch–Nyhan syndrome and Lesch–Nyhan variants. In S. R. Schroeder, M. L. Oster-Granite, & T. Thompson (eds), *Self-injurious behavior: Gene–brain-behavior relationships* (pp. 269–278). Washington, DC: American Psychological Association.

Harris, P., Humphreys, J., & Thomson, G. (1994). A checklist of challenging behaviour: The development of a survey instrument. *Mental Handicap Research, 7*, 118–133.

Hart, B., & Risley, T. R. (1995). *Meaningful differences in the everyday experience of young American children.* Baltimore: Paul H. Brookes.

Hart, B., & Risley, T. R. (1999). *The social world of learning to talk.* Baltimore: Paul H. Brookes.

Harper, D. C., & Wadsworth, J. S. (1993). Grief in adults with mental retardation: Preliminary findings. *Research in Developmental Disabilities, 14*, 313–330.

Harvey, M. T., & Kennedy, C. H. (2002). Polysomnographic phenotypes in developmental disabilities. *International Journal of Developmental Neuroscience, 20*, 443–448.

Hawley, P., Jackson, L., & Kurnit, D. (1985). Sixty-four patients with Brachmann-de Lange syndrome: A survey. *American Journal of Medical Genetics, 20*, 453–459.

Healey, J. J., Ahearn, W. H., Graff, R. B., & Libby, M. E. (2001). Extended analysis and treatment of self-injurious behavior. *Behavioral Interventions, 16*, 181–195.

Heistad, G. T., & Zimmermann, R. L. (1979). Double-blind assessment of Mellaril in a mentally retarded population using detailed evaluations. *Psychopharmacology Bulletin, 15*, 86–88.

Heistad, G. T., Zimmermann, R. L., & Doebler, M. I. (1982). Long-term usefulness of thioridazine for institutionalized mentally retarded patients. *American Journal on Mental Deficiency, 87*, 243–251.

Hellings, J. A. (1999). Psychopharmacology of mood disorders in persons with mental retardation and autism. *Mental Retardation and Developmental Disabilities Research Reviews, 5*, 270–278.

Hellings, J. A., Kelley, L. A., Gabrielli, W. F., Kilgore, E. R., & Shah, P. (1996). Sertraline response in adults with mental retardation and autistic disorder. *Journal of Clinical Psychiatry, 57*, 333–336.

Hellings, J. A., & Warnock, J. K. (1994). Self-injurious behavior and serotonin in Prader–Willi syndrome. *Psychopharmacology Bulletin, 30*, 245–250.

Hellings, J. A., Weckbaugh, M., Nickel, E. J., Cain, S. E., Zarcone, J. R., Reese, R. M., et al. (2005). A double-blind, placebo-controlled study of valproate for aggression in youth with pervasive developmental disorders. *Journal of Child and Adolescent Psychopharmacology, 15*, 682–692.

Hellings, J. A., Zarcone, J. R., Crandall, K., Wallace, D., & Schroeder, S. R. (2001). Weight gain in a controlled study of risperidone in children, adolescents, and adults with mental retardation. *Journal of Child and Adolescent Psychopharmacology, 11*, 229–238.

Hellings, J. A., Zarcone, J. R., Reese, R. M., Valdovinos, M. G., Marquis, J. G., Fleming, K. K., et al. (2006). A crossover study of risperidone in children, adolescents, and adults with mental retardation. *Journal of Autism and Developmental Disorders, 36*, 401–411.

Herpetz, S. (1995). Self-injurious behavior: Psychopathological and nosological characteristics in subtypes of self-injurers. *Acta Psychiatrica Scandinavia, 91*, 57–68.

Hill, B. K., & Bruininks, R. H. (1984). Maladaptive behavior of mentally retarded individuals in residential facilities. *American Journal of Mental Deficiency, 88*, 380–387.

Hillery, J., & Mulcahy, M. (1997). Self-injurious behaviour in persons with a mental handicap: An epidemiological study in an Irish population. *Irish Journal of Psychiatric Medicine, 14*, 12–15.

Hoch, T. A. (2007). Why is my kid doing this and what can I do? Using scatterplots with families of children with disabilities. In D. Linville, & K. M. Hertlein (eds), *The therapist's notebook for family healthcare: Homework, handouts, and activities for individuals, couples, and families coping with illness, loss, and disability* (pp. 83–89). New York, NY: Haworth Press.

Hoch, T. A., Babbitt, R. L., Coe, D. A., Duncan, A., & Trusty, E. (1995). A swallow induction avoidance procedure to establish eating. *Journal of Behavior Therapy and Experimental Psychiatry, 26*, 41–50.

Holden, B., & Gitlesen, J. P. (2006). A total population study of challenging behaviour in the country of Hedmark, Norway: Prevalence, and risk markers. *Research in Developmental Disabilities, 27*, 456–465.

Hollis, J. H. (1968). Chlorpromazine: Direct measurement of differential behavioral effect. *Science, 159*, 1487–1489.

Hollis, J. H., & St. Omer, V. V. (1972). Direct measurement of psychopharmacological response: Effects of chlorpromazine on motor behavior of retarded children. *American Journal of Mental Deficiency, 76*, 397–407.

Holm, V. A. (1996). Prader–Willi syndrome. In A. J. Capute, & P. J. Accardo (eds), *Developmental disabilities in infancy and childhood* (2nd ed.) (pp. 245–254). Baltimore, MD: Paul H. Brookes Publishing Co.

Holman, J. (1977). The moral risk and high cost of ecological concern in applied behavior analysis. In A. Rogers-Warren, & S. Warren (eds), *Ecological perspectives in behavior analysis*. Baltimore: Paul Brookes Publishing Co.

Horner, R. (2000). Positive behavior supports. *Focus on Autism and Other Developmental Disabilities, 15*, 97–105.

Horner, R. H., Day, H. M., & Day, J. R. (1997). Using neutralizing routines to reduce problem behaviors. *Journal of Applied Behavior Analysis, 30*, 601–614.

Horner, R. H., Dunlap, G., & Koegel, R. L. (eds.) (1988). *Generalization and maintenance: Maintaining lifestyle changes in applied settings.* Baltimore: Paul Brookes Publishing Co.

Horner, R. H., Dunlap, G., Koegel, R. L., Carr, E. G., Sailor, W., Anderson, J., et al. (1990). Toward a technology of "non-aversive" behavior support. *Journal of the Association for Persons with Severe Handicaps, 15*, 125–132.

Horrigan, J. P., & Barnhill, L. J. (1997). Risperidone and explosive aggressive autism. *Journal of Autism and Developmental Disorders, 27*, 313–323.

Hoyt, R., & Spradlin, J. (2006). Background: The times. In R. L. Schiefelbusch, & S. R. Schroeder (eds), *Doing science and doing good* (pp. 35–56). Baltimore, MD: Paul Brookes Publishing Co.

Hubel, D. H., & Wiesel, T. N. (1970). The period of susceptibility to the physiological effects of unilateral eye closure in kittens. *Journal of Physiology (London), 206*, 419–436.

Huttenlocher, P. R. (1979). Synaptic density in human frontal cortex-developmental changes and effects of aging. *Brain Research, 163*, 195–205.

International Statistical Classification of Diseases and Related Health Problems 10th Revision (2006). Retrieved on October 14, 2006, from http://www3.who.int/icd/currentversion/ fr-icd.htm

Irle, E. (1987). Lesion size and recovery of function: Some new perspectives. *Brain Research Reviews, 12*, 307–320.

Irvin, D. S., Thompson, T. J., Turner, W. D., & Williams, D. E. (1998). Utilizing increased response effort to reduce chronic hand mouthing. *Journal of Applied Behavior Analysis, 31*, 375–385.

Ishii, N., Kawaguchi, H., Miyakawa, H., & Nakajima, H. (1988). Congenital sensory neuropathy with anhydrosis. *Archives of Dermatology, 124*, 564–566.

Iwata, B. A. (1988). The development and adoption of controversial default technologies. *The Behavior Analyst, 11*, 149–157.

Iwata, B. A., & DeLeon, I. G. (1995). *The functional analysis screening tool* (FAST). Unpublished manuscript, University of Florida.

Iwata, B. A., Dorsey, M. F., Slifer, K. J., Bauman, K. E., & Richman, G. S. (1982). Toward a functional analysis of self-injury. *Analysis and Intervention in Development Disabilities, 2*, 3–20.

Iwata, B. A., Dorsey, M. F., Slifer, K. J., Bauman, K. E., & Richman, G. S. (1982/1994). Toward a functional analysis of self-injury. *Journal of Applied Behavior Analysis, 27*, 197–209.

Iwata, B. A., Pace, G. M., Dorsey, M. F., Zarcone, J. R., Vollmer, T. R., Smith, R. G., et al. (1994). The functions of self-injurious behavior: An experimental-epidemiological analysis. *Journal of Applied Behavior Analysis, 27*, 215–240.

Iwata, B. A., Pace, G. M., Kalsher, M. J., Cowdery, G. E., & Cataldo, M. F. (1990). Experimental analysis and extinction of self-injurious escape behavior. *Journal of Applied Behavior Analysis, 23*(1), 11–27.

Iwata, B. A., Pace, G. M., Kissel, R. C., Nau, P. A., & Farber, J. M. (1990). The self-injury trauma (SIT) scale: A method for quantifying surface tissue damage caused by self-injurious behavior. *Journal of Applied Behavior Analysis, 23*, 99–110.

Iwata, B. A., Pace, G. M., Willis, K. D., Gamache, T. B., & Hyman, S. L. (1986). Operant studies of self-injurious hand biting in Rett syndrome. *American Journal of Medical Genetics, 24*(Suppl.), 157–166.

Jacobson, J. W. (1982). Problem behavior and psychiatric impairment within a developmentally disabled population I: Behavior frequency. *Applied Research in Mental Retardation, 3,* 121–139.

Jacobson, J. W. (1990). Assessing the prevalence of psychiatric disorders in a developmentally disabled population. In E. Dibble, & D. B. Gray (eds), *Assessment of behavior problems with persons with mental retardation living in the community* (pp. 19–70). Rockville, MD: Department of Health and Human Services, National Institutes of Health, Public Health Service, Alcohol, Drug Abuse, and Mental Health Administration.

Jann, M. W. (1991). Clozapine. *Pharmacotherapy, 11,* 179–195.

Johnston, J. M. (2006). "Replacing" problem behavior: An analysis of tactical alternatives. *The Behavior Analyst, 29,* 1–12.

Johnston, J. M., Foxx, R. M., Jacobson, J. W., Green, G., & Mulick, J. M. (2006). Positive behavior support and applied behavior analysis. *The Behavior Analyst, 29,* 51–74.

Johnson, W. L., & Day, R. M. (1992). The incidence and prevalence of self-injurious behavior. In J. K. Luiselli, J. L. Matson, & N. N. Singh (eds), *Self-injurious behavior-analysis, assessment, and treatment* (pp. 21–56). New York: Springer.

Johnson, W. L., Day, R. M., & Hassanian, R. E. S. (1988). *Prevalence of self-injurious behaviors within public school special education program.* Paper presented at the 112th annual Meeting of the American Association on Mental Retardation, Washington, DC, June.

Kaas, J. H. (1991). Plasticity of sensory and motor maps in adult mammals. *Annual Review of Neuroscience, 14,* 137–167.

Kagan, J. (1972). Do infants think? *Scientific American, 226,* 74–82.

Kahan, J., & Pattison, E. M. (1984). Proposal for a distinctive diagnosis: The deliberate self-herm syndrome (DSH). *Suicide and Life-Threatening Behavior, 14,* 17–35.

Kalachnik, J. E. (1999). Measuring side effects of psychopharmacologic medication in individuals with mental retardation and develop mental disabilities. *Mental Retardation and Developmental Disabilities Research Reviews, 5,* 348–356.

Kahng, S., Abt, K. A., & Wilder, D. (2001). Treatment of self-injury correlated with mechanical restraints. *Behavioral Interventions, 16,* 105–110.

Kahng, S., & Iwata, B. A. (1998). Play versus alone conditions as controls during functional analyses of self-injurious escape behavior. *Journal of Applied Behavior Analysis, 31,* 669–672.

Kahng, S., & Iwata, B. A. (1999). Correspondence between outcomes of brief and extended functional analyses. *Journal of Applied Behavior Analysis, 32,* 149–159.

Kahng, S., Iwata, B. A., Fischer, S. M., Page, T. J., Treadwell, K. R., Williams, D. E., et al. (1998). Temporal distributions of problem behavior based on scatter plot analysis. *Journal of Applied Behavior Analysis, 31,* 593–604.

Kahng, S. W., Iwata, B. A., & Lewin, A. B. (2002). Behavioral treatment of self-injury, 1964–2000. *American Journal on Mental Retardation, 107,* 212–221.

Kandel, E. R., Schwarz, J. H., & Jessel, T. M. (eds.) (1991). *Principles of neuroscience* (3rd ed.). Norwalk, CT: Appleton and Lange.

Kanfer, F. H., & Phillips, J. (1970). *Learning foundations of human behavior.* New York: John Wiley.

Kanfer, F. H., & Saslow, G. (1969). Behavioral diagnosis. In C. M. Franks (ed.), *Behavior therapy: Appraisal and status.* New York: McGraw-Hill.

Kantner, R. M., Clark, D. L., Allen, L. C., & Chase, M. F. (1976). Effects of vestibular stimulation on nystagmus response and motor performance in the developmentally delayed infant. *Physical Therapy, 56,* 414–421.

Kasim, S., Kahn, Z., & Jinnah, H. A. (2002). A new animal model for Lesch–Nyhan syndrome: Calcium channel activation with Bay K 8644. In S. R. Schroeder, M. L. Oster-Granite, & T. Thompson (eds), *Self-injurious behavior: Gene–brain-behavior relationships* (pp. 289–298). Washington, DC: American Psychological Association.

Kastner, T., Finesmith, R., & Walsh, K. (1993). Long-term administration of valproic acid in the treatment of affective symptoms in people with mental retardation. *Journal of Clinical Psychopharmacology, 13*, 448–451.

Kazdin, A. E. (1980). Acceptability of alternative treatments for deviant child behavior. *Journal of Applied Behavior Analysis, 13*, 259–273.

Kazdin, A. E., & Matson, J. L. (1981). Social validation in mental retardation. *Applied Research in Mental Retardation, 1*, 39–53.

Kearney, C. A. (1994). Interrater reliability of the Motivation Assessment Scale: Another, closer look. *Journal of the Association for Persons with Severe Handicaps, 19*, 139–142.

Kebbon, L., & Windahl, S. I. (1985). *Self-injurious behavior: Results of a nation-wide survey among mentally retarded persons in Sweden.* Paper presented at the 7th World Congress of the International Association for the Scientific Study of Mental Deficiency, New Delhi, March 24–28.

Kellaway, P. (1979). An orderly approach to visual analysis: Parameters of the normal EEG in adults and children. In D. W. Klass, & D. D. Daly (eds), *Current practice of clinical electroencephalography* (pp. 69–147). New York: Raven.

Kelley, W. N., & Wyngaarden, J. B. (1983). Clinical syndromes associated with hypoxanthine-guanine phosphoribosyltransferase deficiency. In J. B. Stanbury, J. B. Wyngaarden, D. S. Frederickson, J. L. Goldstein, & M. S. Brown (eds), *The metabolic basis of inherited disease* (5th ed.) (pp. 1115–1143). New York: McGraw-Hill.

Kennedy, C., & Sokoloff, L. (1957). An adaptation of the nitrous oxide method to the study of the cerebral circulation in children: Normal values for cerebral blood flow and cerebral metabolic rate in childhood. *Journal of Clinical Investigation, 36*, 1130–1137.

Kennedy, C. H. (1992). Concurrent operants: A model for stimulus control using delayed prompting. *The Psychological Record, 42*, 525–540.

Kennedy, C. H. (2002). Evolution of stereotypy into self-injury. In S. R. Schroeder, M. L. Oster-Granite, & T. Thompson (eds), *Self-injurious behavior: Gene–brain-behavior relationships* (pp. 133–144). Washington, DC: American Psychological Association.

Kennedy, C. H., & Souza, G. (1995). Functional analysis and treatment of eye poking. *Journal of Applied Behavior Analysis, 28*, 27–37.

Kern, L., Carberry, N., & Haidara, C. (1997). Analysis and intervention with two topographies of challenging behavior exhibited by a young woman with autism. *Research in Developmental Disabilities, 18*, 257–287.

Kerr, A. M. (1992). *The significance of the Rett syndrome phenotype.* In From genes to behavior, Society for the Study of Behavioral Phenotypes, 2nd International Symposium, Paper No. 1, Welshpool, UK, November 19–21.

Kiernan, C., & Qureshi, H. (1986). *Setting interview.* Manchester: Hester Adrian Research Centre.

Kiley, M., & Lubin, R. (1983). Epidemiological methods. In J. L. Matson, & J. A. Mulick (eds), *Handbook of mental retardation* (pp. 541–556). New York: Pergamon.

King, B. H. (1993). Self-injury by people with mental retardation: A compulsive behavior hypothesis. *American Journal on Mental Retardation, 98*, 93–112.

Klonsky, E. D. (2007). The functions of deliberate self-injury: A review of the evidence. *Clinical Psychology Review, 27*, 226–239.

Klonsky, E. D., Oltmanns, T. F., & Turkheimer, E. (2003). Deliberate self-harm in a nonclinical population: Prevalence and psychological correlates. *American Journal of Psychiatry, 160*, 1501–1508.

Koegel, L. K., Koegel, R. L., & Dunlap, G. (1996). *Positive behavioral support*. Baltimore, MD: Brooks.

Kolko, D. J., Kazdin, A. E., Thomas, A. M., & Day, B. (1993). Heightened child physical abuse potential: Child, parent, and family dysfunction. *Journal of Interpersonal Violence, 8*, 169–192.

Kraemer, G. W. (1992). A psychobiological theory of attachment. *Behavioral and Brain Sciences, 15*, 493–541.

Kraemer, G. W., & Clarke, H. S. (1990). The behavioral neurobiology of self-injurious behavior in rhesus monkeys. *Progress in Neuropsychopharmacology and Biological Psychiatry, 14*, 141–168.

Kraemer, G. W., Ebert, M. H., Schmidt, D. E., & McKinney, W. T. (1989). A longitudinal study of the effect of different social rearing conditions on cerebrospinal fluid norepinephrine and biogenic amine metabolites in rhesus monkeys. *Neuropsychopharmacology, 2*, 175–189.

Kraemer, G. W., Schmidt, D. E., & Ebert, M. H. (1997). The behavioral neurobiology of self-injurious behavior in rhesus monkeys: Current concepts and relations to impulsive behavior in humans. *Annals of the New York Academy of Sciences, 836*, 12–38.

Kravitz, H., & Boehm, J. (1971). Rhythmic habit patterns in infancy: Their sequence, age of onset, and frequency. *Child Development, 42*, 399–413.

Kravitz, H., Rosenthal, V., Teplitz, Z., Murphy, J. B., & Lesser, R. E. (1960). A study of head-banging in infants and children. *Diseases of the Nervous System, 21*, 203–208.

Kreitman, N., Philip, A. N., Greer, S., & Bagley, C. R. (1969). Parasuicide (letter to the editor). *British Journal of Psychiatry, 115*, 746–747.

Kroeker, R., Touchette, P. E., & Engleman, L. (2004). Quantifying temporal distributions of self-injurious behavior: Defining bouts versus discrete events. *American Journal on Mental Retardation, 109*, 1–8.

Kroeker, R., Touchette, P., Engleman, L., & Sandman, C. A. (2004). Quantifying temporal distributions of self-injurious behavior: Defining bouts versus discrete events. *American Journal on Mental Retardation, 109*, 1–8.

Kurtz, P. F., Chin, M. D., Huete, J. M., Tarbox, R. S. F., O'Connor, J. T., Paclawskyj, T. R., et al. (2003). Functional analysis and treatment of self-injurious behavior in young children: A summary of 30 cases. *Journal of Applied Behavior Analysis, 36*, 205–219.

Kwok, H. M., To, Y. F., & Sung, H. F. (2003). The application of a multisensory Snoezelen room for people with learning disabilities – Hong Kong experience. *Hong Kong Medical Journal, 9*, 122–126.

LaChapelle, D. L., Hadjistavropoulos, T., & Craig, K. D. (1999). Pain measurement in persons with intellectual disabilities. *The Clinical Journal of Pain, 15*, 13–23.

Lalli, J. S., Browder, D. M., Mace, F. C., & Brown, D. K. (1993). Teacher use of descriptive analysis to implement interventions to decrease students' problem behaviors. *Journal of Applied Behavior Analysis, 26*, 227–238.

Lalli, J. S., Casey, S. D., & Kates, K. (1997). Noncontingent reinforcement as treatment for severe problem behaviors: Some procedural variations. *Journal of Applied Behavior Analysis, 30*, 127–137.

Lalli, J. S., Mace, F. C., Wohn, T., & Liverzy, K. (1995). Identification and modification of a response-class hierarchy. *Journal of Applied Behavior Analysis, 28*, 551–559.

Lalli, J. S., Vollmer, T. R., Progar, P. R., Wright, C., Borrero, J., Daniel, D., et al. (1999). Competition between positive and negative reinforcement in the treatment of escape behavior. *Journal of Applied Behavior Analysis, 32*, 285–296.

Lam, K. S. L. (2005). The Repetitive Behavior Scale – Revised: Independent validation and the effects of subject variables. *Dissertation Abstracts International, Section B: The Sciences and Engineering, 65*(9-B), 4812.

Lambert, N., Nihira, K., & Leland, H. (1993). AAMR Adaptive Behavior Scales-School (ABS-S:2). Pro-Ed, Inc.

Lancioni, G. E., Cuvo, A. J., & O'Reilly, M. F. (2002). Snoezelen: An overview of research with people with developmental disabilities and dementia. *Disability and Rehabilitation, 24*, 175–184.

Langbehn, D. R., & Pfohl, B. (1993). Clinical correlates of self-mutilation among psychiatric inpatients. *Annals of Clinical Psychiatry, 5*, 45–51.

Laraway, S., Snycerski, S., Michael, J., & Poling, A. (2003). Motivating operations and terms to describe them: Some further refinements. *Journal of Applied Behavior Analysis, 36*, 407–414.

Larrington, G. G. (1987). A sensory integration based program with a severely retarded/autistic teenager: An occupational therapy case report. *Occupational Therapy in Health Care, 4*, 101–117.

Larson, S. A., Lakin, K. C., & Anderson, L. (2001). Prevalence of mental retardation and developmental disabilities: Estimates from the 1995/1995 National Health Interview Survey Disability Supplements. *American Journal on Mental Retardation, 106*, 231–252.

LaVigna, G. W., & Donnellan, A. M. (1986). *Alternatives to punishment: Solving behavior problems with non-aversive strategies.* New York: Irvington.

Le, D. D., & Smith, R. G. (2002). Functional analysis of self-injury with and without protective equipment. *Journal of Developmental and Physical Disabilities, 14*, 277–290.

Lecavalier, L., & Aman, M. G. (2004). Rating instruments. In J. L. Matson, R. B. Laud, & M. L. Matson (eds), *Behavior modification for persons with developmental disabilities: Treatments and supports* (pp. 160–189). Kingston, NY: NADD.

Lecavalier, L., Aman, M. G., Hammer, D., Stoica, W., & Mathews, G. L. (2004). Factor analysis of the nisonger child behavior rating form in children with autism spectrum disorders. *Journal of Autism and Developmental Disorders, 34*, 709–721.

Lecavalier, L., Leone, S., & Wiltz, J. (2006). The impact of behavior problems on caregiver stress in young people with autism spectrum disorders. *Journal of Intellectual Disability Research, 50*, 172–183.

Lees, A. L., Robertson, M., Trimble, M. R., & Murray, N. M. (1984). A clinical study of Gilles de la Tourette syndrome in the United Kingdom. *Journal of Neurology, Neurosurgery and Psychiatry, 47*, 1–8.

Leibenluft, E., Gardner, D. L., & Cowdry, R. W. (1987). The inner experience of the borderline self-mutilator. *Journal of Personality Disorders, 1*, 317–324.

Lemke, H., & Mitchell, R. (1972). Controlling the behavior of a profoundly retarded child. *The American Journal of Occupational Therapy, 26*, 261–264.

Lenneberg, D. (1967). *Biological foundations of language.* New York: Wiley.

Lerman, D. C., Iwata, B. A., Shore, B. A., & DeLeon, I. G. (1997). Effects of intermittent punishment on self-injurious behavior: An evaluation of schedule thinning. *Journal of Applied Behavior Analysis, 30*, 187–201.

Lerman, D. C., Iwata, B. A., Shore, B. A., & Kahng, S. W. (1996). Responding maintained by intermittent reinforcement: Implications for the use of extinction with problem behavior in clinical settings. *Journal of Applied Behavior Analysis, 29*, 153–171.

Lerman, D. C., Iwata, B. A., & Wallace, M. D. (1999). Side effects of extinction: Prevalence of bursting and aggression during the treatment of self-injurious behavior. *Journal of Applied Behavior Analysis, 32*, 1–8.

Lerman, D. C., Iwata, B. A., Zarcone, J. R., & Ringdahl, J. (1994). Assessment of stereotypic and self-injurious behavior as adjunctive responses. *Journal of Applied Behavior Analysis, 27,* 715–728.

Lerman, D. C., Kelley, M. E., Vorndran, C. M., Kuhn, S. A. C., & LaRue, R. H. (2002). Reinforcement magnitude and responding during treatment with differential reinforcement. *Journal of Applied Behavior Analysis, 35,* 29–48.

Lesch, M., & Nyhan, W. L. (1964). A familial disorder of uric acid metabolism and central nervous system 22 function. *American Journal of Medicine, 36,* 561–570.

Leudar, I., Fraser, W. I., & Jeeves, M. A. (1984). Behaviour disturbance and mental handicap: Typology and longitudinal trends. *Psychological Medicine, 14,* 923–935.

Lewis, M. H. (2004). Environmental complexity and central nervous system development function. *Mental Retardation and Developmental Disabilities Research Reviews, 10,* 91–95.

Lewis, M. H., & Baumeister, A. A. (1982). Stereotyped mannerisms in mentally retarded persons: Animal models and theoretical analyses. In N. R. Ellis (ed.), *International review of research in mental retardation* (Vol. 12) (pp. 123–161). New York, NY: Academic.

Lewis, M. H., & Bodfish, J. W. (1998). Repetitive behavior disorders in autism, Special Issue: "Autism". *Mental Retardation Development Disabilities Research Review, 4,* 80–89.

Lewis, M. H., Bodfish, J. W., Powell, S. B., Parker, D. E., & Golden, R. N. (1996a). Clomipramine treatment of self-injurious behavior of individuals with mental retardation: A double-blind comparison with placebo. *American Journal on Mental Retardation, 100,* 654–665.

Lewis, M. H., Bodfish, J. W., Powell, S. B., & Golden, R. N. (1995). Clomipramine treatment for stereotypy and related repetitive movement disorders associated with mental retardation. *American Journal on Mental Retardation, 100,* 299–312.

Lewis, M. H., Bodfish, J. W., Powell, S. B., Wiest, K., Darling, M., & Golden, R. N. (1996b). Plasma HVA in adults with mental retardation and stereotyped behavior: Biochemical evidence for a dopamine deficiency model. *American Journal on Mental Retardation, 100,* 413–417.

Lewis, M. H., Gluck, J. P., Beauchamp, A. J., Keresztury, M. F., & Mailman, R. B. (1990). Long-term effects of early social isolation in Macaca mulatta: In vivo evidence for changes in dopamine receptor function. *Brain Research, 513,* 67–73.

Lewis, M. H., Gluck, J. P., Bodfish, J., & Mailman, R. B. (1996c). Neurobiological basis of stereotyped behavior in animals and humans. In R. L. Sprague, & K. M. Newell (eds), *Stereotypies: Brain-behavior relationships.* Washington, DC: American Psychological Association Press.

Lewis, M. H., MacLean Jr., W. E., Bryson-Brockmann, W., Arendt, R., Beck, B., Fidler, P. S., et al. (1984). Time-series analysis of stereotyped movements: Relationship of body rocking to cardiac activity. *American Journal on Mental Retardation, 89,* 287–294.

Lewis, M. H., MacLean Jr., W. E., Johnson, W. L., & Baumeister, A. A. (1981). Ultradian rhythms in stereotyped and self-injurious behavior. *American Journal of Mental Deficiency, 85,* 601–610.

Lewis, M. H., Schroeder, S., Aman, M., Gadow, K., & Thompson, T. (1996d). Psychopharmacology. In J. W. Jacobson, & J. A. Mulick (eds), *Manual of diagnosis and professional practice in mental retardation* (pp. 323–340). Washington: American Psychological Association.

Lewis, M. H., Silva, J. R., & Gray-Silva, S. (1995). Cyclicity of aggression and self-injurious behavior in individuals with mental retardation. *American Journal on Mental Retardation, 29,* 436–444.

Lindauer, S. E., DeLeon, I. G., & Fisher, W. W. (1999). Decreasing signs of negative affect and correlated self-injury in an individual with mental retardation and mood disturbance. *Journal of Applied Behavior Analysis, 32,* 103–106.

Lindberg, J. S., Iwata, B. A., Roscoe, E. M., Wordsell, A. S., & Hanley, G. P. (2003). Treatment efficacy of noncontingent reinforcement during brief and extended application. *Journal of Applied Behavior Analysis, 36,* 1–19.

Linehan, M. M. (1993). *Cognitive-behavioral treatment of borderline personality disorder.* New York: Guiford.

Linn, D. M., Rojahn, J., Helsel, W. J., & Dixon, J. (1988). Acute effects of transcutaneous electric nerve stimulation on self-injurious behavior. *Journal of the Multihandicapped Person, 1,* 105–119.

Linscheid, T. R., Iwata, B. A., Ricketts, R. W., Williams, D. E., & Griffin, J. C. (1990). Clinical evaluation of the self-injurious behavior inhibiting system (SIBIS). *Journal of Applied Behavior Analysis, 23,* 53–78.

Lipman, R. S. (1970). The use of psychopharmacological agents in residential facilities for the retarded. In F. Menolascino (ed.), *Psychiatric approached to mental retardation* (pp. 387–398). New York, NY: Basic Books.

Lloyd, E., Kelly, M. L., & Hope, T. (1997). *Self-mutilation in a community sample of adolescents: Descriptive characteristics and provisional prevalence rates.* Paper presented at the Annual Meeting of the Society for Behavioral Medicine, New Orleans, LA.

Lloyd, K. G., Hornykiewicz, O., Davidson, L., Shannak, K., Farley, I., Goldstein, M., et al. (1981). Biochemical evidence of dysfunction of brain neurotransmitters in the Lesch–Nyhan syndrome. *The New England Journal of Medicine, 305,* 1106–1111.

Locke, J. L. (1994). Phases in the child's development of language. *American Scientist, 82,* 436–445.

Loupe, P., Schroeder, S. R., & Tessel, R. E. (1995). FR discrimination training effects in SHR and microcephalic rats. *Pharmacology, Biochemistry and Behavior, 51,* 869–876.

Lovaas, O. I., & Smith, T. (1991). There is more to operant theory and practice: Comment on Guess and Carr. *American Journal on Mental Retardation, 96,* 324–326.

Lovaas, O. I., Freitag, G., Gold, V. J., & Kassorla, I. C. (1965). Experimental studies in childhood schizophrenia. *Journal of Experimental Child Psychology, 2,* 67–84.

Lovaas, O. I., & Simmons, J. Q. (1969). Manipulation of self-destruction in three retarded children. *Journal of Applied Behavior Analysis, 2,* 143–157.

Lowe, K., Allen, D., & Jones, E. (2007). Challenging behaviours: Prevalence and topographies. *Journal of Intellectual Disability Research, 51,* 625–636.

Lowry, M. A. (1998). Assessment and treatment of mood disorders in persons with developmental disabilities. *Journal of Developmental and Physical Disabilities, 10,* 387–406.

Lowry, M. A., & Sovner, R. (1992). Severe behaviour problems associated with rapid cycling bipolar disorder in two adults with profound mental retardation. *Journal of Intellectual Disability Research, 36,* 269–281.

Luchins, D. J., & Dojka, M. S. (1989). Lithium and propranolol in aggression and self-injurious behavior in the mentally retarded. *Psychopharmacology Bulletin, 25,* 372–375.

Luiselli, J. K. (1986). Behavior analysis of pharmacological and contingency management QJ;interventions for self-injury. *Behavior Therapy and Experimental Psychiatry, 17,* 275–284.

Luiselli, J. K. (1992). Protective equipment. In J. K. Luiselli, J. L. Matson, & N. N. Singh (eds), *Self-injurious behavior: Analysis, assessment, and treatment* (pp. 235–292). New York, NY: Springer-Verlag.

Luiselli, J. K., Cochran, M. L., & Huber, S. A. (2005). Effects of otitis media on a child with autism receiving behavioral intervention for self-injury. *Child & Family Behavior Therapy, 27,* 51–56.

Luthar, S. S., Burack, J. A., Cicchetti, D., & Weisz, J. R. (eds.) (1997). *Developmental psychopathology: Perspectives on risk, adjustment, and disorder.* New York: Cambridge University Press.

Lutz, C., Well, A., & Novak, M. (2003). Stereotypic and self-injurious behavior in Rhesus Macaques: A survey and retrospective analysis of environment and early experience. *American Journal of Primatology, 60,* 1–15.

Mace, A. B., Shapiro, E. S., & Mace, F. C. (1999). Effects of warning stimuli for reinforcer withdrawal and task onset on self-injury. *Journal of Applied Behavior Analysis, 31,* 679–682.

Mace, F. C., Blum, N. J., Sierp, B. J., Delaney, B. A., & Mauk, J. E. (2001). Differential response of operant self-injury to pharmacologic versus behavioral treatment. *Journal of Developmental and Behavioral Pediatrics, 22,* 85–91.

Mace, F. C., Hock, M. L., Lalli, J. S., West, B. J., Belfiore, P., Pinter, E., et al. (1988). Behavioral momentum in the treatment of noncompliance. *Journal of Applied Behavior Analysis, 21,* 123–141.

MacHale, R., & Carey, S. (2002). An investigation of the effects of bereavement on the mental health and challenging behaviour in adults with learning disability. *British Journal of Learning Disabilities, 30,* 113–117.

MacKay, D., McDonald, G., & Morrissey, M. (1974). Self-mutilation in the mentally subnormal. *Journal of Psychological Research in Mental Subnormality, 1,* 25–31.

MacLean Jr., W. E., & Baumeister, A. A. (1981). Effects of vestibular stimulation on motor development and stereotyped behavior of developmentally delayed children. *Journal of Abnormal Child Psychology, 10,* 229–245.

Maddux, J. E., Gosselin, J. T., & Winstead, B. A. (2004). Conceptions of psychopathology: A social constructionist perspective. In J. E. Maddux, & B. A. Winstead (eds), *Psychopathology – Foundations for a contemporary understanding* (pp. 3–18). Mahwah, NJ: Lawrence Erlbaum.

Maisto, C. R., Baumeister, A. A., & Maisto, A. A. (1978). An analysis of variables related to self-injurious behavior among institutionalized retarded persons. *Journal of Mental Deficiency Research, 22,* 27–36.

Marcus, B. A., & Vollmer, T. R. (1996). Combining noncontingent reinforcement and differential reinforcement schedules as treatment for aberrant behavior. *Journal of Applied Behavior Analysis, 29,* 43–51.

Marg, E. (1982). Prentice Memorial Lecture: Is the animal model for stimulus deprivation amblyopia in children valid or useful? *American Journal of Optometry and Physiological Optics, 59,* 451–464.

Marholin, D., & Luiselli, J. K. (1979). The question of cause and effect: A response to Steen and Zuriff. *Journal of Behavior Therapy and Experimental Psychiatry, 10,* 89–90.

Marion, S. D., Touchette, P. E., & Sandman, C. A. (2003). Sequential analysis reveals a unique structure for self-injurious behavior. *American Journal on Mental Retardation, 108,* 301–313.

Marquis, J. G., Horner, R. H., Carr, E. G., Turnbull, A. P., Thompson, M., Behrens, G. A., et al. (2000). A meta-analysis of positive behavior support. In R. Gersten, E. P. Schiller, & S. Vaughn (eds), *Contemporary special education research: Synthesis of the knowledge base on critical issues* (pp. 137–178). Mahwah, NJ: Erlbaum.

Marshburn, E. C., & Aman, M. G. (1992). Factor validity and norms for the Aberrant Behavior Checklist in a community sample of children with mental retardation. *Journal of Autism and Developmental Disorders, 22,* 357–373.

Martin, G., Bergen, H. A., Richardson, A. S., Roeger, L., & Allison, S. (2004). Sexual abuse and suicidality: Gender differences in a large community sample of adolescents. *Child Abuse and Neglect, 25*, 491–503.

Martin, J. P., & Bell, J. (1943). A pedigree of mental defect showing sex-linkage. *Journal of Neurology and Psychiatry, 6*, 151–154.

Martin, L., Spicer, D. W., Lewis, M. H., Gluck, J. P., & Cork, L. C. (1991). Social deprivation in infant rhesus monkeys alters the chemoarchitecture of the brain: I. Subcortical regions. *Journal of Neuroscience, 11*, 3344–3358.

Mason, S. M., & Iwata, B. A. (1990). Artifactual effects of sensory-integrative therapy on self-injurious behavior. *Journal of Applied Behavior Analysis, 23*, 361–370.

Mason, W.A. (1992). Does function imply structure? *Behavioral and Brain Sciences, 15*, 519–520.

Matson, J. L. (1986). Self-injury and its relationship to diagnostic schemes in psychopathology. *Applied Research in Mental Retardation, 7*, 223–228.

Matson, J. L. (1989). Self-injurious and stereotyped behavior. In T. H. Ollendick, & M. Hersen (eds), *Handbook of child psychopathology* (2nd ed.) (pp. 265–275). New York: Plenum Press.

Matson, J. L. (1995). *Manual for the diagnostic assessment for the severely handicapped-II*. Baton Rouge, LA: Louisiana State University.

Matson, J. L. (1997). *Manual for the assessment of dual diagnosis*. Baton Rouge, LA: Louisiana State University.

Matson, J. L. (1998). *Diagnostic assessment for the severely handicapped II – manual*. Baton Rouge, LA: Scientific Publishers Incorporated.

Matson, J. L., & Bamburg, J. W. (1998). Reliability of the assessment of dual diagnosis (ADD). *Research in Developmental Disabilities, 19*, 89–95.

Matson, J. L., Bamburg, J. W., Cherry, K. E., & Paclawskyj, T. R. (1999). A validity study on the Questions About Behavioral Function (QABF) Scale: Predicting treatment success for self-injury, aggression, and stereotypies. *Research in Developmental Disabilities, 20*, 163–176.

Matson, J. L., & DiLorenzo, T. M. (1984). *Punishment and its alternatives*. New York: NYL Springer.

Matson, J. L., Gardner, W. I., Coe, D. A., & Sovner, R. (1991). A scale for evaluating emotional disorders in severely and profoundly mentally retarded persons: Development of the Diagnostic Assessment for the Severely Handicapped (DASH) scale. *British Journal of Psychiatry, 159*, 404–409.

Matson, J. L., Hamilton, M., Duncan, D., Bamburg, J., Smiroldo, B., Anderson, S., et al. (1997). Characteristics of stereotypic movement disorder and self-injurious behavior assessed with the Diagnostic Assessment for the Severely Handicapped (DASH-II). *Research in Developmental Disabilities, 18*, 457–469.

Matson, J. L., & Kazdin, A. E. (1981). Punishment in behavior modification: Pragmatic, ethical, and legal issues. *Clinical Psychology Review, 1*, 197–210.

Matson, J. L., Kiely, S. L., & Bamburg, J. W. (1997). The effect of stereotypies on adaptive skills as assessed with the DASH-II and Vineland Adaptive Behavior Scales. *Research in Developmental Disabilities, 18*, 471–476.

Matson, J. L., Kuhn, D. E., Dixon, D. R., Mayville, S. B., Laud, R. B., Cooper, C. L., et al. (2003). The development and factor structure of the Functional Assessment for Multiple Causality (FACT). *Research in Developmental Disabilities, 24*, 485–495.

Matson, J. L., Smiroldo, B. B., & Bamburg, J. W. (1998). The relationship of social skills to psychopathology for individuals with severe or profound mental retardation. *Journal of Intellectual & Developmental Disability, 23*, 137–145.

Matson, J. L., Smiroldo, B. B., Hamilton, M., & Baglio, C. S. (1997). Do anxiety disorders exist in persons with severe and profound mental retardation? *Research in Developmental Disabilities, 18,* 39–44.

Matson, J. L., Smiroldo, B. B., & Hastings, T. L. (1998). Validity of the autism/pervasive developmental disorder subscale of the diagnostic assessment for the severely handicapped-II. *Journal of Autism and Developmental Disorders, 28,* 77–81.

Maurice, P., & Trudel, G. (1982). Self-injurious behavior: Prevalence and relationship to environmental events. In J. H. Hollis, & C. E. Meyers (eds), *Life-threatening behavior: Analysis and Intervention* (pp. 81–103). Washington, DC: American Association on Mental Retardation.

McAdam, D. B., Zarcone, J. R., Hellings, J. A., Napolitano, D. A., & Schroeder, S. R. (2002). Effects of risperidone on aberrant behavior in persons with developmental disabilities: II. Social validity measures. *American Journal on Mental Retardation, 107,* 261–269.

McCord, B. E., Thompson, R. J., & Iwata, B. A. (2001). Functional analysis and treatment of self-injury associated with transitions. *Journal of Applied Behavior Analysis, 34,* 195–210.

McDonough, M., Hillery, J., & Kennedy, N. (2000). Olanzapine for chronic, stereotypic self-injurious behavior: A pilot study in seven adults with intellectual disability. *Journal of Intellectual Disability Research, 44,* 677–684.

McDougle, C. J., Brodkin, E. S., Naylor, S. T., Carlson, D. C., Cohen, D. J., & Price, L. H. (1998a). Sertraline in adults with pervasive developmental disorders: A prospective open-label investigation. *Journal of Clinical Psychopharmacology, 18,* 62–66.

McDougle, C. J., Holmes, J. P., Carlson, D. C., Pelton, G. H., Cohen, D. J., & Price, L. H. (1998b). A double-blind, placebo-controlled study of risperidone in adults with autistic disorder and other pervasive developmental disorders. *Archives in General Psychiatry, 55,* 633–641.

McDougle, C. J., Naylor, S. T., Cohen, D. J., Aghajanian, G. K., Heninger, G. R., & Price, L. H. (1996a). Effects of tryptophan depletion in drug-free adults with autistic disorder. *Archives of General Psychiatry, 53,* 993–1000.

McDougle, C. J., Naylor, S. T., Cohen, D. J., Volkmar, F. R., Heninger, G. R., & Price, L. H. (1996b). A double-blind, placebo-controlled study of fluvoxamine in adults with autistic disorder. *Archives of General Psychiatry, 53,* 1001–1008.

McEvoy, J., & Smith, E. (2005). Families perceptions of the grieving process and concept of death in individuals with intellectual disabilities. *British Journal of Developmental Disabilities, 51,* 17–25.

McGonigle, J. J., Rojahn, J., Dixon, J., & Strain, P. S. (1987). Multiple treatment interference in the alternating treatments design as a function of the intercomponent interval length. *Journal of Applied Behavior Analysis, 20,* 171–178.

McKerchar, T. L., Kahng, S. W., Casioppo, E., & Wilson, D. (2001). Functional analysis of self-injury maintained by automatic reinforcement: Exposing masked functions. *Behavioral Interventions, 16,* 59–63.

Meins, W. (1996). A new depression scale designed for use with adults with mental retardation. *Journal of Intellectual Disability Research, 40,* 222–226.

Meltzer, H. Y. (1991). The mechanisms of action in novel antipsychotic drugs. *Schizophrenia Bulletin, 17,* 263–287.

Melzack, R., & Wall, P. D. (1983). *The challenge of pain.* New York: Basic Books.

Menninger, K. (1935). A psychoanalytic study of the significance of self-mutilation. *Psychoanalytic Quarterly, 4,* 408–466.

Menninger, K. (1938). *Man against himself.* New York: Harcourt Brace World.

Mikhail, A. G., & King, B. H. (2001). Self-injurious behavior in mental retardation. *Current Opinion in Psychiatry, 14*, 457–461.

Miller, M., Canen, E., Roebel, A., & MacLean, W. (2000). *Prevalence of behavior problems in people with mental retardation.* Poster session presented at the 108th annual convention of the American Psychological Association, Washington, DC, August.

Miltenberger, R. G. (2007). *Behavior modification: Principles and procedures* (4th ed.). Belmont, CA: Thompson and Wadsworth.

Mizuno, T. L., & Yugari, Y. (1974). Self-mutilation in the Lesch–Nyhan syndrome. *Lancet, 1*, 761.

Moore, J. M., Mueller, M. M., Dubard, M., Roberts, D. S., & Sterling-Turner, H. E. (2002). The influence of therapist attention on self-injury during a tangible condition. *Journal of Applied Behavior Analysis, 35*, 283–286.

Moore, J. W., Fisher, W. W., & Pennington, A. (2004). Systematic application and removal of protective equipment in the assessment of multiple topographies of self-injury. *Journal of Applied Behavior Analysis, 37*, 73–77.

Moser, H. W. (1995). A role of gene therapy in mental retardation. *Mental Retardation and Developmental Disabilities Research Reviews, 1*, 4–6.

Mossman, D. A., Hastings, R. P., & Brown, T. (2002). Mediators' emotional responses to self-injurious behavior: An experimental study. *American Journal on Mental Retardation, 107*, 252–260.

Muehlenkamp, J. J., & Gutierrez, P. M. (2007). Risk for suicide attempts among adolescents who engage in non-suicidal self-injury. *Archives of Suicide Research, 11*, 69–82.

Mulick, J., Hoyt, R., Rojahn, J., & Schroeder, S. R. (1978). Reduction of a "nervous habit" in a profoundly retarded boy by increasing toy play: A case study. *Journal of Behavior Therapy and Experimental Psychiatry, 26*, 223–229.

Mulick, J. A., Barbour, R., Schroeder, S. R., & Rojahn, J. (1980). Overcorrection of pica in two profoundly retarded adults: Analysis of setting effects, stimulus and response generalization. *Applied Research in Mental Retardation, 1*, 241–252.

Mulick, J. A., Dura, J. R., Rasnake, L. K., & Callahan, C. (1986). *Prevalence of SIB in in-stitutionalized nonambulatory profoundly retarded people.* Poster session presented at the 94th annual convention of the American Psychological Association, Washington, DC, August.

Mulick, J. A., & Meinhold, P. M. (1991). Evaluating models for the emergence and maintenance of stereotypy and self-injury. *American Journal on Mental Retardation, 96*, 327–334.

Mulick, J. A., Schroeder, S. R., & Rojahn, J. (1980). Chronic ruminative vomiting: A comparison of four treatment procedures. *Journal of Autism and Developmental Disorders, 10*, 203–213.

Murphy, G., Hall, S., Oliver, C., & Kissi-Debra, R. (1999). Identification of early self-injurious behaviour in young children with intellectual disability. *Journal of Intellectual Disability Research, 43*, 149–163.

Murphy, G., Oliver, C., Corbett, J., Crayton, L., Hales, J., Head, D., et al. (1993). Epidemiology of self-injury, characteristics of people with self-injury and initial treatment outcome. In C. Kiernan (ed.), *Research to practice: Implication of research on the challenging behaviour of people with learning disabilities* (pp. 1–35). Clevedon: British Institute of Learning Disabilities.

Musafar, F. (1996). Body play: State of grace or sickness? In: A.R. Favazza, (ed.), *Bodies under siege: Self-mutilation in culture and psychiatry* (2nd ed.). Baltimore: Johns Hopkins University Press.

Naidu, S. (1992). Rett syndrome: An update. In Y. Fukuyama, Y. Suzuki, S. Kamashita, & P. Casaer (eds), *Fetal and perinatal neurology* (pp. 79–92). Basel, Switzerland: Karger.

Napolitano, D. A., Jack, S. I., Sheldon, J. B., Williams, D. C., McAdam, D. B., & Schroeder, S. R. (1999). Drug-behavior interactions in persons with mental retardation and developmental disabilities. *Mental Retardation and Developmental Disabilities Research Reviews, 5,* 322–334.

National Institutes of Health. (1991). National Institutes of Health Consensus Development Conference Statement. In *Treatment of destructive behaviors in persons with developmental disabilities* (NIH Publication No. 91-2410). Washington, DC: U.S. Department of Health and Human Services.

National Institute of Mental Health (1970). CGI: Clinical Global Impressions. In W. Guy, & R. R. Bonato (eds), *Manual for the ECDEU Assessment Battery* (2nd rev. ed.) (pp. 121–126). Chevy Chase, MD: Author.

Neef, N. A., Iwata, B. A., & Page, T. J. (1980). The effects of interspersal training versus high-density reinforcement on spelling acquisition and retention. *Journal of Applied Behavior Analysis, 13,* 153–158.

Neidert, P. L., Iwata, B. A., & Dozier, C. L. (2005). Treatment of multiply controlled problem behavior with procedural variants of differential reinforcement. *Exceptionality, 13,* 45–53.

Newell, K. M., & Bodfish, J. W. (2002). Temporal and force dynamics and self-injury. In S. R. Schroeder, M. L. Oster-Granite, & T. Thompson (eds), *Self-injurious behavior: Gene–brain relationships* (pp. 235–250). Washington, DC: American Psychological Association.

Newell, K. M., Sprague, R. L., Pain, M. T., Deutsch, K. M., & Meinhold, P. (1999). Dynamics of self-injurious behaviors. *American Journal on Mental Retardation, 104,* 11–21.

Newsome, C. D., Favell, J., & Rincover, A. (1983). The side effects of punishment. In S. Axlrod, & J. Apsche (eds), *The effects of punishment on human behavior* (pp. 285–316). NY: Academic Press.

Newton, J. T. (1991). The Motivation Assessment Scale: Inter-rater reliability and internal consistency in a British sample. *Journal of Mental Deficiency Research, 35,* 472–474.

Nihira, K., Foster, R., Shellhaas, M., & Leland, H. (1974). *AAMD Adaptive Behavior Scale.* Washington, DC: American Association on Mental Deficiency.

Nijman, H. L. I., Dautzenberg, M., & Merkelbach, H. L. G. J. (1999). Self-mutilating behaviour of psychiatric inpatients. *European Psychiatry, 14,* 4–10.

Nock, M. K., & Prinstein, M. J. (2004). A functional approach to the assessment of self-mutilative behavior. *Journal of Consulting and Clinical Psychology, 72,* 885–890.

Nock, M. K., & Prinstein, M. J. (2005). Contextual features and behavioral functions of self-mutilation among adolescents. *Journal of Abnormal Psychology, 114,* 10–146.

Northup, J., Broussard, C., Jones, K., George, T., Vollmer, T. R., & Herring, M. (1995). The differential effects of teacher and peer attention on disruptive classroom behavior of three children with a diagnosis of attention deficit hyperactivity disorder. *Journal of Applied Behavior Analysis, 28,* 227–228.

Northup, J., Kodak, T., Grow, L., Lee, J., & Coyne, A. (2004). Instructional influences on analogue functional analysis outcomes. *Journal of Applied Behavior Analysis, 37*(4), 509–512.

Northup, J., Wacker, D., Sasso, G., Steege, M., Cigrand, K., Cook, J., et al. (1991). A brief functional analysis of aggressive and alternative behavior in an outpatient clinic setting. *Journal of Applied Behavior Analysis, 24,* 509–522.

Nottestad, J. A., & Linaker, O. M. (2001). Self-injurious behaviour before and after deinstitutionalization. *Journal of Intellectual Disability Research, 45,* 121–129.

Novak, M. (2003). Self-injurious behavior in Rhesus monkeys: New insights into its etiology, physiology, and treatment. *American Journal of Primatology, 59,* 3–19.

Novak, M. A., Crockett, C. M., & Sackett, G. P. (2002). Self-injurious behavior in captive Macaque monkeys. In S. R. Schroeder, M. L. Oster-Granite, & T. Thompson (eds), *Self-injurious behavior: Gene–brain-behavior relationships* (pp. 151–161). Washington, DC: American Psychological Association.

Nudo, R. J., Wise, B. M., SiFuentes, F., & Milliken, G. W. (1996). Neural substrates for the effects of rehabilitative training on motor recovery after ischemic infarct. *Science, 272*, 1791–1794.

Nyhan, W. L. (1967a). The Lesch–Nyhan syndrome: Self-destructive biting, mental retardation neurological disorder and hyperuricaemia. *Developmental Medicine and Child Neurology, 9*, 563–572.

Nyhan, W. L. (1972). Behavioral phenotypes in organic genetic disease. Presidential address to Society of Pediatric Research, May 1, 1971. *Pediatric Research, 6*, 1–9.

Nyhan, W. L. (1994). The Lesch–Nyhan disease. In T. Thompson, & D. Gray (eds), *Destructive behavior in developmental disabilities* (pp. 181–197). Thousand Oaks, CA: Sage Publication.

Nyhan, W. L. (2002). Lessons from Lesch–Nyhan Syndrome. In S. R. Schroeder, M. L. Oster-Grantie, & T. Thompson (eds), *Self-injurious behavior: Gene–brain-behavior relationships* (pp. 251–267). Washington, DC: American Psychological Association.

Nyhan, W. L., Johnson, H., Kaufman, I., & Jones, K. (1980). Serotonergic approaches to modification of behavior in the Lesch–Nyhan syndrome. *Applied Research in Mental Retardation, 1*, 25–40.

Nyhan, W. L., Pesek, J., Sweetman, L., Carpenter, D., & Carter, C. (1967b). Genetics of an X-linked disorder of uric acid metabolism and cerebral function. *Pediatric Research, 1*, 5–13.

Oberlander, T. F., Gilbert, C. A., Chambers, C. T., O'Donnell, M. E., & Craig, K. D. (1999). Biobehavioral responses to acute pain in adolescents with a significant neurologic impairment. *The Clinical Journal of Pain, 15*, 201–209.

Obi, C. (1997). Restraint fading and alternative management strategies to treat a man with Lesch–Nyhan syndrome over a two year period. *Behavioral Interventions, 12*, 195–202.

Office for Victims of Crime (2002). *First response to victims of crime who have a disability*. Washington, DC: U.S. Department of Justice.

Oliver, C., Hall, S., Hales, J., Murphy, G., & Watts, D. (1998). The treatment of severe self-injurious behavior by the systematic fading of restraints: Effects on self-injury, self-restraint, adaptive behavior, and behavioral correlates of affect. *Research in Developmental Disabilities, 19*, 143–165.

Oliver, C., Hall, S., & Murphy, G. (2005). The early development of self-injurious behavior: Evaluating the role of social reinforcement. *Journal of Intellectual Disability Research, 49*, 591–599.

Oliver, C., McClintock, K., Hall, S., Smith, M., Dagnan, D., & Stenfert-Kroese, B. (2003). Assessing the severity of challenging behaviour: Psychometric properties of the challenging behavior interview. *Journal of Applied Research in Intellectual Disabilities, 16*, 53–61.

Oliver, C., Murphy, G., Crayton, L., & Corbett, J. (1993). Self-injurious behavior in Rett syndrome: Interactions between features of Rett syndrome and operant conditioning. *Journal of Autism and Developmental Disorders, 23*, 91–109.

Oliver, C., Murphy, G. H., & Corbett, J. A. (1987). Self-injurious behavior in people with mental handicap: A total population study. *Journal of Mental Deficiency Research, 31*, 147–162.

O'Neill, R. E., Horner, R. H., Albin, R. W., Sprague, J. R., Storey, K., & Newton, J. S. (1997). *Functional assessment and program development for problem behavior: A practical handbook*. New York, NY: Brooks/Cole.

O'Reilly, M., Lacey, C., & Lancioni, G. (2001). A preliminary investigation of the assessment and treatment of tantrums with two post-institutionalized Romanian adoptees. *Scandinavian Journal of Behavior Therapy, 30,* 179–187.

O'Reilly, M., & Lancioni, G. (2000). Response covariation of escape-maintained aberrant behavior correlated with sleep deprivation. *Research in Developmental Disabilities, 21,* 125–136.

O'Reilly, M. F. (1996). Assessment and treatment of episodic self-injury: A case study. *Research in Developmental Disabilities, 17,* 349–361.

O'Reilly, M. F. (1997). Functional analysis of episodic self-injury correlated with recurrent otitis media. *Journal of Applied Behavior Analysis, 30,* 165–167.

O'Reilly, M. F., Lancioni, G. E., King, L., Lally, G., & Dhomhnaill, O. N. (2000). Using brief assessments to evaluate aberrant behavior maintained by attention. *Journal of Applied Behavior Analysis, 33,* 109–112.

O'Reilly, M. F., Murray, N., Lancioni, G. E., Sigafoos, J., & Lacey, C. (2003). Functional analysis and intervention to reduce self-injurious and agitated behavior when removing protective equipment for brief time periods. *Behavior Modification, 27,* 538–559.

Ornitz, E. M., Brown, M. B., Sorosky, A. D., Ritvo, E. R., & Dietrich, L. (1970). Environmental modification of autistic behavior. *Archives of General Psychiatry, 22,* 560–565.

Osuch, E. A., Noll, J. G., & Putnam, F. W. (1999). The motivation for self-injury in psychiatric patients. *Psychiatry, 62,* 334–346.

Owens, D., Horrocks, J., & House, A. (2002). Fatal and non-fatal repetition of self-harm: Systematic review. *British Journal of Medicine, 181,* 193–199.

Pace, G. M., Iwata, B. A., Edwards, G. L., & McCosh, K. C. (1986). Stimulus fading and transfer in the treatment of self-restraint and self-injurious behavior. *Journal of Applied Behavior Analysis, 19,* 381–389.

Paclawskyj, T. R., Matson, J. L., Bamburg, J. W., & Baglio, C. S. (1997). A comparison of the Diagnostic Assessment for the Severely Handicapped-II (DASH-II) and the Aberrant Behavior Checklist (ABC). *Research in Developmental Disabilities, 18,* 289–298.

Paclawskyj, T. R., Matson, J. L., Rush, K. S., Smalls, Y., & Vollmer, T. R. (2000). Questions about behavioral function (QABF): A behavioral checklist for functional assessment of aberrant behavior. *Research in Developmental Disabilities, 21,* 223–229.

Paivio, Sandra, C., & McCulloch, C. R. (2004). Alexithymia as a mediator between childhood trauma and self-injurious behaviors. *Child Abuse and Neglect, 28,* 339–354.

Parmelee, A. H., & Sigman, M. D. (1983). Perinatal brain development and behavior. In M. Haith, & J. Campos (eds), *Biology and infancy* (Vol. 2) (pp. 95–155). New York: Wiley.

Pary, R. J. (1991). Towards defining adequate lithium trials for individuals with mental retardation and mental illness. *American Journal on Mental Retardation, 95,* 681–691.

Pary, R. J. (1994). Clozapine in three individuals with mild mental retardation and treatment refractory psychiatric disorders. *Mental Retardation, 32,* 323–327.

Pary, R.M., & Khan, S. (2002). Cyclic behaviors in persons with developmental disabilities: Are cluster and migraine headaches being overlooked? *Mental Health Aspects of Developmental Disabilities, 5,* 125–129.

Patel, M. R., Carr, J. E., Kim, C., Robles, A., & Eastridge, D. (2000). Functional analysis of aberrant behavior maintained by automatic reinforcement: Assessment of specific sensory reinforcers. *Research in Developmental Disabilities, 21,* 393–407.

Pattison, E. M., & Kahan, J. (1983). The deliberate self-harm syndrome. *American Journal of Psychiatry, 140,* 867–872.

Pelios, L., Morren, J., Tesch, D., & Axelrod, S. (1999). The impact of functional analysis methodology on treatment choice for self-injurious behavior and aggressive behavior. *Journal of Applied Behavior Analysis, 32*, 185–195.

Persel, C. S., Persel, C. H., Ashley, M. J., & Krych, D. K. (1997). The use of noncontingent reinforcement and contingent restraint to reduce physical aggression and self-injurious behavior in a traumatically brain injured adult. *Brain Injury, 11*, 751–760.

Petersilia, J. R. (2001). Crime victims with developmental disabilities: A review essay. *Criminal Justice and Behavior, 28*, 655–694.

Piazza, C. C., Adelinis, J. D., Hanley, G. P., Goh, H., & Delia, M. D. (2000). An evaluation of the effects of matched stimuli on behaviors maintained by automatic reinforcement. *Journal of Applied Behavior Analysis, 33*, 13–27.

Plant, K. M., & Sanders, M. R. (2007). Predictors of caregiver-stress in families of preschool-aged children with developmental disabilities. *Journal of Intellectual Disabilities Research, 51*, 109–124.

Poindexter, A. R., Cain, N., Clarke, D. J., Cook, E. H., Corbett, J. A., & Levitas, A. (1998). Mood stabilizers. In S. Reiss, & M. G. Aman (eds), *Psychotropic medication and developmental disabilities: The international consensus handbook* (pp. 215–227). Columbus, OH: The Ohio State University.

Poling, A., Gadow, K., & Cleary, J. (1991). *Drug therapy for behavior disorders.* New York, NY: Pergamon Press.

Poling, A., & Normand, M. (1999). Noncontingent reinforcement: An inappropriate description of time-based schedules that reduce behavior. *Journal of Applied Behavior Analysis, 32*, 237–238.

Polleux, F., & Lauder, J. M. (2004). Toward a neurobiology of autism. *Mental Retardation and Developmental Disabilities Research Reviews, 10*, 303–317.

Pomerantz, B. (1987). Scientific basis of acupuncture. In G. Stux, & B. Pomeranz (eds), *Acupuncture: Textbook and atlas* (pp. 1–34). New York: Springer-Verlag.

Potenza, M. N., Holmes, J. P., Kanes, S. J., & McDougle, C. J. (1999). Olanzapine treatment of children, adolescents, and adults with pervasive developmental disorders: An open-label pilot study. *Journal of Clinical Psychopharmacology, 19*, 37–44.

Powell, S., Bodfish, J., Parker, D., Crawford, T., & Lewis, M. (1996). Self-restraint and self-injury: Occurrence and motivational significance. *American Journal of Mental Retardation, 101*, 41–48.

Prader, A., Labhart, A., & Willi, H. (1956). Ein Syndrom von Adipositas, Kleinwuchs, Kryptorchismus und Oligophrenie nach myatonicartigem Zustand im Neugeborenenalter. *Schweizerische Medizinische Wochenschrift, 86*, 1260–1261.

Pyles, D. A. M., Muniz, K., Cade, A., & Silva, R. (1997). A behavioral diagnostic paradigm for integrating behavior-analytic psychopharmacological interventions for people with a dual diagnosis. *Research in Developmental Disabilities, 18*, 185–214.

Rapp, J. T., Miltenberger, R. G., Galensky, T. L., Ellingson, S. A., & Long, E. S. (1999). A functional analysis of hair pulling. *Journal of Applied Behavior Analysis, 32*, 329–337.

Ratey, J. J. (ed.) (1991). *Mental retardation: Developing pharmacotherapies.* Washington, DC: American Psychiatric Press.

Ratey, J. J., Mikkelson, E. J., Smith, G. B., Upadhyaya, A., Zuckerman, H. S., Martell, D., et al. (1986). Beta blockers in the severely and profoundly mentally retarded. *Journal of Clinical Psychopharmacology, 6*, 103–107.

Ratey, J. J., Sorgi, P., O'Driscoll, G. A., Sands, S. K., Dachler, M. L., Fletcher, J. R., et al. (1992). Nadolol to treat aggression and psychiatric symptomatology in chronic psychiatric patients: A double blind-placebo controlled study. *Journal of Clinical Psychiatry, 53*, 41–46.

Ratey, J. J., Sovner, R., Mikkelson, E., & Chmielinski, H. E. (1989). Buspirone therapy for maladaptive behavior and anxiety in developmentally disabled persons. *Journal of Clinical Psychiatry, 50*, 382–384.

Ratey, J. J., Sovner, R., Parks, A., & Rogentine, K. (1991). Buspirone treatment of aggression and anxiety in mentally retarded patients: A multiple baseline, placebo lead-in study. *Journal of Clinical Psychiatry, 52*, 159–162.

Ratey, R. J., Leveroni, C., Kilmer, D., Gutheil, C., & Swartz, B. (1993). The effects of clozapine on severely aggressive psychiatric inpatients in a state hospital. *Journal of Clinical Psychiatry, 54*, 349–413.

Reese, R. M., Hellings, J., & Schroeder, S. R. (2007). Treatment methods for destructive and aggressive behavior in people with severe mental retardation/developmental disabilities. In N. Bouras (ed.), *Psychiatric and behavioural disorders in developmental disabilities and mental retardation* (pp. 269–282). London: Cambridge University Press.

Reid, A. H. (1972). Psychosis in mental defectives: I Manic depressive psychosis. *British Journal of Psychiatry, 120*, 205–212.

Reid, A.H., Ballinger, B.R., Heather, B.B., & Melvin, S.J. (1984). The natural history of behavioural symptoms among severely and profoundly mentally retarded patients, *British Journal of Psychiatry, 145*, 289–293.

Reid, A. H., Naylor, G. S., & Kay, D. S. G. (1981). A double-blind placebo controlled crossover trial of carbamazepine in overactive severely mentally handicapped patients. *Psychological Medicine, 11*, 109–113.

Reiss, S. (1988). *Test manual for the Reiss Screen for maladaptive behavior*. Orland Park, IL: International Diagnostic Systems.

Reiss, S., & Rojahn, J. (1993). Joint occurrence of depression and aggression in children and adults with mental retardation. *Journal of Intellectual Disability Research, 37*, 287–294.

Repp, A. C., & Deitz, S. M. (1974). Reducing aggressive and self-injurious behavior of institutionalized retarded children through reinforcement of other behaviors. *Journal of Applied Behavior Analysis, 7*, 313–325.

Repp, A. C., Felce, D., & Barton, L. E. (1988). Basing the treatment of stereotypic and self-injurious behaviors on hypotheses of their causes. *Journal of Applied Behavior Analysis, 21*, 281–289.

Repp, A. C., & Singh, N. N. (eds.) (1990). *Perspectives on the use of nonaversive and aversive interventions for persons with developmental disabilities*. Sycamore, IL: Sycamore Publishing Co.

Research Units on Pediatric Psychopharmacology Autism network (2002). Risperidone in children with autism and serious problems. *New England Journal of Medicine, 347*, 1361–1369.

Rett, A. (1966). Über ein eigenartiges hirnatrophisches Syndrom bei Hyperammoniamie in Kindesalter. *Wiener Medizinische Wochenschrift, 116*, 723–738.

Richdale, A. L. (1999). Sleep problems in autism: Prevalence, cause, and intervention. *Developmental Medicine and Child Neurology, 41*, 60–66.

Richman, D., & Hagopian, L. P. (1999). On the effects of "quality" of attention in the functional analysis of destructive behavior. *Research in Developmental Disabilities, 20*, 51–62.

Richman, D. M., & Lindauer, D. M. (2005a). Longitudinal assessment of stereotypic, proto-injurious, and self-injurious behavior exhibited by young children with developmental delays. *American Journal on Mental Retardation, 110*, 439–450.

Richman, D. M., & Lindauer, S. E. (2005b). Longitudinal assessment of self-injurious and stereotypic behavior. *American Journal on Mental Retardation, 110*, 439–450.

Richman, D. M., Teichman, H., & Kolb, J. (2006). *Early intervention and prevention of severe behavior problems in children with developmental disabilities.* Paper given at the Annual Gatlinburg Conference on Research and Theory in Mental Retardation and Developmental Disabilities. San Diego, CA, March 15–18.

Ricketts, R. W., Goza, A. B., Ellis, C. R., Singh, Y. N., Chambers, L. V. N., Singh, N. N., et al. (1994). Clinical effects of buspirone on intractable self-injurious behavior in adults with mental retardation. *Journal of the American Academy of Child and Adolescent Psychiatry, 33,* 270–276.

Riley, C. M., Day, R. L., Greeley, D. M., & Langford, W. S. (1949). Central autonomic dysfunction with defective lacrimation. *Pediatrics, 3,* 468–478.

Rinck, C. (1998). Epidemiology of psychotropic medication. In S. Reiss, & M. G. Aman (eds), *Psychotropic medication and developmental disabilities* (pp. 31–44). Columbus, OH: The Ohio State University.

Rincover, A. (1978). Sensory extinction: A procedure for eliminating self-stimulatory behavior in developmentally disabled children. *Journal of Abnormal Child Psychology, 6,* 299–310.

Rincover, A., Cook, R., Peoples, A., & Packard, D. (1979). Sensory extinction and sensory reinforcement principles for programming multiple adaptive behavior change. *Journal of Applied Behavior Analysis, 12,* 221–233.

Rincover, A., Newsom, C. D., & Carr, E. G. (1979). Using sensory extinction procedures in the treatment of compulsive like behavior of developmentally disabled children. *Journal of Consulting and Clinical Psychology, 47,* 695–701.

Ringdahl, J. E., Vollmer, T. R., Marcus, B. A., & Roane, H. S. (1997). An analogue evaluation of environmental enrichment: The role of stimulus preference. *Journal of Applied Behavior Analysis, 30,* 203–216.

Risley, T. R. (1970). Behavior modification: An experimental therapeutic endeavor. In L. A. Hamerlynch, P. O. Davidson, & L. E. Acker (eds), *Behavior modification and ideal health services* (pp. 123–162). Calgary, Alberta, Canada: University of Calgary Press.

Rivinus, T., & Harmatz, J. (1979). Diagnosis and lithium treatment of affective disorder in the retarded: Five case studies. *American Journal of Psychiatry, 136,* 551–554.

Roberts, M. L., Mace, F. C., & Daggett, J. A. (1995). Preliminary comparison of two negative reinforcement schedules to reduce self-injury. *Journal of Applied Behavior Analysis, 28,* 579–580.

Robertson, M. M. (1992). Self-injurious behavior and Tourette syndrome. In T. N. Case, A. J. Friedhoff, & D. J. Cohen (eds), *Advances in neurology* (Vol. 58) (pp. 105–114). New York, NY: Raven Press.

Robertson, M. M., Trimble, M. R., & Lees, A. J. (1989). Self-injurious behavior and the Gilles de la Tourette syndrome: A clinical study and review of the literature. *Psychological Medicine, 19,* 611–625.

Rodham, K., Hawton, K., & Evans, E. (2004). Reasons for deliberate self harm: Comparison of self-poisoners and self-cutters in a community sample of adolescents. *Journal of American Child and Adolescent Psychiatry, 43,* 80–87.

Rodier, P. M., Ingram, J. L., Tisdale, B., Nelson, S., & Romano, J. (1996). Embryological origin for autism: Developmental anomalies of the cranial nerve motor nuclei. *Journal of Comparative Neurology, 370,* 247–261.

Roeleveld, N., Zielhuis, G. A., & Gabreëls, F. (1997). The prevalence of mental retardation: A critical review of recent literature. *Developmental Medicine and Child Neurology, 39,* 125–132.

Rogers-Warren, A., Warren, S. F. (eds.) (1977). *Ecological perspectives in behavior analysis.* Baltimore: Paul Brookes Publishing Co.

Rojahn, J. (1984). Self-injurious behavior in institutionalized, severely/profoundly retarded adults – prevalence data and staff agreement. *Journal of Behavioral Assessment, 6*, 13–27.

Rojahn, J. (1986). Self-injurious and stereotypic behavior of non-institutionalized mentally retarded people: Prevalence and classification. *American Journal on Mental Deficiency, 91*, 268–276.

Rojahn, J. (1994). Epidemiology and topographic taxonomy of self-injurious behavior. In T. Thompson, & D. Gray (eds), *Destructive behavior and developmental disabilities* (pp. 49–67). Thousand Oaks, CA: Sage Publications.

Rojahn, J., Aman, M. G., Matson, J. L., & Mayville, E. (2003). The Aberrant Behavior Checklist and the Behavior Problems Inventory: Convergent and divergent validity. *Research in Developmental Disabilities, 24*, 391–404.

Rojahn, J., Hoch, T., Whittaker, K., & Gonzalez, M. (in press). Assessment of Self-injurious and aggressive behavior. In J. L. Matson, & L. Glidden (eds), *International Review of Research in Mental Retardation* (Vol. 34). San Diego: Elsevier.

Rojahn, J., Borthwick-Duffy, S., & Jacobson, J. (1993). The association between psychiatric diagnoses and severe behavior problems in mental retardation. *Annals of Clinical Psychiatry, 5*, 163–170.

Rojahn, J., & Esbensen, A. (2002). Epidemiology of self-injurious behavior in mental retardation. In S. Schroeder, M. L. Oster-Granite, & T. Thompson (eds), *Self-injurious behavior: Gene–brain–behavior relationships* (pp. 41–77). Washington, DC: APA Books.

Rojahn, J., & Helsel, W. J. (1991). The Aberrant Behavior Checklist in children and adolescents with dual diagnosis. *Journal of Autism and Developmental Disorders, 1*, 17–28.

Rojahn, J., Matson, J. L., Lott, D., Esbensen A., & Smalls, Y. (1999). *Epidemiology and topographic assessment of SIB.* Invited address, Cosponsored Conference on Self-Injurious Behavior by National Institute for Child Health and Human Development and Merrill Advanced Study Center, University of Kansas, Rockville, MD, December 6.

Rojahn, J., Matson, J. L., Lott, D., Esbensen, A. J., & Smalls, Y. (2001). The Behavior Problems Inventory: An instrument for the assessment of self-injury, stereotyped behavior and aggression/destruction in individuals with developmental disabilities. *Journal of Autism and Developmental Disorders, 31*, 577–588.

Rojahn, J., Matson, J. L., Naglieri, J. A., & Mayville, E. (2004). Relationships between psychiatric conditions and behavior problems among adults with mental retardation. *American Journal on Mental Retardation, 109*, 21–33.

Rojahn, J., Mulick, J., McCoy, D., & Schroeder, S. R. (1978). Setting effects, adaptive clothing, and the modification of head banging and self-restraint in two profoundly retarded adults. *Behaviour Analysis and Modification, 2*, 185–196.

Rojahn, J., Schroeder, S. R., & Mulick, J. A. (1980). Ecological assessment of self-protective devices in three profoundly retarded adults. *Journal of Autism and Developmental Disorders, 10*, 59–66.

Rojahn, J., Tassé, M. J., & Morin, D. (1998). Self-injurious behavior and stereotypies. In T. H. Ollendick, & M. Hersen (eds), *Handbook of child psychopathology* (3rd ed.) (pp. 307–336). New York: Plenum Press.

Romanczyk, R. G. (1986). Self-injurious behavior: Conceptualization, assessment, and treatment. In K. D. Gadow (ed.), *Advances in learning and behavioral disabilities*. Greenwich, CT: JAI Press.

Romanczyk, R. G., Gordon, W. C., Crimmins, D. B., Wenzel, Z. M., & Kistner, J. A. (1980). Childhood psychosis and 24h rhythms: A behavioral and psychophysiological analysis. *Chronobiologia, 7*, 1–14.

Romanczyk, R. G., Lockshin, S., & O'Connor, J. (1992). Psychophysiology and issues of anxiety and arousal. In J. K. Luiselli, J. L. Matson, & N. N. Singh (eds), *Self-injurious behavior: Analysis, assessment, and treatment* (pp. 93–121). New York: Springer.

Roscoe, E. M., Iwata, B. A., & Goh, H. L. (1998). A comparison of noncontingent reinforcement and sensory extinction as treatments for self-injurious behavior. *Journal of Applied Behavior Analysis, 31,* 635–646.

Rosenquist, P. B., Bodfish, J. W., & Thompson, R. (1997). Tourette Syndrome associated with mental retardation: A single-subject treatment study with haloperidol. *American Journal of Mental Retardation, 101,* 497–504.

Rosenzweig, M. R., & Bennett, E. L. (1976). Enriched environments: Facts, factors, and fantasies. In L. Petrinovich, & I. L. McGaugh (eds), *Knowing, thinking, and believing* (pp. 170–213). New York: Plenum Press.

Ross, R. T. (1972). Behavioral correlates of levels of intelligence. *American Journal of Mental Deficiency, 76,* 545–549.

Ross, S., & Heath, N. L. (2003). Two models of adolescent self-mutilation. *Suicide and Life-Threatening Behavior, 33,* 277–287.

Routh, D. K., & Schroeder, S. R. (2003). A history of psychological theory and research in mental retardation since World War II. In L. Masters-Glidden (ed.), *International review of research in mental retardation* (Vol. 26) (pp. 1–59). New York: Academic Press.

Ruedrich, S., & Erhardt, L. (1999). Beta-blockers in mental retardation and developmental disabilities. *Mental Retardation and Developmental Disabilities Research Reviews, 5,* 290–298.

Ruedrich, S., Swales, T. P., Fossaceca, C., Toliver, J., & Rutkowski, A. (1999). Effect of divalproex sodium on aggression and self-injurious behavior in adults with intellectual disability: A retrospective review. *Journal of Intellectual Disability Research, 43,* 105–111.

Ruedrich, S. L., Grush, L., & Wilson, J. (1990). Beta adrenergic blocking medications for the treatment of rage outbursts in mentally retard persons. *American Journal on Mental Retardation, 95,* 110–119.

RUPP Autism Network (2002). Resperidone in children with autism and serious behavior problems. *New England Journal of Medicine, 347,* 314–321.

Rush, A. J., & Frances, A. (2000). Treatment of psychiatric and behavioral problems in mental retardation. *American Journal on Mental Retardation, 105,* 159–228.

Rush, K. S., Crockett, J. L., & Hagopian, L. P. (2001). An analysis of the selective effects of NCR with punishment targeting problem behavior associated with positive affect. *Behavioral Interventions, 16,* 127–135.

Ryan, E. P., Helsel, W. J., Lubetsky, M. J., Miewald, B. K., Hersen, M., & Bridge, J. (1989). Use of naltrexone in reducing self-injurious behavior. *Journal of Developmental and Physical Disabilities, 2,* 295–309.

Sachsse, U. (1999). *Selbstverletzendes Verhalten. Psychodynamik – Psychotherapie (Self-injurious behavior. Psychodynamic – Psychotherapy)*. Goettingen: Vandenhoeck & Ruprecht.

Sackett, G. P. (1968). Abnormal behavior in laboratory reared rhesus monkeys. In F. W. Fox (ed.), *Abnormal behavior in animals* (pp. 293–331). Philadelphia: Saunders.

Saloviita, T. (2000). The structure and correlates of self-injurious behavior in an institutional setting. *Research in Developmental Disabilities, 21,* 501–511.

Salvy, S. J., Mulick, J. A., Butter, E., Bartlett, R. K., & Linscheid, T. R. (2004). Contingent electric shock (SIBIS) and a conditioned punisher eliminate severe head banging in a pre-school child. *Behavioral Interventions, 19,* 59–72.

Sameroff, A., & Chandler, M. J. (1976). Reproductive risk and the continuum of caretaker casualty. In F. Horowitz (ed.), *Review of research in child development* (Vol. 4) (pp. 187–244). Chicago, IL: University of Chicago Press.

Sandler, A. G. (2001). Sensory reinforcement strategies for the treatment of nonsocially mediated self-injury. *Journal of Developmental and Physical Disabilities, 13*, 307–316.

Sandman, C. A. (1988). B-endorphin dysregulation in autistic and self-injurious behavior: A neurodevelopmental hypothesis. *Synapse, 2*, 193–199.

Sandman, C. A. (1990/1991). The opiate hypothesis in autism and self-injury. *Journal of Child and Adolescent Psychopharmacology, 1*, 237–248.

Sandman, C. A., Datta, P., Barron, J. L., Hoehler, F., Williams, C., & Swanson, J. (1983). Naloxone attenuates self-abusive behavior in developmentally disabled subjects. *Applied Research in Mental Retardation, 4*, 5–11.

Sandman, C. A., & Hetrick, W. P. (1995). Opiate mechanisms in self-injury. *Mental Retardation and Developmental Disabilities Research Reviews, 1*, 130–136.

Sandman, C. A., Hetrick, W. P., Taylor, D. V., Barron, J. L., Touchette, P., Lott, I., et al. (1993). Naltrexone reduces self-injury and improves learning. *Experimental and Clinical Psychopharmacology, 1*, 242–258.

Sandman, C. A., Hetrick, W., Taylor, D. V., & Chicz-Demet, A. (1997). Dissociation of POMC peptides after self-injury predicts responses to centrally acting opiate blockers. *American Journal on Mental Retardation, 102*, 182–199.

Sandman, C. A., Hetrick, W., Tayler, D. V., Marion, S. D., Touchette, P., Barron, J. L., et al. (2000). Long-term effects of naltrexone on self-injurious behavior. *American Journal on Mental Retardation, 105*, 103–117.

Sandman, C. A., Spence, M. A., & Smith, M. (1999). Proopiomelanocortin (POMC) dysregulation and response to opiate blockers. *Mental Retardation and Developmental Disabilities Research Reviews, 5*, 314–321.

Sandman, C. A., & Touchette, P. (2002). Opioids and the maintenance of self-injurious behavior. In S. R. Schroeder, M. L. Oster-Granite, & T. Thompson (eds), *Self-injurious behavior: Gene–brain-behavior relationships* (pp. 191–203). Washington, DC: American Psychological Association.

Sandman, C. A., Touchette, P., Marion, S., Lenjavi, M., & Chicz-Demet, A. (2002). Dysregulation of proopiomelanocortin and contagious maladaptive behavior. *Regulatory Peptide, 108*, 179–185.

Sandman, C. A., Touchette, P., Marion, S., Lenjavi, M., & Chicz-Demet, A. (2003). Beta-Endorphin and ACTH are dissociated after self-injury in adults with developmental disabilities. *American Journal on Mental Retardation, 108*, 414–424.

Sansom, D., Krishnan, V. H. R., Corbett, J., & Kerr, A. (1993). Emotional and behavioral aspects of Rett syndrome. *Developmental Medicine and Child Neurology, 35*, 340–345.

Sarimski, K. (1997). Communication, social-emotional development and parenting stress in Cornelia-de-Lange syndrome. *Journal of Intellectual Disability Research, 41*, 70–75.

Schaal, D. W., & Hackenburg, T. (1994). Toward a functional analysis of drug treatment for behavior problems of people with developmental disabilities. *American Journal on Mental Retardation, 99*, 123–140.

Schade, J. P., & van Groenigen, W. B. (1961). Structural organization of the human cerebral cortex. *Acta Anatomica, 47*, 74–111.

Schaefer, H. H. (1970). Self-injurious behavior: Shaping "head-banging" in monkeys. *Journal of Applied Behavior Analysis, 3*, 111–116.

Schmahl, C., Bohus, M., & Esposito, F. (2006). Neural correlates of antinociception in borderline personality disorder. *Archives of General Psychiatry, 63*, 659–667.

Schopler, E., Reichler, R. J., De Vellis, R. F., & Daly, K. (1980). Toward objective classification of childhood autism: Childhood Autism Rating Scale. *Journal of Autism and Developmental Disorders, 10*, 91–103.

Schroeder, S. R. (1984). Neurochemical and behavioral interactions with stereotyped self-injurious behavior. In J. C. Griffin, M. T. Stark, D. E. Williams, B. K. Altmeyer, & H. K. Griffin (eds), *Advances in the treatment of SIB* (pp. 61–88). Austin, TX: Griffin.

Schroeder, S. R. (1988). Neuroleptic medications for persons with developmental disabilities. In M. G. Aman, & N. N. Singh (eds), *Psychopharmacology of the developmental disabilities* (pp. 82–100). New York: Springer-Verlag.

Schroeder, S. R. (ed.). (1999). Psychopharmacology in developmental disabilities. *Mental Retardation and Developmental Disabilities Research Reviews, 5*, 251–359.

Schroeder, S. R., Bickel, W. K., & Richmond, G. (1986). Primary and secondary prevention of self-injurious behavior. In K. Gadow, & I. Bialer (eds), *Advances in learning and behavioral disabilities* (Vol. 5) (pp. 65–87). Greenwich, CT: JAI.

Schroeder, S. R., Breese, G. R., & Mueller, R. A. (1990). Dopaminergic mechanisms in self-injurious behavior. In D. K. Routh, & M. Wolraich (eds), *Advances in developmental and behavioral pediatrics* (pp. 183–200). Greenwich, CT: JAI.

Schroeder, S. R., & Gualtieri, C. T. (1985). Behavioral interactions induced by chronic neuroleptic therapy with persons with mental retardation. *Psychopharmacology Bulletin, 21*, 310–315.

Schroeder, S. R., Hammock, R. G., Mulick, J. A., Rojahn, J., Walson, P., Fernald, W., et al. (1995). Clinical trails of D1 and D2 dopamine modulating drugs and self-injury in mental retardation and developmental disability. *Mental Retardation and Developmental Disabilities Research Reviews, 1*, 120–129.

Schroeder, S. R., Kanoy, R., Thios, S., Mulick, J., Rojahn, J., Stephens, M., et al. (1982a). Antecedent conditions affecting management and maintenance of programs for the chronically self-injurious. In J. Hollis, & C. E. Meyers (eds), *Life threatening behavior* (pp. 105–159). Washington, DC: AAMD Monograph Series, No. 5.

Schroeder, S. R., Lewis, M. A., & Lipton, M. A. (1983). Interactions of pharmacotherapy and behavior therapy among children with learning behavioral disorders. In K. D. Gadow, & I. Bialer (eds), *Advances in learning and behavioral disabilities* (Vol. 2) (pp. 179–225). Greenwich, CT: JAI.

Schroeder, S. R., Loupe, P. S., & Tessel, R. E. (2006). *Training-induced recovery from SIB in 6-OHDA depleted rats.* Poster given at the Annual Gatlinburg Conference on Research and Theory in Mental Retardation and Developmental Disabilities. San Diego, CA, March 15–18.

Schroeder, S. R., & MacLean, W. (1987). If it isn't one thing, it's another: Experimental analysis of covariation in behavior management data of severely disturbed retarded persons. In S. Landesman-Dwyer, & P. Vietze (eds), *Living environments and mental retardation* (pp. 315–338). Washington, DC: AAMD Monograph Series.

Schroeder, S. R., Mulick, J., & Schroeder, C. (1979). Management of severe behavior problems of the retarded. In N. Ellis (ed.), *Handbook of mental deficiency* (2nd ed.) (pp. 341–366). New York, NY: Erlbaum.

Schroeder, S. R., Mulick, J. A., & Rojahn, J. (1980). The definition, taxonomy, epidemiology, and ecology of self-injurious behavior. *Journal of Autism and Developmental Disorders, 10*, 417–432.

Schroeder, S. R., Oldenquist, A., & Rojahn, J. (1990). A conceptual framework for judging the humaneness and effectiveness of behavioral treatment. In A. Repp, & N. N. Singh (eds), *Aversive and non-aversive treatment: The great debate in developmental disabilities* (pp. 103–118). Sycamore, IL: Sycamore Press.

Schroeder, S. S., Oster-Granite, M. L., Thompson, T. (eds.) (2002). *Self-injurious behavior: Gene–brain-behavior relationships.* American Psychological Association, Washington, DC.

Schroeder, S. R., Peterson, C. R., & Solomon, L. J. (1977). EMG feedback and the contingent restraint of self-injurious behavior among the severely retarded: Two case illustrations. *Behavior Therapy, 8,* 738–741.

Schroeder, S. R., Reese, R. M., Hellings, J., Loupe, J., & Tessel, R. E. (1999). The causes of self-injurious behavior and their implications. In N. A. Wieseler, & R. Hanson (eds), *Challenging behavior with mental health disorders and severe developmental disabilities* (pp. 65–87). Washington, DC: AAMR Monograph Series.

Schroeder, S. R., Rojahn, J., & Mulick, J. A. (1978). Ecobehavioral organization of developmental day care for the chronically self-injurious. *Journal of Pediatric Psychology, 3,* 81–88.

Schroeder, S. R., Rojahn, J., & Oldenquist, A. (1991). *Treatment of destructive behaviors among people with mental retardation and developmental disabilities: An overview of the program.* Paper presented at the Consensus Development Conference on Destructive Behavior, National Institutes of Health, Bethesda, MD. NIH Publication No. 91-2410.

Schroeder, S. R., Rojahn, J., & Reese, R. M. (1997). Reliability and validity of instruments for assessing psychotropic medication effects on self-injurious behavior in mental retardation. *Journal of Autism and Developmental Disorders, 27,* 89–102.

Schroeder, S. R., & Schroeder, C. S. (1989). The role of the AAMR in the aversives controversy. *Mental Retardation, 27,* 3–4.

Schroeder, S. R., Schroeder, C., Rojahn, J., & Mulick, J. A. (1982b). Analysis of self-injurious behavior: Its development and management. In J. L. Matson, & J. R. McCartney (eds), *Handbook of behavior modification for the mentally retarded.* New York: Plenum.

Schroeder, S. R., Schroeder, C. S., Smith, B., & Dalldorf, J. (1978). Prevalence of self-injurious behaviors in a large state facility for the retarded: A three-year follow-up study. *Journal of Autism and Childhood Schizophrenia, 8,* 261–269.

Schroeder, S. R., & Tessel, R. (1994). Dopaminergic and serotonergic mechanisms in self injury and aggression. In T. Thompson, & D. Gray (eds), *Treatment of destructive behavior in developmental disabilities* (pp. 198–212). Newbury Park, CA: Sage Publications.

Schwartz, T. L., Linberg, J. V., Tillman, W., & Odom, J. V. (1987). Monocular depth and vernier acuities: A comparison of binocular and uniocular subjects. *Investigative Ophthalmology Visual Science, 28*(Suppl.), 304.

Schwatka, F. (1889/1890). The sun-dance of the Sioux. *Century Magazine, 39.*

Seignot, M. J. N. (1961). Un cas de maladie de tics de Gilles de la Tourette gueri par le R. -1625. *Annales Medico-Psychologicues (Paris), 119,* 578–579.

Seltzer, M. M., & Heller, T. (1997). Families and caregiving across the life course: Research advances on the influence of context. *Family Relations, 46,* 395–405.

Sequeira, H., & Hollins, S. (2003). Clinical effects of sexual abuse on people with learning disability: Critical literature review. *British Journal of Psychiatry, 182,* 13–19.

Sevin, J. A., Matson, J. L., Williams, D., & Kirkpatrick-Sanchez, S. (1995). Reliability of emotional problems with the Diagnostic Assessment for the Severely Handicapped (DASH). *British Journal of Clinical Psychology, 34,* 93–94.

Shapira, N. A., Lessig, M. C., Lewis, M. H., Goodman, W. K., & Driscoll, D. J. (2004). Effects of Topiramate in adults with PraderWilli syndrome. *American Journal on Mental Retardation, 109,* 301–309.

Shaywitz, B. A., Yager, R. D., & Klopper, J. H. (1976). Selective brain dopamine depletion in developing rats: An experimental model of minimal brain dysfunction. *Science, 191,* 305–308.

Sheiner, L. B., Beal, S. L., & Sambol, S. C. (1989). Study designs for dose-ranging. *Clinical Pharmacology and Therapeutics, 46,* 63–77.

Shirley, M. J., Iwata, B. A., & Kahng, S. W. (1999). False–positive maintenance of self-injurious behavior by access to tangible reinforcers. *Journal of Applied Behavior Analysis, 32,* 201–204.

Shneidman, E. S. (1985). *Definition of suicide.* New York: Wiley.

Shore, B. A., Iwata, B. A., DeLeon, I. G., Kahng, S., & Smith, R. G. (1997). An analysis of reinforcer substitutability using object manipulation and self-injury as competing responses. *Journal of Applied Behavior Analysis, 30,* 21–41.

Shott, S.R., Amin, R., Chini, B., Heubi, C., Hotze, S., & Akers, R. (2006). Obstructive sleep apnea: Should all children with down syndrome be tested? *Archives of Otolaryngology, Head, and Neck Surgery, 132,* 432–436.

Sidman, M. (1978). Remarks. *Behaviorism, 6,* 265–268.

Sidman, M., & Stoddard, L. T. (1966). Programming perception and learning for retarded children. In N. R. Ellis (ed.), *International review of research in mental retardation* (Vol. 2) (pp. 152–208). New York: Academic Press.

Sigafoos, J., & Meikle, B. (1996). Functional communication training for the treatment of multiply determined challenging behavior in two boys with autism. *Behavior Modification, 20,* 60–84.

Simon, E. W., Blubaugh, K. M., & Pippidis, M. (1996). Substituting traditional antipsychotics with risperidone for individuals with mental retardation. *Mental Retardation, 34,* 359–366.

Simonoff, E. (1998). Genetic counseling in autism and pervasive developmental disorders. *Journal of Developmental Disorders, 28,* 447–456.

Simpson, M. (1975). The phenomenology of self mutilation in a general hospital setting. *Canadian Psychiatric Association Journal, 20,* 429–544.

Simpson, M. A. (1976). Self-mutilation and suicide. In E. S. Shneidman (ed.), *Suicidology: Contemporary developments* (pp. 281–315). New York: Grune & Stratton.

Simpson, M. A. (1980). Self-mutilation as indirect self destructive behavior. In L. N. Faberow (ed.), *The many faces of suicide* (pp. 257–283). New York: McGraw-Hill.

Singer, H. S. (1992). Neurochemical analysis of post-mortem cortical and striatal brain tissue in patients with Tourette syndrome. *Advances in Neurology, 58,* 135–144.

Singh, N. N. (1977). Prevalence of self-injury in institutionalized retarded children. *New Zealand Medical Journal, 86,* 325–327.

Singh, N. N., & Aman, M. G. (1983). Effects of thioridazine dosage on the behavior of severely retarded persons. *American Journal of Mental Deficiency, 85,* 580–587.

Singh, N. N., & Millichamp, C. J. (1985). Pharmacological treatment of self-injurious behavior in mentally retarded persons. *Journal of Autism and Developmental Disorders, 15,* 257–267.

Singh, N. N., Singh, Y. N., & Ellis, C. R. (1992). Psychopharmacology of self-injury. In J. K. Luiselli, J. L. Matson, & N. N. Singh (eds), *Self-injurious behavior: Analysis, assessment, and treatment* (pp. 307–351). New York: Springer-Verlag.

Singh, N. N., Watson, J. E., & Winton, A. S. W. (1986). Treating self-injury: Water mist spray versus facial screening or forced arm exercise. *Journal of Applied Behavior Analysis, 19,* 403–410.

Skinner, B. F. (1953). *Science and human behavior.* New York: MacMillen.

Skinner, B. F. (1968). *The technology of teaching*. New York, NY: Appleton-Century-Crofts.

Skinner, B. F. (1974). *About behaviorism*. New York: Random House.

Smalley, S. L., Asarnow, R. F., & Spence, M. A. (1988). Autism and genetics: A decade of research. *Archives of General Psychiatry, 45*, 953–961.

Smathers, S. A., Wilson, J. G., & Nigro, M. A. (2003). Topiramate effectiveness in Prader–Willi syndrome. *International Journal of Neuropsychopharmacology, 5*, 141–145.

Smeets, P. M. (1971). Some characteristics of mental defectives displaying self-mutilative behaviors. *Training School Bulletin, 68*, 131–135.

Smith, A. C. M., McGavran, L., Robinson, J., Waldstein, G., Macfarlane, J., Zonona, J., et al. (1986). Interstitial deletion of (17) (p11.2) in nine patients. *American Journal of Medical Genetics, 4*, 393–414.

Smith, R. G., & Churchill, R. M. (2002). Identification of environmental determinants of behavior disorders through functional analysis of precursor behaviors. *Journal of Applied Behavior Analysis, 35*, 125–136.

Smith, R. G., Iwata, B. A., Goh, H. L., & Shore, B. A. (1995a). Analysis of establishing operations for self-injury maintained by escape. *Journal of Applied Behavior Analysis, 28*, 515–535.

Smith, T., Mruzek, D. W., & Mozingo, D. (2005). Sensory integrative therapy. In J. W. Jacobson, R. M. Foxx, & J. A. Mulick (eds), *Controversial therapies for developmental disabilities: Fad, fashion, and science in professional practice* (pp. 331–350). Mahwah, NJ: Lawrence Erlbaum Associates.

Smith, T., Klevstrand, M., & Lovaas, O. I. (1995b). Behavioral treatment of Rett's disorder: Ineffectiveness in three cases. *American Journal on Mental Retardation, 100*, 317–322.

Smotherman, W. (1995). *Caveats in the study of early development*. Paper presented at NICHD Conference on Animal Models for the Study of Mental Retardation. Bethesda, MD, September 21–22.

Snyder, R., Turgay, A., Aman, M. G., Binder, C., Fisman, S., Carroll, A. & The Risperidone Conduct Study Group (2002). Effects of risperidone on conduct and disruptive disorders in children with subaverage IQ's. *Journal of the American Academy of Child and Adolescent Psychiatry, 41*, 1026–1036.

Solnick, J., Rincover, A., & Peterson, C. (1977). Some determinants of the reinforcing and punishing effects of time-out. *Journal of Applied Behavior Analysis, 10*, 415–424.

Soule, B., & O'Brien, D. (1974). Self-injurious behavior in a state center for the retarded: Incidence. *Research and the Retarded, Spring*, 1–8.

Sovner, R. (1989). The use of valproate in the treatment of mentally retard persons with typical and atypical bipolar disorders. *Journal of Clinical Psychiatry, 50*(Suppl.), 40–43.

Sovner, R., Fox, C., Lowry, M. J., & Lowry, M. A. (1993). Fluoxetine treatment of depression and associated self-injury in two adults with mental retardation. *Journal of Intellectual Disability Research, 37*, 301–312.

Sovner, R., Hurley, A. (1983). Do the mentally retarded suffer from affective illness? *Archives of General Psychiatry, 40*, 61–67.

Sovner, R., & Lowry, M. (1990). A behavioral methodology for diagnosing affective disorders in individuals with mental retardation. *The Habilitative Mental Healthcare Newsletter, 9*, 56–61.

Sovner, R., Pary, R. J., Dosen, A., Gedye, A., Barrera, F. J., Cantwell, D. P., et al. (1998). Antidepressant drugs. In S. Reiss, & M. G. Aman (eds), *Psychotropic medications and developmental disabilities: The international consensus handbook* (pp. 179–200). Columbus, OH: the Ohio State University.

Sparrow, S. S., Balla, D. A., & Cicchetti, D. V. (1984). *Vineland adaptive behavior scales, interview edition, survey Form manual.* Circle Pines, MN: American Guidance Service.

Sparrow, S. S., Cicchetti, D. V. & Balla, D. A. (2005a). *Vineland II – Vineland Adaptive Behavior Scales.* (2nd ed.) Survey Forms Manual. Circle Pines, MN: AGS Publishing.

Sparrow, S. S., Cicchetti, D. V., & Balla, D. A. (2005b). *Vineland II – Vineland Adaptive Behavior Scales.* (2nd ed.) Teacher Rating Form Manual. Circle Pines, MN: AGS Publishing.

Spradlin, J. E. (1963). Assessment of speech and language of retarded children: The parsons language sample. In R.L. Schiefelbusch (ed.), *Language studies of mentally retarded children. Journal of Speech and Hearing Disorders Monograph, 10*, 8–31.

Sprague, J., Holland, K., & Thomas, K. (2005a). The effect of noncontingent sensory reinforcement, contingent sensory reinforcement, and response interruption on stereotypical and self-injurious behavior. *Research in Developmental Disabilities, 18*, 61–77.

Sprague, R. L., Kalachnik, J. E., & Slaw, K. M. (1989). Psychometric properties of the dyskinesia identification system: Condensed user scale (DISCUS). *Mental Retardation, 27*, 141–148.

Sprague, R. L., & Newell, K. M. (1996). *Stereotyped movements: Brain and behavior relationships.* Washington, DC: American Psychological Association.

Sprague, R. L., & Sleator, E. K. (1977). Methylphenidate in hyperkinetic children: Differences in dose effects on learning a social behavior. *Science, 198*, 1274–1276.

Sprague, R. L., & Werry, J. S. (1971). Methodology of psychopharmacological studies with the retarded. In N. R. Ellis (ed.), *International review of research in mental retardation* (Vol. 5) (pp. 148–220). New York, NY: Academic Press.

Stadele, N. D., & Malaney, L. A. (2001). The effects of a multisensory environment on negative behavior and functional performance of individuals with autism. *University of Wisconsin-LaCrosse Undergraduate Research Journal, 4*, 211–216.

Stainback, W., & Stainback, S. (1983). A review of research on the educability of profoundly retarded persons. *Education and Training of the Mentally Retarded, 18*, 90–100.

Steege, M. W., Wacker, D. P., Cigrand, K. C., Berg, W. K., Novak, C. G., Reimers, T. M., et al. (1990). Use of negative reinforcement in the treatment of self-injurious behavior. *Journal of Applied Behavior Analysis, 23*, 459–467.

Steen, P. L., & Zuriff, G. E. (1977). The use of relaxation in the treatment of self-injurious behavior. *Journal of Behavior Therapy and Experimental Psychiatry, 8*, 447–448.

Stein, D. J., Keating, J., & Zar, H. (1993). *Compulsive and impulsive symptoms in Prader–Willi syndrome.* Abstracts in New Research (NR 33), Annual Meeting of the American Psychiatric Association, San Francisco, CA, May.

Stein, M. T. (2005). Challenging case. *Journal of Developmental & Behavioral Pediatrics, 26*, 241–245.

Stigler, K. A., Posey, D. J., & McDougle, C. J. (2004). Aripiprazole for maladaptive behavior in pervasive developmental disorders. *Journal of Child and Adolescent Psychopharmacology, 14*, 455–463.

Stoddart, K. P., Burke, L., & Temple, V. (2002). Outcome evaluation of bereavement groups for adults with intellectual disabilities. *Journal of Applied Research in Intellectual Disabilities, 15*, 28–35.

Stodgell, C. J., Schroeder, S. R., Hyland, J. M., & Tessel, R. E. (1997). Effect of repeated footshock stress, apomorphine and their combination on the incidence of apomorphine (APO)-elicited self-injurious behavior (SIB) in juvenile neonatal 6-hydroxydopamine (6HD)-treated rats. *Neuroscience Abstracts, 20*, 1444.

Stodgell, C. J., Schroeder, S. R., & Tessel, R. E. (1996). FR discrimination training reverses 6HD-induced striatal dopamine depletion of a rat with Lesch–Nyhan syndrome. *Brain Research, 713,* 246–252.

Stokes, T. F., & Baer, D. M. (1977). An implicit technology of generalization. *Journal of Applied Behavior Analysis, 10,* 349–367.

Sturmey, P. (1994). Assessing the functions of aberrant behavior: A review of psychometric instruments. *Journal of Autism and Developmental Disabilities, 24,* 293–304.

Sturmey, P., Fink, C., & Sevin, J. (1993). The behavior problems inventory: A replication and extension of its psychometric properties. *Journal of Developmental and Physical Disabilities, 5,* 327–336.

Sturmey, P., Sevin, J., & Williams, D. E. (1995). The behavior problems inventory: A further replication of its factor structure. *Journal of Intellectual Disability Research, 39,* 353–356.

Summers, S. J., & Witts, P. (2003). Psychological intervention for people with learning disabilities who have experienced bereavement: A case study illustration. *British Journal of Learning Disabilities, 31,* 37–41.

Sundberg, M. L., & Partington, J. W. (1998). *Teaching language to children with autism or other developmental disabilities.* Pleasant Hills, CA: Behavior Analysts, Inc.

Suyemoto, K. L. (1998). The functions of self-mutilation. *Clinical Psychology Review, 18,* 531–554.

Suyemoto, K. L., & MacDonald, M. L. (1995). Self-cutting in female adolescents. *Psychotherapy: Theory, Research, Practice, Training, 32,* 162–171.

Symons, F. J., Clark, R. D., Hatton, D. D., Skinner, M., & Bailey, D. B. (2003). Self-injurious behavior in young boys with fragile X syndrome. *American Journal of Medical Genetics, 118,* 115–121.

Symons, F. J., & Danov, S. (2005). A prospective clinical analysis of pain behavior and self-injurious behavior. *Pain, 117,* 473–477.

Symons, F. J., Davis, M. L., & Thompson, T. (2000). Self-injurious behavior and sleep disturbance in adults with developmental disabilities. *Research in Developmental Disabilities, 21,* 115–123.

Symons, F. J., Sperry, L. A., Dropik, P. L., & Bodfish, J. W. (2005). The early development of stereotypy and self-injury: A review of research methods. *Journal of Intellectual Disability Research, 49,* 144–158.

Symons, F. J., Sutton, K. A., & Bodfish, J. W. (2001a). Preliminary study of altered skin temperature at body sites associated with self-injurious behavior in adults who have developmental disabilities. *American Journal on Mental Retardation, 106,* 336–343.

Symons, F. J., Sutton, K. A., Walker, C., & Bodfish, J. W. (2003). Altered diurnal pattern of salivary substance P in adults with developmental disabilities and chronic self-injury. *American Journal on Mental Retardation, 108,* 13–18.

Symons, F. J., Tapp, J., Wulfsberg, A., Sutton, K. A., Heeth, W. L., & Bodfish, J. W. (2001b). Sequential analysis of the effects of naltrexone on the environmental mediation of self-injurious behavior. *Experimental and Clinical Psychopharmacology, 99,* 269–276.

Symons, F. J., & Thompson, T. (1997). A review of self-injurious behavior and pain in persons with developmental disabilities. In N. W. Bray (ed.), *International Review of Research in Mental Retardation* (Vol. 21) (pp. 69–111). New York: Academic Press.

Symons, F. J., Thompson, A., & Rodriguez, M. C. (2004). Self-injurious behavior and the efficacy of naltrexone treatment: A quantitative synthesis. *Mental Retardation and Developmental Disabilities Research Reviews, 10,* 193–200.

Symons, F. J., Wendelschafer-Crabb, G., Kennedy, W., Hardict, R., Dahl, N., & Bodfish, J. W. (2005). *A preliminary study of epidermal nerve fibers and self-injury.* Poster presented at the Annual Gatlinburg Conference on Research in Mental Retardation and Developmental Disabilities. Annapolis, MD, March 16.

Symons, F. S. (2002). Self-injury and pain: Models and mechanisms. In S. R. Schroeder, M. L. Oster-Granite, & T. Thompson (eds), *Self-injurious behavior: Gene–brain-behavior relationships* (pp. 223–234). Washington, DC: American Psychological Association.

Tanner, B. A., & Zeiler, M. (1975). Punishment of self-injurious behavior using aromatic ammonia as the aversive stimulus. *Journal of Applied Behavior Analysis, 8,* 53–57.

Tapp, J., Wehby, J., & Ellis, D. (1995). A multiple option observation system for experimental studies: MOOSES. *Behavior Research Methods, Instruments, and Computers, 27,* 25–31.

Tarbox, J., Wallace, M. D., Tarbox, R. S. F., Landaburu, H. J., & Williams, L. (2004). Functional analysis and treatment of low rate problem behavior in individuals with developmental disabilities. *Behavioral Interventions, 19,* 187–204.

Tarpley, H., & Schroeder, S. R. (1979). A comparison of DRO and DRI procedures in the treatment of self-injurious behavior. *American Journal of Mental Deficiency, 84,* 188–194.

Tassé, M. J., Aman, M. G., Hammer, D., & Rojahn, J. (1996). The Nisonger child behavior rating form: Age and gender effects and norms. *Research in Developmental Disabilities, 17,* 59–75.

Tassé, M. J., & Lecavalier, L. (2000). Comparing parent and teacher ratings of social competence and problem behaviors. *American Journal on Mental Retardation, 105,* 252–259.

Tate, B. G., & Baroff, G. S. (1966). Aversive control of self-injurious behavior in a psychotic boy. *Behavior Research and Therapy, 4,* 281–287.

Taylor, D. V., Rush, D., Hetrick, W. P., & Sandman, C. A. (1993). Self-injurious behavior within the menstrual cycle of women with developmental delays. *American Journal on Mental Retardation, 97,* 659–664.

Tessel, R. E., Schroeder, S. R., Loupe, P. S., & Stodgell, C. J. (1995a). Reversal of 6HD-induced neonatal brain catecholamine depletion after operant training. *Pharmacology, Biochemistry, and Behavior, 51,* 861–868.

Tessel, R. E., Schroeder, S. R., Stodgell, C. J., & Loupe, P. S. (1995b). Rodent models of mental retardation: Self-injury, aberrant behavior and stress. *Mental Retardation and Developmental Disabilities Reviews, 1,* 99–103.

The Columbia Encyclopedia (2002). *Flagellants* (6th ed.). New York: Bartleby.com.

Thelen, E. (1979). Rhythmical stereotypies in normal human infants. *Animal Behaviour, 27,* 699–715.

Thelen, E. (1995). Motor development: A new synthesis. *American Psychologist, 50,* 79–95.

Thompson, T., Felce, D., & Symons, F. J. (eds.). (2000). *Behavioral observation.* Baltimore, MD: Brookes.

Thompson, C. I., Games, P. A., & Koons, P. B. (1967). Effects of punishment as positive reinforcement for the punisher. *Perceptual and Motor Skills, 24,* 887–898.

Thompson, R. H., Iwata, B. A., Connors, J., & Roscoe, E. M. (1999). Effects of reinforcement for alternative behavior during punishment of self-injury. *Journal of Applied Behavior Analysis, 32,* 317–328.

Thomson, S., & Emerson, E. (1995). Inter-informant agreement on the Motivation Assessment Scale: Another failure to replicate. *Mental Handicap Research, 8,* 203–208.

Thompson, T., & Caruso, M. (2002). Self-injurious behavior: Knowing what we're looking for. In S. R. Schroeder, M. L. Oster-Granite, & T. Thompson (eds), *Self-injurious behavior: Gene–brain-behavior relationships* (pp. 3–21). Washington, DC: American Psychological Association.

Thompson, T., Hackenberg, T., Cerutti, D., Baker, D., & Axtell, S. (1994). Opioid antagonist effects on self-injury in adults with mental retardation: Response form and location as determinants of medication effects. *American Journal on Mental Retardation, 99,* 85–102.

Thompson, T., Hackenberg, T., & Schaal, D. (1991). *Pharmacological treatments for behavior problems in developmental disabilities.* Paper presented at the Consensus Development Conference on Destructive Behavior, National Institutes of Health, Bethesda, MD, NIH Publication No. 01-2410.

Thompson, T., Symons, F., Delaney, D., & England, C. (1995). Self-injurious behavior as endogenous neurochemical self-administration. *Mental Retardation and Developmental Disabilities Research Reviews, 1,* 137–148.

Thyer, B. A. (1987). Punishment-induced aggression: A possible mechanism of child abuse? *Psychological Reports, 60,* 129–130.

Tiefenbacher, S., Novak, M. A., Jorgensen, M. J., & Meyer, J. S. (2000). Physiological correlates of self-injurious behavior in captive, socially reared, rhesus monkeys. *Psychoneuroimmunology, 25,* 799–817.

Toole, L. M., DeLeon, I. G., Kahng, S., Ruffin, G. E., Pletcher, C. A., & Bowman, L. G. (2004). Re-evaluation of constant versus varied punishers using empirically derived consequences. *Research in Developmental Disabilities, 25,* 557–586.

Touchette, P. E., & Howard, J. S. (1984). Errorless learning: Reinforcement contingencies and stimulus control transfer in delayed prompting. *Journal of Applied Behavior Analysis, 17,* 175–188.

Touchette, P. E., MacDonald, R. F., & Langer, S. N. (1985). A scatter plot for identifying stimulus control of problem behavior. *Journal of Applied Behavior Analysis, 18,* 343–351.

Tu, J. B., Hartridge, C., & Izawa, J. (1992). Psychopharmacogenetic aspects of Prader–Willi syndrome. *Journal of the American Academy of Child and Adolescent Psychiatry, 31,* 1137–1140.

Tucker, M., Sigafoos, J., & Bushell, H. (1998). Use of noncontingent reinforcement in the treatment of challenging behavior. *Behavior Modification, 22,* 529–547.

Turnbull, H. R., Guess, D., Backus, L., Barber, P., Fiedler, C., Helmstetter, E., et al. (1986). A model for analyzing the moral aspects of special education and behavioral interventions: The moral aspects of aversive procedures. In P. Dokecki, & R. Zaner (eds), *Ethics and decision-making for persons with severe handicaps: Toward an ethically relevant research agenda* (pp. 167–210). Baltimore: Paul Brookes Publishing Co.

Turner, C. A., & Lewis, M. H. (2002). Dopaminergic mechanisms in self-injurious behavior and related disorders. In S. R. Schroeder, M. L. Oster-Granite, & T. Thompson (eds), *Self-injurious behavior: Gene–brain–behavior relationships* (pp. 165–179). Washington, DC: American Psychological Association.

Turp, M. (2002). *Hidden self-harm: Narratives from psychotherapy.* London, England: Jessica Kingsley Publishers.

Ullman, L. P., & Krasner, L. (1965). *Case studies in behavior modification.* New York, NY: Holt, Rinehart & Winston.

Vaegan, T. D. (1979). Critical period for deprivation amblyopia in children. *Transactions of the Opthalmological Societies of the United Kingdom, 99,* 432–439.

Valdovinos, M. G., Napolitano, D. A., Zarcone, J. R., Hellings, J. A., Williams, D. C., & Schroeder, S. R. (2002). Multimodal evaluation of risperidone for destructive behavior: Functional analysis, direct observation, rating scales and psychiatric impressions. *Experimental and Clinical Psychopharmacology, 10,* 268–275.

Valdovinos, M., Schroeder, S. R., & Kim, G. (2003). Prevalence and correlates of psychotropic medication use among adults with developmental disabilities: 1970–2000. In L. M. Glidden (ed.), *International review of research in mental retardation* (Vol. 26) (pp. 175–220). New York: Academic Press.

Vale, V., & Juno, A. (1989). *Modern primitives*. San Francisco, CA: ReSearch.

Van Camp, C. M., Lerman, D. C., Kelley, M. E., Roane, H. S., Contrucci, S. A., & Vorndran, C. M. (2000). Further analysis of idiosyncratic antecedent influences during the assessment and treatment of problem behavior. *Journal of Applied Behavior Analysis, 33*, 207–221.

Van Camp, C. M., Vollmer, T. R., & Daniel, D. (2002). A systematic evaluation of stimulus preference, response effort, and stimulus control in the treatment of automatically reinforced self-injury. *Behavior Therapy, 32*, 603–613.

Van de Wetering, B. J. M., & Heutink, P. (1993). The genetics of Gilles de la Tourette syndrome: A review. *Journal of Laboratory and Clinical Medicine, 121*, 638–645.

Van den Borre, R., Vermote, R., Buttiens, M., Thiry, P., Dierick, G., Gentjens, J., et al. (1993). Risperidone as add-on therapy in behavioural disturbance in mental retardation: A double-blind placebo-controlled cross-over study. *Acta Psychiatrica Scandinavica, 87*, 167–171.

Van Houten, R. (1993). The use of wrist weights to reduce self-injury maintained by sensory reinforcement. *Journal of Applied Behavior Analysis, 26*, 197–203.

Vanstraelen, M., & Tyrer, S. P. (1999). Rapid cycling bipolar affective disorder in people with intellectual disability: A systematic review. *Journal of Intellectual Disability Research, 43*, 349–359.

Verkerk, A. J. M. H., Pieretti, M., Sutcliffe, J. S., Fu, Y. H., Kuhl, D. P., Pizzuti, A., et al. (1991). Identification of a gene (FMR-1) containing a CGG repeat coincident with a break-point cluster region exhibiting length variation in fragile X syndrome. *Cell, 65*, 905–914.

Visser, J. E., Bar, P. R., & Jinnah, H. A. (2000). Lesch–Nyhan disease and the basal ganglia. *Brain Research Reviews, 32*, 449–475.

Von Hofsten, C. (1982). Eye-hand coordination in the newborn. *Developmental Psychology, 18*, 450–461.

Vollmer, T. R., Borrero, J. C., Wright, C. S., Van Camp, C., & Lalli, J. S. (2001). Identifying possible contingencies during descriptive analyses of severe behavior disorders. *Journal of Applied Behavior Analysis, 34*, 269–287.

Vollmer, T. R., & Iwata, B. A. (1992). Differential reinforcement as treatment for behavior disorders: Procedural and functional variations. *Research in Developmental Disabilities, 13*, 393–417.

Vollmer, T. R., Iwata, B. A., Zarcone, J. R., Smith, R. G., & Mazaleski, J. L. (1993). The role of attention in the treatment of attention-maintained self-injurious behavior: Noncontingent reinforcement and differential reinforcement of other behavior. *Journal of Applied Behavior Analysis, 26*, 9–21.

Vollmer, T. R., Marcus, B. A., & LeBlanc, L. (1994). Treatment of self-injury and hand mouthing following inconclusive functional analysis. *Journal of Applied Behavior Analysis, 27*, 331–344.

Vollmer, T. R., Marcus, B. A., & Ringdahl, J. E. (1995a). Noncontingent escape as treatment for self-injurious behavior maintained by negative reinforcement. *Journal of Applied Behavior Analysis, 28*, 15–26.

Vollmer, T. R., Marcus, B. A., Ringdahl, J. E., & Roane, H. S. (1995b). Progressing from brief assessments to extended experimental analysis in the evaluation of aberrant problem behavior. *Journal of Applied Behavior Analysis, 28*, 561–576.

Vollmer, T. R., & Matson, J. L. (1995). *Questions About Behavioral Functions*. Baton Rouge, LA: Scientific Publishers, Inc.

Vollmer, T. R., Progar, P. R., Lalli, J. S., Van Camp, C. M., Sierp, B. J., Wright, C. S., et al. (1998). Fixed time schedules attenuate extinction induced phenomena in the treatment of severe aberrant behavior. *Journal of Applied Behavior Analysis, 31,* 529–542.

Vollmer, T. R., & Vorndran, C. M. (1998). Assessment of self-injurious behavior maintained by access to self-restraint materials. *Journal of Applied Behavior Analysis, 31,* 647–650.

Wacker, D. P., & Berg, W. K. (2002). PBS as a service delivery system. *Journal of Positive Behavior Interventions, 4,* 25–28.

Wacker, D. P., Berg, W. K., & Harding, J. W. (2006). *Long-term follow-up of destructive behavior in home settings.* Paper given at the Annual Convention of the Gatlinburg Conference on Research and Theory in Mental Retardation. San Diego, CA, March 15–18.

Wacker, D. P., Berg, W. K., Harding, J. W., Derby, M. K., Asmus, J. M., & Healy, A. (1998). Evaluation and long-term treatment of aberrant behavior displayed by young children with developmental disabilities. *Journal of Developmental and Behavioral Pediatrics, 19,* 260–266.

Wacker, D. P., Harding, J., Cooper, L. J., Derby, K. M., Peck, S., Asmus, J., et al. (1996). The effects of meal schedule and quantity on problematic behavior. *Journal of Applied Behavior Analysis, 29,* 79–87.

Wahler, R., House, A., & Stambaugh, E. (1976). *Ecological assessment of child problem behavior.* New York: Pergamon Press.

Walkup, J. T., Labellarte, M. J., & Riddle, M. A. (1998). Commentary: Unmasked and uncontrolled medication trials in child and adolescent psychiatry. *Journal of the American Academy of Child and Adolescent Psychiatry, 37,* 360–363.

Wall, P. D., & Melzack, R. (eds.) (1989). *Textbook of pain* (2nd ed.) New York: Churchill Livingstone.

Wallace, M. D., & Iwata, B. A. (1999). Effects of session duration on functional analysis outcome. *Journal of Applied Behavior Analysis, 32,* 175–183.

Walsh, B. W., & Rosen, P. M. (1988). *Self-mutilation: Theory, research and treatment.* New York: The Guilford Press.

Warnock, J. K., & Kestenbaum, M. D. (1992). Pharmacologic treatment of severe skin-picking behaviors in Prader–Willi syndrome. *Archives of Dermatology, 128,* 1623–1625.

Wenk, G. L., Naidu, S., & Moser, H. (1989). Altered neurochemical markers in Rett syndrome. *Annals of Neurology, 26,* 466–468.

Werry, J. S. (1999). Anxiolytics in MRDD. *Mental Retardation and Developmental Disabilities Research Reviews, 5,* 299–304.

Werry, J. S., Aman, M. G. (eds.) (2001). *A practitioner's guide to psychoactive drugs for children and adolescents* (3rd ed.) New York: Plenum Press.

White, G. D., Nielsen, G., & Johnson, S. M. (1972). Timeout duration and the suppression of deviant behavior in children. *Journal of Applied Behavior Analysis, 5,* 111–120.

Whitney, L. R. (1966). The effects of operant conditioning on the self-destructive behavior of retarded children. In *Exploring Progress in Maternal and Child Health Nursing Practice.* American Nursing Association, 1965, Regional Conference No. 3. New York: Appleton-Century-Crofts.

Wieseler, N. A., Hanson, R. H., Chamberlain, T. P., & Thompson, T. (1985). Functional taxonomy of stereotypic and self-injurious behavior. *Mental Retardation, 25,* 230–234.

Wieseler, N. A., Hanson, R. H., Chamberlain, T. P., & Thompson, T. (1988). Stereotypic behavior of mentally retarded adults as adjunctive to a positive reinforcement schedule. *Research in Developmental Disabilities, 9,* 393–403.

Wieseler, N. A., Hanson, R. H., & Nord, G. (1995). Investigation of mortality and morbidity associated with severe self-injurious behavior. *American Journal on Mental Retardation, 100,* 1–5.

Wilder, D. A., & Carr, J. E. (1998). Recent advances in the modification of establishing operations to reduce aberrant behavior. *Behavioral Interventions, 13*, 43–59.

Wilder, D. A., Fisher, W. W., Anders, B. M., Cercone, J. J., & Neidert, P. L. (2001). Operative mechanisms of noncontingent reinforcement at varying magnitudes and schedules. *Research in Developmental Disabilities, 22*, 117–124.

Williams, D. C., & Saunders, K. J. (1997). Methodological issues in the study of drug effects on cognitive skills in mental retardation. In N. W. Bray (ed.), *International Review of Research in Mental Retardation*, (Vol. 21) (pp. 147–185). New York: Academic press.

Williams, H., Clarke, R., Bouras, N., Martin, J., & Holt, G. (2000). Use of the atypical antipsychotics olanzapine and risperidone in adults with intellectual disability. *Journal of Intellectual Disability Research, 44*, 164–169.

Winchel, R. M., & Stanley, M. (1991). Self-injurious behavior: A review of the behavior and biology of self-mutilation. *American Journal of Psychiatry, 148*, 306–317.

Winnicott, D. (1953). Transitional objects and transitional phenomena. *International Journal of Psychoanalysis, 34*, 89–97.

Winnicott, D. (1960). The theory of the parent–child relationship. *International Journal of Psychoanalysis, 41*, 585–595.

Wisely, J. H., Hare, D. J., & Fernandez-Ford, L. (2002). A study of the topography and nature of self-injurious behaviour in people with learning disabilities. *Journal of Learning Disabilities, 6*, 61–71.

Wolf, M. M. (1978). Social validity: The case for subjective measurement or how applied behavior analysis is finding its heart. *Journal of Applied Behavior Analysis, 11*, 203–214.

Wolff, P. (1967). The role of biological rhythms in early psychological development. *Bulletin of the Menninger Clinic, 31*, 197–218.

Wong, D. F., Harris, J. C., Naidu, S., Yokoi, F., Marenco, S., Dannals, R. F., et al. (1996). Dopamine transporters are markedly reduced in Lesch–Nyhan disease in vivo. *Proceedings of the National Academy of Science, 93*.

Woods, T.S. (1983). DRO and DRI: A false dichotomy? *Psychological Record, 33*, 59–66.

Wordsell, A. S., Iwata, B. A., Hanley, G. P., Thompson, R. H., & Kahng, S. W. (2000). Effects of continuous and intermittent reinforcement for problem behavior during functional communication training. *Journal of Applied Behavior Analysis, 33*, 167–179.

Wyatt v. Stickney. (1972). 344 F. Supp. 373 (M.D. Ala. 1972), 503 F.2d 507 5th Circuit, 1974.

Yates, T. M. (2004). The developmental psychopathology of self-injurious behavior: Compensatory regulation in posttraumatic adaptation. *Clinical Psychology Review, 24*, 35–74.

Yates, T. M. (2006). A longitudinal study of self-injurious behavior in a community sample. *Dissertation Abstracts International, Section B: The Sciences and Engineering, 66*(8-B), 4518.

Yoo, J. H., Williams, D. C., Napolitano, D. A., Peyton, R. T., Baer, D. E., & Schroeder, S. R. (2003). Rate-decreasing effects of the atypical neuroleptic risperidone attenuated by conditions of reinforcement in a woman with mental retardation. *Journal of Applied Behavior Analysis, 36*, 245–248.

Yudofsky, S. C., Silver, J. M., Jackson, W., Endicott, J., & Williams, D. (1986). The Overt Aggression Scale for the objective rating of verbal and physical aggression. *American Journal of Psychiatry, 143*, 35–39.

Zahl, D. L., & Hawton, K. (2004). Repetition of deliberate self-harm and subsequent suicide risk: Long-term follow-up study of 11,583 patients. *British Journal of Psychiatry, 185*, 70–75.

Zarcone, J. R., Hellings, J. A., Crandall, K., Reese, R. M., Marquis, J., Fleming, K., et al. (2001). Effects of risperidone on aberrant behavior of persons with developmental disabilities: I. Double-blind crossover study using multiple measures. *American Journal on Mental Retardation, 106*, 525–538.

Zarcone, J. R., Iwata, B. A., Hughes, C. E., & Vollmer, T. R. (1993). Momentum versus extinction effects in the treatment of self-injurious escape behavior. *Journal of Applied Behavior Analysis, 26*, 135–136.

Zarcone, J. R., Iwata, B. A., Mazaleski, J. L., & Smith, R. G. (1994). Momentum and extinction effects on self-injurious behavior and noncompliance. *Journal of Applied Behavior analysis, 27*, 649–658.

Zarcone, J. R., Iwata, B. A., Vollmer, T. R., Jagtiani, S., Smith, R. G., & Mazaleski, J. L. (1993). Extinction of self-injurious escape behavior with and without instructional fading. *Journal of Applied Behavior Analysis, 26*, 353–360.

Zarcone, J. R., Rodgers, T., Iwata, B. A., Rourke, D. A., & Dorsey, M. (1991). Reliability analysis of the Motivation Assessment Scale: A failure to replicate. *Research in Developmental Disabilities, 12*, 349–360.

Zarcone, J. R., Valdovinos, M. G., Lindauer, S. E., Crosland, K. A., Morse, P., McKerchar, T., et al. (2004). Functional analysis and the effects of risperidone: Review of 20 cases. *American Journal on Mental Retardation, 109*, 310–321.

Zhou, L., Goff, G. A., & Iwata, B. A. (2000). Effects of increasing response effort on self-injury and object manipulation as competing responses. *Journal of Applied Behavior Analysis, 33*, 29–40.

Zimmermann, R. L., & Heistad, G. T. (1982). Studies of long term efficacy of antipsychotic drugs in the control of behavior. *Journal of the American Academy of Child Psychiatry, 21*, 136–143.

Zlotnick, C., Shea, M. T., & Pearlstein, T. (1996). The relationship between dissociative symptoms, alexithymia, impulsivity, sexual abuse, and self-mutilation. *Comprehensive Psychiatry, 37*, 12–16.

Zoghbi, H. Y. (ed.). (2002). Rett syndrome. *Mental Retardation and Developmental Disabilities Research Reviews, 8*, 59–111.

Author Index

Subject Index